GUIDE TO FIRST-YEAR

Writing

Fourth Edition

2015–2016

Dr. Lynée Gaillet, Director

Dr. Angela Hall-Godsey, Associate Director

Jennifer L. Vala, Assistant Director

Kristen A. Ruccio, Assistant Director

Georgia State University

Lower Division Studies

FOUNTAINHEAD
PRESS

As a textbook publisher, we are faced with enormous environmental issues due the large amount of paper contained in our print products. Since our inception in 2002, we have worked diligently to be as eco-friendly as possible.

Our "green" initiatives include:

Electronic Products
We deliver products in non-paper form whenever possible. This includes pdf downloadables, flash drives, & CD's.

Electronic Samples
We use a new electronic sampling system, called Xample. Instructor samples are sent via a personalized web page that links to pdf downloads.

FSC Certified Printers
All of our Printers are certified by the Forest Service Council which promotes environmentally and socially responsible management of the world's forests. This program allows consumer groups, individual consumers and businesses to work together hand in hand to promote responsible use of the world's forests as a renewable and sustainable resource.

Recycled Paper
Almost all of our products are printed on a minimum of 10-30% post consumer waste recycled paper.

Support of Green Causes
When we do print, we donate a portion of our revenue to Green causes. Listed below are a few of the organizations that have received donations from Fountainhead Press. We welcome your feedback and suggestions for contributions, as we are always searching for worthy initiatives.
Rainforest 2 Reef
Environmental Working Group

Cover Designer: Doris Bruey
Book Layout: OffCenter Concept House

Books may be purchased for educational purpose.

For information, please call or write:

1-800-586-0030

Fountainhead Press
Southlake, TX 76092

Web site: www.fountainheadpress.com

Email: customerservice@fountainheadpress.com

ISBN: 978-1-68036-024-0

Printed in the United States of America

CONTENTS

ACKNOWLEDGEMENTS

The Guide to First-Year Writing, 4th edition is the product of hard work by faculty, staff, and teachers in the Lower Division Studies program of the Department of English at Georgia State University. In addition to authoring this text, participants on various committees gathered information, organized essays and art submissions, as well as conducted several rounds of student and faculty-centered surveys. The feedback from instructors and students was instrumental in creating the fourth edition of the *Guide to First-Year Writing*.

Editors

General Editor

Lynée Lewis Gaillet

Managing and Contributing Editor

Angela Hall-Godsey

Production and Contributing Editors

Jennifer L. Vala

Kristen A. Ruccio

Editorial Staff

Dan Abitz, Cristine Busser, Deborah D'Cruze, Stephanie Devine, Matt Donald, Andy Fentem, Donald Gammill, Nancy Paxton-Wilson, Stephanie Little Rountree

Chapter Nine Contributing Editorial Staff

Deborah D'Cruze, Stephanie Devine, Matt Donald, Andy Fentem, Valerie Robin

Website Contributors

Deborah D'Cruze, Jennifer L. Vala, Lelania Ottoboni Watkins, Stephanie Devine

Student Art Contributors

Courtney Anderson, Alesa Barron, Michael Black-Akert, Charles Clark, Moira Catherine Clark, Nadia Deljou, Marissa Graziano, Kaylin James, Justin Jordan, Judith Kim, Alexandra Linne, Lorelei Crystalilly Marden, Alexander Thomas Mitchell, Steve Osborne, Shedaria Presley, Courtney Jane Richir, Joshua Sheridan, James Supreme, Fenton Thompson, Lillia Tran, Jiri Vala Jr., William Walsh, Teal Waxelbaum, Eun Kyoung Yang

Student Writing Contributors

Joe Beard, Nicole Berne, Carla Marie Bazemore-Colclough, Jessie Giles, Angell Green, Randall Harrell, Justin Jones, Pam Logan, Jessica Martinez, Ryan Ocampo, KaTerra Smith, Amanda Tice

Cover Photo

Hollace Bain (back cover), Austin Sak (motion shot, front cover), GSU Digital Asset Library (panther, front cover)

Mitchell, Alexander Thomas. *Splash*.

INTRODUCTION

What Is Lower Division Studies?

By now you have attended several orientation programs introducing you to university life. As a first-year student, you are probably excited to start on this path toward your degree. The Lower Division Studies program for the Department of English welcomes you to Georgia State University. Our program comprises all first- and second-year composition (English 1101, English 1102, and English 1103) and literature survey courses (English 2110, 2120, and 2130). Our directors and staff oversee the pedagogical design and curriculum for all Lower Division courses. In addition to this work, our program trains and supports all instructors who teach 1000 and 2000 level English courses. Since every student must complete first-year writing courses (part of the University's CORE classes), our program seeks to provide assistance and direction to over three thousand students a semester. One way we manage contact with so many students is by creating a centralized location for Lower Division information – the Lower Division Office, which is housed in the English Department (25 Park Place). Another way we monitor the progress of our first-year students is through the creation of this textbook and companion website for use in all composition courses. The material you learn in these introductory courses will serve as the foundation of your academic pursuits. No matter what your major, you will need to become an effective communicator. These CORE courses prepare you for academic and professional discourse. We encourage you to become familiar with Lower Division Studies (LDS).

Lower Division Studies Administration

Dr. Lynée Lewis Gaillet, Director, Lower Division Studies
lgaillet@gsu.edu

Dr. Angela Hall-Godsey, Associate Director, Lower Division Studies
ahallgodsey1@gsu.edu

Kristen Ruccio, Assistant Director, Lower Division Studies
kruccio1@gsu.edu

Web Resources

Lower Division Studies maintains its own webpage, which houses valuable administrative information. To visit this site, go to http://lds.gsu.edu/

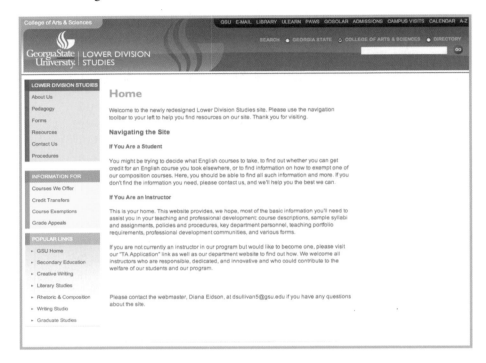

Guide to First-Year Writing also hosts a companion site, which is a good place to find supplemental leaning resources. Please visit this site to search for information on the *Guide*, writing tutorials, links to educational resources, grammar tutorials, and sample student essays. You can find Lower Division Policy information pertinent to GSU students on this site. To visit this site, go to guidetowriting.gsu.edu

Why Do I Have To Take A Writing Class?

Regardless of your major and intended career path, all students and professionals must know how to write well. Mastering course content and conducting research isn't enough – you will need to know

how to appropriately and effectively articulate your findings and demonstrate mastery of subject matter. Most college classes require writing as one of the ways instructors assess what you know. So, English courses are not the only courses that require writing. More pointedly, writing involves critical thinking. Those who learn how to write well must also learn valuable skills in reading comprehension, synthesizing, argumentation, rhetorical analysis, and organization. As you learn how to write better, you will also learn how to articulate your point of view, develop clear and ethically-driven arguments, and how to become stronger *thinkers*. As a critical thinker, your role as a student, and later as a professional, strengthens. In addition, your participation in a university community and your ability to articulate your experiences can benefit your outside and personal interests.

What kind of writing do you imagine you will do as a professional in the work force? You may be surprised by the amount of writing required in most professions. The College Board's National Com-

Sheridan, Joshua. *Lord of the Arts*

mission on Writing compiled a report representing responses from over 100 corporate leaders of American companies. This report, "Writing A Ticket to Work ... Or a Ticket Out: A Survey of Business Leaders," outlines the expectations those in the corporate world have regarding employee writing competencies. The research found that writing is not only a "threshold skill of employment and promotion, particularly among salaried employees," but that two-thirds of all salaried employees in industry has some writing responsibility" (3). Of course, a published report shouldn't be the only evidence to convince you of the benefit of effective writing skills. Have you ever sent an email to a coworker, teacher, or family member that didn't "say" what you meant? In every job, regardless of the industry, you will be required to communicate in writing: including, memos, emails, proposals, reports, formal findings analysis, and summaries of company materials. Research suggests that effective writers are hirable, marketable, and promotable.

What Happens In A Writing Class?

Georgia State University's composition courses are capped at 25 students per class, which allows more direct and individual classroom instruction. Instead of sitting in a lecture hall taking notes with one hundred other students, you will engage with the writing process through what's known as active and student-centered learning. What are these modes of learning? Well, your class may involve in-class writing assignments, oral presentations, classroom debates, community-driven assignments, peer editing, blog post discussion forums, and group projects. The classroom becomes a community of writers, who are all interested in developing modes of written expression. As a first-year composition student, you will be expected to engage in classroom discussions, to complete reading and writing assignments outside of class, and to participate in the peer editing process with your peers. Additionally, all first-year students at Georgia State will share in a communal reading experience through their participation in the First-Year Book Program. By the time you find your classroom and meet your Composition instructor, you should already be familiar with (indeed, read) the 2015 book selection. According to the program's homepage,

> *The First-Year Book Program at Georgia State University aims to provide all incoming freshmen with a common intellectual experience to stimulate discussion, to promote critical thinking, and to develop a sense of community among first-year students, faculty, and staff. (http://success.students. gsu.edu/first-year-programs/first-year-book/)*

Previous selections have asked students to consider their role as academics within the context of citizenship. Our program works to weave the content of the selected book into the 1101 and 1102 curriculum. In addition to what you will find here, our companion site will house writing and discussion activities for the committee's 2015 selection.

The *Guide*, the companion website, first-year initiative programs like PEP and Success Academy, and the First-Year Book program work to develop the composition learning space in a way that permits exploration, inquiry, and development. By the time you complete composition 1101 and 1102 at GSU, you should recognize in your own writing the skills and techniques you see in the writers you read. Think of the writing classroom as a space where you can both learn how to write and write in order to learn. The writing class invites inquiry and offers instruction for developing your initial questions and research plan, then articulating your findings. In addition to learning how to write better, your instructor will help you become an authority on a subject, express yourself, and refine your abilities to research, reflect, read actively, organize findings, and engage in critique.

Yes, mastering grammar conventions and mechanics are fundamental to developing clear writing and to illustrating credibility for your audience. However, effective compositing involves logic, organization, research support, and consideration of the rhetorical situation in addition to correct grammar usage. In composition classes, we ask you to assess your writing weaknesses (as well as your strengths) and work on demonstrating scholarly writing skills. Your instructors are trained to help you through this process. So, be sure to become familiar with the classroom rules, the course expectations, and ways in which you can improve your writing by visiting your instructor during office hours and making appointments with a Writing Studio tutor: http://www.writingstudio.gsu.edu/.

How Do I Use This Book?

Your 1101 or 1102 instructor has assigned this book (and possibly others) in order to facilitate your understanding of the writing and critical thinking process. The first section of the *Guide to First-Year Writing* provides a rhetorical basis for learning. Chapters one through six from *Praxis: A Brief Rhetoric* (Fountainhead Press) introduce fundamental elements of collegiate-level writing—principles and advice about invention, writing, and revising. The *Praxis* chapters also include writing activities.

Barron, Alesa. *The Art of Writing*

The second part of the *Guide to First-Year Writing* is Georgia State specific. This fourth edition reflects the feedback we received from students in previous semesters as well as feedback from instructors who used the book in class. These thoughtfully revised chapters address civil engagement, public literacy, writing and culture, media literacy, writing and editing in public spaces, and visual analysis. The authors of these chapters incorporate student writing (from students just like you), campus-based assignments, and discussion prompts related to GSU and the surrounding Atlanta community. The *Guide to First-Year Writing* combines traditional information about research and composing with localized instructional materials that invite you to write and reflect about the GSU community and your experiences as a Georgia State student/scholar.

Lower Division Studies welcomes you to GSU. Since the *Guide to First-Year Writing* represents the ideas and work of our student body, we hope that you will add your voice to the 5th edition of the *Guide to First-Year Writing*. Be on the lookout for email invitations to submit your art work and writing for inclusion in the next edition.

1

PRACTICING RHETORIC

Why Rhetoric Is Important in My Writing by Elizabeth Jimenez

Rhetoric is an intangible power that has the ability to motivate and manipulate. If I master rhetoric, I know I possess the ability to move my audience toward my goal.

I communicate effectively when I gain the confidence of the audience. Influencing my class and professor is my number one goal and is done so by my ethos. My use of rhetoric is validated by my credibility in the subject I disseminate. I must possess credibility if I am to be a reputable source of information.

Once I have gained the attention of the audience, I obtain logos when I clearly and logically disseminate my thoughts. I accomplish my purpose when I prove my statements. This is done by substantiating my thoughts with supporting evidence. Many contributing factors that come into play have an influence on my argument, such as bias. If my argument is biased, this can strongly detract from my goal.

Persuasive rhetoric is not necessarily accomplished when I use too much emotion. I find if I overuse pathos, the general idea gets lost. If I want my idea to be well received, it is important for me to communicate with levelheadedness.

These elements help me to establish effective rhetoric, which is crucial as I write for different audiences in college. Rhetoric will open doors throughout my college career as I discover new ways of conveying information and opinions.

Elizabeth Jimenez writes that understanding rhetoric gives her the power to persuade an audience.

Through *Praxis*, Theory Becomes Action

The word ***praxis*** can be translated as "process" or "practice." Aristotle, the great Greek rhetorician, employed the term in a special way to mean practical reasoning, for which the goal was action. To be practical in the Aristotelian sense is a little different from what being practical means today. It indicates the ability to apply abstract theory to concrete situations and thus, to move from theory to action. Moreover, praxis embodies a creative element that raises it above the mundane or merely pragmatic. Therefore, "practicing rhetoric" is not practice in the sense of rehearsal. Rather, it is performing, or applying, or acting out rhetoric—taking theory and turning it into action.

So, if we understand praxis or the "practicing" part of "practicing rhetoric," what does the "rhetoric" part of the chapter title mean? In common usage, the word *argument* has a narrow definition that emphasizes heated or angry exchanges of clashing and often irreconcilable viewpoints. Moreover, sides in such arguments are limited to black and white opposites and include no shades of gray. If one person is right, then the other must be wrong.

In academia, in contrast, we argue because it causes us to examine critically our own as well as others' ideas. Argument compels us to consider conflicting claims, to evaluate evidence, and to clarify our thoughts. We know that even wise, well-intentioned people don't always agree, so we consider others' ideas respectfully. After one person presents an argument, either orally or in writing, others respond with arguments that support, modify, or contradict the original one. Then, in turn, more individuals counter with their own versions, and thus, the interchange becomes a conversation.

Academic arguments can be divided into several different categories, depending upon the extent of the writer's desire to persuade and the scope of the conversational exchange.

1. **One type of argument simply makes a point about the topic.** For example, later in this chapter you will read an article titled, "San Ysidro Shooting Survivor Lives His Dream of Being a Cop." In the article, the author describes the wounds inflicted on a young man during the McDonald's Massacre in San Ysidro in 1984 and then explains how and why this young man later became a cop. No one is likely to disagree with the writer's line of reasoning, at least not if the author offers sufficient evidence to back up the original statement that, for this man, being a cop is his dream. This article is a profile, a type of argument more often seen in magazines and newspapers than in journals.

2. A second type of argument involves a controversial issue, and the writer's aim is to persuade the audience to change its stance on the matter. The ideal result, for the writer, would be that members of the audience alter their positions to coincide with the writer's viewpoint. In this second type of argument, it is essential that the writer offer the complete structure of thesis, evidence, possible opposition viewpoints which are discussed and countered, and a conclusion. "The Sleepover Question," another reading in this chapter, presents this kind of argument. The author, who has conducted research in both America and Holland, argues the controversial position that if American parents would adopt more liberal attitudes toward their children's sexuality, like the parents in Holland, "the transition into adulthood need not be so painful for parents or children." A reading in Chapter 3, "Why Executions Should Be Televised," offers a more extreme version of this type of argument. Either executions are televised or they aren't, and the writer advocates that they should be.

3. A third type of argument emphasizes multiple perspectives and viewpoints and tries to find common ground that participants can agree upon. In Chapter 4, several readings are collected in a casebook called "The $300 House." The *Harvard Business Review* initiated a design competition intended to spark inclusive argument with the aim of gathering ideas about how to build inexpensive but adequate homes for the poor in the world's slums. "Hands Off Our Houses," one response to the competition that appears in the casebook, argues, for example, that bringing $300 houses into the slums of Mumbai is not the answer to the housing problem. In contrast, other responses posted on a website associated with the competition suggest ways the idea of the $300 house might work, while admitting enormous difficulties.

These three types of arguments represent points in a spectrum, and all persuasive texts may not neatly fit into one of the three categories. A crucial thing to remember, though, is that all arguments involve the presentation of a line of reasoning about a topic or an issue—a thesis, hypothesis, or claim—and the support of that reasoning with evidence.

Become Part of the Academic Conversation

As a student, you are expected to join academic conversations that are already in progress. How do you do that? How do you know what kind of response is appropriate? Have you ever entered a party where everyone is talking excitedly? Most likely, you paused near the doorway to get a sense of who was there and what they were discussing before you decided who to talk to and what to say. Or, have you become part of a Facebook group or a listserv discussion group? If so, you know it is a good idea to "lurk" for a while before asking questions or contributing a remark. Writing an academic paper involves a similar process. You read about a subject until you have a good grasp of the points authorities are debating. Then you find a way to integrate your own ideas about that subject with the ideas of others and create an informed contribution to the conversation.

For example, the following students' introductions to movie reviews demonstrate they not only understand the films and have interesting things to say about them; their writing also displays knowledge of what others have written about the films, whether the students agree with those evaluations or not.

■ Roger Ebert claims that audience members who haven't seen the first two *Lord of the Rings* films (Peter Jackson, 2001, 2002) will likely "be adrift during the early passages of [the third] film's 200 minutes." But then again, Ebert continues, "to be adrift occasionally during this nine-hour saga comes with the territory" (par. 3). Ebert, though, misses one crucial fact regarding *Lord of the Rings: The Return of the King* (2003). This third installment opens with a flashback intended to familiarize new spectators about what happened in the previous two films. Within these five minutes, the audience discovers how Gollum (Andy Serkis) came to be corrupt through the destructive power of the Ring. The viewer, therefore, will not necessarily be "adrift," as Ebert claims, since the lighting, setting, and sound in the opening of *The Return of the King* show the lighter, more peaceful world before Gollum finds the ring, compared to the darker, more sinister world thereafter.

■ "It's hard to resist a satire, even when it wobbles, that insists the most unbelievable parts are the most true" (*Rolling Stone* par. 1). This is Peter Travers's overarching view of Grant Heslov's satire, *The Men Who Stare at Goats* (2009). Travers is correct here; after all, Goats's opening title card, which reads, "More of this is real than you would believe," humorously teases the viewer that some of the film's most "unbelievable parts" will, in fact, offer the most truth. We experience this via Bill Wilson's (Ewan McGregor) interview of an ex "psy-ops" soldier, when Wilson's life spirals out of control, and all the other farfetched actions presenting "reality." But again, it is the film's opening—specifically, its setting, camera movements and angles, dialogue, effects, and ambient noise—that sets the foundation for an unbelievably realistic satire.*

In both of these introductions, the students quote reviews by professional film critics and respond to the critics' opinions. Moreover, the students continue their arguments by using the critics' ideas as springboards for their own arguments. These two short examples indicate these students have learned how to counter positions advocated by authorities without losing their own voices. If the rest of their essays continue as they have begun, the students will have written essays to which others can reply, thus continuing the conversation. Later in this textbook, you will have your own chance to enter the conversation of film reviews by reviewing a favorite movie of your own.

Collaborative Groups Help Students Enter the Academic Conversation

Likely, your writing class will include collaborative group work as part of the mix of activities, along with lecture, class discussion, and in-class writing. You may wonder why there is so much talk in a writing class, which is a good question. Use of collaborative groups is based on extensive research, which shows that students who work in small groups as part of their courses tend to learn more and retain the knowledge longer than students who are not asked to work in groups. Also, research shows students who participate in collaborative group work generally are more satisfied with the course. Groups give students a chance to apply knowledge they have learned and provide a change of pace from lectures or other class activities. There are several types of groups, and your class may include one or all of them:

- Informal, one-time pairs or groups. After presenting some material, your instructor may ask you to turn to the person next to you and discuss the topic or answer a question.

- Ongoing small classroom groups. Usually, these groups work together for a significant part of the semester, and your instructor may assign roles to members of the group such as recorder, facilitator, editor, and spokesperson. Often, the roles will rotate, so that everyone has a chance to try out each job. Your instructor may give you a job description for each role or train the class in the tasks for each role.

---

* Kelli Marshall. "Entering a Conversation, Teaching the Academic Essay," *Unmuzzled Thoughts about Teaching and Pop Culture*, October 23, 2010, http://kellimarshall.net/unmuzzledthoughts/teaching/academic-essay/. Accessed August 30, 2011.

- Task groups. These groups are formed to write a report, complete a project, or do some other task together. These groups meet several times, often outside of class. The products of these groups are usually graded, and your instructor will often require members to rate each other on their performance.

- Peer editing groups. When you have completed a draft of an essay or other text, your instructor may ask you to exchange papers in pairs or within small groups. You will be asked to read your classmate's paper carefully and make comments, either on a peer editing form or on the paper itself. Likewise, your classmate will read and make comments on your paper. Then, when you receive your paper back, you can make revisions based on your classmate's comments.

An added benefit to the use of collaborative groups in writing classes is that students can help each other figure out what the ongoing conversation is for a particular topic or issue before writing about it. Also, groups provide a forum where students can practice making comments that are part of that conversation.

Rhetoric and Argument

The structure of an argument—introduction (including a thesis), supporting evidence, counterarguments, and conclusion—will be familiar to you from previous English classes. What you may not realize is that ancient Greeks developed this argumentative structure out of necessity. Their democratic system of government required that citizens be able to speak persuasively in public, as there were no attorneys or professional politicians. Ancient Greeks called their persuasive strategies rhetoric, and rhetoric became the primary means of education of the elite youth in Athens.

Rhetoric, like argument, is a word that has both a popular meaning and an academic meaning. You have probably heard someone say of a politician's speech, "Oh, that's just rhetoric," meaning the politician's words are empty verbiage or hot air. The politician is attempting to sound impressive while saying nothing that has real meaning. Or perhaps the politician is making promises that listeners believe he or she has no intention of keeping. Politicians who engage in verbal deception often succeed only in acquiring the reputation of dishonesty.

In the field of rhetoric and composition today, rhetoric has a much different meaning. Though definitions vary somewhat from one practitioner to another, rhetoric generally means the study and use of persuasive communication (or argument), a meaning that traces its roots back to the original use of the term by ancient Greeks. Rhetoric, in the form of oratory, was essential to the Greeks, as they used it to resolve disputes in the law courts and to promote political action in the Assembly.

Are We All Greeks?

As Americans, we owe an immense debt to ancient Greek civilization. Our laws, our democratic form of government, our literature, and our art have their roots in ancient Athens. Earlier generations of Americans and Western Europeans, who often studied Latin and Greek, may have had a clearer understanding of the direct connections of our culture to Athens of the 4th and 5th centuries BCE. Indeed, the English poet Percy Bysshe Shelley famously said, "We are all Greeks" because of the essential influence of ancient Greek culture upon Western civilization. However, even translated into 21st century American English, the linkage is still there.

Something quite amazing happened in Athens, around 500 BCE. Instead of being invaded by a foreign country who appointed a puppet ruler or experiencing a coup in which a strong man seized power, the people peaceably chose to put in place a direct democracy. Attica was not the only city-state to have a democracy, but it was the most successful. During the golden age of Greece, from roughly 500 BCE to 300 BCE, art, architecture, and literature thrived.

Direct or radical democracy meant all male citizens of Attica over the age of 20 could vote in the Assembly, the policy-making body of the city-state. They did not elect senators or representatives as we do today. Each of these men *voted directly*. Moreover, they could settle differences with fellow citizens by suing in the law courts. Out of 250,000 to 300,000 residents in Attica, some 30,000 were citizens. Amazingly, it was not unusual for 10,000 of these eligible men to vote in the Assembly. The law courts had juries of 500 or more. Imagine trying to speak to an audience of 10,000 people without modern loudspeakers. Even with the wonderful acoustics in Greek theatres, it would have been a challenge.

Ordinary citizens were required to speak in the Assembly or the courts to promote laws or defend themselves from lawsuits, as there were no attorneys or professional politicians. Certainly, speaking before such large audiences necessitated special skills acquired only through extensive training and practice. Many sought out teachers to help them learn how to speak persuasively, and, indeed, training in rhetoric became the primary method of education for the elite young men of Athens. A few women were also educated in rhetoric, but they were in the minority.

The earliest teachers of verbal persuasive skills we now call rhetoric were Sophists who migrated from Sicily and other Greek states. Some of their viewpoints were curiously modern—for example, that knowledge is relative and that pure truth does not exist. However, they became known for teaching their pupils to persuade an audience to think whatever they wanted them to believe. Sophists such as Gorgias themselves often presented entertainment speeches during which they would argue, on the spur of the moment, on any topic raised by the audience, just to show they were able to construct effective arguments on any subject.

The term rhetoric comes from the Greek word *rhetorike*, which Plato coined as a criticism of the Sophists, claiming the Sophists' rhetoric could be employed to manipulate the masses for good or ill, and that rhetoricians used it irresponsibly. Ironically, Plato demonstrates excellent rhetorical techniques himself when he condemns rhetoric and argues that only the elite who are educated in philosophy are suited to rule, not the rhetoricians. Aristotle, Plato's student, took a more moderate viewpoint toward rhetoric. Indeed, he was the first philosopher to classify rhetoric as a tool for practical debate with general audiences. His book *On Rhetoric* (though it was probably lecture notes possibly combined with student responses, rather than a manuscript intended for publication) is the single most important text that establishes rhetoric as a system of persuasive communication.

Athens, even in its glory days, seethed with controversy and bickering over the many inefficiencies of democracy. Men trained in rhetoric executed two coups, the Tyranny of the Four Hundred in 411 BCE and the Tyranny of the Thirty in 404 BCE, neither of which was an improvement; after each coup, democracy returned. Moreover, Athenians fought wars with Persia (the Battle of Marathon in 490 BCE and the Battle of Thermopylae in 480 BCE) and Sparta (the Peloponnesian War in 431–404 BCE and the Corinthian War of 395–387 BCE). Finally, the armies of Philip II of Macedonia defeated Athens at the Battle of Chaeronea in 338 BCE, ending Athenian independence. Despite coups and wars, democracy remained in place in Athens for nearly 200 years.

If Americans might be called Greeks because our country is based on Greek traditions, this is not to say that rhetoric appears in all cultures. True, one might say that all civilizations have some sort of persuasive negotiation process; but profound differences exist between cultures in terms of what verbal strategies are persuasive. Indeed, disparity in expectations and the actions of individuals and groups from different traditions can be a cause of strife.

Rhetoric and Power

Aristotle defined rhetoric as "the faculty of discovering, in a given instance, the available means of persuasion," which we might paraphrase as the power to see the means of persuasion available in any given situation. Each part of this definition is important. Rhetoric is power; the person who is able to speak eloquently, choosing the most suitable arguments about a topic for a specific audience in a particular situation, is the person most likely to persuade. In both Greece and Rome, the primary use of rhetoric was oratory—persuasion through public speaking. However, the texts of many famous speeches were recorded and studied as models by students, and prominent rhetoricians wrote treatises and handbooks for teaching rhetoric. To Greeks and Romans, a person who could use rhetoric effectively was a person of influence and power because he could persuade his audience to action. The effective orator could win court cases; the effective orator could influence the passage or failure of laws; the effective orator could send a nation to war or negotiate peace.

Skill with rhetoric has conveyed power through the ages, though in our contemporary world, rhetoric is often displayed in written text such as a book, newspaper or magazine article, or scientific report, rather than presented as a speech. Persuasive communication also can be expressed visually, as an illustration that accompanies a text or a cartoon that conveys its own message. Indeed, in our highly visual society, with television, movies, video games, and the Internet, images can often persuade more powerfully than words alone.

Using rhetoric effectively means being able to interpret the rhetoric we are presented with in our everyday lives. Knowledge of persuasive communication or rhetoric empowers us to present our views and persuade others to modify their ideas. Through changes in ideas, rhetoric leads to action. Through changes in actions, rhetoric affects society.

Selected Definitions of Rhetoric

Aristotle, 350 BCE—*Rhetoric is "the faculty of discovering, in a given instance, the available means of persuasion."*

Cicero, 90 BCE—*Rhetoric is "speech designed to persuade" and "eloquence based on the rules of art."*

Quintilian, 95 CE—*Rhetoric is "the science of speaking well."*

Augustine of Hippo, ca. 426 CE—*Rhetoric is "the art of persuading people to accept something, whether it is true or false."*

Anonymous, ca. 1490–1495—*Rhetoric is "the science which refreshes the hungry, renders the mute articulate, makes the blind see, and teaches one to avoid every lingual ineptitude."*

Heinrich Cornelius Agrippa, 1531—*"To confess the truth, it is generally granted that the entire discipline of rhetoric from start to finish is nothing other than an art of flattery, adulation, and, as some say more audaciously, lying, in that, if it cannot persuade others through the truth of the case, it does so by means of deceitful speech."*

Hoyt Hudson, 1923—*"In this sense, plainly, the man who speaks most persuasively uses the most, or certainly the best, rhetoric; and the man whom we censure for inflation of style and strained effects is suffering not from too much rhetoric, but from a lack of it."*

I. A. Richards, 1936—*"Rhetoric, I shall urge, should be a study of misunderstanding and its remedies."*

Sister Miriam Joseph, 1937—*Rhetoric is "the art of communicating thought from one mind to another, the adaptation of language to circumstance."*

Kenneth Burke, 1950—*"[T]he basic function of rhetoric [is] the use of words by human agents to form attitudes or to induce actions in other human agents."*

Gerard A. Hauser, 2002—*"Rhetoric, as an area of study, is concerned with how humans use symbols, especially language, to reach agreement that permits coordinated effort of some sort."*

Activity 1.1 Historical Usage of the Word "Rhetoric"

Read through the list of historical definitions of the word "rhetoric" on the previous page, and choose one that you find interesting. In a discussion, compare your chosen definition with those of your classmates.

Activity 1.2 Contemporary Usage of the Word "Rhetoric"

Find at least two recent but different examples involving use of the word "rhetoric." For example, search your local newspaper for an example of how the word "rhetoric" is being used. A search of the *Dallas Morning News* for the word "rhetoric" led to a story about citizen efforts to clean up a neglected area of town: "He now hopes for help to finally fill the gap between rhetoric and reality." Or ask a friend, fellow employee, or a family member to tell you what the word "rhetoric" means and write down what they say. Discuss your examples in your small group and present the best ones to the class.

Visual Map of Meanings for the Word "Rhetoric"

The word map for the word "rhetoric" shown in figure 1.1 has branches for different meanings of the word, with some branches splitting again to display subtle subsets of connotation. It was created by a website, Visual Thesaurus (www.visualthesaurus.com), which computes visual word maps for any word inputted in its search box. The idea is that words lead to branches that lead to more words, inspiring users to think of language in new ways.

At the Visual Thesaurus site, if you place your cursor over one of the circles connecting the branches, a small box will pop up that defines that connection. One of these connection boxes is visible. Notice it says, "using language effectively to please or persuade." This is the branch of the visual map that is closest to the meaning of "rhetoric" as used in this book. The other branches illustrate other contemporary uses of the word.

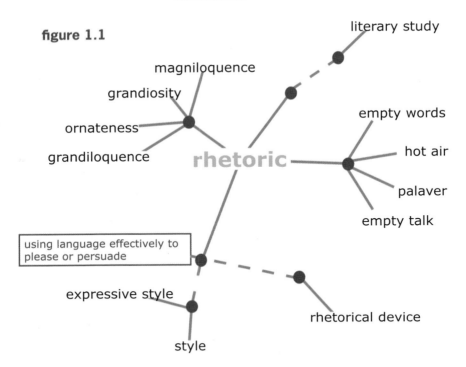

figure 1.1

Activity 1.3 **Explore the Visual Map of the Word "Rhetoric"**

In your small group, choose one of the five branches of words in the visual map of the word "rhetoric." Go to one or more good dictionaries and explore the meanings of the words in that branch. A good place to start would be the *Oxford English Dictionary*, which your college library may offer online. The *OED* offers intricate analyses of the histories of word meanings. Report to the class what you find out about the words on your particular branch.

Rhetorical Argument

Often, in our culture, the word "argument" is taken to mean a disagreement or even a fight, with raised voices, rash words, and hurt feelings. We have the perception of an argument as something that has victory and defeat, winners and losers. Argument, in the sense of a **rhetorical argument**, however, means the carefully crafted presentation of a viewpoint or position on a topic and the giving of thoughts, ideas, and opinions along with reasons for their support. The persuasive strength of an argument rests upon the rhetorical skills of the rhetor (the speaker or the writer) in utilizing the tools of language to persuade a particular audience.

Aristotle identified three appeals (see figure 1.2) or three ways to persuade an audience, and we are still using these today, though often without using the Greek terms to identify the means of persuasion:

Ethos—The rhetor convinces an audience by means of his character or credibility. In oratory, the speaker projects an air of confidence and authority. In writing, ethos is conveyed by the qualifications of the writer or the authorities that are cited and also by the quality of the writing.

Pathos—The rhetor persuades by playing upon the listener's (or reader's) emotions. He or she may refer to children, death, disaster, injustice, or other topics that arouse pity, fear, or other emotions.

Logos—The rhetor persuades by the use of reasoning and evidence. Arguments based on logos employ deductive or inductive reasoning.

figure 1.2

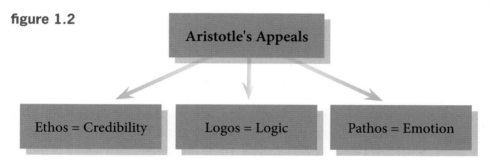

Although a good argument will contain at least traces of all three appeals, skilled rhetors analyze their audiences to determine which of the three would be most persuasive to that particular audience. Then, they construct arguments that emphasize that particular appeal.

In addition, a knowledgeable rhetor considers the time, place, audience, topic, and other aspects of the occasion for writing or speaking to determine the **kairos**, or opportune moment of the composition (see figure 1.3). This factor or critical moment both provides and limits opportunities for appeals suitable to that moment. For example, someone giving a commencement address has certain opportunities and constraints. Likewise, an attorney writing a last-minute appeal for someone on death row has a very different set of options.

figure 1.3

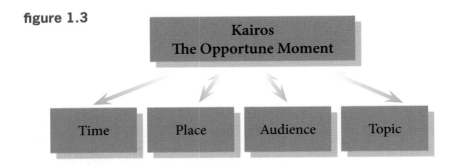

The editorial below addresses the shooting attack on Arizona Congresswoman Gabrielle Giffords that killed six and left Giffords and others seriously wounded. The text, published on *Time* magazine's website shortly after the attack, addresses the kairos of the situation—a United States Congresswoman has been shot, certainly an exceptional moment in many ways. The editorial demonstrates several important things to remember in understanding rhetoric and its use in American society. The author, Nathan Thornburgh, addresses the controversy about whether "overheated rhetoric" (exaggerated pathos) had inspired the shooting, an important question considering the often-inflammatory language of political rhetoric in the United States. However, his text is not filled with rash or harsh words that could further inflame the controversy. Though the text is an opinion piece, taking a position regarding this controversy and offering evidence to support his opinion, it is not itself "overheated rhetoric." As you read the text, think about whether he emphasizes ethos, pathos, or logos. You may or may not agree with his position. Rhetorical language is never neutral; its purpose is to persuade an audience to share the author's opinion. Good arguments, though, do not use "overheated rhetoric," false evidence, or logical fallacies to win over an audience.

Reading 1.1

Violent Rhetoric and Arizona Politics
by Nathan Thornburgh

This editorial by Nathan Thornburgh was originally printed in *Time* shortly after the shooting of Arizona Congresswoman Gabrielle Giffords.

Sometimes, rumors of violence beget actual violence. Saturday's mass shooting at a Safeway on North Oracle Road in Tucson, which killed six and left Democratic Congresswoman Gabrielle Giffords and others gravely wounded, may well be one of those occasions.

It's impossible to know this early what the motivations for the attack were. Was the alleged shooter—who has been identified as 22-year-old Tucsonan

Jared Loughner—angry about immigration? Or perhaps another hot-button issue? YouTube videos ascribed to him bore the mark of mental illness—they were conspiratorial, unintelligible, espousing no particular cause—but no matter his mental state, his crime took place in an overheated political environment. Last March, at the height of the health care reform battle, Giffords's office was vandalized. She mentioned in an MSNBC interview that a Sarah Palin graphic had depicted her district in the crosshairs of a gun sight. "They've got to realize there are consequences to that," she said. "The rhetoric is incredibly heated." The corner next to her office had also become, she said, a popular spot for Tea Party protests.

As Pima County Sheriff Clarence Dupnik put it in an extraordinary and melancholic press conference after the shooting, "we have become the Mecca for prejudice and bigotry." He added that he's "not aware of any public officials who are not receiving threats."

Another shooting victim, a federal judge named John Roll, had been placed under 24-hour security in 2009 after ruling in favor of illegal immigrants in a high-profile case. It's unclear why he was at the supermarket event. But for almost a year now, Arizona's leaders have been grappling with anti-immigration sentiments, inflamed by reports of crossborder violence. National media attention, with its attendant voices of hysteria, only added to the churn. Pundits spoke gravely about a wave of violence, born in Mexico and now flooding Arizona. Arizona's two most famous politicians fueled the fury. Republican Senator John McCain, facing an unexpected reelection challenge from the right, ran a campaign obsessed with crossborder crime. And GOP Governor Jan Brewer, who invited the national spotlight by championing strict anti-illegal immigrant legislation, talked of beheadings in the desert.

The only problem with all this talk about a massive crossborder crime wave is that it wasn't true. Phoenix had not become one of the world's kidnapping capitals. Crime rates in Arizona had been steady or even fallen in some areas. There had been no beheadings in the desert. There were plenty of deaths there, but they were pathetic and meek tragedies: impoverished border-crossers, abandoned by their heartless guides, dying of exposure and dehydration.

But the idea of a state under siege took hold. When I was on the border last year reporting on the murder of rancher Rob Krentz, I talked to many who sincerely believed that they were under attack. Krentz's murder was a terrible event, but it was an isolated event. The relatively small number of home invasions, holdups and other crimes deeply disturbed border communities, but only because they had been living in such calm for so long. Their crime rates still don't match most cities in the states.

The supermarket meet-and-greet where Giffords was shot was actually a testimony to just how safe southern Arizona is. As a press release from her office last week put it, "'Congress on Your Corner' allows residents of Arizona's 8th Congressional District to meet their congresswoman one-on-one and discuss with her any issue, concern or problem involving the federal government." Not exactly the kind of event a politician would hold in a war zone.

It's true that Giffords was not a fan of the state's anti-immigration bill SB1070, but there were higher-profile opponents, such as her fellow Congressional Representative in Tucson, Raul Grijalva. Yet the idea that Arizona is under attack has been pushed hard enough that it's very possible that the coward who shot her (in the head, according to a Tucson paper) believed that the 40-year-old Democrat, who had been tarred by some as soft on immigration because she didn't support SB1070, was contributing to larger-scale violence against Arizonans.

If that is the case, it would only add to the tragedy. The fact is, that among all the overwrought promises and all the panic I heard last summer in Arizona, I found that Giffords was one of the few politicians offering concrete law enforcement steps that would actually work against the drug cartels and other smugglers. It's not just that she fought for more money and police for border protection, although she did that. She co-sponsored legislation last year with a California Republican that aimed to give law enforcement important new tools in cracking down on the cash cards that were a favored method of money-laundering. It was one of the many sensible, pragmatic ideas she had for cracking down on crime.

Whatever dark fantasies drove someone to try to take her life, Giffords is a sensible politician who was likely shot because she dealt with Arizona's reality, not its rumors.

Activity 1.4 Write a Summary of "Violent Rhetoric and Arizona Politics"

Summarizing is an excellent technique to use when preparing for an exam or doing research for an essay. It allows you to discern the main points of a text and how they fit together. With a classmate, review the editorial by Thornburgh. Read the article together carefully, and list the main points individually. After you've listed the main points, put them into paragraph form.

Caution: Beware of the temptation to add your own analysis of what the text is saying. For example, if you are summarizing a scientist's article on global warming, you need to be careful not to reveal your personal opinion about whether or not global warming is occurring or whether or not human actions are to blame. In this assignment, you summarize only. You do not argue or analyze.

When you're finished, compare your summary with that of your partner.

Activity 1.5 Analyzing "Violent Rhetoric and Arizona Politics"

1. What does Nathan Thornburgh mean when he uses the term "overheated rhetoric"?

2. What is the argument that Thornburgh is making about the cause of the attack on Representative Giffords?

3. What evidence does Thornburgh offer to support his argument?

4. Does Thornburgh make his case? Is he convincing? Why or why not?

Reading 1.2

The Sleepover Question

by Amy Schalet

This text by Amy Schalet was first published in *The New York Times*. "The Sleepover Question" hazards an argument that many Americans—or at least American parents—may find controversial. Backed by her credentials as a professor of sociology, she cites research from 130 interviews, both in the United States and the Netherlands, and tackles the issue of whether or not American parents should allow their adolescent children to have sex in the family home. Pay particular attention, for she shows how to argue a subject that is not only controversial but often ignored.

NOT under my roof. That's the attitude most American parents have toward teenagers and their sex lives. Squeamishness and concern describe most parents' approach to their offspring's carnality. We don't want them doing it—whatever "it" is!—in our homes. Not surprisingly, teenage sex is a source of conflict in many American families.

Would Americans increase peace in family life and strengthen family bonds if they adopted more accepting attitudes about sex and what's allowable under the family roof? I've interviewed 130 people, all white, middle class and not particularly religious, as part of a study of teenage sex and family life here and in the Netherlands. My look into cultural differences suggests family life might be much improved, for all, if Americans had more open ideas about teenage sex. The question of who sleeps where when a teenager brings a boyfriend or girlfriend home for the night fits within the larger world of culturally divergent ideas about teenage sex, lust and capacity for love.

Kimberly and Natalie dramatize the cultural differences in the way young women experience their sexuality. (I have changed their names to protect confidentiality.) Kimberly, a 16-year-old American, never received sex education at home. "God, no! No, no! That's not going to happen," she told me. She'd like to tell her parents that she and her boyfriend are having sex, but she believes it is easier for her parents not to know because the truth would "shatter" their image of her as their "little princess."

Natalie, who is also 16 but Dutch, didn't tell her parents immediately when she first had intercourse with her boyfriend of three months. But, soon after, she says, she was so happy, she wanted to share the good news. Initially her father was upset and worried about his daughter and his honor. "Talk to him," his wife advised Natalie; after she did, her father made peace with the change. Essentially Natalie and her family negotiated a life change together and figured out, as a family, how to adjust to changed circumstance.

Respecting what she understood as her family's "don't ask, don't tell" policy, Kimberly only slept with her boyfriend at his house, when no one was home. She enjoyed being close to her boyfriend but did not like having to keep an important part of her life secret from her parents. In contrast, Natalie and her boyfriend enjoyed time and a new closeness with her family; the fact that her parents knew and approved of her boyfriend seemed a source of pleasure.

The difference in their experiences stems from divergent cultural ideas about sex and what responsible parents ought to do about it. Here, we see teenagers as helpless victims beset by raging hormones and believe parents should protect them from urges they cannot control. Matters aren't helped by the stereotype that all boys want the same thing, and all girls want love and cuddling. This compounds the burden on parents to steer teenage children away from relationships that will do more harm than good.

The Dutch parents I interviewed regard teenagers, girls and boys, as capable of falling in love, and of reasonably assessing their own readiness for sex. Dutch parents like Natalie's talk to their children about sex and its unintended consequences and urge them to use contraceptives and practice safe sex.

Cultural differences about teenage sex are more complicated than clichéd images of puritanical Americans and permissive Europeans. Normalizing ideas about teenage sex in fact allows the Dutch to exert *more* control over their children. Most of the parents I interviewed actively discouraged promiscuous behavior. And Dutch teenagers often reinforced what we see as 1950s-style mores: eager to win approval, they bring up their partners in conversation, introduce them to their parents and help them make favorable impressions.

Some Dutch teenagers went so far as to express their ideas about sex and love in self-consciously traditional terms; one Dutch boy said the advantage of spending the night with a partner was that it was "Like Mom and Dad, like when you're married, you also wake up next to the person you love."

Normalizing teenage sex under the family roof opens the way for more responsible sex education. In a national survey, 7 of 10 Dutch girls reported that by the time they were 16, their parents had talked to them about pregnancy and contraception. It seems these conversations helped teenagers prepare, responsibly, for active sex lives: 6 of 10 Dutch girls said they were on the pill when they first had intercourse. Widespread use of oral contraceptives contributes to low teenage pregnancy rates — more than 4 times lower in the Netherlands than in the United States.

Obviously sleepovers aren't a direct route to family happiness. But even the most traditional parents can appreciate the virtue of having their children be comfortable bringing a girlfriend or boyfriend home, rather than have them sneak around.

Unlike the American teenagers I interviewed, who said they felt they had to split their burgeoning sexual selves from their family roles, the Dutch teens had a chance to integrate different parts of themselves into their family life. When children feel safe enough to tell parents what they are doing and feeling, presumably it's that much easier for them to ask for help. This allows parents to have more influence, to control through connection.

Sexual maturation is awkward and difficult. The Dutch experience suggests that it is possible for families to stay connected when teenagers start having sex, and that if they do, the transition into adulthood need not be so painful for parents or children.

Activity 1.6 Analyze "The Sleepover Question"

1. What do you think about the "not under my roof" approach to a parent controlling a teen's sexuality versus the Dutch approach of allowing a teen's partner to sleep over? Discuss in your small group.

2. How do stereotypes play against the argument for a more open approach to teen sex in America? How much of parents' discomfort with their teen potentially having sex is guided by how their parents treated the subject when they were teens?

3. "The Sleepover Question" emphasizes logos. Can you paraphrase the logic of the argument? How does emotion (pathos) play a role in resistance to this argument?

4. In the article, the writer discusses the link between the use of oral contraceptives and lower teen pregnancy rates but does not mention the risk of STDs or condom use. Is it irresponsible of the author not to discuss the risk of STDs and sex, especially when she is willing to discuss teen pregnancy? Does it feel like an incomplete argument without discussing STDs?

5. If you were going to write a letter to the editor about this article, what would you say?

Why Study Rhetoric?

Rhetoric, or persuasive communication, happens all around us every day, in conversation at the grocery store, in blogs, on television, and in the classroom. We Americans constantly air our opinions about almost everything. Sometimes it is to convince others to share our opinions, sometimes the reason is to engage in a dialogue that will help us understand the world around us, and sometimes it is to persuade others to action.

Argument is essential to human interaction and to society, for it is through the interplay of ideas in argument that we discover answers to problems, try out new ideas, shape scientific experiments, communicate with family members, recruit others to join a team, and work out any of the multitude of human interactions essential for society to function. When issues are complex, arguments do not result in immediate persuasion of the audience; rather, argument is part of an ongoing conversation between concerned parties who seek resolution, rather than speedy answers.

Rhetoric provides a useful framework for looking at the world, as well as for evaluating and initiating communications. In the modern world, writing and communicating persuasively is a necessary skill. Those who can present effective arguments in writing are, in the business world, often the ones who are promoted. In addition, those who are able to evaluate the arguments presented to them, whether by politicians, advertisers, or even family members, are less likely to be swayed by logical fallacies or ill-supported research.

Also, writing rhetorically is a tool with sometimes surprising uses. Research shows that, as students, we are more likely to remember material we have written about rather than simply memorized. Also, through the process of writing, writers often find that they initiate ideas and connections between ideas that they might not otherwise have found. Thus, writing may lead to new discoveries.

Rhetoric is a part of our everyday lives. When we're in a conversation with someone, we use rhetoric on a conscious or subconscious level. If you go to class wearing the T-shirt of your favorite musician or band, you're ultimately sending a rhetorical message identifying you as a fan of that artist or group.

If you've ever written a profile on a dating site, you've used rhetorical principles to convince an audience of potential partners to contact you or to write you back if you have chosen to make the first contact. You build ethos by talking about yourself in order to build credibility among potential partners, and you establish pathos when you talk about an interest that is shared by a potential mate.

Being able to use the tools of rhetoric effectively gives you the power to control your communication—both incoming and outgoing—and to affect your environment in a positive way.

Reading 1.3

San Ysidro Shooting Survivor Lives His Dream of Being a Cop

by Janine Zuniga

In this feature story from the *San Diego Union-Tribune*, Janine Zuniga describes vividly how Alberto Leos, then a 17-year-old cook and high school football star, was shot and left for dead during James Oliver Huberty's rampage at a San Ysidro McDonald's in 1984. The 21 dead and 19 wounded made the massacre the worst one-day shooting by a single individual in United States history at the time. But Leos's story did not end there. The young man underwent surgeries and completed rehabilitation, going on to become a policeman. Notice how the author makes use of both ethos and pathos in writing this profile.

The shots fired at point-blank range pierced both arms, his right leg, stomach and chest, and Alberto Leos crumpled to the kitchen floor next to three co-workers at a San Ysidro McDonald's. Even with his injuries, the 17-year-old cook, three weeks into his first job, knew the others were dead. He could tell by the lifeless positions of their bodies.

During a harrowing 77 minutes 20 years ago today, Leos, a high school football star, watched in helpless horror as a heavily armed James Oliver Huberty "executed, killed families, babies, my manager."

In all, 21 people were killed and 19 wounded in what was, up to that time, the worst one-day massacre by a single gunman in U.S. history. "All I remember is saying a prayer," Leos said. "I prayed to see my family one more time . . . before I died."

The McDonald's Massacre, as it came to be called, has faded for many San Diegans during the past two decades, but for those such as Leos who survived, it became the defining moment of their lives.

Leos's recovery included three months in the hospital, where he underwent five surgeries to remove the bullets and repair damage. He spent two years in therapy, for both physical and emotional injuries.

Despite painful rehabilitation, scars and memories, Leos became even more determined to fulfill his childhood dream of becoming a police officer. He has been a cop for 17 years.

After stints with the National City and Chula Vista police departments, Leos is now a San Diego police sergeant working the Southern Division, which includes routine patrols of San Ysidro.

"I was born to do this work," said Leos, who is married and lives in Chula Vista. "I was born to be in this profession. That's how I feel."

Leos said that while growing up in Cudahy, a city southeast of Los Angeles, the only time he saw deputies was when they were taking someone to jail. But that image changed one day when an L.A. County sheriff's deputy visited his third-grade classroom.

"To see him in the school setting, I was in awe—his uniform, his nice, shiny badge," Leos said. "He told us they were there to help people, to help those who can't help themselves. I told myself that when I was older, I wanted to do that."

But Leos's parents quickly and, for a decade, successfully discouraged him from pursuing the dream, saying it was too dangerous a career for their only son. Their opposition vanished on the day he almost lost his life.

"When I was shot and my friends and co-workers were killed, my parents were very, very supportive of me doing whatever I wanted," Leos said. "I guess they felt I had a second chance."

Photo by Howard Lipin / Union-Tribune

San Diego police sergeant, Alberto Leos, preparing to go out on patrol recently, overcame five surgeries and two years of painful therapy after the McDonald's Massacre to fulfill his childhood dream of becoming a police officer.

The short sleeves of Leos's dark-blue uniform can't hide the scars on his arms, but he doesn't often share the details of that day. The 5-foot-8, clean-shaven officer is soft-spoken and somewhat formal.

"Even as a young, young man, I could tell he was a serious kind of person, not in a sober sense, but in that he had a job and wanted to help his folks, that he was a good kid," said Andrea Skorepa, who as an employee of the local social-services agency Casa Familiar helped administer a $1.4 million fund for survivors and those injured in the McDonald's Massacre.

Skorepa, who has remained friends with the officer, said some who lived through it, such as Leos, have accomplished their goals, while others have succumbed to the tragedy.

"For the people who survived, that day was the beginning of a new life for them," Skorepa said. "What they have done with their lives becomes the important story. He doesn't live as a victim. He's not gone that way."

He tries to get assigned to San Ysidro when he can, because he wants to give back to the community and to Casa Familiar. The agency not only helped with the fund but helped get his family through a very tough time.

"That's when I learned about community service and how much it's needed," Leos said.

Said Skorepa, now executive director of Casa Familiar, "I think it gives you a different perspective, if you've come that close to losing your life and are somehow spared, on how to live your life."

In all his years in law enforcement, Leos has never fired his weapon at anyone. He's sure he will if he has to, but his instincts, which he has learned to trust, help guide him more calmly through tense situations.

Now, if a situation doesn't feel right, he will take a few steps back and think it through. Back on that unforgettable day, Leos said something told him not to go to work, but he didn't listen to his gut.

"I woke up with this feeling that I shouldn't go in," said Leos, who will turn 38 next month. "My friends were going to the beach and invited me to go. But it was the first job I ever had, and I talked myself out of it."

Activity 1.7   Consider a Profile

1. In your small group, decide what argument Janine Zuniga is making in this profile of the San Ysidro massacre survivor.

2. Describe what you think are the best specific details the writer includes, either of the shooting or of Leos's subsequent recovery and career as a policeman. How do these details contribute to the story?

3. A profile generally emphasizes the ethos of the subject. In this profile, how does the author do that? How does the author also make use of pathos?

4. As the readers, what conclusion are you left with after you read the article? Is this the impression that the writer wanted you to have, do you think?

Memories of McDonald's Rhetorical Actions 20 Years Later

In 2004, twenty years after the massacre, a memorial service was held at the site, and the media ran stories about the anniversary. Many people contributed to a blog associated with the anniversary story in the local newspaper:

Shortly after the shooting that injured Alberto Leos, wounded 18 others, and killed 21 people (see the reading on page 22), a committee in San Ysidro, California, collected 1,400 signatures asking that the McDonald's be razed and a memorial park built. Although McDonald's was in no way responsible for the attack, it responded to the committee's rhetorical appeal. Bob Kaiser, director of media relations for McDonald's, said, "The concern is for the people, not simply business" and reported that the company's decision whether to reopen the restaurant was being held in abeyance. Later, the company tore down the restaurant and donated the land to the city. After debating what to do with the land, the city used it to build a community college.

Jennifer wrote: "I live in La Jolla, exactly twenty five miles north of the former McDonald's where this tragedy took place some twenty plus years ago. The site is now the home of Southwestern College, but I have seen the memorial and am always filled with sadness when I go there. They have done a wonderful job on the memorial which is just in front of the former McDonald's building which you can tell was once the eatery, but has been painted grey, though the general shape of the building is still there. I am especially touched by the and it is great that the memory of what happened not so long ago in our city is kept alive. ALL those that survived or not on that very sad day, were heroes, but their memories will never be in vain and we, as the citizens of this beautiful city will always be proud of their bravery and courage."

Leonor wrote: "I was seven at the time and I lived half a block from McDonald's. I saw bullets flying in the air and I remember police officers not letting us go to our house. They told us to get down in our car and not move. It was scary because we did not know what was going on. We were going to eat at McDonald's but my grandma invited us to her house. I still live in San Ysidro and I graduated from Southwestern College and I see the area everyday. It's not easy to forget what I do remember."

Armida wrote: "I remember that day. I was there. I had just turned 17. This was my first job. I lost my cousin and two friends because they threw a coffee pot at him to save this guy who became a cop. I saved a co-worker. I never told anybody or wrote about this day till now."

Sergio wrote: "I still remember this event. I'm now 33 years old and I was 9 years old. I still remember the gun shots, many of them. I grew up about 3 blocks away. I remember the countless police officers blocking the streets of Sunset Lane, which was my street. Two of my friends were murdered. I could have been there. My best friend died that day. This has been a funeral I will always remember. I just like to share a tiny bit on that day in the summer of July."

Joe Bloggs wrote: "I remember this happening. I was only about 12 years old at the time and living in Australia, but it is something I never forget about. Why America is so obsessed with guns I will never understand. Nobody except the police and army should have access to firearms. The private ownership of guns should be illegal and there should be gun amnesty days where guns can be handed in to be crushed. This is going to happen time and time again, people, unless you stand up and say no to gun ownership."

The blog entries show the impact of the event, even 20 years later. Notice that there are no negative comments about the McDonald's, nor about what the community decided to do with the land. Nothing McDonald's could have done would have erased the pain of the event, but its rhetorical actions, in both word and deed, did not add to the trauma of the event. McDonald's response to the citizens' request to tear down the building and donate the land to the city continues to be praised 20 years later.

Activity 1.8 Blogging and Responding to Blogging

Collaborate

In your group, discuss the blog entries above about the San Ysidro shooting. Which blog entry attracts your attention the most? What do you think was the author's rhetorical purpose?

Write your own blog entry in response to the McDonald's story. What would you say to the citizens who remember the event? What would you say to the people at McDonald's who made the decision to tear down the building and donate the land to the city?

Do you blog? Why? Do you check your blog frequently? How do you feel if there are responses to your comments? How do you feel if there are no responses to your comments? Does it matter if the response is positive or negative?

Compose Activity 1.9 Write about Everyday Arguments

Read your local newspaper or magazines such as *Time* or *Fortune* or search the Internet and bring to class a copy of a recent text or visual image that makes an argument about an issue. You might find, for example, an editorial in your local newspaper about recycling efforts in your community or a blog entry about parenting practices. Be sure, however, that the text or image takes a position on the issue. Write a paragraph of approximately 100 to 150 words describing the argument to your classmates and your reaction to it.

Encountering Visual Rhetoric

Why is a visual so powerful? Colors, shapes, and symbols impact viewers in ways text alone cannot. Many images present arguments and, because they are visual, they communicate more quickly and, sometimes, more powerfully than words.

The images on the next page are covers from *GQ* magazine. On the left, Sacha Baron Cohen, in the Bruno character, graces the humor edition of the magazine in a pose echoing that of Jennifer Aniston, on the right, which was printed on a cover a few months previously. What do you think when you see a man positioned in a way that is typical for a scantily dressed (or nude) female? Is it funny? Many think so, but not everyone. A posting on a blog called thesocietypages.org says of Cohen, "The contrast between the meaning of the pose (sexy and feminine) with the fact that he's male draws attention to how powerfully gendered the pose is… women look sexy when they pose like this, men look stupid when they do."

A photo's ability to persuade can be significant, whether it is a news photo or an advertisement. However, not everyone interprets images the same way, especially when they evoke stereotypes of gender, race, or religion.

Compare these two cover photos from *GQ* magazine. Though the poses are similar, because the figure on the left is a man and the one on the right is a woman, they evoke very different responses from readers. Some see the photo on the left as paying humorous tribute to the one on the right. Others interpret both images as exploiting feminine gender stereotypes.

Activity 1.10 **Write a Caption for a Photo or a Pair of Photos**

Choose a news photo or advertisement from a newspaper, magazine, or the Internet that presents an argument. Alternatively, compare two news photos or advertisements. Copy or paste the photo or photos on a piece of paper and write a caption that expresses the argument(s) you see in the photo.

Rhetorical Arguments Stand the Test of Time

Abraham Lincoln's Gettysburg Address is the short speech that the president delivered at the site of the battle of Gettysburg where, four months previously, the Union Army defeated Confederate forces. His was not the only talk that day at the dedication of the Soldiers' National Cemetery, but it is the only one remembered. In just over two minutes, he was able to reframe the Civil War not just as a victory for the North but as a "new birth of freedom" for all

Americans. Now, during the 150th anniversary of the Civil War, is a good time to remember Lincoln's rhetoric—in terms of both the content and the style of his speech.

Reading 1.5

Text of the Gettysburg Address

Four score and seven years ago our fathers brought forth on this continent, a new nation, conceived in Liberty, and dedicated to the proposition that all men are created equal.

Now we are engaged in a great civil war, testing whether that nation, or any nation so conceived and so dedicated, can long endure. We are met on a great battlefield of that war. We have come to dedicate a portion of that field, as a final resting place for those who here gave their lives that that nation might live. It is altogether fitting and proper that we should do this.

But, in a larger sense, we cannot dedicate—we cannot consecrate—we cannot hallow—this ground. The brave men, living and dead, who struggled here, have consecrated it, far above our poor power to add or detract. The world will little note, nor long remember what we say here, but it can never forget what they did here. It is for us the living, rather, to be dedicated here to the unfinished work which they who fought here have thus far so nobly advanced. It is rather for us to be here dedicated to the great task remaining before us—that from these honored dead we take increased devotion to that cause for which they gave the last full measure of devotion—that we here highly resolve that these dead shall not have died in vain—that this nation, under God, shall have a new birth of freedom—and that government of the people, by the people, for the people, shall not perish from the earth.

Though no actual recording exists of Lincoln giving the speech, you can listen to it if you search on the Internet for "recording of Gettysburg Address." Listen to the speech, noting the phrase "Four score and seven years ago," which is so famous that Americans know instantly, when it is quoted by orators or writers, that it is a reference to Lincoln. Consider what arguments the president makes in his speech. Think about their relevance today.

Activity 1.11 Paraphrase the Gettysburg Address

Rephrase each sentence of the Gettysburg Address, one by one, in your own words, putting it in 21st century wording rather than Lincoln's ceremonial, 19th century phrasing. In a paraphrase, the text does not become shorter; it is recreated in different words. This is a useful technique in helping you understand a text. It is also helpful when you are writing an analysis of a text because you can use your paraphrase rather than long, block quotes. Remember, though, when you are writing an essay, you must cite a paraphrase in the text and also include it in your list of references.

Activity 1.12 Keep a Commonplace Book

Ancient rhetoricians performed speeches with little warning, often to advertise their services as teachers of rhetoric. Thus, they frequently memorized arguments about specific topics that could be adapted to the audience and situation on a moment's notice. They called these memorized arguments "commonplaces." Commonplace books are an outgrowth of the Greek concept of commonplaces, but they are a little different. They became popular in the Middle Ages as notebooks in which individuals would write down quotes or ideas about a particular topic.

For thousands of years, people have been keeping commonplace books, a kind of journal or diary in which the author includes quotes, drawings, and images.

These notations might later be used to generate an idea for a composition. In more modern times, people have created commonplace books in the form of scrapbooks in which they collect quotes as well as drawings and clippings. Thus, they become a record of a person's intellectual life and can be saved for later reference.

For this class, take a notebook, perhaps one with a colorful or interesting cover, and keep notes, quotes, vocabulary words, and clippings related to the topics discussed in class. As your instructor directs, this commonplace book may be graded as evidence of class participation or it may be a private journal. Take a look at the commonplace books shown here for ideas. Be creative and enjoy adapting this ancient journal form to record ideas that interest you.

Activity 1.13 Create Your Own Blog

Create a home page for a professional blog using a site like Blogger, WordPress, or Weebly. Blogger is the easiest to use, but the others have more flexible options. Read the help screens for instructions on how to create your blog. Your design choices should reflect your personality. Keep in mind, though, that you are building an "academic self," so all the topics you write about should be of an academic nature and in an academic tone. Some students decide to have two blogs, one for their friends and one for professional networking, so you may want to do this, especially if you already have a blog.

Home   About Me   My Videos   My CMC Degree

End of the Year... My Favorite Memory
May 15, 2011

Exactly one week ago, I was at my graduation ceremony receiving my college degree. Normally graduating would be the last thing a student would do before summer vacation however I am still at CMC working away. You see, me and my RA crew had to stay in the residence halls for a few days after graduation to close down the building. Although they left 2 days ago, I am still here working on a special project. Sitting in an empty 250 bedroom mansion has given me a lot of time to think about my year. With all this reminiscing, I tried to think of my favorite memory of 2nd semester. It was difficult to choose but my 2nd semester Sky Club trip was my favorite memory of all.

For our 2nd semester Sky Club trip, we went to the McDonald Observatory in Fort David Texas. This was the 2nd trip we took and it was my favorite. We embarked out on April Fools Day (no joke) and headed south towards Texas. It was nice because we took two 11 man vans and only had 14 people on the trip so the drive was very comfortable. We stopped in several spots throughout the day and finally 15 hours later we arrived in the famous town of Fort Davis! We were all shocked to actually be in Texas because our amusement for the entire ski season in Steamboat was making fun of Texan tourists. Since we were now tourists in Texas, we began acting like tourists. Immediately we busted out cameras and took pictures of anything and everything we could see.

During this class, you'll use the blog to explore different aspects of each chapter in the textbook (and other topics that your instructor directs). You can also blog about other topics related to your writing this semester, and you can link to other blogs that you think your readers would find of interest.

After you have created the look of your blog, write a first entry that introduces you to your readers. You might include your major, your college, and something interesting that might attract readers to your blog.

Mitchell, Alexander Thomas. *Bae Feelings*.

2
RESPONDING RHETORICALLY

Praxis in Action

Why I Annotate Readings by Lauren Connolly

Annotating a reading gives me the ability to participate in a conversation with the author of the text in order to develop my ideas for writing and understanding the information presented. My annotation style uses two methods: one is with a pencil and the other is with a highlighter.

As with a conversation, my side comments may be to protest the author's ideas or to make connections with other things in my life, other readings for the class, or my other classes. By making notes, I am actively participating in the conversation, opposed to passively taking in the information presented, and it gives me an opportunity to create something meaningful from the text. Using the highlighter sparingly, I only mark a word or phrase, in order to point out specific ideas or words that I want to reference, understand, or quote in my writing at a later point in time. The meaningful interaction is when, using a pencil, I write comments in the margins in response to these highlights. These comments are frequently a part of my prewriting stage, as I use my marginal comments directly in my early written drafts. Annotating allows me to respond, clarify, and develop my ideas about what I have learned, enabling me to use the ideas later in both my writing and research.

Lauren Connolly likes to annotate readings because it allows her to have a conversation with the writer.

33

Thinking Critically, Reading Rhetorically

In contemporary times we study texts to encourage students to develop critical thinking, a skill which is essential for understanding the scientific method and for making effective judgments in the workplace and in civil life. This student-centered emphasis would have seemed strange to ancient Greek and Roman rhetoricians and their students. They believed that a rhetor's skill was best developed by honoring the skills of those who excelled in the past. Therefore, a large part of the educational process involved having students study the texts of well-regarded speeches, memorize and recite them, and model new compositions based on their approaches to topics and language style. As Isocrates explained:

> Since language is of such a nature that it is possible to discourse on the same subject matter in many different ways—to represent the great as lowly or invest the little with grandeur, to recount the things of old in a new manner or set forth events of recent date in an old fashion—it follows that one must not shun the subjects upon which others have composed before, but must try to compose better than they . . . (Panegyricus).

Thus, students in ancient Greece or Rome would have been presented with a text, often read aloud by a teacher, and they would be asked to transcribe or copy it down with the idea that they would internalize the skills of the master rhetor who had originally given the speech. Then, they would be asked to write about the same subject in a way that built upon what they had learned from the master text but incorporated their own personal attitudes or perspectives.

Today, rather than being asked to model new compositions based upon the techniques of classic texts, students are asked to read texts carefully and then to engage in critical thinking and discussion about those texts.

Critical thinking involves considering issues thoughtfully and independently. Critical thinkers do not believe facts or opinions just because they are published—whether it is in newspapers, textbooks, on television, or on the Internet. Nor do they focus upon just understanding or memorizing information, as in facts and figures. Critical thinkers examine the reasoning of the information in front of them, looking for premises and considering the inferences drawn from those premises. They are able to think for themselves, making logical connections between ideas, seeing cause and effect relationships, and using information to solve problems.

Reading rhetorically makes use of critical thinking skills, but it also involves looking at texts as arguments and evaluating them for validity, adequacy of evidence, and presence of bias. Moreover, reading rhetorically involves having a knowledge of rhetoric and specialized Greek terms such as logos, pathos, ethos, and kairos—words that were defined briefly in Chapter 1 and will be discussed more extensively in Chapter 3. Practice reading rhetorically as you read the following article on the Strauss-Kahn sexual assault case.

Reading 2.1

A wealthy public figure accused of sexual misconduct in a swanky hotel says that the charge is trumped up, that his alleged victim lacks credibility.

In their eagerness to bag a famous name, the defendant says, investigators have rushed to judgment. He says they have failed to carefully consider whether the woman who reported being accosted had a motive to lie.

That's what Dominque Strauss-Kahn says, through his attorneys.

And that's what lawyer A. Scott Bolden says. He represents Washington Redskins lineman Albert Haynesworth, awaiting trial on a misdemeanor charge that he indecently groped a waitress at the posh W Hotel in Washington.

In Sex-Crime Cases, Credibility a Thorny Issue

by Paul Duggan

In 2011, Dominique Strauss-Kahn, the head of the International Monetary Fund (IMF), was accused of sexual assault by a housekeeper at the Sofitel New York hotel. He pled not guilty. During the case, the victim's credibility was called into question, as she had reportedly lied to the police in her first statement about the case. The following article, by Paul Duggan, published in *The Washington Post*, talks about the credibility of alleged victims in sex-crime cases, and how, in the Strauss-Kahn case, it could affect the outcome. To begin a critical reading of an article, you want to read the entire piece first for content. Then, reread the introduction. How does the author attempt to capture the audience's attention? How does the author use the Lanigan case as a frame of reference?

"Let me tell you something about sex-crimes prosecutors," said Bolden, a former sex-crimes prosecutor. "They tend to be true believers. I mean, they've never met a victim they don't want to save or who they don't believe. . . . And when credibility issues arise, they tend to just want to explain them away."

As authorities Friday acknowledged doubts about the credibility of Strauss-Kahn's accuser in New York, and the rape case against the former head of the International Monetary Fund seemed in jeopardy, Bolden and other lawyers said the news highlights one of the thorniest issues in sex-crimes prosecutions:

Will jurors believe the alleged victim?

Sometimes the believability issue has nothing to do with the allegation itself. The witness may have a troubled past that could cast doubt on her testimony.

Harry O'Reilly, a retired New York City police detective who helped create the department's Special Victims Unit in the early 1970s—the unit that handled the Strauss-Kahn case—said investigators often deal with accusers who have less-than-savory backgrounds and who offer changing accounts of alleged assaults.

"It's quite common for there to be credibility issues," he said. He said detectives initially should focus only on whether the alleged crime occurred, and not be deterred by the woman's personal history, even if it involves dishonesty.

"If someone makes an allegation, we listen," he said. "And then we look for chinks in the story. And if the story begins to dissipate, then we go from there. But at the onset, we're not looking at things in her past that aren't relevant to the allegation."

Attorney Peter Greenspun, who defended Fairfax County teacher Sean Lanigan, acquitted this year of sexually molesting a 12-year-old female student, said authorities have to proceed in such cases with caution.

"These are the kinds of cases where the most care has to be exercised before anyone is charged, because of what allegations like this do to people," Greenspun said.

Jurors in the Fairfax trial later voiced outrage at the dearth of evidence against Lanigan, a married father of three whose life was shattered by the allegations.

"These are devastating charges," Greenspun said. "There's an assumption of guilt by the public, and reputations and life trajectories are destroyed."

In New York, prosecutors acknowledged that the hotel maid who accused Strauss-Kahn of raping her in his luxury suite May 14 later lied to investigators about her personal history and gave them inconsistent accounts of the moments after the alleged assault.

Strauss-Kahn, 62, who was arrested hours after the allegation and resigned from the IMF, was ordered released from home confinement in Manhattan on Friday. But the district attorney's office has not moved to dismiss the rape case.

"She said it happened, and he's sort of a pompous guy with a reputation ... for grabbing women, so they thought, well, of course, it must have happened," Greenspun said. He said police generally spend too little time investigating such cases before making arrests, especially when the suspects are prominent men.

Even if Strauss-Kahn's attorneys have information about his accuser that they could use in court to cast doubt on her veracity, prosecutors have a "moral obligation" to proceed with the case if they believe that the woman is being truthful, said lawyer Mai Fernandez, director of the National Center for Victims of Crime.

"You could have Attila the Hun come to you and say he's a victim, and the truth of the matter is, in this particular case, he may be," Fernandez said.

"You have to look first at the evidence that's directly related to the case at hand," she added. "The victim? Well, everybody has a past. None of us is without sin. There's always something that a defense lawyer can use to tarnish your reputation."

Kristina Korobov, a former prosecutor, agreed with Fernandez, but only to an extent.

"It's true that you can't just say to a victim, 'Well, you have a credibility problem, so too bad,' and then, based on that, you don't proceed with the case," Korobov said. "Because that just rewards offenders who choose victims with credibility problems."

In a case like Strauss-Kahn's, she said, prosecutors are probably weighing whether the woman's credibility is so badly damaged that a conviction would be highly unlikely.

"There were a number of victims in my lifetime who I legitimately believed had been victimized, but I didn't file a charge," said Korobov, now a senior attorney with the National Center for the Prosecution of Violence Against Women. "You've got to be very selective about what cases you bring, based on what you think you can prove."

Activity 2.1 Analyze a Text

In your small group, discuss the following questions and then report your group's opinion(s) to the class.

1. What is the problem that the author is concerned about in regard to prosecuting sex crimes?

2. What court cases does he mention? How was the victim's ethos involved?

3. How does the writer appeal to logos? To pathos?

4. If your group were writing a letter to the editor of the *Washington Post* commenting about this article, what might you say about the controversy the writer presents?

Rhetoric's Visual Heritage and Impact

The first televised presidential debate in September 1960 is a famous example of the power of visual rhetoric and a vivid illustration of the fact that visual elements must be considered when "reading" rhetorical situations. Radio listeners who could hear but not see the debate rated Vice President Richard Nixon as the winner over Senator John F. Kennedy—Nixon's arguments sounded more logical and were more clearly expressed. However, the television audience experienced a new element in the history of presidential debates: They could see the performances of the handsome and tan Senator Kennedy and the pasty-white and ill-looking Vice President Nixon, and they clearly preferred Kennedy. He *looked and acted presidential*, which overcame the drawbacks that had troubled his campaign previously—that he was relatively unknown, young, and Catholic. It overcame any advantage that Nixon may have had in presenting logical arguments and also by being an incumbent vice president. And unfortunately for Nixon, by 1960, 88 percent of Americans had televisions. "It's one of those unusual points on the timeline of history where you can say things changed very dramatically—in this case, in a single night," says Alan Schroeder, a media historian who authored the book, *Presidential Debates: Forty Years of High-Risk TV.** Indeed, after the unexpected impact of the Kennedy-Nixon debates, presidential candidates were so apprehensive about competing on television that it was 16 years

---

*Webley, Kayla. "How the Nixon-Kennedy Debate Changed the World." *Time* 23 September 2010. Web. 30 July 2011.

before candidates (President Gerald R. Ford and former Governor Jimmy Carter) were again willing to risk presenting themselves side by side on television.

Why did the experience of seeing the two candidates, rather than hearing them or reading their speeches, make such a difference? The ancient Greeks and Romans who developed rhetoric would have understood the reason: It was what they called ethos, which can be translated only imperfectly as credibility. A person's ethos is determined partially by his or her reputation, but as Richard Nixon learned the hard way, it is conveyed even more powerfully by appearance, gestures, tone, and cadence of speech. It is important to remember that the standards and perceptions of Americans are heavily influenced by rhetoric as it was defined and implemented by the Greeks and Romans—first in oral presentations. Many of the attributes of rhetoric translate to written texts, but not all. Thus, when considering a text that was originally presented as a speech, reading rhetorically means thinking about visual rhetoric—the impact the speech would have had on an audience that was *watching and listening to the presentation.*

The first presidential debate between Vice President Richard Nixon and Senator John F. Kennedy illustrated the power of visual rhetoric.

Moreover, the impact of visual rhetoric involves more than speeches: It concerns television shows, films, photographs, paintings, advertisements, and even the typesetting layout of a text that has no illustrations. We will consider these types of visual rhetoric in more detail later in this chapter.

On page 41, we reprint President Barack Obama's speech announcing the death of Osama bin Laden. This speech is available widely on the Internet at such sites as AmericanRhetoric.com, NYTimes.com, and YouTube.com. If possible, watch the speech before you read the text, and as you do so think about the impact of the speech, including the president's verbal presentation and the setting at the White House, as well as the content of the speech. Think about the various audiences President Obama was speaking to—Americans and people around the world who might be watching at that moment, as well as a historic audience of people such as yourself who would be viewing the speech months or years later.

The Rhetorical Triangle

When reading a text or listening to a speech, keep in mind the three parts of the rhetorical triangle—writer, audience, and subject (see figure 2.1). Each of these can be framed as a question:

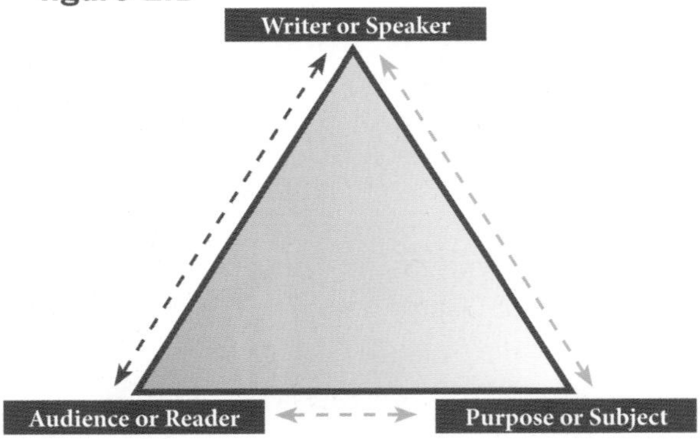

■ Who is the writer? What is the impression the writer wants to make on the audience? What does the writer do to establish credibility (ethos)? How does the writer create common ground with the audience?

figure 2.1

Writer or Speaker

Audience or Reader ← - - - → Purpose or Subject

■ Who is the intended audience? How would a logical appeal influence the audience? An ethical appeal? An emotional appeal? What does the audience anticipate in terms of organization and format of the presentation or paper? What is the extent of their knowledge about the subject, and do they have prejudices or preferences?

■ What is the purpose of the communication? In the case of an argument, the purpose would be to persuade. Is that the case with this reading? Is it clear what the writer wants to persuade the audience to believe or to do? Is the request phrased in a logical manner?

Activity 2.2 Apply the Rhetorical Triangle

For each of the readings presented thus far in the textbook, identify the speaker, the audience, and the purpose. Then analyze how each of those elements affects the content of the reading.

1. "Violent Rhetoric and Arizona Politics" (Chapter 1, p. 14)

2. "The Sleepover Question" (Chapter 1, p. 18)

3. "San Ysidro Shooting Survivor Lives His Dream of Being a Cop" (Chapter 1, p. 22)

4. "In Sex-Crime Cases, Credibility a Thorny Issue" (Chapter 2, p. 35)

Reading 2.2

President Barack Obama on the Death of Osama bin Laden

Good evening. Tonight, I can report to the American people and to the world that the United States has conducted an operation that killed Osama bin Laden, the leader of al Qaeda, and a terrorist who's responsible for the murder of thousands of innocent men, women, and children.

It was nearly 10 years ago that a bright September day was darkened by the worst attack on the American people in our history. The images of 9/11 are seared into our national memory— hijacked planes cutting through a cloudless September sky; the Twin Towers collapsing to the ground; black smoke billowing up from the

President Barack Obama announced the death of Osama bin Laden.

Pentagon; the wreckage of Flight 93 in Shanksville, Pennsylvania, where the actions of heroic citizens saved even more heartbreak and destruction.

And yet we know that the worst images are those that were unseen to the world. The empty seat at the dinner table. Children who were forced to grow up without their mother or their father. Parents who would never know the feeling of their child's embrace. Nearly 3,000 citizens taken from us, leaving a gaping hole in our hearts.

On September 11, 2001, in our time of grief, the American people came together. We offered our neighbors a hand, and we offered the wounded our blood. We reaffirmed our ties to each other, and our love of community and country. On that day, no matter where we came from, what God we prayed to, or what race or ethnicity we were, we were united as one American family.

We were also united in our resolve to protect our nation and to bring those who committed this vicious attack to justice. We quickly learned that the 9/11 attacks were carried out by al Qaeda—an organization headed by Osama bin Laden, which had openly declared war on the United States and was committed to killing innocents in our country and around the globe. And so we went to war against al Qaeda to protect our citizens, our friends, and our allies.

Over the last 10 years, thanks to the tireless and heroic work of our military and our counterterrorism professionals, we've made great strides in that effort. We've disrupted terrorist attacks and strengthened our homeland defense. In Afghanistan, we removed the Taliban government, which had given Bin Laden and al Qaeda safe haven and support. And around the globe, we worked with our friends and allies to capture or kill scores of al Qaeda terrorists, including several who were a part of the 9/11 plot.

Yet Osama bin Laden avoided capture and escaped across the Afghan border into Pakistan. Meanwhile, al Qaeda continued to operate from along that border and operate through its affiliates across the world. And so shortly after taking office, I directed Leon Panetta, the director of the CIA, to make the killing or capture of Bin Laden the top priority of our war against al Qaeda, even as we continued our broader efforts to disrupt, dismantle, and defeat his network.

Then, last August, after years of painstaking work by our intelligence community, I was briefed on a possible lead to Bin Laden. It was far from certain, and it took many months to run this thread to ground. I met repeatedly with my national security team as we developed more information about the possibility that we had located Bin Laden hiding within a compound deep inside of Pakistan. And finally, last week, I determined that we had enough intelligence to take action, and authorized an operation to get Osama bin Laden and bring him to justice.

Today, at my direction, the United States launched a targeted operation against that compound in Abbottabad, Pakistan. A small team of Americans carried out the operation with extraordinary courage and capability. No Americans were harmed. They took care to avoid civilian casualties. After a firefight, they killed Osama bin Laden and took custody of his body.

For over two decades, Bin Laden has been al Qaeda's leader and symbol, and has continued to plot attacks against our country and our friends and allies. The death of Bin Laden marks the most significant achievement to date in our nation's effort to defeat al Qaeda.

Yet his death does not mark the end of our effort. There's no doubt that al Qaeda will continue to pursue attacks against us. We must—and we will—remain vigilant at home and abroad.

As we do, we must also reaffirm that the United States is not—and never will be—at war with Islam. I've made clear, just as President Bush did shortly after 9/11, that our war is not against Islam. Bin Laden was not a Muslim leader; he was a mass murderer of Muslims. Indeed, al Qaeda has slaughtered scores of Muslims in many countries, including our own. So his demise should be welcomed by all who believe in peace and human dignity.

Over the years, I've repeatedly made clear that we would take action within Pakistan if we knew where Bin Laden was. That is what we've done. But it's important to note that our counterterrorism cooperation with Pakistan helped lead us to Bin Laden and the compound where he was hiding. Indeed, Bin Laden had declared war against Pakistan as well, and ordered attacks against the Pakistani people.

Tonight, I called President Zardari, and my team has also spoken with their Pakistani counterparts. They agree that this is a good and historic day for both of our nations. And going forward, it is essential that Pakistan continue to join us in the fight against al Qaeda and its affiliates.

The American people did not choose this fight. It came to our shores, and started with the senseless slaughter of our citizens. After nearly 10 years of service, struggle, and sacrifice, we know well the costs of war. These efforts weigh on me every time I, as Commander-in-Chief, have to sign a letter to a family that has lost a loved one, or look into the eyes of a service member who's been gravely wounded.

So Americans understand the costs of war. Yet as a country, we will never tolerate our security being threatened, nor stand idly by when our people have been killed. We will be relentless in defense of our citizens and our friends and allies. We will be true to the values that make us who we are. And on nights like this one, we can say to those families who have lost loved ones to al Qaeda's terror: Justice has been done.

Tonight, we give thanks to the countless intelligence and counterterrorism professionals who've worked tirelessly to achieve this outcome. The American people do not see their work, nor know their names. But tonight, they feel the satisfaction of their work and the result of their pursuit of justice.

We give thanks for the men who carried out this operation, for they exemplify the professionalism, patriotism, and unparalleled courage of those who serve our country. And they are part of a generation that has borne the heaviest share of the burden since that September day.

Finally, let me say to the families who lost loved ones on 9/11 that we have never forgotten your loss, nor wavered in our commitment to see that we do whatever it takes to prevent another attack on our shores.

And tonight, let us think back to the sense of unity that prevailed on 9/11. I know that it has, at times, frayed. Yet today's achievement is a testament to the greatness of our country and the determination of the American people.

The cause of securing our country is not complete. But tonight, we are once again reminded that America can do whatever we set our mind to. That is the story of our history, whether it's the pursuit of prosperity for our people, or the struggle for equality for all our citizens; our commitment to stand up for our values abroad, and our sacrifices to make the world a safer place.

Let us remember that we can do these things not just because of wealth or power, but because of who we are: one nation, under God, indivisible, with liberty and justice for all.

Thank you.

May God bless you.

And may God bless the United States of America.

Activity 2.3 **Evaluate the President's Speech**

After you have both watched President Obama's speech on the Internet and read the text, discuss these questions in your small group and then present the consensus of your group's answers to the class.

1. Discuss the president's presentation of the speech. Do you think the speech had a different impact on those who watched it on television versus those who heard it on the radio? What about those who neither saw nor heard it but rather read the speech?

2. How would you describe the president's tone, appearance, and mannerisms (all part of his ethos)? What about the location he chose for the speech and the timing just after news agencies had announced Bin Laden's death (the kairos)?

3. Summarize what the president says about the government's reasons for seeking Osama bin Laden and killing him. Does the president make a good argument for the necessity and importance of this act?

4. Notice that the president uses visual imagery in his speech. For example, in paragraph two, immediately after he announces his news, he refers to 9/11—"a bright September day was darkened by the worst attack on the American people in our history." What is the purpose of the visual descriptions in his speech?

5. Do you agree or disagree with what the president has to say? How so?

Activity 2.4 **Research Reactions to President Obama's Speech**

Using Google or another search engine, research the reactions to the president's speech announcing the death of Bin Laden.

1. In the days after the speech, what did the media report about the attack on Bin Laden's compound?

2. What were some American reactions to the speech and to the killing of Bin Laden?

3. What was the reaction around the world, both in Muslim and non-Muslim countries?

4. Did you learn anything during your research that surprised you? How so?

As your instructor directs, either discuss these questions in class or turn in written answers to the questions.

Reading 2.3

The Lexicon
by Charles McGrath

A *lexicon* is a synonym for dictionary, thesaurus, and wordlist. Charles McGrath, in his *New York Times* essay, "The Lexicon," examines the changes that 9/11 wrought in the English language. The attack on the World Trade Center, unlike other world-changing violent events, hasn't yet created many new words, he decides. Rather, it has brought already-existing words to our everyday vocabulary—such as jihad, T.S.A. shoe bomber, and sleeper cell. These not-so-pretty words are the lexicon of 9/11.

Ground zero, sleeper cells, progressive vertical collapse: The most resonant phrases of 9/11 are imbued with what might be called antipoetry, a resistance to prettification.

Unlike some other momentous events in our history—World War II, say, or the Vietnam War—the attacks that took place on Sept. 11, 2001, have not particularly changed or enriched our vocabulary. Sometimes these things take a while. It wasn't until the 1960s, for example, that the term "holocaust," which used to mean any large-scale massacre, took on the specific connotations it has today. For now, though, you could argue that the events of 9/11 still seem so unfathomable that they have actually impoverished the language a little, leaving us with a vacuous phrase like **war on terror**, which manages to empty both "war" and "terror" of much their meaning, or the creepy, Nazi-sounding **homeland**, which seems a far less pleasant place to live than just plain America.

We do know a lot of words now that we probably should have known before, like **jihad, Taliban, mujahedeen** and **Al Qaeda**. And some that we'd just as soon forget, like **T.S.A., security checkpoint, shoe bomber** and **progressive vertical collapse**. A term like **sleeper cell** probably sticks in our heads because it contains a tiny hint of embedded poetry, and for the same reason it's hard to forget those **72 black-eyed virgins** whom the terrorists believed they were on their way to meet. The "black-eyed" bit is a brilliant touch, even if it's probably a mistranslation.

But the most resonant phrases that have taken residence in our consciousness since that September morning are ones imbued with what might be called antipoetry, a resistance to metaphor or to prettification. **Ground zero**, for example—a term that originated with the Manhattan Project and was originally used in connection with nuclear explosions—seems particularly apt in this new context, with its sense of absolute finality, of a point that is both an end and a beginning and to which everything else refers.

And even **9/11** itself has a kind of rightness. No one says "September 11th" anymore as shorthand for that awful day. (To do so, a friend once joked, would be "so September 10th.") There's a pleasing, no-nonsense simplicity and precision to the expression—the same effect created by "24/7," only starker, and with none of the exaggeration. These four syllables are right at the end of language, where words turn into abstraction. Individually, they're just random, empty numbers, but yoked by that fateful slash they contain volumes. 9/11—everyone knows what that means, and to say any more would be pointless. Sometimes words fail.

Activity 2.5 **Develop a Lexicon**

Choose one of the following activities and create a lexicon as a group or individually:

1. Reread President Obama's speech about the death of Osama bin Laden. What words have become a more frequent part of the nation's vocabulary as a result of Bin Laden's actions? Al Qaeda and Taliban are two. Can you find others? Do an Internet search for Osama bin Laden, until you have five to seven words. Then write a 250 to 300 word essay, similar to McGrath's, in which you consider how Bin Laden's life and death have affected our country's vocabulary.
2. Do a search on the Internet for "new words." You will find lists of words and phrases that have been added to new editions of dictionaries. Examples may include such words as "aquascape," "soul patch," and "sandwich generation." Choose five to seven new words that are related to each other in some way. Create a lexicon of your own with a paragraph about each word that emphasizes the invention or recent history of the word. Give examples of each word's usage in blogs or other publications.

Ways of Reading Rhetorically

Reading theorist Louise Rosenblatt suggests a technique for analyzing written texts—particularly those with few visual cues other than words on paper or a computer screen. She says that we take the pattern of verbal signs left by the author and use them to recreate the text, not in the exact way the author perceived the text, but guided by it.

So, as we read, there is a constant stream of response to the text. However, Rosenblatt says that even as the reader is recreating the text, he or she is also reacting to it. Thus, there are two interacting streams of response involved as the person moves through the text. The reader, rather than being a passive receptor for the author's text, actually participates in the creative process during reading.

However, we read differently depending on the text and the occasion. For example, if you take a paperback novel on an airplane trip, you probably read simply for entertainment and to pass the time in the air. If you read *King Lear* for a literature class, you read for the plot, characterization, and other elements that you know will be discussed in class. If you read a chapter in your chemistry textbook before an exam, you are focusing on remembering concepts and details that might be on the test. Reading as a writer is another type of reading. You examine the text with an eye for the choices the writer made when crafting the text, such as whether the writer begins with a narrative introduction, a quote from a noted authority, or a startling statement. You notice, for example, what people are mentioned in the text, either as authorities or participants in activities.

Rosenblatt also makes a useful distinction between two main kinds of reading—aesthetic reading and efferent reading. In **aesthetic reading**, the reader is most interested in what happens "during the reading event, as he fixes his attention on the actual experience he is living through," according to Rosenblatt. Readers focus upon the ideas, images, and story of the text that evoke an aesthetic experience in the moment of reading. **Efferent readers**, in contrast, read to learn from the text, and, thus, according to Rosenblatt, "concentrate on the information, the concepts, the guides to action, that will be left with him when the reading is over."

Reading rhetorically is efferent reading, focusing not on the experience of reading but on the information the text conveys and upon the way an argument is established and supported in a text. Some arguments are written in an engaging style that is a pleasure to read, while others are written in a highly emotional tone that arouses a visceral response in the reader. A text that inspires aesthetic reading must sometimes be read several times in order for the reader to focus on the structure of the argument beneath the creative language.

Some theorists say that critical thinking is "thinking about thinking" or "reasoning about reasoning," and that is exactly what reading rhetorically involves—reasoning about whether or not a text presents a reasoned argument. A good way to begin reading rhetorically is to be aware of the essential elements of an argument and identify these elements in the text you are evaluating. See the Checklist of Essential Elements in an Argument presented below.

Checklist of Essential Elements in an Argument

☑ *A debatable issue.* By definition, for a text to be an argument, there must be at least two sides that can be asserted and supported.

☑ *A clearly stated position, claim statement, or thesis.* Arguments assert different kinds of claims, such as taking a position on an issue of fact, asserting a cause and effect relationship, declaring the value of some entity, or advocating a solution to a problem; but, in each case, after you read the argument, you should be able to restate or summarize the position, claim, or thesis in one or two sentences.

☑ *An audience.* To evaluate an argument, you need to know the original intended audience or place of publication, so that you can decide if the argument takes into account the audience's attitudes, background, and other factors. Ask yourself, for example, if the writer is assuming too much or too little background knowledge on the part of the audience or if the writer is using language that assumes the reader's agreement on the issue when that assumption is not warranted.

☑ *Evidence from reliable sources.* Quotes, statistics, and other evidence should be credited to reputable sources, even if your text is not a document that offers academic-style citations. The evidence should be sufficient to support the author's position or thesis.

☑ *Acknowledgment of the opposing argument.* A good rhetorician does not ignore any potential weaknesses in the argument. It is better to acknowledge points in favor of the opposing argument and then, if possible, refute the opposition's strong points than it is to allow an audience to poke holes in an argument.

☑ *A conclusion and/or call to action.* An argument can be concluded in a variety of effective ways, but it is important to note that it does, indeed, conclude. The conclusion can be a call to action on the part of the audience, but it should not be the beginning of an additional argument that is not supported by the evidence presented.

Reading 2.4

The Web Means the End of Forgetting

by Jeffrey Rosen

Several years ago, Stacy Snyder was a fairly typical 25-year-old college student training to be a teacher. That all changed forever when she did something that she probably thought was harmless fun—she posted a photo of herself on a social network site. In this article published in *The New York Times*, Jeffrey Rosen uses Snyder's case to illustrate how notions of privacy are changing because of the ever-growing presence and popularity of social networking sites. What is even more alarming, according to Rosen, is that photos and information, once posted on the web, are there forever. The web does not forget, and this lack of forgetting is changing society's ability to forgive and forget.

You may enjoy posting status updates about your life on a MySpace, Facebook, or Twitter account; however, with employers increasingly conducting background checks on such sites, it's very important to be careful about what you choose to post. This includes status updates, photographs, and videos. If you read the following article carefully, you may never look at social networking sites quite the same again.

Four years ago, Stacy Snyder, then a 25-year-old teacher in training at Conestoga Valley High School in Lancaster, Pa., posted a photo on her MySpace page that showed her at a party wearing a pirate hat and drinking from a plastic cup, with the caption "Drunken Pirate." After discovering the page, her supervisor at the high school told her the photo was "unprofessional," and the dean of Millersville University School of Education, where Snyder was enrolled, said she was promoting drinking in virtual view of her underage students. As a result, days before Snyder's scheduled graduation, the university denied her a teaching degree. Snyder sued, arguing that the university had violated her First Amendment rights by penalizing her for her (perfectly legal) after-hours behavior. But in 2008, a federal district judge rejected the claim, saying that because Snyder was a public employee whose photo didn't relate to matters of public concern, her "Drunken Pirate" post was not protected speech.

When historians of the future look back on the perils of the early digital age, Stacy Snyder may well be an icon. The problem she faced is only one example of a challenge that, in big and small ways, is confronting millions of people around the globe: how best to live our lives in a world where the Internet records everything and forgets nothing—where every online photo, status update, Twitter post and blog entry by and about us can be stored forever. With websites like LOL Facebook Moments, which collects and shares embarrassing personal revelations from Facebook users, ill-advised photos and online chatter are coming back to haunt people months or years after the fact.

Examples are proliferating daily: there was the 16-year-old British girl who was fired from her office job for complaining on Facebook, "I'm so totally bored!!"; there was the 66-year-old Canadian psychotherapist who tried to enter the United States but was turned away at the border—and barred permanently from visiting the country—after a border guard's Internet search found that the therapist had written an article in a philosophy journal describing his experiments 30 years ago with LSD. According to a recent survey by Microsoft, 75 percent of U.S. recruiters and human-resource professionals report that their companies require them to do online research about candidates, and many use a range of sites when scrutinizing applicants—including search engines, social networking sites, photo- and video-sharing sites, personal websites and blogs, Twitter and online gaming sites. Seventy percent of U.S. recruiters report that they have rejected candidates because of information found online, like photos and discussion-board conversations and membership in controversial groups.

Technological advances, of course, have often presented new threats to privacy. In 1890, in perhaps the most famous article on privacy ever written, Samuel Warren and Louis Brandeis complained that because of new technology—like the Kodak camera and the tabloid press—"gossip is no longer the resource of the idle and of the vicious but has become a trade." But the mild society gossip of the Gilded Age pales before the volume of revelations contained in the photos, video and chatter on social media sites and elsewhere across the Internet. Facebook, which surpassed MySpace in 2008 as the largest social-networking site, now has nearly 500 million members, or 22 percent of all Internet users, who spend more than 500 billion minutes a month on the site. Facebook users share more than 25 billion pieces of content each month (including news stories, blog posts and photos), and the average user creates 70 pieces of content a month. There are more than 100 million registered Twitter users, and the Library of Congress recently announced that it will be acquiring—and permanently storing—the entire archive of public Twitter posts since 2006.

In Brandeis's day—and until recently, in ours—you had to be a celebrity to be gossiped about in public: today all of us are learning to expect the scrutiny that used to be reserved for the famous and the infamous. A 26-year-old Manhattan woman told *The New York Times* that she was afraid of being tagged in online photos because it might reveal that she wears only two outfits when out on the town—a Lynyrd Skynyrd T-shirt or a basic black dress. "You have movie-star issues," she said, "and you're just a person."

We've known for years that the web allows for unprecedented voyeurism, exhibitionism and inadvertent indiscretion, but we are only beginning to understand the costs of an age in which so much of what we say, and of what others say about us, goes into our permanent—and public—digital files. The fact that the Internet never seems to forget is threatening, at an almost existential level, our ability to control our identities; to preserve the option of reinventing ourselves and starting anew; to overcome our checkered pasts.

In a recent book, "Delete: The Virtue of Forgetting in the Digital Age," the cyberscholar Viktor Mayer-Schönberger cites Stacy Snyder's case as a reminder of the importance of "societal forgetting." By "erasing external memories," he says in the book, "our society accepts that human beings evolve over time, that we have the capacity to learn from past experiences and adjust our behavior." In traditional societies, where missteps are observed but not necessarily recorded, the limits of human memory ensure that people's sins are eventually forgotten. By contrast, Mayer-Schönberger notes, a society in which everything is recorded "will forever tether us to all our past actions, making it impossible, in practice, to escape them." He concludes that "without some form of forgetting, forgiving becomes a difficult undertaking."

It's often said that we live in a permissive era, one with infinite second chances. But the truth is that for a great many people, the permanent memory bank of the web increasingly means there are no second chances—no opportunities to escape a scarlet letter in your digital past. Now the worst thing you've done is often the first thing everyone knows about you.

THE CRISIS—AND THE SOLUTION?

Concern about these developments has intensified this year, as Facebook took steps to make the digital profiles of its users generally more public than private. Last December, the company announced that parts of user profiles that had previously been private—including every user's friends, relationship status and family relations—would become public and accessible to other users. Then in April, Facebook introduced an interactive system called Open Graph that can share your profile information and friends with the Facebook partner sites you visit.

What followed was an avalanche of criticism from users, privacy regulators and advocates around the world. Four Democratic senators—Charles Schumer of New York, Michael Bennet of Colorado, Mark Begich of Alaska and Al Franken of Minnesota—wrote to the chief executive of Facebook, Mark Zuckerberg, expressing concern about the "instant personalization" feature and the new privacy settings. In May, Facebook responded to all the criticism by introducing a new set of privacy controls that the company said would make it easier for users to understand what kind of information they were sharing in various contexts.

Facebook's partial retreat has not quieted the desire to do something about an urgent problem. All around the world, political leaders, scholars and citizens are searching for responses to the challenge of preserving control of our identities in a digital world that never forgets. Are the most promising solutions going to be technological? Legislative? Judicial? Ethical? A result of shifting social norms and cultural expectations? Or some mix of the above? Alex Türk, the French data protection commissioner, has called for a "constitutional right to oblivion" that would allow citizens to maintain a greater degree of anonymity online and in public places. In Argentina, the writers Alejandro Tortolini and Enrique Quagliano have started a campaign to "reinvent forgetting on the Internet," exploring a range of political and technological ways of making data disappear. In February, the European Union helped finance a campaign called "Think B4 U post!" that urges young people to consider the "potential consequences" of publishing photos of themselves or their friends without "thinking carefully" and asking permission. And in the United States, a group of technologists, legal scholars and cyberthinkers are exploring ways of recreating the possibility of digital forgetting. These approaches share the common goal of reconstructing a form of control over our identities: the ability to reinvent ourselves, to escape our pasts and to improve the selves that we present to the world. [. . .]

[. . .] In the near future, Internet searches for images are likely to be combined with social-network aggregator search engines, like today's Spokeo and Pipl, which combine data from online sources—including political contributions, blog posts, YouTube videos, web comments, real estate listings and photo albums. Increasingly these aggregator sites will rank people's public and private reputations, like the new website Unvarnished, a reputation marketplace where people can write anonymous reviews about anyone. In the Web 3.0 world, Michael Fertik, a Harvard Law School graduate, predicts people will be rated, assessed and scored based not on their creditworthiness but on their trustworthiness as good parents, good dates, good employees, good baby sitters or good insurance risks.

One legal option for responding to online setbacks to your reputation is to sue under current law. There's already a sharp rise in lawsuits known as Twittergation—that is, suits to force websites to remove slanderous or false posts. Last year, Courtney Love was sued for libel by the fashion designer Boudoir Queen for supposedly slanderous comments posted on Twitter, on Love's MySpace page and on the designer's online marketplace-feedback page. But even if you win a U.S. libel lawsuit, the website doesn't have to take the offending material down any more than a newspaper that has lost a libel suit has to remove the offending content from its archive.

Some scholars, therefore, have proposed creating new legal rights to force websites to remove false or slanderous statements. Cass Sunstein, the Obama administration's regulatory czar, suggests in his new book, "On Rumors," that there might be "a general right to demand retraction after a clear demonstration that a statement is both false and damaging." (If a newspaper or blogger refuses to post a retraction, they might be liable for damages.) Sunstein adds that websites might be required to take down false postings after receiving notice that they are false—an approach modeled on the Digital Millennium Copyright Act, which requires websites to remove content that supposedly infringes intellectual property rights after receiving a complaint.

As Stacy Snyder's "Drunken Pirate" photo suggests, however, many people aren't worried about false information posted by others—they're worried about true information they've posted about themselves when it is taken out of context or given undue weight. And defamation law doesn't apply to true information or statements of opinion. Some legal scholars want to expand the ability to sue over true but embarrassing violations of privacy—although it appears to be a quixotic goal.

Daniel Solove, a George Washington University law professor and author of the book, *The Future of Reputation*, says that laws forbidding people to breach confidences could be expanded to allow you to sue your Facebook friends if they share your embarrassing photos or posts in violation of your privacy settings. Expanding legal rights in this way, however, would run up against the First Amendment rights of others. Invoking the right to free speech, the U.S. Supreme Court has already held that the media can't be prohibited from publishing the name of a rape victim that they obtained from public records. Generally, American judges hold that if you disclose something to a few people, you can't stop them from sharing the information with the rest of the world.

That's one reason that the most promising solutions to the problem of embarrassing but true information online may be not legal but technological ones. Instead of suing after the damage is done (or hiring a firm to clean up our messes), we need to explore ways of preemptively making the offending words or pictures disappear.

Zuckerberg said in January to the founder of the publication TechCrunch that Facebook had an obligation to reflect "current social norms" that favored exposure over privacy. "People have really gotten comfortable not only sharing more information and different kinds but more openly and with more people, and that social norm is just something that has evolved over time," he said.

However, norms are already developing to recreate off-the-record spaces in public, with no photos, Twitter posts or blogging allowed. Milk and Honey, an exclusive bar on Manhattan's Lower East Side, requires potential members to sign an agreement promising not to blog about the bar's goings on or to post photos on social-networking sites, and other bars and nightclubs are adopting similar policies. I've been at dinners recently where someone has requested, in all seriousness, "Please don't tweet this"—a custom that is likely to spread.

But what happens when people transgress those norms, using Twitter or tagging photos in ways that cause us serious embarrassment? Can we imagine a world in which new norms develop that make it easier for people to forgive and forget one another's digital sins? [. . .]

[. . .] Perhaps society will become more forgiving of drunken Facebook pictures in the way Samuel Gosling, the University of Texas, Austin, psychology professor says he expects it might. And some may welcome the end of the segmented self, on the grounds that it will discourage bad behavior and hypocrisy: it's harder to have clandestine affairs when you're broadcasting your every move on Facebook, Twitter and Foursquare. But a humane society values privacy, because it allows people to cultivate different aspects of their personalities in different contexts; and at the moment, the enforced merging of identities that used to be separate is leaving many casualties in its wake. Stacy Snyder couldn't reconcile her "aspiring-teacher self" with her "having-a-few-drinks self": even the impression, correct or not, that she had a drink in a pirate hat at an off-campus party was enough to derail her teaching career.

That doesn't mean, however, that it had to derail her life. After taking down her MySpace profile, Snyder is understandably trying to maintain her privacy: her lawyer told me in a recent interview that she is now working in human resources; she did not respond to a request for comment. But her success as a human being who can change and evolve, learning from her mistakes and growing in wisdom, has nothing to do with the digital file she can never entirely escape. Our character, ultimately, can't be judged by strangers on the basis of our Facebook or Google profiles; it can be judged by only those who know us and have time to evaluate our strengths and weaknesses, face to face and in context, with insight and understanding. In the meantime, as all of us stumble over the challenges of living in a world without forgetting, we need to learn new forms of empathy, new ways of defining ourselves without reference to what others say about us and new ways of forgiving one another for the digital trails that will follow us forever.

Activity 2.6 Discuss "The Web Means the End of Forgetting"

1. What is the significance of the title, "The Web Means the End of Forgetting"?

2. What does Jeffrey Rosen mean when he suggests that in the future Stacy Snyder may be an icon?

3. What is the main point in Jeffrey Rosen's main essay? What is he arguing?

4. Does Rosen offer sufficient evidence to make you take his argument seriously? Why or why not?

5. Are you a member of any social networking sites? What can you do in order to protect your reputation?

6. A woman interviewed in the article said, in regard to being tagged in online photos, "you have movie-star issues—and you're just a person." If you are a member of any social networking sites, do you tag friends in photos? Is it important to be careful about this? Why or why not?

Activity 2.7 What Is the Current State of Identity Protection in Social Networking Sites?

In your group, explore news, watchdog, and government sites to see if any new laws or other protections have been implemented to safeguard individuals posting personal information on the web. Report what you learn to the class.

Close Reading of a Text

Rhetorical reading involves careful and patient attention to the text, even reading the text several times. Following are several strategies for reading critically. You do not need to use all of the reading strategies suggested for each essay you read, but as you begin to read critically, you should try all of the strategies at least once to see which ones supplement your natural reading and learning style.

1. **Learn about the author.** Knowing whether an author is a biologist, a professional writer, or a politician can guide your expectations of the essay. If you are reading in a magazine or journal, you can often discover information in the contributor's notes at the beginning or end of the essay or at the beginning or end of the magazine. Many books have a dust jacket or a page giving a short biography of the author. As you learn about the author, jot down any impressions you may have about the author's purpose in writing the essay. Does the author have an obvious agenda in promoting a certain viewpoint on the topic?

2. **Skim the text.** Once you've gotten to know the author a little, it is helpful to read the essay quickly and superficially by reading the introduction, the first sentence in every paragraph, and the conclusion. Read quickly. When you skim a text, you are not trying to understand it. You are preparing for the more careful read that will follow. If the essay tells a story, skimming will give you a good sense of the chronology of the story. When is the story taking place? How much time seems to pass? If the essay is argumentative, skimming will provide knowledge of the basic structure of the argument and will introduce you to the main points of support. If the essay is primarily informative, you will learn some of the important distinctions and classifications the author uses to organize the information.

It may be interesting to note whether you can get the gist of the reading by skimming. Has the writer provided topic sentences for paragraphs or sections? If so, the writer is trying to make his or her message easily accessible.

3. **Explore your own knowledge and beliefs on the subject.** Make a list of what you already know about the topic of the text. Then make a list of what you believe about this topic. Finally, make a note beside each entry that marks where that information or belief came from.

4. **Reflect on the topic.** The final step before reading is reflecting on what you expect from the essay before you begin a careful reading. What does the title lead you to expect from the essay? Does your quick glance at the essay seem to support the title? How do you feel about the essay so far? Does it anger you, interest you, bore you? Do you think you have any experience that relates to the essay? Will your experience and the

author's experience lead you to the same conclusions? One effective way to reflect is to freewrite on the topic of the essay. Exploring what you know before you embark on a careful reading of the essay can deepen your responses.

5. **Annotate.** Read the essay slowly, thinking about what meaning the author is trying to convey. It is a good idea to annotate as you read, particularly points that seem important and/or raise questions in your mind. If you don't want to write in your text, try photocopying assigned essays so you can annotate them. You'll probably develop your own system of annotation as you begin to use this technique more often, but here are some basic guidelines to help you begin your annotations:

- Underline sentences, phrases, and words that seem important to the essay.

- Circle words you don't know but think you understand from the context. Then you can look them up later to see if the dictionary definition matches the definition you assumed from the context.

- Write questions in the margins. If the margins aren't large enough to write a complete question, a couple of words to remind you of what you were thinking and a question mark will do. You can also write brief comments in the margins, again just a few words to remind you of your thoughts.

- Number or put check marks in the margin by major points. Careful annotation of each point in the margin will help you later if you choose to outline.

- Use arrows, lines, and symbols in the margins to connect ideas in the essay that seem related or depend on each other.

- Note transitions, sentence structures, examples, topic sentences, and other rhetorical moves that seem particularly effective in the essay by writing a brief comment or an exclamation mark in the margin next to the underlined text.

See figure 2.2 on page 60 for an example of an annotated article.

6. **Outline.** An excellent way to distill the meaning of a text is to create an informal outline of the argument. If, as part of annotating the essay, you jot down the main subject of each paragraph in the margin, this will allow you to see the organization of the essay and outline it easily. An outline should list the focus of the essay and track how that focus unfolds paragraph by paragraph. If you are outlining a narrative essay, the outline will probably follow the chronology of the events. Outlining an informative essay, you might find that the outline tracks the steps of a process or reveals divisions and classifications. Outlining an argumentative essay, you'll probably find your outline works to prove a thesis by making statements which support that thesis, raising objections and refuting them, or, perhaps, proposing solutions to solve a problem.

7. **Freewrite about the text.** Another way to distill the meaning of a text after you have read it carefully is to lay the essay aside and freewrite for a few minutes about the content and purpose of the essay. If you have not tried freewriting before, it is easy. You simply put your pen to the paper, focus the topic in your mind, and write whatever comes to mind about the topic for a set period of time, perhaps five minutes. If you cannot think of anything to write, you write, "I can't think of anything to write," and then you continue writing what is in your mind. You may find it helpful to begin your freewriting by writing, "This essay is about . . ." and continue writing, explaining to yourself what you think the essay is about.

8. **Summarize the text.** Write a summary of what you consider to be the primary meaning of the text. Your summary should answer these questions about claims, support, purpose, and audience:

- What is the author of the essay trying to show or prove (claim)?

- What does the writer use to convince me that he or she is well informed or right (support)?

- Why did the writer choose to write this essay (purpose)?

- Who is the author addressing or writing for (audience)?

To write a clear summary, you have to understand the essay. You might test your understanding by reading the essay again and deciding whether your summary is accurate. Writing summaries helps you understand your assignments and prepares you for the numerous summaries you will complete.

Responding to Oral and Visual Media

Increasingly, young "politically minded viewers" are plugging into YouTube, Facebook, and comedy shows like "The Daily Show" and other alternative media instead of traditional news outlets. According to a *New York Times*

figure 2.2   **Reading 2.2**

One man affected so many

Where was I when it happened?

visual image—good technique

strong verbs

President Barack Obama on the Death of Osama bin Laden

Good evening. Tonight, I can report to the American people and to the world that the United States has conducted an operation that killed Osama bin Laden, the leader of al Qaeda, and a terrorist who's responsible for the murder of thousands of innocent men, women, and children.

It was nearly 10 years ago that a bright September day was darkened by the worst attack on the American people in our history. The images of 9/11 are seared into our national memory— hijacked planes cutting through a cloudless September sky; the Twin Towers collapsing to the ground; black smoke billowing up from the

President Barack Obama announced the death of Osama bin Laden.

Presidential seal—ethos

refers to children—pathos

Pentagon; the wreckage of Flight 93 in Shanksville, Pennsylvania, where the actions of heroic citizens saved even more heartbreak and destruction.

And yet we know that the worst images are those that were unseen to the world. The empty seat at the dinner table. Children who were forced to grow up without their mother or their father. Parents who would never know the

article, surveys and interviews during the 2008 presidential election indicate that "younger voters tend to be not just consumers of news and current events but conduits as well—sending out e-mailed links and videos to friends and their social networks. And in turn, they rely on friends and online connections for news to come to them." **Word of mouth** (via e-mail) is replacing traditional media as the major news filter, at least for young viewers. In this new process, moreover, "viewers" or "writers of e-mail" move seamlessly back and forth between e-mail, text-messaging, television viewing, and Internet surfing, appreciating and sharing the choicest rhetorical pieces with others. "We're talking about a generation that doesn't just like seeing the video in addition to the story—they expect it," said Danny Shea, 23, the associate media editor for *The Huffington Post* (huffingtonpost.com). "And they'll find it elsewhere if you don't give it to them, and then that's the link that's going to be passed around over e-mail and instant message." This multistream, cross-platform method of communication among younger viewers/readers is a fertile forum for rhetorical analysis.

Actually, the lines between oral, written, and visual "texts" have always been somewhat blurred. Speeches delivered orally in person or on television have a visual component, as the audience sees the speaker present the text. A written text is also, in a sense, visual because the audience's mind must process the little squiggles of ink on paper or on the computer screen into words. A visual text such as an advertisement or cartoon often includes written text, and, even if it does not, the image will inspire thoughts that are often distilled into language for expression. Reasonably, many of the same techniques used to analyze written and oral texts also can be applied to visual media (cartoons, advertisements, television, etc.).

Reading 2.5

I know I said I love you,

I know you know it's true,
I've got to put the phone down,
and do what we got to do.

One's standing in the aisleway,
Two more at the door,
We've got to get inside there,
Before they kill some more.

Time is runnin' out,
Let's roll.
Time is runnin' out,
Let's roll.

No time for indecision,
We've got to make a move,
I hope that we're forgiven,
For what we got to do

Let's Roll
by Neil Young

Music lyrics are performance texts, just as are speeches. They are written to be heard, not written to be read. However, you can analyze the argument in song lyrics, such as "Let's Roll," reprinted here, which was written by Neil Young. The song was inspired by the last words of a passenger named Todd Beamer, who died in the hijacking of Flight 93 on September 11, 2001. To analyze the song's lyrics rhetorically, you can consider whether the lyrics have a debatable issue, a clear thesis or claim, evidence to support that claim, a particular audience, and a conclusion. With a song, moreover, you can also consider the impact of the lyrics as they are presented by a vocalist accompanied by musical instruments. How does the musical presentation of the lyrics affect their impact as an argument?

How this all got started,
I'll never understand,
I hope someone can fly this thing,
And get us back to land.

Time is runnin' out,
Let's roll.
Time is runnin' out,
Let's roll.

No one has the answer,
But one thing is true,
You've got to turn on evil,
When it's coming after you,
You've gotta face it down,
And when it tries to hide,
You've gotta go in after it,
And never be denied,

Time is runnin' out,
Let's roll.

Let's roll for freedom,
Let's roll for love,
We're going after Satan,
On the wings of a dove,
Let's roll for justice,
Let's roll for truth,
Let's not let our children,
Grow up fearful in their youth.

Time is runnin' out,
Let's roll.
Time is runnin' out,
Let's roll.
Time is runnin' out,
Let's roll.

Activity 2.8 Respond to Song Lyrics

1. Reflect on what you know about the September 11 attacks. At the end of the first stanza, Young writes, "I've got to put the phone down, and do what we got to do." What is the call to action he is making here? What rhetorical significance does it have in this historical context?

2. Who is Young referring to when he says, "We're going after Satan"? What action is he advocating?

Activity 2.9 Consider a Song as an Argument

In your small group, explore the Internet for a song that seems to make an argument, and answer the following questions. Share your findings with the class.

1. What message is the artist/group trying to transmit with the song?

2. What are some lyrics that help to support this message?

3. How would you describe the musical style of the song? In what ways does the style of singing and instrumentation help the rhetorical message?

Responding to Visual Rhetoric

Methods of analyzing visual rhetoric draw upon several theoretical traditions. In art criticism, viewers may look for symbolism in an image or consider what meaning the artist was trying to convey. Semiotics views images as having intertextuality, as similar images come to have similar meanings, and those meanings may create similar emotions in the viewer. Rhetoricians, as you might expect, consider the argument that an image may present to a viewer. They think about how the subject of the image is presented in relation to other elements in the visual, how the image is cropped, and what types of lighting and colors are present. Rhetoricians also pay particular attention to the interplay between the visual image and any text that may appear with the image and how the two together construct an argument.

You know you're not the first.

BMW Premium
Selection
Used Cars

www.bmw.gr

Sheer
Driving Pleasure

Courtesy BMW premium advertising.

In the BMW advertisement shown above, for example, a beautiful blonde-haired young woman is presented without clothes and lying down with her hair artfully arranged in waves. *Salon* magazine reprinted a copy of the BMW advertisement, pointing out that, "in small print scrawled across her bare shoulder, it reads: 'You know you're not the first.' As your eyes drift to the bottom of the advertisement—and the top of her chest—you learn that it's an advertisement for BMW's premium selection of used cars."

Of course, sexual appeal has been used for decades to sell a whole range of products. However, what do you think is BMW's argument here? *Salon* thinks the ad is implying, "Used cars, used women" and that the ad gives a "whole new meaning" to BMW's slogan, printed in the ad: "Sheer Driving Pleasure."

The image that appears below, surprisingly, isn't advertising a car. No, it is selling a community college, West Hills College, capitalizing on the idea that with all the money you would save by going to a community college, you could buy a nice car.

"YOU'D BE AMAZED WHAT YOU CAN LEARN IN TWO YEARS."
and save

Two years at West Hills College: $600
vs.
Two years at a UC school: $28,000·
Why not spend $27,400 on something else?

ONCE YOU GO HERE,
YOU CAN GO ANYWHERE.

WEST HILLS COMMUNITY COLLEGE DISTRICT

1-800-266-1114 or www.westhillscollege.com

Courtesy West Hills College

Activity 2.10 Interpret Advertisements

1.   What is the symbolism of the beautiful young woman (presumably naked) posed as she is in the BMW advertisement?

2.   What meaning do you think the tag line, "You know you're not the first," adds to the image? Then, when you realize that the image is an ad for BMW used cars, does your interpretation of this tag line's meaning change?

3. What are the creators of the West Hills College advertisement trying to say by showing the image of the student sitting on the car?

4. The use of fonts is another important element in transmitting a message in an advertisement. In the West Hills College ad, why are the words "and save" written in a different font and inserted with the caret?

5. As a college student, would you be convinced by the West Hills advertisement? Why or why not? What elements exist in the ad that would or would not convince you to attend the college mentioned?

6. Do you find the BMW advertisement amusing, objectionable, or appealing? Does it make you want to buy a used BMW?

Activity 2.11 Find Advertisements with Effective Arguments

Bring to class an advertisement that you think makes an effective argument. It can be torn from a magazine or downloaded from the Internet. In your small group, evaluate each advertisement for its effectiveness in selling something, and choose the one with the most effective argument. Present your choice to the class along with an explanation of why you think it is effective.

Interaction between Texts and Images

Many of the texts we encounter in everyday life—in newspapers, magazines, and on the Internet—are not texts in isolation but texts combined with images. Indeed, when readers first glance at one of these media, likely their attention is caught first by photos, then by headlines. Only after being engaged by these attention-getting visual elements (for headlines are visual elements as well as written) are readers likely to focus on the written text. Student writers today, like professionals, have access to the use of visual elements in their compositions, and adding photos can not only catch the reader's attention but also emphasize particular points of an argument or create an overall mood.

All-Star Rockers Salute Buddy Holly

by Andy Greene

R&R

All-Star Rockers Salute Buddy Holly

McCartney, Cee Lo, the Black Keys, Kid Rock and more cut killer covers disc

When Buddy Holly died in a plane crash in 1959, he was just 22 years old and had been writing and recording songs for only about two years. But that music—including immortal hits like "Not Fade Away" and "Peggy Sue"—has had an incalculable impact on rock history. "He was a major influence on the Beatles," Paul McCartney told Rolling Stone recently. "John and I spent hours trying to work out how to play the opening riff to "That'll Be the Day," and we were truly blessed by the heavens the day we figured it out. It was the first song John, George and I ever recorded."

A half-century later, McCartney has returned to Holly's catalog, cutting a smoking rendition of "It's So Easy." It's one of 19 newly recorded Holly covers—by an all-star lineup including the Black Keys, My Morning Jacket, Kid Rock Fiona Apple, Patti Smith, and Lou Reed—for the tribute

NOT FADE AWAY
Holly in 1950. McCartney and Cee Lo recorded new songs commemorating Holly's 75th birthday.

disc *Rave on Buddy Holly*, spearheaded by Randall Poster, music supervisor of movies such as *The Royal Tenenbaums* and *I'm Not There*. "We wanted to commemorate Buddy's 75th birthday," Poster says. "I've used a lot of his songs in movies, and they're so powerful and so ripe for interpretation."

Florence and the Machine cut a New Orleans-flavored version of "Not Fade Away" while on tour in the Big Easy last year. "My grandmother took me to the musical *Buddy: The Buddy Holly Story* when I was a kid, and it changed my life," says singer Florence Welch. "When we were in New Orleans, we decided

it would be good to use the environment around us, so we brought in local Cajun musicians." Cee Lo Green tackled the relatively obscure "You're So Square (Baby, I Don't Care)." "We wanted to keep the rockabilly intact," he says. "But we broadened it and gave it a bit of something unique to me. There's something Americana about it, something country and something African." Smith selected "Words of Love." "During the song she talks in Spanish and is sort of channeling [Holly's widow] Maria Elena Holly," says Poster. "It's so romantic and so novel. More times than not, we were just overwhelmed by the power of the renditions that we received." Despite Holly's extremely brief career, Poster thinks the set could have been even longer: "There's probably a half-dozen more songs we could have done. If I had more time and more of a budget, I would have kept on going." ANDY GREENE

Activity 2.12 **Analyze Interaction between Texts and Images**

Read the article, "All-Star Rockers Salute Buddy Holly," by Andy Greene, published in *Rolling Stone* magazine. Look at how the images and layout work together and answer the questions:

1. What rhetorical purpose do the photos of these musicians achieve in relation to the article? Hint: think about the ethos (credibility, reputation, power) of these particular musicians, especially when they appear together on the page.

2. Consider the way the text is wrapped around the pictures. In particular, notice how this layout suggests a close relationship between Buddy Holly, Paul McCartney, and Cee Lo Green. What does this layout signify?

Activity 2.13   Write a Summary

Summarizing is an excellent technique to use when preparing for an exam or researching for an essay. It allows you to discern the main points of a text to see what is beneficial for you to know for the exam or paper. With a classmate, search for an article from a newspaper or magazine that presents a strong argument. Read the article, and list the main points individually. After you've listed the main points, put them into paragraph form. Caution: Beware of the temptation to add your own analysis of what the text is saying. For example, if you are summarizing a scientist's article on global warming, you need to be careful not to reveal your personal opinion about whether or not global warming is occurring or whether or not human actions are to blame. In this assignment, you summarize only. You do not argue or analyze.

When you're finished, compare your summary with that of your partner.

Reading 2.7

How to Make a Kindle Cover from a Hollowed Out Hardback Book

by Justin Meyers

The author of the following article explains why you would want to make a Kindle cover out of an old book instead of buying a new Kindle cover. What does the article say are the drawbacks of the Kindle? Think about it. These instructions are an argument, saying in text and photos that as wonderful as the Kindle is, it does not satisfy the needs of a reader to touch and smell a book. The author attempts to rectify the Kindle's shortcomings through these instructions for making a cover out of a book.

Notice also how the author uses photos to illustrate his text. If you had just the text and no photos, following the instructions would be much more difficult.

Kindle users love reading. But let's face it— a book is in your hands.

Sure, Amazon's Kindle makes it possible to read more books, clears up a lot of shelf space, fits snugly in anyone's baggage and can actually be cheaper in the long run. But each reading feels the same. The only difference is the words you read and your reaction to them. You begin to miss that sometimes rough feel of a hardback book, along with the slick, almost slippery design

of a paperback. Each book seems to have a smell of its own, something unique. And getting your hands dirty with ink from the finely written words was half the journey.

The Kindle erases that part of your reading experience. It feels the same, smells the same and even looks the same. Instead of turning pages, which is different sizes, thicknesses and colors from book to book, you're pressing the same button over and over again. In some ways, reading a classic on your Kindle actually devalues its adventure. But the eBook reader is convenient, practically weightless and serves up immediate literature consumption.

So where's the compromise?

Well, you can have the best of both worlds—sort of . . .

ebonical has crafted the perfect Kindle case—out of a hardcover book. Kindle cases can be expensive, so making a homemade Kindle cover is the perfect weekend project. And chances are you already have the perfect book for your Kindle collecting dust on your bookshelf. If not, you'll need to shop the local bookstores.

"I decided to carve out the pages of a printed book and thus complete the poetic circle of digital book readers destroying the printed word.

"Getting the right book turned out to be harder than I thought as most hardcover books are designed to be a particular size and variance is slight. Too small and the edges would be brittle. Too large and it would just become a hassle and ruin the point of having the small digital reader in the first place. With some time spent scouring thrift shops and second hand book stalls I managed, with some luck, to find what seemed to be the right book."

So, then how do you actually make the Kindle book cover?

STEP 1   **Gather the Materials**

- Your perfectly-sized hardcover book
- Hobby PVA glue (polyvinyl acetate) or Elmer's white glue
- Paintbrush
- Scalpel, box cutter or other sharp utility knife
- Ruler
- Pencil
- More books (for use as weights)

STEP 2   **Crafting Your Kindle Case**

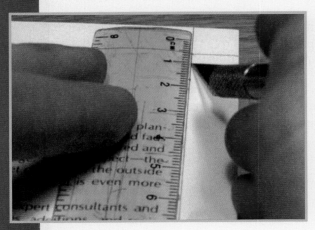

Getting your book ready for your Kindle is an easy process, though a lengthy one.

You begin by choosing where you want your hole to start. Once you have your spot picked, you use the paintbrush to spread the glue onto the edges of the pages where the hole will be cut. Use your extra books to weigh it down during the drying process.

When dry, open the book back up to your chosen starting point. Use the ruler and pencil to mark your hole the size of the Kindle. Once all marked, use your utility knife to start cutting on the outline. It's probably best to use your ruler as a straight edge to help guide the blade along, for a better, straighter cut. This is the longest step, because you have a lot to cut through. The time will vary depending on how deep your book is. I wouldn't recommend *War and Peace*.

Once you've gotten all the way to the back cover, the rest is easy. Just clean up the edges of your cuts as best you can, then use your paintbrush again to spread some glue along the cut edges.

TIP: When choosing your first page to cut, it's good to actually save it for later. Don't cut with the rest of them. When you have your hole fully cut open and have applied the glue, apply another thin line on the top border of your actual first page cut (essentially, the second page). Then close the book and add the weights to the top and let dry. Saving the first page helps reduce the chance of you accidentally gluing unwanted pages to cut ones, causing you to have to cut the pages you didn't want to cut to open the hole back up. Saving your first page makes it premeditated.

After fully dried, open it up and cut the final page (first page) to open the hole up. Then, you'll need to let it dry again, with the book open. After dried, that's it. You're done!

Activity 2.14 Write and Illustrate Instructions

Write and illustrate your own set of instructions for an activity that includes an argument. For example, during a lawn party at the White House, First Lady Michelle Obama served Carrot Lemonade to children who gave the drink rave reviews. Such a recipe could include an introduction explaining that creating healthy adaptations of popular foods and drinks for children only works if they taste good. Or, you might write instructions for how to remove geotags from photos before posting them on Facebook or other social networking sites. In your instructions you could explain that this process prevents people that you don't know from learning where you took the picture—and possibly learning where you live if you took it at home. Your argument would be that it is important to protect your privacy when you post photos on the Internet.

Try out your instructions on a friend, so you are sure you have included all the necessary steps and illustrated them adequately. Don't forget to include a brief statement of your argument, as does the writer of the Kindle cover article.

Activity 2.15 Create Your Own Blog

Read an article on the Internet related to a topic in which you're interested. Make sure the article has a substantial amount of text, as well as related images. In your blog, discuss how the text and the images both contribute to the article's rhetorical message. Include the title of the article, the author, the name of the publication or web page, and a link to the article.

Activity 2.16 Write in Your Commonplace Book

What do you read for fun? Magazines, blogs, books? Do you engage in what Louise Rosenblatt calls "aesthetic reading"? (See the section titled, "Ways of Reading Rhetorically") Write down a quote in your commonplace book from something that you have read for fun. First, reflect about what the quote means to you. Then, comment about why it is important to read things for fun and how that experience is different than reading to learn.

3
ANALYZING RHETORICALLY

Praxis in Action

Analyzing Arguments Improves My Writing by Eurydice Saucedo

Reading enables my creative mind to soar to undreamed-of worlds, to visit the deepest of memories, and to laugh as words describe a child's joy. Yes, reading enables me to be a bigger dreamer, but it also opens my eyes to better understand this world we live in.

Reading essays teaches me definitions and meanings, and, with practice, allows me to discern the validity and reliability of arguments. I can distinguish between fair representation of an issue, embellishment of truth, and bitter sarcasm. Every sentence has more than just simple grammar and punctuation. Every text, just like everything else in life, needs to be taken with a grain of salt, slowly simmered, and thought about before the final evaluation can be made. If I know rhetorical concepts, I can recognize when a text is trying to persuade me of something, and I can decide if the writer presents a good argument and sufficient evidence to merit serious consideration.

Reading and analyzing texts helps me learn how to structure my own argument. I may find a flaw in an argument, for example, a lack of acknowledgement of a counterargument that causes me to distrust a text. This causes me to be more careful to include the counterargument in my own text. And when I read and reread a classic argument such as Martin Luther King's "I Have a Dream" speech, I may make note of a strategy that I can use later. For example, Dr. King's adapting of President Lincoln's memorable language, saying, "five score years ago" instead of Lincoln's "four score and seven years ago" is highly effective. Perhaps I will try adapting a highly memorable quote when it fits in my argument.

One of the best ways to become a better writer is to read good writing.

Eurydice Saucedo writes, "Every text, just like everything else in life, needs to be taken with a grain of salt, slowly simmered, and thought about before the final evaluation can be made."

Discover the Kairos—The Opening for Argument

Ancient Greek archer

Kairos is a Greek word often translated as the right or opportune moment to do something, though it has no exact English translation. The first recorded use of the word kairos is in Homer's *Iliad*, where it appears as an adjective referring to an arrow striking the "deadliest spot" on the human body. When the word appears again later in Greek writing as a noun—a kairos—it retains this essential meaning as an opening or aperture. Twelve bronze axes with ring openings for wooden shanks are positioned in a line, so archers can practice by aiming at the kairos or ring opening, with the arrow passing down the line, through each ax. Clearly, launching an arrow through the kairos of twelve axes placed a yard apart required strength, training, practice, and a precise visual and muscle awareness of place. When people today say, "I saw my opening, and I took it, " they are conveying this meaning of kairos as an opening, combined with the idea of kairos as an opportunity.[1]

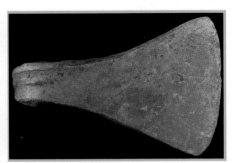

Ancient bronze ax with a ring hole
for a wooden shank

Each time a rhetor (a speaker or writer) constructs an argument, he or she is working within a context of a certain moment, a particular time and place, that come together in a unique opportunity or opening for action—a kairos. A kairos both constrains and enables what a rhetor can say or write effectively in a particular situation. So, to compose the most effective text, a rhetor must do more than develop a thesis or statement of the main idea that takes a position about the subject—he or she must discover the kairos of the argument and its ramifications. What opportunities does the kairos present for making a persuasive argument, and what restrictions may be wise in consideration of the audience or occasion?

Use Kairos to Make Your Own Argument

Consider the following suggestions for determining the kairotic moment for your argument—the opening of sensitivity where you can shoot your metaphoric arrow:

- *Consider timeliness.* What is going on right now with the issue and how can you emphasize that in an argument? For example, if you are writing

---

[1] Thomas Rickert, "Invention in the Wild: On Locating Kairos in Space-Time," in *The Locations of Composition.* eds. Christopher J. Keller and Christian R. Weisser (Albany: SUNY Press, 2007) pp. 72–73.

about the death penalty, choose to write about the current cases on death row or the most recent person to be executed. Or, if your topic is about the unemployed exhausting their government benefits and you have, yourself, recently become unemployed, you can use your own experience as an illustration of the problem.

- *Know your audience.* What are the characteristics of the audience? Do they agree with your position on the issue or not? What is their educational level and the extent of their knowledge about the subject? For example, if you are writing about immigration policy reform, does your audience believe there is a need for reform? Do they have personal experience with illegal or legal immigrants? You can judge the amount of background information you need to provide based upon the characteristics of your audience. Also, the most important members of the audience, so far as an argument is concerned, are not those who already agree with you but those who are neutral or even slightly opposed to your position but willing to listen. Be careful not to phrase your argument in ways that are insulting to people who do not agree with you, for if you do so, they will stop listening to you.

- *Find a place to stand.* In the reading that follows, Martin Luther King, Jr., stood in front of the Lincoln Memorial as he gave his famous speech, "I Have a Dream." This location greatly impacts the speech and increases King's ethos, which we discuss in more detail below. You can make a similar rhetorical move, for example, if you live in a border community because you stand, metaphorically and physically, at an important juncture for issues such as immigration, free trade, and national security.

When Martin Luther King, Jr., gave his "I Have a Dream" speech, his words were carefully crafted to take into consideration the setting in front of the Lincoln Memorial. He said, "Five score years ago, a great American, in whose symbolic shadow we stand today, signed the Emancipation Proclamation." The words "five score" recall the "four score and seven years ago" of Lincoln's words in the Gettysburg Address. And King also pointed out that he and his audience that day stood in the "symbolic shadow" of the president who signed the Emancipation Proclamation. In these ways, he made use of Lincoln's shadow to legitimize what he was saying about civil rights.

In other ways, however, the kairos of the moment limited what he could say. His audience included both the thousands of people in front of him who were dedicated to the cause of racial equality and also the audience of those millions watching on television who may or may not have agreed with his message. Thus, the tone of his message needed to be subtly measured not to antagonize those among his audience, particularly the television audience, who may have opposed aspects of the civil rights movement such as school integration. However, he spoke to let both his supporters and his opponents know, "The whirlwinds of revolt will continue to shake the foundations of our nation until the bright day of justice emerges." Yes, King advocated nonviolent demonstrations, but they were demonstrations nonetheless; he was putting opponents on notice that the disruptions caused by demonstrations would continue "until justice emerges." King consistently took the high road, while maintaining the power of the kairotic moment when he spoke. This is one reason why his words continue to be studied decades after his death.

Reading 3.1

I Have a Dream

by Martin Luther King, Jr.

Martin Luther King, Jr., delivered this speech on August 28, 1963, at the Lincoln Memorial in Washington, D.C., as part of the March on Washington for Jobs and Freedom. A Baptist minister, King received the Nobel Peace Prize in 1964 for his efforts to end racial discrimination through nonviolent means. He was assassinated in 1968.

I am happy to join with you today in what will go down in history as the greatest demonstration for freedom in the history of our nation.

Five score years ago, a great American, in whose symbolic shadow we stand today, signed the Emancipation Proclamation. This momentous decree came as a great beacon light of hope to millions of Negro slaves who had been seared in the flames of withering injustice. It came as a joyous daybreak to end the long night of their captivity.

But one hundred years later, the Negro still is not free. One hundred years later, the life of the Negro is still sadly crippled by the manacles of segregation and the chains of discrimination. One hundred years later, the Negro lives on a lonely island of poverty in the midst of a vast ocean of material prosperity. One hundred years later, the Negro is still languished in the corners of American society and finds himself an exile in his own land. And so we've come here today to dramatize a shameful condition.

In a sense we've come to our nation's capital to cash a check. When the

architects of our republic wrote the magnificent words of the Constitution and the Declaration of Independence, they were signing a promissory note to which every American was to fall heir. This note was a promise that all men, yes, black men as well as white men, would be guaranteed the "unalienable Rights" of "Life, Liberty and the pursuit of Happiness." It is obvious today that America has defaulted on this promissory note, insofar as her citizens of color are concerned. Instead of honoring this sacred obligation, America has given the Negro people a bad check, a check which has come back marked "insufficient funds."

But we refuse to believe that the bank of justice is bankrupt. We refuse to believe that there are insufficient funds in the great vaults of opportunity of this nation. And so, we've come to cash this check, a check that will give us upon demand the riches of freedom and the security of justice.

We have also come to this hallowed spot to remind America of the fierce urgency of Now. This is no time to engage in the luxury of cooling off or to take the tranquilizing drug of gradualism. Now is the time to make real the promises of democracy. Now is the time to rise from the dark and desolate valley of segregation to the sunlit path of racial justice. Now is the time to lift our nation from the quicksands of racial injustice to the solid rock of brotherhood. Now is the time to make justice a reality for all of God's children.

It would be fatal for the nation to overlook the urgency of the moment. This sweltering summer of the Negro's legitimate discontent will not pass until there is an invigorating autumn of freedom and equality. Nineteen sixty-three is not an end, but a beginning. And those who hope that the Negro needed to blow off steam and will now be content will have a rude awakening if the nation returns to business as usual. And there will be neither rest nor tranquility in America until the Negro is granted his citizenship rights. The whirlwinds of revolt will continue to shake the foundations of our nation until the bright day of justice emerges.

But there is something that I must say to my people, who stand on the warm threshold which leads into the palace of justice: In the process of gaining our rightful place, we must not be guilty of wrongful deeds. Let us not seek to satisfy our thirst for freedom by drinking from the cup of bitterness and hatred. We must forever conduct our struggle on the high plane of dignity and discipline. We must not allow our creative protest to degenerate into physical violence. Again and again, we must rise to the majestic heights of meeting physical force with soul force.

The marvelous new militancy which has engulfed the Negro community must not lead us to a distrust of all white people, for many of our white brothers, as evidenced by their presence here today, have come to realize that their destiny is tied up with our destiny. And they have come to realize that their freedom is inextricably bound to our freedom.

We cannot walk alone.

And as we walk, we must make the pledge that we shall always march ahead.

We cannot turn back.

There are those who are asking the devotees of civil rights, "When will you be satisfied?" We can never be satisfied as long as the Negro is the victim of the unspeakable horrors of police brutality. We can never be satisfied as long as our bodies, heavy with the fatigue of travel, cannot gain lodging in the motels of the highways and the hotels of the cities. We cannot be satisfied as long as the negro's basic mobility is from a smaller ghetto to a larger one. We can never be satisfied as long as our children are stripped of their selfhood and robbed of their dignity by a sign stating: "For Whites Only." We cannot be satisfied as long as a Negro in Mississippi cannot vote and a Negro in New York believes he has nothing for which to vote. No, no, we are not satisfied, and we will not be satisfied until "justice rolls down like waters, and righteousness like a mighty stream."[2]

I am not unmindful that some of you have come here out of great trials and tribulations. Some of you have come fresh from narrow jail cells. And some of you have come from areas where your quest—quest for freedom left you battered by the storms of persecution and staggered by the winds of police brutality. You have been the veterans of creative suffering. Continue to work with the faith that unearned suffering is redemptive. Go back to Mississippi, go back to Alabama, go back to South Carolina, go back to Georgia, go back to Louisiana, go back to the slums and ghettos of our northern cities, knowing that somehow this situation can and will be changed.

Let us not wallow in the valley of despair, I say to you today, my friends.

And so even though we face the difficulties of today and tomorrow, I still have a dream. It is a dream deeply rooted in the American dream.

I have a dream that one day this nation will rise up and live out the true meaning of its creed: "We hold these truths to be self-evident, that all men are created equal."

I have a dream that one day on the red hills of Georgia, the sons of former slaves and the sons of former slave owners will be able to sit down together at the table of brotherhood.

I have a dream that one day even the state of Mississippi, a state sweltering with the heat of injustice, sweltering with the heat of oppression, will be transformed into an oasis of freedom and justice.

I have a dream that my four little children will one day live in a nation where they will not be judged by the color of their skin but by the content of their character.

I have a dream today!

I have a dream that one day, down in Alabama, with its vicious racists, with its governor having his lips dripping with the words of "interposition" and "nullification"—one day right there in Alabama little black boys and black girls will be able to join hands with little white boys and white girls as sisters and brothers.

I have a dream today!

I have a dream that one day every valley shall be exalted, and every hill and mountain shall be made low, the rough places will be made plain, and the crooked places will be made straight; "and the glory of the Lord shall be revealed and all flesh shall see it together."[3]

This is our hope, and this is the faith that I go back to the South with.

With this faith, we will be able to hew out of the mountain of despair a stone of hope. With this faith, we will be able to transform the jangling discords of our nation into a beautiful symphony of brotherhood. With this faith, we will be able to work together, to pray together, to struggle together, to go to jail together, to stand up for freedom together, knowing that we will be free one day.

And this will be the day—this will be the day when all of God's children will be able to sing with new meaning:

> My country 'tis of thee, sweet land of liberty, of thee I sing.
> Land where my fathers died, land of the Pilgrim's pride,
> From every mountainside, let freedom <u>ring</u>!

And if America is to be a great nation, this must become true.

And so let freedom ring from the prodigious hilltops of New Hampshire.
Let freedom ring from the mighty mountains of New York.
Let freedom ring from the heightening Alleghenies of Pennsylvania.
Let freedom ring from the snow-capped Rockies of Colorado.
Let freedom ring from the curvaceous slopes of California.

But not only that:
Let freedom ring from Stone Mountain of Georgia.
Let freedom ring from Lookout Mountain of Tennessee.
Let freedom ring from every hill and molehill of Mississippi.
From every mountainside, let freedom ring.

And when this happens, when we allow freedom to ring, when we let it ring from every village and every hamlet, from every state and every city, we will be able to speed up that day when all of God's children, black men and white men, Jews and Gentiles, Protestants and Catholics, will be able to join hands and sing in the words of the old Negro spiritual:

Free at last! Free at last!

Thank God Almighty, we are free at last![4]

[2] Amos 5:24 (rendered precisely in The American Standard Version of the Holy Bible)

[3] Isaiah 40:4–5 (King James Version of the Holy Bible). Quotation marks are excluded from part of this moment in the text because King's rendering of Isaiah 40:4 does not precisely follow the KJV version from which he quotes (e.g., "hill" and "mountain" are reversed in the KJV). King's rendering of Isaiah 40:5, however, is precisely quoted from the KJV.

[4] "Free at Last" from American Negro Songs by J. W. Work.

Activity 3.1 Use Microsoft's Comment Feature to Annotate a Text

If you download Dr. Martin Luther King's speech from AmericanRhetoric.com, you can make use of Microsoft's Comment feature to annotate the speech with your comments, as is done in the example below. In Microsoft Word, highlight the text you want to annotate, go to the "Insert" pull-down menu, and select "Comment." A box will appear where you can enter your comment.

> I am happy to join with you today in what will go down in history as the greatest demonstration for freedom in the history of our nation.
>
> Five score years ago, a great American, in whose symbolic shadow we stand today, signed the Emancipation Proclamation. This momentous decree came as a great beacon light of hope to millions of Negro slaves who had been seared in the flames of withering injustice. It came as a joyous daybreak to end the long night of their captivity.
>
> But one hundred years later, the Negro still is not free. One hundred years later, the life of the Negro is still sadly crippled by the manacles of segregation and the chains of discrimination. One hundred years later, the Negro lives on a lonely island of poverty in the midst of a vast ocean of material prosperity. One hundred years later, the Negro is

2/7/09 12:38 AM
Comment: Reference to Lincoln's Gettysburg Address

Activity 3.2 Discuss "I Have a Dream"

Read the "I Have a Dream" speech by Rev. Martin Luther King, Jr., and, if possible, watch the speech. It is archived at http://www.americanrhetoric.com, where it is listed as the most requested speech and #1 in its list of the top 100 American speeches.

1. Discuss the kairos of Dr. King's speech. What was the occasion? Who was his audience, both present and absent? What were the issues he spoke about?

2. How did Dr. King take advantage of the kairos of the situation in the wording of his speech?

3. Why do you think the speech continues to be so popular and influential?

Activity 3.3 Identify the Kairos

Identifying the kairos in Martin Luther King's speech in front of the Lincoln Memorial is easy. In some speeches, however, identifying the kairos is more difficult. Every speech and every text has a kairos, but some rhetors are better at identifying it and utilizing it than others. Identify the kairos in the following readings that have appeared thus far in the text. Then discuss in your group how the writer or speaker does or does not utilize kairos to maximum effect.

1. "Violent Rhetoric and Arizona Politics" (Chapter 1, p. 14)

2. "The Sleepover Question" (Chapter 1, p. 18)

3. "San Ysidro Shooting Survivor Lives His Dream of Being a Cop" (Chapter 1, p. 22)

4. "President Barack Obama on the Death of Osama bin Laden" (Chapter 2, p. 41)

5. "The Web Means the End of Forgetting" (Chapter 2, p. 50)

Activity 3.4 Analyze an Audience

Select a group that you do not belong to and analyze it as a potential audience. As one method, you might locate a blog on the Internet that advocates a point of view different from your own. For example, if you believe in global warming, read a blog frequented by those who do not share that belief. If you are a Democrat, look for a Tea Party or Republican blog. Find a yoga blog if you are a football fan. Read blog entries for a week and write a one-page analysis. Answer these questions:

1. What are the two or three issues of primary interest to the group? What is the general position on each issue?

2. Who are these people? Where do they live? What is their educational level?

3. What is the extent of their knowledge about the issues of primary interest? Are they familiar with the evidence, or do they just repeat opinions?

4. What types of appeals would make a difference to the readers of this blog: ethos, pathos, or logos? How so?

Aristotle's Persuasive Appeals

Some theorists associate the rhetorical triangle directly with Aristotle's **appeals** (or proofs): ethos, pathos, and logos. **Ethos** refers to the writer's (or speaker's) credibility; **pathos** refers to emotion used to sway the audience; and, finally, **logos** refers to the writer's purpose (or subject), for an effective argument will include evidence and other supporting details to back up the author's claims.

Aristotle wrote:

> Of those proofs that are furnished through the speech there are three kinds. Some reside in the character [*ethos*] of the speaker, some in a certain disposition [*pathos*] of the audience and some in the speech itself, through its demonstrating or seeming to demonstrate [*logos*].

Contemporary theorist Wayne C. Booth said something similar:

> The common ingredient that I find in all writing that I admire— excluding for now novels, plays, and poems—is something that I shall reluctantly call the rhetorical stance, a stance which depends upon discovering and maintaining in any writing situation a

proper balance among the three elements that are at work in any communicative effort: the available arguments about the subject itself [*logos*], the interests and peculiarities of the audience [*pathos*], and the voice, the implied character of the speaker [*ethos*].

Arguments from Logos

Logos or reason was Aristotle's favorite of the three persuasive appeals, and he bemoaned the fact that humans could not be persuaded through reason alone, indeed that they sometimes chose emotion over reason. Aristotle also used the term *logos* to mean rational discourse. To appeal to logos means to organize an argument with a clear claim or thesis, supported by logical reasons that are presented in a well-organized manner that is internally consistent. It can also mean the use of facts and statistics as evidence. However, logos without elements of pathos and ethos can be dry, hard to understand, and boring.

Consider the following logical argument that advocates the televising of executions.

Reading 3.2

Earlier this month, Georgia conducted its third execution this year. This would have passed relatively unnoticed if not for a controversy surrounding its videotaping. Lawyers for the condemned inmate, Andrew Grant DeYoung, had persuaded a judge to allow the recording of his last moments as part of an effort to obtain evidence on whether lethal injection caused unnecessary suffering.

Though he argued for videotaping, one of Mr. DeYoung's defense lawyers, Brian Kammer, spoke out against releasing the footage to the public. "It's a horrible thing that Andrew DeYoung had to go through," Mr. Kammer said, "and it's not for the public to see that."

We respectfully disagree. Executions in the United States ought to be made public.

Executions Should Be Televised

by Zachary B. Shemtob and David Lat

In this opinion piece published in *The New York Times*, Zachary B. Shemtob and David Lat argue what they know is going to be an unpopular position in the United States—that executions should be televised.

Shemtob is an assistant professor of criminal justice at Connecticut State University and Lat is a former federal prosecutor who also founded a legal blog, *Above the Law*. They reason, "democracy demands maximum accountability and transparency." Knowing that their position contradicts present policy, they carefully address possible objections to their position, such as the idea that executions are too gruesome to put on television.

Right now, executions are generally open only to the press and a few select witnesses. For the rest of us, the vague contours are provided in the morning paper. Yet a functioning democracy demands maximum accountability and transparency. As long as executions remain behind closed doors, those are impossible. The people should have the right to see what is being done in their name and with their tax dollars.

This is particularly relevant given the current debate on whether specific methods of lethal injection constitute cruel and unusual punishment and therefore violate the Constitution.

There is a dramatic difference between reading or hearing of such an event and observing it through image and sound. (This is obvious to those who saw the footage of Saddam Hussein's hanging in 2006 or the death of Neda Agha-Soltan during the protests in Iran in 2009.) We are not calling for opening executions completely to the public—conducting them before a live crowd—but rather for broadcasting them live or recording them for future release, on the Web or TV.

When another Georgia inmate, Roy Blankenship, was executed in June, the prisoner jerked his head, grimaced, gasped and lurched, according to a medical expert's affidavit. The *Atlanta Journal-Constitution* reported that Mr. DeYoung, executed in the same manner, "showed no violent signs in death." Voters should not have to rely on media accounts to understand what takes place when a man is put to death.

Cameras record legislative sessions and presidential debates, and courtrooms are allowing greater television access. When he was an Illinois state senator, President Obama successfully pressed for the videotaping of homicide interrogations and confessions. The most serious penalty of all surely demands equal if not greater scrutiny.

Opponents of our proposal offer many objections. State lawyers argued that making Mr. DeYoung's execution public raised safety concerns. While rioting and pickpocketing occasionally marred executions in the public square in the 18th and 19th centuries, modern security and technology obviate this concern. Little would change in the death chamber; the faces of witnesses and executioners could be edited out, for privacy reasons, before a video was released.

Of greater concern is the possibility that broadcasting executions could have a numbing effect. Douglas A. Berman, a law professor, fears that people might come to equate human executions with putting pets to sleep. Yet this seems overstated. While public indifference might result over time, the initial broadcasts would undoubtedly get attention and stir debate.

Still others say that broadcasting an execution would offer an unbalanced picture—making the condemned seem helpless and sympathetic, while keeping the victims of the crime out of the picture. But this is beside the point: the defendant is being executed precisely because a jury found that his crimes were so heinous that he deserved to die.

Ultimately the main opposition to our idea seems to flow from an unthinking disgust—a sense that public executions are archaic, noxious, even barbarous. Albert Camus related in his essay "Reflections on the Guillotine" that viewing executions turned him against capital punishment. The legal scholar John D. Bessler suggests that public executions might have the same effect on the public today; Sister Helen Prejean, the death penalty abolitionist, has urged just such a strategy.

That is not our view. We leave open the possibility that making executions public could strengthen support for them; undecided viewers might find them less disturbing than anticipated.

Like many of our fellow citizens, we are deeply conflicted about the death penalty and how it has been administered. Our focus is on accountability and openness. As Justice John Paul Stevens wrote in *Baze v. Rees*, a 2008 case involving a challenge to lethal injection, capital punishment is too often "the product of habit and inattention rather than an acceptable deliberative process that weighs the costs and risks of administering that penalty against its identifiable benefits."

A democracy demands a citizenry as informed as possible about the costs and benefits of society's ultimate punishment.

Activity 3.5 Analyze an Argument from Logos

1. In your small group, go over the Checklist of Essential Elements in an Argument (Chapter 2), and decide if the authors of this article fulfill each one. Be prepared to defend your decisions to the class.

2. Shemtob and Lat present a logical argument about why executions should be televised. Ignoring your own reaction to their editorial, outline the main points.

3. How do the authors handle their audience's possible emotional objections to their argument? Give an example.

4. What is your reaction to the argument that executions should be televised? Did reading and evaluating the article cause you to see the issue differently? If so, in what way?

Deductive Reasoning

Aristotle was the first person in Western culture to write systematically about logic, and he is credited with developing and promoting syllogistic or **deductive reasoning** in which statements are combined to draw a **conclusion**. He wrote that "a statement is persuasive and credible either because it is directly self-evident or because it appears to be proved from other statements that are so." This logical structure is called a **syllogism**, in which premises lead to a conclusion. The following is perhaps the most famous syllogism:

Major premise: All humans are mortal.

Minor premise: Socrates is human.

Conclusion: Socrates is mortal.

The **major premise** is a general statement accepted by everyone that makes an observation about all people. The second statement of the syllogism is the **minor premise**, which makes a statement about a particular case within the class of all people. Comparison of the two premises, the general class of "all humans" and the particular case of "Socrates" within the class of "all humans" leads to the conclusion that Socrates also fits in the class "mortal," and thus his death is unavoidable. Thus, the logic moves from the general to the particular.

Similarly, if you try the pumpkin bread at one Starbucks and like it, you may infer that you will like the pumpkin bread at another Starbucks. The argument would look like this:

Major premise: Food products at Starbucks are standardized from one Starbucks to another.

Minor premise: You like the pumpkin bread at one Starbucks.

Conclusion: You will like the pumpkin bread at another Starbucks.

However, if your major premise is wrong, and the owner of one Starbucks substitutes an inferior stock of pumpkin bread, then your conclusion is wrong. Deductive reasoning is dependent upon the validity of each premise; otherwise the syllogism does not hold true. If the major premise that food products are standardized at all Starbucks franchises does not hold true, then the argument is not valid. A good deductive argument is known as a valid argument and is such that if all its premises are true, then its conclusion must be true. Indeed, for a deductive argument to be valid, it must be absolutely impossible for both its premises to be true and its conclusion to be false.

Inductive Reasoning

Aristotle identified another way to move logically between premises, which he called "the progress from particulars to universals." Later logicians labeled this type of logic as **inductive reasoning**. Inductive arguments are based on probability. Even if an inductive argument's premises are true, that doesn't establish with 100 percent certainty that its conclusions are true. Even the best inductive argument falls short of deductive validity.

Consider the following examples of inductive reasoning:

Particular statement: Milk does not spoil as quickly if kept cold.

General statement: All perishable foods do not spoil as quickly if kept cold.

Particular statement: Microwaves cook popcorn more quickly than conventional heat.

General statement: All foods cook more quickly in a microwave.

In the first example, inductive reasoning works well because cold tends to prolong the useable life of most perishable foods. The second example is more problematic. While it is true that popcorn cooks more quickly in a microwave oven, the peculiarities of microwave interaction with food molecules does not produce a uniform effect on all food stuffs. Rice, for example, does not cook much, if any, faster in a microwave than it does on a stovetop. Also, whole eggs may explode if cooked in their shells.

A good inductive argument is known as a strong (or "cogent") inductive argument. It is such that if the premises are true, the conclusion is likely to be true.

Activity 3.6 Identify Deductive and Inductive Reasoning

Collaborate

In your small group, identify an example of a deductive argument and list the premises and conclusion. Then identify an inductive argument and identify the particular statement and the general statement. Report to the class.

Logical Fallacies

Generally speaking, a **logical fallacy** is an error in reasoning, as opposed to a factual error, which is simply being wrong about the facts. A **deductive fallacy** (sometimes called a *formal fallacy*) is a deductive argument that has premises that are all true, but they lead to a false conclusion, making it an invalid argument. An **inductive fallacy** (sometimes called an *informal fallacy*) appears to be an inductive argument, but the premises do not provide enough support for the conclusion to be probable. Some logical fallacies are more common than others and, thus, have been labeled and defined. Following are a few of the most well-known types:

Ad hominem (to the man) are arguments that attempt to discredit a point of view through personal attacks upon the person who has that point of view. These arguments are not relevant to the actual issue because the character of the person that holds a view says nothing about the truth of that viewpoint.

> *Example*: Noam Chomsky is a liberal activist who opposes American intervention in other countries. Noam Chomsky's theory of transformational grammar, which suggests that humans have an innate ability to learn language, is ridiculous.

Non sequitur (Latin for "it does not follow") arguments have conclusions that do not follow from the premises. Usually, the author has left out a step in the logic, expecting the reader to make the leap over the gap.

> *Example*: "Well, look at the size of this administration building; it is obvious this university does not need more funding."

Either/or or **false dichotomy** arguments force an either/or choice when, in reality, more options are available. Issues are presented as being either black or white.

> *Example*: With all the budget cuts, "we either raise tuition or massively increase class size."

Red herring arguments avoid the issue and attempt to distract with a side issue.

> *Example*: "Why do you question my private life issues, when we have social problems with which to deal?"

Ad populum (Latin for "appeal to the people") arguments appeal to popularity. If a lot of people believe it, it must be true.

> *Example*: "Why shouldn't I cheat on this exam? Everyone else cheats."

Ad verecundium (Latin for "argument from that which is improper") arguments appeal to an irrelevant authority.

> *Example*: "If the President of Harvard says it is a good idea, then we should follow suit." Or, "That is how we have always done it."

Begging the question arguments simply assume that a point of view is true because the truth of the premise is assumed. Simply assuming a premise is true does not amount to evidence that it *is* true.

> *Example*: A woman's place is in the home; therefore, women should not work.

Confusing cause and effect is a common problem with scientific studies in which the fact that two events are correlated implies that one causes the other.

> *Example*: Obese people drink a lot of diet soda; therefore, diet soda causes obesity.

Post hoc (from the Latin phrase "Post hoc, ergo proper hoc," or after this, therefore because of this) is a fallacy that concludes that one event caused another just because one occurred before the other.

Example: The Great Depression caused World War II.

In a **straw man** fallacy, a position of an opponent is exaggerated or weakened, so that it is easier for the opponent to argue against it.

Example: Pro-choice advocates believe in murdering unborn children.

A **slippery slope** argument asserts that one event will inevitably lead to another event.

Example: the Dilbert cartoon below:

DILBERT: © Scott Adams/Dist. by United Feature Syndicate, Inc.

These logical fallacies are summarized in table 3.1.

Chart of Fallacies and Examples		
Fallacy	**The Error in Reasoning**	**Example**
Ad hominem	When speakers attack the person making the argument and not the argument itself.	"We can't believe anything he says; he is a convicted felon."

table 3.1

Fallacy	The Error in Reasoning	Example
Ad populum	When we attempt to persuade people by arguing our position is reasonable because so many other people are doing it or agree with it.	"Why shouldn't I cheat on this exam? Everyone else cheats."
Ad verecundium	An appeal to persuasion based on higher authority or tradition.	"If the president of Harvard says it is a good idea, then we should follow suit." Or, "That is how we have always done it."
Begging the question	When a speaker presumes certain things are facts when they have not yet been proven to be truthful.	"Oh, everyone knows that we are all Christians."
Confusing cause and effect	A common problem with scientific studies in which the fact that two events are correlated implies that one causes the other.	"Obese people drink a lot of diet soda; therefore, diet soda causes obesity."
Either/or	Presents two options and declares that one of them must be correct while the other must be incorrect.	"We either raise tuition or massively increase class size."
Non sequitur	When you make an unwarranted move from one idea to the next.	"Well, look at the size of this administration building; it is obvious this university does not need more funding."
Post hoc	Assumes that because one event happened after another, then the preceding event caused the event that followed.	"Every time Sheila goes to a game with us, our team loses. She is bad luck."
Red herring	When a speaker introduces an irrelevant issue or piece of evidence to divert attention from the subject of the speech.	"Why do you question my private life issues, when we have social problems with which to deal?"
Slippery slope	Assumes that once an action begins it will follow, undeterred, to an eventual and inevitable conclusion.	"If we let the government dictate where we can pray, soon the government will tell us we cannot pray."

Fallacy	The Error in Reasoning	Example
Straw man	When a speaker ignores the actual position of an opponent and substitutes a distorted and exaggerated position.	"Oh, you think we should agree to a cut in our salaries. Why do you want to bleed us dry?"

Activity 3.7 Identify Logical Fallacies

Match the following types of logical fallacies with the examples below:

Types:
Ad hominem   Post hoc
Begging the question   Straw man
Confusing cause and effect   Slippery slope

Examples:

1. Legalization of medical marijuana will lead to increased marijuana use by the general population.

2. Twenty-one is the best age limit for drinking because people do not mature until they are 21.

3. If you teach birth control methods, more teenage girls will get pregnant.

4. The culture wars of the 1960s were a result of parents being unable to control their children after the post–World War II baby boom.

5. Al Gore claims that global warming is a dangerous trend. Al Gore is a liberal. Therefore, there is no global warming.

6. Immigration reform advocates want to separate families and children.

Activity 3.8 Create Examples of Logical Fallacies

In your small group, work through the chart of logical fallacies above and create a new example for each type of fallacy. Then report to the class, one fallacy at a time, with the instructor making a list of each group's examples on the chalk board. Discuss any examples that are not clear cases of a particular fallacy.

Arguments from Pathos

Pathos makes use of emotion to persuade an audience.

Aristotle wrote:

> Proofs from the disposition of the audience are produced whenever they are induced by the speech into an emotional state. We do not give judgment in the same way when aggrieved and when pleased, in sympathy and in revulsion.

Effective rhetors know their audiences, particularly what emotions they hold that are relevant to the issue under consideration. What motivates them? What are their fears, their hopes, their desires, and their doubts? If the audience has the same emotions as you do, fine. However, if they do not already hold those emotions, you need to bring them to share the hurt, the anger, or the joy that will persuade them to share your viewpoint—through the stories you tell, the statistics you cite, and the reasoning you offer.

For example, when Martin Luther King, Jr., in his "I Have a Dream" speech (reprinted earlier in this chapter) referred to the "hallowed spot" of the Lincoln Memorial, he was appealing to his audience's feelings of patriotism and reverence for the accomplishments of President Lincoln. Subtly, he was also garnering this emotion toward Lincoln in contemporary support of civil rights. Lincoln had issued the Emancipation Proclamation that declared all slaves to be free, yet, according to King, America had not lived up to Lincoln's promise.

Reading 3.3

People for Sale
by E. Benjamin Skinner

Most people imagine that slavery died in the 19th century. Since 1810, more than a dozen international conventions banning the slave trade have been signed. Yet today there are more slaves than at any time in human history.

E. Benjamin Skinner has written on a wide range of topics. His articles have appeared in *Newsweek International, Travel and Leisure,* and other magazines. This essay was adapted from *A Crime So Monstrous: Face-to-Face with Modern-Day Slavery* and appeared in *Foreign Policy.*

And if you're going to buy one in five hours, you'd better get a move on. First, hail a taxi to JFK International Airport and hop on a direct flight to Port-au-Prince, Haiti. The flight takes three hours. After landing, take a tap-tap, a flatbed pickup retrofitted with benches and a canopy, three-quarters of the way up Route de

Delmas, the capital's main street. There, on a side street, you will find a group of men standing in front of Le Réseau (the Network) barbershop. As you approach, a man steps forward: "Are you looking to get a person?"

Meet Benavil Lebhom. He smiles easily. He has a trim mustache and wears a multicolored striped golf shirt, a gold chain, and Doc Martens knockoffs. Benavil is a courtier, or broker. He holds an official real estate license and calls himself an employment agent. Two-thirds of the employees he places are child slaves. The total number of Haitian children in bondage in their own country stands at 300,000. They are restavèks, the "stay-withs," as they are euphemistically known in Creole. Forced, unpaid, they work in captivity from before dawn until night. Benavil and thousands of other formal and informal traffickers lure these children from desperately impoverished rural parents with promises of free schooling and a better life.

The negotiation to buy a child slave might sound a bit like this:

"How quickly do you think it would be possible to bring a child in? Somebody who could clean and cook?" you ask. "I don't have a very big place; I have a small apartment. But I'm wondering how much that would cost? And how quickly?"

"Three days," Benavil responds.

"And you could bring the child here?" you inquire. "Or are there children here already?"

"I don't have any here in Port-au-Prince right now," says Benavil, his eyes widening at the thought of a foreign client. "I would go out to the countryside."

You ask about additional expenses. "Would I have to pay for transportation?"

"Bon," says Benavil. "A hundred U.S."

Smelling a rip-off, you press him, "And that's just for transportation?"

"Transportation would be about 100 Haitian," says Benavil, "because you'd have to get out there. Plus, [hotel and] food on the trip. Five hundred gourdes"—around $13.

"OK, 500 Haitian," you say.

Now you ask the big question: "And what would your fee be?" Benavil's eyes narrow as he determines how much he can take you for.

"A hundred. American."

"That seems like a lot," you say, with a smile so as not to kill the deal. "Could you bring down your fee to 50 U.S.?"

Benavil pauses. But only for effect. He knows he's still got you for much more than a Haitian would pay. "Oui," he says with a smile.

But the deal isn't done. Benavil leans in close. "This is a rather delicate question. Is this someone you want as just a worker? Or also someone who will be a 'partner'? You understand what I mean?"

You don't blink at being asked if you want the child for sex. "Is it possible to have someone who could be both?"

"Oui!" Benavil responds enthusiastically.

If you're interested in taking your purchase back to the United States, Benavil tells you that he can "arrange" the proper papers to make it look as though you've adopted the child.

He offers you a 13-year-old girl.

"That's a little bit old," you say.

"I know of another girl who's 12. Then ones that are 10, 11," he responds.

The negotiation is finished, and you tell Benavil not to make any moves without further word from you. You have successfully arranged to buy a human being for 50 bucks.

It would be nice if that conversation were fictional. It is not. I recorded it in October 2005 as part of four years of research into slavery on five continents. In the popular consciousness, "slavery" has come to be little more than just a metaphor for undue hardship. Investment bankers routinely refer to themselves as "high-paid wage slaves." Human rights activists may call $1-an-hour sweatshop laborers slaves, regardless of the fact that they are paid and can often walk away from the job.

The reality of slavery is far different. Slavery exists today on an unprecedented scale. In Africa, tens of thousands are chattel slaves, seized in war or tucked away for generations. Across Europe, Asia, and the Americas, traffickers have forced as many as 2 million into prostitution or labor. In South Asia, which has the highest concentration of slaves on the planet, nearly 10 million languish in bondage, unable to leave their captors until they pay off "debts," legal fictions that in many cases are generations old.

Few in the developed world have a grasp of the enormity of modern-day slavery. Fewer still are doing anything to combat it. . . . Between 2000 and 2006, the U.S. Justice Department increased human trafficking prosecutions from 3 to 32, and convictions from 10 to 98. By the end of 2006, 27 states had passed anti-trafficking laws. Yet, during the same period, the United States liberated only about 2 percent of its own modern-day slaves. As many as 17,500 new slaves continue to enter bondage in the United States every year . . . Many feel that sex slavery is particularly revolting—and it is. I saw it firsthand. In a Bucharest brothel, I was offered a mentally handicapped suicidal girl in exchange for a used car. But for every woman or child enslaved in commercial sex, there are some 15 men, women, and children enslaved in other fields, such as domestic work or agricultural labor.

Save for the fact that he is male, Gonoo Lal Kol typifies the average slave of our modern age. (At his request, I have changed his name.) Like a majority of the world's slaves, Gonoo is in debt bondage in South Asia. In his case, in an Indian quarry. Like most slaves, Gonoo is illiterate and unaware of the Indian laws that ban his bondage and provide for sanctions against his master. His story, told to me near his four-foot-high stone and grass hutch, represents the other side of the "Indian Miracle."

Gonoo lives in Lohagara Dhal, a forgotten corner of Uttar Pradesh, a north Indian state that contains 8 percent of the world's poor. I met him one evening in December 2005 as he walked with two dozen other laborers in tattered and filthy clothes. Behind them was the quarry. In that pit, Gonoo, a member of the historically outcast Kol tribe, worked with his family 14 hours a day. His tools were a hammer and a pike. His hands were covered in calluses, his fingertips worn away.

Gonoo's master is a tall, stout, surly contractor named Ramesh Garg. He makes his money by enslaving entire families forced to work for no pay beyond alcohol, grain, and subsistence expenses. Slavery scholar Kevin Bales estimates that a slave in the 19th-century American South had to work 20 years to recoup his or her purchase price. Gonoo and the other slaves earn a profit for Garg in two years.

Every single man, woman, and child in Lohagara Dhal is a slave. But, in theory at least, Garg neither bought nor owns them. The seed of Gonoo's slavery, for instance, was a loan of 62 cents. In 1958 his grandfather borrowed that amount from the owner of a farm where he worked. Three generations and three slave masters later, Gonoo's family remains in bondage.

Recently, many bold, underfunded groups have taken up the challenge of tearing out the roots of slavery. Some gained fame through dramatic slave rescues. Most learned that freeing slaves is impossible unless the slaves themselves choose to be free. Among the Kol of Uttar Pradesh, for instance, an organization called Pragati Gramodyog Sansthan (PGS)—the Progressive Institute for Village Enterprises—has helped hundreds of families break the grip of the quarry contractors.

The psychological, social, and economic bonds of slavery run deep, and for governments to be truly effective in eradicating slavery, they must partner with groups that can offer slaves a way to pull themselves up from bondage. One way to do that is to replicate the work of grassroots organizations such as the India-based MSEMVS (Society for Human Development and Women's Empowerment). In 1996 the group launched free transitional schools where children who had been enslaved learned skills and acquired enough literacy to move on to formal schooling. The group also targeted mothers, providing them with training and start-up materials for microenterprises. . . . In recent years, the United States has shown an increasing willingness to help fund these kinds of organizations, one encouraging sign that the message may be getting through.

For four years, I encountered dozens of enslaved people, several of whom traffickers like Benavil actually offered to sell to me. I did not pay for a human life anywhere. And, with one exception, I always withheld action to save any one person, in the hope that my research would later help to save many more. At times, that still feels like an excuse for cowardice. But the hard work of real emancipation can't be the burden of a select few. For thousands of slaves, grassroots groups like PGS and MSEMVS can help bring freedom. Until governments define slavery in appropriately concise terms, prosecute the crime aggressively in all its forms, and encourage groups that empower slaves to free themselves, however, millions more will remain in bondage. And our collective promise of abolition will continue to mean nothing at all.

Activity 3.9 Analyze an Argument from Pathos

After reading Skinner's essay on slavery, reread the passage in which he negotiated to buy a child slave. Then freewrite for five minutes about how that negotiation made you feel.

Most people feel emotional when they read about a child in distress, and Skinner further highlights that emotional effect by putting this particular episode in dialogue, always a point of emphasis in an essay. Do you think Skinner deliberately appealed to pathos in this part of his essay? Discuss in your group.

List other areas where the essay evokes an emotional response. Consider why, and freewrite on the feelings and beliefs that are brought into play. How did the author know that you would probably react this way?

Although much of Skinner's argument relies on pathos, he also provides statistics and references to authorities to bolster his argument. Identify the paragraphs which provide statistics or other evidence that would qualify as logos.

Arguments from Ethos

No exact translation exists in English for the word *ethos*, but it can be loosely translated as the credibility of the speaker. This credibility generates good will which colors all the arguments, examples, and quotes the rhetor utilizes in his text. Rhetors can enhance their credibility by evidence of intelligence, virtue, and goodwill and diminish it by seeming petty, dishonest, and mean-spirited. In addition, a speaker or writer can enhance his or her own credibility by references to quotes or the actions of authorities or leaders.

Aristotle wrote:

> Proofs from character [ethos] are produced, whenever the speech is given in such a way as to render the speaker worthy of credence—we more readily and sooner believe reasonable men on all matters in general and absolutely on questions where precision is impossible and two views can be maintained.

For example, Martin Luther King, Jr., pointed out in his "I Have a Dream" speech, that, according to the framers of the Constitution and the Declaration of Independence, "unalienable Rights" of "Life, Liberty and the pursuit of Happiness" apply equally to black men and white men. He was, in effect, borrowing the ethos of Thomas Jefferson and the framers of the Constitution in support of the unalienable rights of blacks.

Consider the following article and how the author's credibility or ethos enhances the appeal of his arguments.

Reading 3.4

I remember the first time the concept of another world entered my mind. It was during a walk with my father in our garden in Sri Lanka. He pointed to the Moon and told me that people had walked on it. I was astonished: Suddenly that bright light became a place that one could visit.

Alien Life Coming Slowly into View
by Ray Jayawardhana

Ray Jayawardhana, the author of "Alien Life Coming Slowly into View," which was originally published in *The New York Times*, is a professor of astronomy and astrophysics at the University of Toronto. He is also the author of *Strange New Worlds: The Search for Alien Planets and Life Beyond Our Solar System.*

Schoolchildren may feel a similar sense of wonder when they see pictures of a Martian landscape or Saturn's rings. And soon their views of alien worlds may not be confined to the planets in our own solar system.

After millenniums of musings and a century of failed attempts, astronomers first detected an exoplanet, a planet orbiting a normal star other than the Sun, in 1995. Now they are finding hundreds of such worlds each year. Last month, NASA announced that 1,235 new possible planets had been observed by Kepler, a telescope on a space satellite. Six of the planets that Kepler found circle one star, and the orbits of five of them would fit within that of Mercury, the closest planet to our Sun.

By timing the passages of these five planets across their sun's visage—which provides confirmation of their planetary nature—we can witness their graceful dance with one another, choreographed by gravity. These discoveries remind us that nature is often richer and more wondrous than our imagination. The diversity of alien worlds has surprised us and challenged our preconceptions many times over.

It is quite a change from merely 20 years ago, when we knew for sure of just one planetary system: ours. The pace of discovery, supported by new instruments and missions and innovative strategies by planet seekers, has been astounding.

What's more, from measurements of their masses and sizes, we can infer what some of these worlds are made of: gases, ice or rocks. Astronomers have been able to take the temperature of planets around other stars, first with telescopes in space but more recently with ground-based instruments, as my collaborators and I have done.

Two and a half years ago, we even managed to capture the first direct pictures of alien worlds. There is something about a photo of an alien planet—even if it only appears as a faint dot next to a bright, overexposed star—that makes it "real." Given that stars shine like floodlights next to the planetary embers huddled around them, success required painstaking efforts and clever innovations. One essential tool is adaptive optics technology, which, in effect, takes the twinkle out of the stars, thus providing sharper images from telescopes on the ground than would otherwise be possible.

At the crux of this grand pursuit is one basic question: Is our warm, wet, rocky world, teeming with life, the exception or the norm? It is an important question for every one of us, not just for scientists. It seems absurd, if not arrogant, to think that ours is the only life-bearing world in the galaxy, given hundreds of billions of other suns, the apparent ubiquity of planets, and the cosmic abundance of life's ingredients. It may be that life is fairly common, but that "intelligent" life is rare.

Of course, the vast majority of the extra-solar worlds discovered to date are quite unlike our own: many are gas giants, and some are boiling hot while others endure everlasting chills. Just a handful are close in size to our planet, and only a few of those may be rocky like the Earth, rather than gaseous like Jupiter or icy like Neptune.

But within the next few years, astronomers expect to find dozens of alien earths that are roughly the size of our planet. Some of them will likely be in the so-called habitable zone, where the temperatures are just right for liquid water. The discovery of "Earth twins," with conditions similar to what we find here, will inevitably bring questions about alien life to the forefront.

Detecting signs of life elsewhere will not be easy, but it may well occur in my lifetime, if not during the next decade. Given the daunting distances between the stars, the real-life version will almost certainly be a lot less sensational than the movies depicting alien invasions or crash-landing spaceships.

The evidence may be circumstantial at first—say, spectral bar codes of interesting molecules like oxygen, ozone, methane and water—and leave room for alternative interpretations. It may take years of additional data-gathering, and perhaps the construction of new telescopes, to satisfy our doubts. Besides, we won't know whether such "biosignatures" are an indication of slime or civilization. Most people will likely move on to other, more immediate concerns of life here on Earth while scientists get down to work.

If, on the other hand, an alien radio signal were to be detected, that would constitute a more clear-cut and exciting moment. Even if the contents of the message remained elusive for decades, we would know that there was someone "intelligent" at the other end. The search for extraterrestrial intelligence with radio telescopes has come of age recently, 50 years after the first feeble attempt. The construction of the Allen Telescope Array on an arid plateau in northern California greatly expands the number of star systems from which astronomers could detect signals.

However it arrives, the first definitive evidence of life elsewhere will mark a turning point in our intellectual history, perhaps only rivaled by Copernicus's heliocentric theory or Darwin's theory of evolution. If life can spring up on two planets independently, why not on a thousand or even a billion others? The ramifications of finding out for sure that ours isn't the only inhabited world are likely to be felt, over time, in many areas of human thought and endeavor—from biology and philosophy to religion and art.

Some people worry that discovering life elsewhere, especially if it turns out to be in possession of incredible technology, will make us feel small and insignificant. They seem concerned that it will constitute a horrific blow to our collective ego.

I happen to be an optimist. It may take decades after the initial indications of alien life for scientists to gather enough evidence to be certain or to decipher a signal of artificial origin. The full ramifications of the discovery may not be felt for generations, giving us plenty of time to get used to the presence of our galactic neighbors. Besides, knowing that we are not alone just might be the kick in the pants we need to grow up as a species.

Activity 3.10 **Analyzing an Argument from Ethos**

1. In the above article, Ray Jayawardhana draws upon the ethos of his position as a professor of astronomy and astrophysics to formulate a convincing argument for the strong possibility of the existence of alien life. In your group, discuss how Jayawardhana's profession increases the credibility of his argument.

2. How do you think this essay would compare to essays by people of more credentials who argue that no alien life exists? What kinds of other evidence could Jayawardhana have offered that would strengthen his argument?

3. Is Jayawardhana appealing to pathos with his opening narrative? What effect does he want to have on his audience by describing this childhood memory?

Combining Ethos, Pathos, and Logos

The ethos, pathos, and logos appeals are equally important and merit equal attention in the writing process. No text is purely based on one of the three appeals, though more of the argument in a particular text may be based on one appeal rather than another. In each writing situation, however, an effective rhetor will think about how each plays into the structure of the argument.

In today's world, for example, a public speaker's effectiveness is affected by the ability to use a teleprompter, or, if one is not available, to memorize a speech well enough so he or she can speak without frequently referring to notes. If a speaker's eyes flit from left to right across the text of a teleprompter, it shows on television. This reduces the credibility, or ethos, of the speaker, no matter how well the other appeals are executed in the speech. The equivalent of presentation for a written text would be to produce a document that is essentially free from grammatical errors, spell-checked, and printed on good paper stock with the correct margins and type size. If the document does not look professional, it will lose credibility or ethos no matter what it says.

To give another example, E. Benjamin Skinner's essay, "People for Sale," relies on the highly emotional image of a child being sold into slavery for its major appeal. However, if you read back through the essay, you will see that it has a clear thesis, which could be stated as the following: Slavery exists in the present time, even in the United States, and it is not even that difficult to buy a slave. The essay is well organized and offers a variety of evidence, including statistics and first-person observation. Logos may not stand out as the primary appeal in Skinner's essay, but it is nevertheless strong in its appeal to logos.

If you want to develop your writing skills, it is essential that you pay attention to each of Aristotle's appeals—ethos, pathos, and logos.

Activity 3.11 Writing about Ethos, Pathos, and Logos

Choose one of the texts in Chapters 1, 2, or 3 and write an essay that identifies the ethos, pathos, and logos of the particular text. Then discuss how the three appeals together are used by the author to produce an effective essay. Alternatively, discuss which of the appeals is weak in the particular essay and how that affects the effectiveness of the essay.

Photos Heighten Ethos or Pathos

When Steve Jobs was in the process of turning over the reins of Apple to Tim Cook, the two appeared in a series of photos in a variety of publications. For example, see the photo below (from wired.com). Notice the "twinning effect," as both Jobs and Cook wear blue jeans and black pullover sweaters. In a not-so-subtle way, Apple was using ethos to visually state that since Jobs and Cook look alike, they must be alike. Thus, Cook would be successful in running Apple.

Photos can be equally effective in presenting pathos, though logos is more problematic.

Meet Tim Cook: The Man in Charge of Apple

© EPA/Monica M. Davey

For millions of Apple fans, Steve Jobs is irreplaceable. But if there's one man Jobs himself trusts to stand in his shoes it is his second in command Apple Chief Operating Officer Tim Cook.

Activity 3.12 Logos Activity: Write a Letter to the Editor

In the following letter, originally published on the blog, *The Frisky* (www.thefrisky.com), the author uses both humor and logic to argue that *The New Yorker* reviews shouldn't give away the ending of movies.

An Open Letter To The New Yorker
via The Frisky on 4/25/11

Dear *New Yorker*,

Obviously, you are an awesome magazine. However, I have one small, teensy weensy beef. Could you please—possibly—stop ruining the ending of movies for me? Last night, on a 10-hour flight from Buenos Aires to New York, I sat down determined to catch up on your last three issues. In one, I read a review of Jake Gyllenhaal's newish movie, "Source Code." I had been planning to see it. Emphasis on the *had*. While you didn't go into details, you told me how it unfolds in the end. Which sort of takes the wind out of a movie's sail, doesn't it? But even worse, in a fantastic article about Anna Faris and her specific brand of girl humor, you let me know the surprise twist ending of her upcoming click, "What's Your Number?" Which. Doesn't. Even. Come. Out. Until. SEPTEMBER. Reading this reminded me of the collective sigh of 100 students in my Intro to Film Studies class in college when our professor told us the secret to "Chinatown" before we watched.

Choose one of your favorite magazines and write a letter to the editor. You can protest something the magazine has done recently that bothered you, or you can praise something that it has done well. Your letter does not need to be long, but you need to make your argument clear and support it with specific examples. If appropriate for your target publication, use humor as does the author of the letter to the editor of *The New Yorker*.

After you have written your letter to the editor, write a paragraph describing your target publication, what you have written in your letter, and why your letter is an illustration of logos.

Activity 3.13 Pathos Activity: Portray an Emotion in a Collage

Think of an emotion that you've been feeling lately and that you are willing to explore. Create a collage to express that emotion. Use these criteria.

- You can create your collage with cut and paste paper or you can create it through a computer program.

- Have little white space. Use colors with emotional connotations (blue for calm, for example).

- Have at least three images. You can find these on the Internet or in magazines, or take your own photos.

- Before you begin your collage, write down the emotion you are trying to explore and describe how you plan to represent it. In other words, make a plan, even though you will likely deviate from it.

- When you finish, write a paragraph describing the experience of creating the collage. Turn your paragraph in with your collage.

Compose

Activity 3.14 Ethos Activity: Create a Professional Facebook Page

Facebook is not just used to tell your friends about what you did over the weekend. Corporations use it as a networking tool. As you learned in the reading in Chapter 2, "The Web Means the End of Forgetting," it is a good idea to be cautious about what you post about yourself on Facebook because information and photos may be seen by unintended audiences, including future employers. Some individuals choose to have two Facebook pages, one for their personal friends and one for networking.

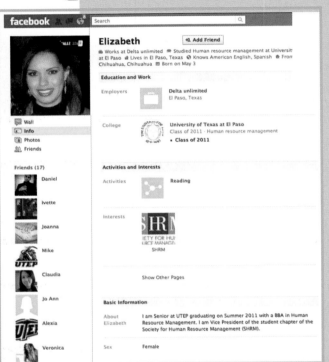

For this assignment, create a professional Facebook page similar to the one shown here. Consider in your small group what information and photos you want to post on a page you will use for networking. In effect, you are creating an ethos for yourself by these choices.

After you have completed your Facebook page, write a paragraph that explains the ethos you wanted to project in your page and how your content choices project that ethos.

Activity 3.15 Write a Rhetorical Analysis

In this essay you will make use of rhetorical vocabulary to analyze a text or combined text and images. The sample student essay in Chapter 7 (see page 190) analyzes a speech archived on the American Rhetoric website (http://www.americanrhetoric.com), which features many presidential and other prominent speeches. Alternatively, you can write a rhetorical analysis of a Facebook page, a newspaper or magazine article, or website.

In your analysis, apply several of the rhetorical concepts you have studied this semester:

- Speaker or writer—Does the speaker's identity affect the text?

- Purpose—What was the speaker or writer trying to achieve?

- Audience—Who was the speech/text directed to? Are there multiple audiences?

- Rhetorical appeals—How does the speaker or writer use ethos, pathos, and logos?

- Kairos—What is special about the rhetorical moment of the text/speech in terms of place and time?

Activity 3.16 Write on Your Blog

In your blog, do a freewrite exercise in which you argue for some type of policy change related to a topic you are interested in writing about. What is the kairos of your topic? Where can you use the three rhetorical appeals (pathos, ethos, and logos)?

Activity 3.17 Write in Your Commonplace Book

Do a search on the Internet for kairos, ethos, pathos, and logos. Print out and paste a short section about each from the Internet. Then comment briefly about each section.

Linne, Alexandra. *The Psychology of Contentment.*

4

INVENTING RHETORICALLY

Praxis in Action

How I Do Invention by Adam Webb

Before I start a research and writing project, I like to explore as many perspectives, arguments, or interpretations of a topic as possible. After I have chosen my topic, I write down everything I know about it. Next, I read broadly about my topic. I call this early stage of the research process "reading around," similar to information gathering.

Then, I usually ask myself a series of questions, such as: (1) Why is this topic important to me? (2) What has been said or written on this topic? (3) Who has already written on this topic? (4) How do these perspectives or arguments relate to my own perspective on this topic? and (5) How has media, such as television or the Internet, portrayed this topic? If I don't know the answers, either from my personal knowledge or my "reading around," I ask individuals who are knowledgeable about my topic. By answering these questions, I usually develop a larger contextual framework in which I can better understand and situate myself within the various perspectives on my topic. This is all before I start to integrate specific material from research sources.

Next, I start locating any recurring terms, themes, symbols, connections, or references as well as listing other ideas, beliefs, or values that might be relevant to my topic. In order to keep track of my ideas and information, I like to use Dragon Dictation, a note-taking and voice recording program application on my smartphone. I sometimes use this application to start writing an outline of my ideas.

By this time, I know what I want to argue and the general framework of my project. Then I can begin adding in specific paraphrases and quotes from my research.

Adam Webb has developed his own process for doing research that he applies to different projects.

Aristotle's Classification of Rhetoric

Aristotle, in *The Art of Rhetoric* (or *On Rhetoric*), laid the groundwork for today's persuasive writing by being the first to write systemically about how to teach rhetoric. His teacher Plato, in contrast, had distrusted rhetoric. Plato deplored the way rhetoricians (or politicians) of his era skillfully manipulated the people of Athens, particularly the masses of up to 10,000 voters in the Assembly or 500 in the juries of the law courts. Aristotle, on the other hand, perceived great potential in rhetoric, when taught properly. Rhetoric, as he envisioned it, could be both persuasive and ethical, and in *The Art of Rhetoric* he laid out an organization and classification of rhetoric as he believed it should be taught.

Aristotle divided the process of writing and delivering a composition into five parts. The first of these was **invention**, during which the writer or speaker expanded a topic into ideas that were later arranged into a text or speech. According to the ancient Greeks, the rhetor *invented* these ideas, though they may have mirrored or adapted thoughts presented by previous rhetors. Today, we call this the **prewriting stage** of the writing process, an adaptation of Aristotle's invention stage.

In the previous chapter, we discussed the three appeals or means that a rhetor can use to persuade an audience: ethos, pathos, and logos. In *The Art of Rhetoric*, Aristotle divides these appeals or means of persuasion into two types of proofs: artistic and inartistic. Today, these proofs are still part of the writing process though we call them by different names.

Artistic Proofs

Artistic proofs are logical arguments constructed by rhetors from ideas plucked from their minds. An individual then develops these thoughts into a line of reasoning and, in the process, explores and narrows the topic, creates a thesis, and determines the ideas that need to be conveyed to the audience. These proofs are the ones that Aristotle and other ancient rhetoricians believed were critically important, for they are the ones developed from the *rhetor's own mind* and, thus, *invented*. These ideas can be shaped into two types of arguments—deductive and inductive—which we will discuss in the next few pages.

Inartistic Proofs

Inartistic proofs are direct evidence that the speaker might use to support the argument, such as testimony, documents, and anything else that rhetors do not invent through their own thinking. Today, we would call these proofs research. They, also, are essential to writing, but they should *support* the writer's ideas, rather than lead them.

For Aristotle's students, the use of artistic and inartistic proofs might not have been a two-step process—first one and then the other, though the proofs are arranged that way in *The Art of Rhetoric*, as they are in this book. Rather, similar to the process used by Adam Webb (see the *Praxis in Action* at the beginning of this chapter), they might have developed both proofs in an alternating or recursive process. After developing basic ideas for a composition through invention, these students would then collect information from authorities (testimony), what Webb refers to as "reading around." Then they would return to inventing artistic proofs about the project, followed by more references to inartistic proofs. Today, we have more resources for research than did the ancient Greeks, but this does not make artistic proofs any less important. The differences between artistic and inartistic proofs are summarized in table 4.1 below.

Aristotle's Artistic and Inartistic Proofs	
Artistic	**Inartistic**
Ideas from the rhetor's own mind, thus *invented*	Information gained from external sources
Personal knowledge	Authorities
Observation	Testimony
Patterns of reasoning	Documents

table 4.1

The Five Canons of Rhetoric

Greek and Roman teachers of rhetoric divided rhetoric into five parts or canons. These canons corresponded to the order of activities in creating a speech, as they perceived the process: Invention, arrangement, style, memory, and delivery. These five parts are described in many handbooks of rhetorical instruction, including the *Rhetorica ad Herennium*, which was composed by an unknown author between 86 and 82 CE:

> The speaker . . . should possess the faculties of Invention, Arrangement, Style, Memory, and Delivery. Invention is the

devising of matter, true or plausible, that would make the case convincing. Arrangement is the ordering and distribution of the matter, making clear the place to which each thing is to be assigned. Style is the adaptation of suitable words and sentences to the matter devised. Memory is the firm retention in the mind of the matter, words, and arrangement. Delivery is the graceful regulation of voice, countenance, and gesture.

Today, classes in composition or writing studies still emphasize the necessity of **invention**, now interpreted as prewriting activities that enable writers to develop the logic and words needed for effective arguments. **Arrangement** involves organizing an argument into a logical format that leads the reader easily from the thesis to the conclusion. **Style** has to do with the author's voice and tone and the structure of sentences and paragraphs. **Memory** is used somewhat differently today, as students are no longer required to memorize compositions for oral presentation. Instead, memory is utilized in ways such as remembering how and where to retrieve information from the Internet, books, and other reference materials. Finally, **delivery**, which once involved gestures and tone of voice in an oral presentation, today has to do with document design, so that the final product is presented in a professional manner according to Modern Language Association (MLA) or American Psychological Association (APA) style. Delivery also involves grammatical accuracy because surface errors detract from the effective impact of a document. See table 4.2 below for a summary of the five parts of rhetoric.

The Five Parts (or Canons) of Rhetoric		
English	Greek	Latin
invention	*heuresis*	*inventio*
arrangement	*taxis*	*dispositio*
style	*lesis*	*elocutio*
memory	*mneme*	*memoria*
delivery	*hypocrisis*	*actin*

table 4.2

The Modern Writing Process Overview

Prewriting (Inventing)

Writing is not only about putting the pen to paper. As did rhetors in ancient Greece and Rome, you have to think deeply and critically about a subject before you begin a composition. The "invention" step of the writer's process is designed to help you find a worthwhile topic and develop your ideas about that topic before you start to write a draft. It includes writing, discussion, and research, as well as informal writing to help you explore your thoughts and feelings about a subject. Whatever method you choose, keep a record of your thoughts and discoveries as you spend this time in close examination of your subject.

Drafting

It may seem odd that writing a draft should come in the middle of the writer's process. However, research has shown that students and professionals alike write more effective essays when they don't reach for the pen too quickly. If you have spent enough time in the invention stage, the actual drafting stage may go more quickly. After writing the first draft, in succeeding drafts you can add details, observations, illustrations, examples, expert testimony, and other support to help your essay entertain, illuminate, or convince your audience.

Revising

Today, we talk more about the revision stage of writing than did ancient rhetoricians. If you are a student who tends to write assigned essays at the last minute, you may have missed this step entirely, yet many writers claim this is the longest and most rewarding step in the writing process. To revise, you must, in a sense, learn to let go of your writing. Some students think their first drafts should stay exactly the way they are written because they are true to their feelings and experience. Many writers find, however, that first drafts assume too much about the reader's knowledge and reactions. Sometimes readers, reading a first draft essay, are left scratching their heads and wondering what it is the writer is trying to convey. Writers who revise try to read their writing as readers would, taking note of gaps in logic, the absence of clear examples, the need for reordering information, and so on. Then they can revise their content with the reader in mind.

Editing and Polishing

Once writers have clarified their messages and the methods by which they will present those messages, one more step must be taken. Particularly because their compositions are written, rather than presented orally, they must go over their work again to check for correct spelling, grammar, and punctuation, as well as the use of Standard Written English. Some students finish with an essay, print it, and turn it in without ever examining the final copy. This is a critical mistake, because misspelled words and typographical and formatting errors can make an otherwise well-written essay lose its credibility. The five canons of rhetoric and the modern writing process are summarized in table 4.3 below.

The Five Canons of Rhetoric and the Modern Writing Process	
Five Canons of Rhetoric	**Modern Writing Process**
Invention—Devising the arguments that will make the case convincing, often basing them on models of famous speeches.	Prewriting—Determining the thesis, points of argument, counterargument, and rebuttal. Researching evidence to support the argument.
Arrangement—Ordering the argument into a logical format. Style—Finding suitable words and figures of speech. [Note: This may have been a recursive process, but the ancients did not consider that aspect important.]	Drafting, revising, and editing—Putting ideas and prewriting into a useable form through a recursive process of drafting, revising, and editing.
Memory—Retaining the argument in the mind, including its content and arrangement.	Remembering how and where to retrieve information from the Internet, books, and other reference materials.
Delivery—Effective use of voice and gestures to present argument.	Publication—Putting text, images, and other elements in a suitable format and releasing the document to an audience.

table 4.3

Activity 4.1 Compare the Five Canons of Rhetoric and the Modern Writing Process

Collaborate

In your group, reread the discussions in this chapter on the five canons of rhetoric and the modern writing process and review the table above. What parts of the five canons correspond to the modern writing process?

What step in the five canons is not included in the contemporary writing process? If the similarities and differences are not clear to you, consult the Internet. If you search for either "Five Canons of Rhetoric" or "Writing Process" you will find resources. What explanations can you offer for the differences? The similarities?

Stasis Theory Identifies Critical Point in Controversy

Stasis theory presents a series of four questions that were developed by Greek and Roman rhetoricians, primarily Aristotle, Quintilian, and Hermagoras. Answering these questions for an issue enabled rhetors to determine the critical (or stasis) point in a disagreement. This was a technique the ancients developed for the law courts to enable advocates to focus their arguments on the crux of the case. Quintilian, the great Roman teacher of rhetoric, explained in regard to a defendant:

> By far the strongest mode of defense is if the charge which is made can be denied; the next, if an act of the kind charged against the accused can be said not to have been done; the third, and most honorable, if what is done is proved to have been justly done. If we cannot command these methods, the last and only mode of defense is that of eluding an accusation, which can neither be denied nor combated, by the aid of some point of law, so as to make it appear that the action has not been brought in due legal form.

In other words, Quintilian is saying that in law cases, advocates have four choices in developing a focus for their arguments. You have probably watched a courtroom drama on television or film and can recall various defenses made on behalf of defendants. The strongest and most obvious defense is that the defendant is not guilty, that is, he or she did not do the deed in question. The same was true in Quintilian's day. However, sometimes an argument of innocence is not possible, perhaps because it seems obvious that the defendant did perform the deed in question. Thus, the advocate must develop a different strategy. For example, in defense of one accused of murder, the attorney may argue self-defense or mitigating circumstances (such as that the killing was an act of war). In rare cases, other defenses are offered; for example, if the supposed victim's body has not been found, the advocate can argue that the victim

Marcus Fabius Quintilianus (Quintilian) was a Roman orator from Spain who taught stasis theory.

may still be alive. An attorney can discover these possible defenses by using stasis theory to analyze the situation.

Another great advantage of stasis theory is that, if pursued diligently, it prevents the rhetor from making the mistake of organizing an argument by simply forwarding reasons why he or she is correct and the opposition is wrong. That approach may please people who agree with the rhetor, but it will not likely gain any support from the opposition. Answering the stasis questions carefully forces the writer to consider aspects of the issue that may have been overlooked but are crucial to an effective argument.

The wording of the four questions has varied somewhat over time, but essentially they are questions of fact, definition, quality, and policy. The same questions can be applied to any issue, not only issues of law. The four stasis questions are as follows:

1. What are the facts? (conjecture)
2. What is the meaning or nature of the issue? (definition)
3. What is the seriousness of the issue? (quality)
4. What is the best plan of action or procedure? (policy)

Many writers prefer stasis theory to other prewriting techniques because answering the questions determines whether or not the different sides of an argument are at stasis. Being at **stasis** means that the opponents are in agreement about their disagreement—the stasis point—which can be identified by one of the four stasis questions. If the sides are at stasis, they have common ground to build upon, for they are arguing the same issue. There is, thus, a greater chance the sides can reach a workable consensus or compromise. If opponents are not at stasis, there is much more work to be done to reach consensus.

The point where the opposing sides agree upon their disagreement is the stasis point.

For example, in the argument about the teaching of evolution and/or intelligent design in schools, the two sides are not in agreement about how to discuss the issue. Those in favor of teaching evolution claim intelligent design should not be called science, which is an issue of definition. Those who propose teaching intelligent design along with (or instead of) evolution tend to focus on "proving" evidence, an issue of fact. Until the two sides can agree upon what is the stasis point, or crux of the issue, they cannot debate effectively. They are not presenting arguments about the same question.

The four stasis questions can be broken into the subquestions listed in table 4.4. If you want to find the stasis point, work through the list for your issue, answering all of the subquestions. However, for each question, you must identify not only how *you* would answer the question but also how the opposing side or sides would answer. For example, if you are considering the issue of global warming, people with different positions will not agree on the facts. Thus, you must identify the basic facts of global warming represented by your side, and then identify the facts that might be presented by the opposing side.

Stasis Questions
Fact
• Did something happen?
• What are the facts?
• Is there a problem/issue?
• How did it begin and what are its causes?
• What changed to create the problem/issue?
• Can it be changed?
It also may be useful to ask the following critical questions of your own research and conclusions:
• Where did I obtain my data and are these sources reliable?
• How do I know they're reliable?
Definition
• What is the nature of the problem/issue?
• What exactly is the problem/issue?
• What kind of a problem/issue is it?
• To what larger class of things or events does it belong?
• What are its parts, and how are they related?
It also may be useful to ask the following critical questions of your own research and conclusions:
• Who/what is influencing my definition of this problem/issue?
• How/why are these sources/beliefs influencing my definition of the issue?

table 4.4

Quality

- Is it a good thing or a bad thing?
- How serious is the problem/issue?
- Who might be affected by this problem/issue (stakeholders)?
- What happens if we don't do anything?
- What are the costs of solving the problem/issue?

It also may be useful to ask the following critical questions of your own research and conclusions:

- Who/what is influencing my determination of the seriousness of this problem/issue?
- How/why are these sources/beliefs influencing my determination of the issue's seriousness?

Policy

- Should action be taken?
- Who should be involved in helping to solve the problem/address the issue?
- What should be done about this problem?
- What needs to happen to solve this problem/address this issue?

It also may be useful to ask the following critical questions of your own research and conclusions:

- Who/what is influencing my determination of what to do about this problem/issue?
- How/why are these sources/beliefs influencing my determination of what to do about this issue?

Source: Adapted from Purdue Owl Resource on Stasis Theory, http://owl.english .purdue.edu/owl/resource/736/1.

Using Stasis Questions

To illustrate the use of stasis questions, a team of writers working together to compose a report on racism in America might use the stasis questions to talk through information they will later use in their report. In the following sample dialogue, team members disagree about what actions are racist.

"Flying the Confederate battle flag is racist."

"Flying the Confederate battle flag is *not* racist."

"Yes, it is, because it represents the Confederate states that supported slavery, and it's generally accepted that slavery in America was racist."

"Flying the Confederate battle flag is not racist, because it's a part of American history and Southern heritage."

These two team members disagree about whether or not flying the Confederate battle flag is a racist act. This sort of disagreement might lead to a complete breakdown of group work if common ground cannot be found.

In this example, the team members go on to agree that some people still exhibit the Confederate battle flag (*fact*) on their vehicles and on their clothes, but that the flag is also displayed in museums (*fact*). They go on to agree that the issue is still very important to some people since a number of American states have recently debated the flag in legislatures and assemblies (*quality*). Moreover, group members note that a number of legal suits have been filed for and against the display of the flag in public places, so it's clear the issue still matters to a lot of people (*quality*).

In this sense, the team members have achieved stasis on two of the four stases—*fact* (people still display the flag, though in different places) and *quality* (it's a very important issue). Where the team members disagree, however, is in the stases of *definition* (is the display of the flag "racist"?) and *policy* (what should we do about this?).

Thinking about this disagreement using stasis theory allows people to build common ground so that parties who disagree can move toward resolution and action even if they can't agree on all levels. For example, team members who disagree about whether or not flying the Confederate battle flag is racist might still be able to agree on what to do about it.

"Ok, we disagree about whether flying the flag is racist, but we can agree that flying the flag is probably protected under the First Amendment to the United States Constitution—that flying the flag is protected by our freedom of speech."

"Yeah."

"So, people are free to display the flag on their vehicles, on their clothes, and on their property, as well as in museums. But, state legislatures and assemblies will have to debate and vote on whether or not the flag can be displayed on publicly funded property or in public symbols, such as state flags and seals."

"That sounds pretty democratic. Sure."

Not every team situation is going to end this amicably; however, by using the stasis questions to help keep the dialogue going—on a reasonable course— team members can find common ground and work toward action that is acceptable to most, if not all, of the group members.*

Stasis Theory and Kairos

As you will remember from Chapter 3, the *kairos* of an argument is the context, opportune moment, or point in time in which the rhetor, the audience, the issue, and the current situation provide opportunities and constraints for an argument. If you keep kairos in mind as you analyze an issue, you take advantage of timeliness. For example, if you want to write an argument about the death penalty, you might consider that United States courts are increasingly questioning the validity of eyewitness testimony, evidence which has been the deciding factor in many death penalty cases.

As part of your use of stasis theory, consider the four questions in relation to kairos:

1. How do recent developments (new facts) or the local situation affect the issue? Will it change your audience's perception of the facts?

2. Does the current situation affect your audience's definition of the issue? Is it defined differently by an audience in this location than elsewhere?

3. Have recent events made the issue more or less important to your audience? Is it more or less important in your location than elsewhere?

4. Do recent events, locally or widely, affect the need or lack of need for action, in your audience's perception?

As a rhetorician, it is important for you to be aware of the history of a controversy. But it is equally important to have an awareness of the kairos of the argument. Such an awareness enables you to adopt a "ready stance" and adjust your argument, so that it reflects an awareness of your audience's position and interests, as well as contemporary developments in the issue.

---

* Allen Brizee, "Stasis Theory for Teamwork," *Purdue Owl*, April 17, 2010, http://owl.english.purdue.edu/owl/ (Accessed October 3, 2011).

Such a flexible stance may afford you an opportunity to be persuasive that you might otherwise miss.

Activity 4.2 Identify the Defense in a Television or Film Courtroom Drama

As your instructor directs, watch a courtroom drama on television or film and decide what defense the defendant's attorney is offering. Report your conclusion to your small group or the class. Then, after you have discussed the stasis questions, identify which of the four questions the attorney in the drama is focusing upon as the crux of the defense. Discuss with your group or the class.

Activity 4.3 Use Stasis Theory to Explore Your Topic

Choose an issue that interests you and answer all the stasis questions in the table on pages 117-118, both for your position and for the opposing argument. Elaborate with three or four sentences for each subquestion that is particularly relevant to your topic. Is your issue at stasis for any of the questions? Report to your group or to the class.

Activity 4.4 Evaluate a Public Debate

Locate a public debate that has been reported recently in newspaper editorials, television programs, or other media that can be analyzed by using stasis theory. In a paper of 350 to 500 words, do the following:

- Describe the context (kairos).

- Identify the sides of the argument and their principal points.

- Decide which stasis question each side is primarily addressing.

- Determine whether or not the issue is at stasis and explain your answer.

- Include a citation in MLA or APA format for your source or sources.

Activity 4.5: Use Stasis Theory to Analyze a Case

Professors Vijay Govindarajan and Christian Sarkar launched a competition on the *Harvard Business Network* blog for designs to build $300 houses for the poor. Word of the competition spread quickly, and a wide variety of people began to write about the competition—in editorials in *The New York Times*, the *Economist,* and in a companion blog, http://www.300house.com/blog.

Your Task: Read the four articles written about the $300 house competition that appear on the following pages. Discuss them in class and in small groups. In particular, note that Matias Echanove and Rahul Srivastava write in their *New York Times* op-ed essay, "Hands Off Our Houses," that the idea of a $300 house is impractical and will fail in places such as Mumbai, India. In contrast, "A $300 Idea that Is Priceless," the editorial from the *Economist,* praises the design competition for initiating an "explosion of creativity." Work through the stasis questions, with one side of the controversy being those who support this design initiative. The other side would be those who foresee problems in applying this idealistic initiative in the real world, a viewpoint that is expressed in "Hands Off Our Houses."

Write a paper of approximately 750 words in which you do the following:

- Briefly present the idea of the design competition.

- Summarize the arguments of those in favor of the initiative.

- Explain the reservations expressed in "Hands Off Our Houses."

- Identify a stasis point, if one exists, and explain why you think the sides have common ground on that particular stasis question.

- Discuss whether the discovery of common ground might allow individuals involved in this debate to talk to one another and work toward solutions for the problem of substandard housing in slums worldwide.

- As your instructor directs, cite your sources in APA or MLA style.

Reading 4.1

David A. Smith, the founder of the Affordable Housing Institute (AHI) tells us that "markets alone will never satisfactorily house a nation's poorest citizens ... whether people buy or rent, housing is typically affordable to only half of the population."

The $300 House: A Hands-On Lab for Reverse Innovation?

by Vijay Govindarajan

Published in the *HBR Blog Network*.

The result? Smith points to a "spontaneous community of self-built or informally built homes—the shanty towns, settlements, and ever-expanding slums that sprout like mushrooms on the outskirts of cities in the developing world."

We started discussing the issue, examining the subject through the lens of reverse innovation.

Here are five questions Christian and I asked ourselves:

1. How can organic, self-built slums be turned into livable housing?

2. What might a house-for-the-poor look like?

3. How can world-class engineering and design capabilities be utilized to solve the problem?

4. What reverse-innovation lessons might be learned by the participants in such a project?

5. How could the poor afford to buy this house?

Livable Housing. Our first thought was that self-built houses are usually built from materials that are available—cardboard, plastic, mud or clay, metal scraps and whatever else is nearby. Built on dirt floors, these structures are prone to collapse and catching fire. Solution: replace these unsafe structures with a mass-produced, standard, affordable, and sustainable solution. We want to create the $300-House-for-the-Poor.

Look and Feel. To designers, our sketch of this house might be a bit of a joke, but it's useful nonetheless to illustrate the concept, to get started. We wanted the house to be an ecosystem of products and solutions designed around the real needs of the inhabitants. Of course it would have to be made out of sustainable, green materials, but more crucially, it would have to be durable enough to withstand torrential rains, earthquakes, and the stress of children playing. The house might be a single room structure with drop-down partitions for privacy. Furniture—sleeping hammocks and fold-down chairs would be built in. The roof would boast an inexpensive solar panel and battery to light the house and charge the mobile phone and tablet computer. An inexpensive water filter would be built in as well.

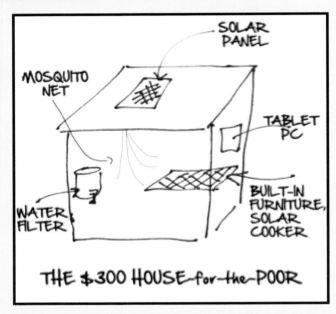

In effect, the house is really a one-room shed designed around the family ecosystem, a lego-like aggregation of useful products that "bring good things to life" for the poor.

World-Class Design. Our next question was: "Who will do this?" We decided that it would have to be a collaboration between global design and engineering companies and non-profits with experience solving problems for the poor. The usual suspects ran through our minds—IDEO, GE, TATA, Siemens, Habitat-for-Humanity, Partners In Health, the Solar Electric Light Fund, the Clinton Global Initiative, the Gates Foundation, Grameen. Governments may play an important part in setting the stage for these types of cross-country innovation projects.

The Reverse Innovation Payoff. Participating companies will reap two rewards. First, they will be able to serve the unserved, the 2.5 billion who make up the bottom of the pyramid. Second, they create new competencies which can help transform lives in rich countries by creating breakthrough innovations to solve several problems (scaled housing for hurricane victims, refugees, and even the armed forces).

A House of One's Own: Affordability. To move beyond charity, the poor must become owners of their homes, responsible for their care and upkeep. The model of social business introduced by Muhammad Yunus resonates strongly with us. Micro-finance must surely play a role in making the $300 House-for-the-Poor a viable and self-sustaining solution.

Of course, the idea we present here is an experiment. Nevertheless, we feel it deserves to be explored. From the one-room shacks in Haiti's Central Plateau to the jhuggi clusters in and around Delhi, to the favelas in São Paulo, the problem of housing-for-the-poor is truly global.

We ask CEOs, governments, NGOs, foundations: Are there any takers?

Reading 4.2

Mumbai, India

Hands Off Our Houses

by Matias Echanove and Rahul Srivastava

Published in *The New York Times.*

Last summer, a business professor and a marketing consultant wrote on The Harvard Business Review's website about their idea for a $300 house. According to the writers, and the many people who have enthusiastically responded since, such a house could improve the lives of millions of urban poor around the world. And with a $424 billion market for cheap homes that is largely untapped, it could also make significant profits.

The writers created a competition, asking students, architects and businesses to compete to design the best prototype for a $300 house (their original sketch was of a one-room prefabricated shed, equipped with solar panels, water filters and a tablet computer). The winner will be announced this month. But one expert has been left out of the competition, even though her input would have saved much time and effort for those involved in conceiving the house: the person who is supposed to live in it.

We work in Dharavi, a neighborhood in Mumbai that has become a one-stop shop for anyone interested in "slums" (that catchall term for areas lived in by the urban poor). We recently showed around a group of Dartmouth students involved in the project who are hoping to get a better grasp of their market. They had imagined a ready-made constituency of slum-dwellers eager to buy a cheap house that would necessarily be better than the shacks they'd built themselves. But the students found that the reality here is far more complex than their business plan suggested.

To start with, space is scarce. There is almost no room for new construction or ready-made houses. Most residents are renters, paying $20 to $100 a month for small apartments.

Those who own houses have far more equity in them than $300—a typical home is worth at least $3,000. Many families have owned their houses for two or three generations, upgrading them as their incomes increase. With additions, these homes become what we call "tool houses," acting as workshops, manufacturing units, warehouses and shops. They facilitate trade and production, and allow homeowners to improve their living standards over time.

None of this would be possible with a $300 house, which would have to be as standardized as possible to keep costs low. No number of add-ons would be able to match the flexibility of need-based construction.

In addition, construction is an important industry in neighborhoods like Dharavi. Much of the economy consists of hardware shops, carpenters, plumbers, concrete makers, masons, even real-estate agents. Importing pre-fabricated homes would put many people out of business, undercutting the very population the $300 house is intended to help.

Worst of all, companies involved in producing the house may end up supporting the clearance and demolition of well-established neighborhoods to make room for it. The resulting resettlement colonies, which are multiplying at the edges of cities like Delhi and Bangalore, may at first glance look like ideal markets for the new houses, but the dislocation destroys businesses and communities.

The $300 house could potentially be a success story, if it was understood as a straightforward business proposal instead of a social solution. Places like refugee camps, where many people need shelter for short periods, could use such cheap, well-built units. A market for them could perhaps be created in rural-urban fringes that are less built up.

The $300 house responds to our misconceptions more than to real needs. Of course problems do exist in urban India. Many people live without toilets or running water. Hot and unhealthy asbestos-cement sheets cover millions of roofs. Makeshift homes often flood during monsoons. But replacing individual, incrementally built houses with a ready-made solution would do more harm than good.

A better approach would be to help residents build better, safer homes for themselves. The New Delhi–based Micro Homes Solutions, for example, provides architectural and engineering assistance to homeowners in low-income neighborhoods.

The $300 house will fail as a social initiative because the dynamic needs, interests and aspirations of the millions of people who live in places like Dharavi have been overlooked. This kind of mistake is all too common in the trendy field of social entrepreneurship. While businessmen and professors applaud the $300 house, the urban poor are silent, busy building a future for themselves.

Reading 4.3

When *The New York Times* printed "Hands Off Our Houses," an op-ed about our idea for a $300 House for the poor, we were both delighted and dismayed—delighted because the $300 House was being discussed, and dismayed because authors Matias Echanove and Rahul Srivastava,

The $300 House: A Hands-On Approach to a Wicked Problem

by Vijay Govindarajan with Christian Sarkar

Published in the *HBR Blog Network*

co-founders of the Institute of Urbanology, didn't seem to have read the series of blog posts about our idea.

Nearly every criticism the authors levy in their op-ed is answered in 12 blog posts, a magazine article from January/February 2011, a video interview, and a slideshow that integrated community and commentary, which were published between last October and this May.

In critiquing our vision, the authors cite Micro Homes Solutions as "a better approach." In fact, the leaders of that venture were invited several months ago to contribute a blog post to our series as a way of joining the discussion and helping us understand what they've seen on the ground there. They declined to be part of the conversation.

The authors also write that students who tried to write a business plan to serve the poor and who visited poor urban areas of India found "the reality here is far more complex than their business plan suggested."

Yet a fundamental tenet of our project and the blog series about it is that slums present complex challenges that can't be fixed with a clever shack alone. Rather than creating an echo chamber of rah-rah rhetoric, we told blog authors to focus on one of the many knotty issues that Echanove and Srivastava cite in their critique. From the start we asked: What are the complexities of financing these homes? How do you get energy and infrastructure into such dwellings? How do you get corporations to invest in a significant way? We acknowledged that we didn't have the answers. "Just because it is going to take longer than it should doesn't mean we should walk away," wrote Seth Godin in one of the posts. "It's going to take some time, but it's worth it."

The op-ed suggests that the $300 House doesn't acknowledge that "space is scarce" in urban poor areas. Yet, Sunil Suri wrote in a post on the urban challenge that "slums by their nature are located where land and space are limited." Suri proposed potential solutions, including innovative materials, new ways of thinking of the construction process, and building up.

The authors also say that "one expert has been left out of the challenge . . . the person who is supposed to live in it." But a post in the series on the co-creation challenge from Gaurav Bhalla addressed this squarely. "It will be unfortunate if the house were to be designed by those who will never live in it," wrote Bhalla. "Investments need to be made understanding the daily habits and practices of people for whom the house is being designed." Bhalla used the case study of the chulha stove, co-created by businesses, NGOs, and slum dwellers, to make his point. We are also bringing students to India and Haiti to do ethnographic research that will inform development of a $300 House, and when prototypes are developed, they will be deployed and tested with those who will live in them.

Echanove and Srivastava also state that a $300 House "would have to be as standardized as possible to keep costs low. No number of add-ons would be able to match the flexibility of need-based construction." While we agree that a one-size-fits-all approach will not work, we disagree that a $300 House would be inflexible. Core tenets from a blog post about the overall design challenge of creating a $300 House by Bill Gross include "give your customers options" and "make it aspirational." And David Smith's entry on the financial challenge shows that flexibility can be born out of financing options as well. A need-based approach alone also ignores the scale of the problem we are facing. "Triple the U.S. population by three. That's how many people around the world live on about a dollar a day," Godin writes. "Triple it again and now you have the number that lives on $2. About 40% of the world lives on $2 or less a day." In any situation where scale is required, so is some level of standardization.

The most puzzling critique in the op-ed was that "construction is an important industry in neighborhoods like Dharavi. Much of the economy consists of hardware shops, carpenters, plumbers, concrete makers, masons, even real-estate agents. Importing prefabricated homes would put many people out of business, undercutting the very population the $300 house is intended to help."

In fact, our contest's design briefing said these dwellings should be "self built and/or self-improvable." It also stated that the design should rely as much as possible on local materials, which of course would be harvested and crafted by local workers. Our goal is to increase demand for local trades, not drive them away. And the idea that jobs would disappear belies the fact that with progress comes new jobs; teachers for the kids who can now go to school; health care professionals for the families that can now afford check-ups; technology professionals who could service solar panels or internet access devices; farmers who could manage shared crop spaces in the neighborhoods. The $300 House project is a housing ecosystem project.

Finally, Echanove and Srivastava state that "The $300 house could potentially be a success story, if it was understood as a straightforward business proposal instead of a social solution."

We disagree completely. We do support other applications for low-cost housing—bringing these dwellings back to the industrialized world for hurricane relief, for example, would be a reverse innovation success story. However, trying to pigeonhole ideas as either "for good" or "for profit" is an outmoded way of thinking.

The authors have an implicit negative view on business. For them, profit seems to be a dirty word. For us, good business and social innovation are one and the same. The rising tide of New Capitalism, what Michael Porter calls "shared value" and what Umair Haque calls "thick value," is perhaps the most important reaction to the corruption and greed that spurred the most recent global economic crisis. The *Economist* was right when it suggested that this is a "can do" moment in history.

Our goal is neither to start yet another charity—one of our advisers, Paul Polak, tells us that "you can't donate your way out of poverty"—nor to start just another business. Rather we must encourage existing businesses to find ways to create new, scalable markets; to get NGOs to share their on-the-ground expertise; and to force governments to make it as simple as possible to work across the hybrid value chain in order to make such a project a reality and begin the process of instilling dignity in and creating options for individuals who now don't have either.

We are happy that Echanove and Srivastava share our passion for the problem of affordable housing, which is a wicked problem. We simply disagree with the idea that if it's a market, it can't also be a socially progressive solution. Trying to categorize the regeneration of slums as either a business problem or social problem is like trying to categorize a flame as either heat or light. It is both, always.

Reading 4.4

A $300 Idea that Is Priceless

from Schumpeter, a column in the *Economist*

Applying the world's business brains to housing the poor.

Friedrich Engels said in "The Condition of the Working Class in England," in 1844, that the onward march of Manchester's slums meant that the city's Angel Meadow district might better be described as "Hell upon Earth." Today, similar earthly infernos can be found all over the emerging world: from Brazil's favelas to Africa's shanties. In 2010 the United Nations calculated that there were about 827m people living in slums—almost as many people as were living on the planet in Engels's time—and predicted that the number might double by 2030.

Last year Vijay Govindarajan, of Dartmouth College's Tuck School of Business, along with Christian Sarkar, a marketing expert, issued a challenge in a *Harvard Business Review* blog: why not apply the world's best business thinking to housing the poor? Why not replace the shacks that blight the lives of so many poor people, thrown together out of cardboard and mud, and prone to collapsing or catching fire, with more durable structures? They laid down a few simple guidelines. The houses should be built of mass-produced materials tough enough to protect their inhabitants from a hostile world. They should be equipped with the basics of civilized life, including water filters and solar panels. They should be "improvable," so that families can adapt them to their needs. And they should cost no more than $300.

Mr. Govindarajan admits that the $300 figure was partly an attention-grabbing device. But he also argues that it has a certain logic. Muhammad Yunus, the founder of Grameen Bank, has calculated that the average value of the houses of people who have just escaped from poverty is $370. Tata Motors has also demonstrated the value of having a fixed figure to aim at: the company would have found it more difficult to produce the Tata Nano if it had simply been trying to produce a "cheap" car rather than a "one lakh" car (about $2,200).

The attention-grabbing certainly worked. The blog was so inundated with positive responses that a dedicated website, 300house.com, was set up, which has attracted more than 900 enthusiasts and advisers from all over the world. On April 20th Mr. Govindarajan launched a competition inviting people to submit designs for a prototype of the house.

Why has a simple blog post led to such an explosion of creativity? The obvious reason is that "frugal innovation"—the art of radically reducing the cost of products while also delivering first-class value—is all the rage at the moment. General Electric has reduced the cost of an electrocardiogram machine from $2,000 to $400. Tata Chemicals has produced a $24 purifier that can provide a family with pure water for a year. Girish Bharadwaj, an engineer, has perfected a technique for producing cheap footbridges that are transforming life in rural India.

Another reason is that houses can be such effective anti-poverty tools. Poorly constructed ones contribute to a nexus of problems: the spread of disease (because they have no proper sanitation or ventilation), the perpetuation of poverty (because children have no proper lights to study by) and the general sense of insecurity (because they are so flimsy and flammable). Mr. Govindarajan's idea is so powerful because he treats houses as ecosystems that provide light, ventilation and sanitation.

Numerous innovators are also worrying away at this nexus of problems. Habitat for Humanity, an NGO, is building durable houses of bamboo in Nepal. Idealab, a consultancy, is on the verge of unveiling a $2,500 house that will be mass-produced in factories, sold in kits and feature breakthroughs in ventilation, lighting and sanitation. Philips has produced a cheap cooking stove, the Chulha, that cuts out the soot that kills 1.6m people a year worldwide. The Solar Electric Light Fund is demonstrating that you can provide poor families with solar power for roughly the same cost as old standbys such as kerosene and candles.

Profits and other problems

These thinkers, like the advocates of the $300 house, must solve three huge problems to succeed. They must persuade big companies that they can make money out of cheap homes, because only they can achieve the economies of scale needed to hit the target price. They need to ensure sufficient access to microloans: $300 is a huge investment for a family of squatters living on a couple of dollars a day. And they need to overcome the obstacle that most slum-dwellers have weak or non-existent property rights. There is no point in offering people the chance to buy a cleverly designed house if they have no title to the land they occupy. Solving these problems will in turn demand a high degree of co-operation between people who do not always get on: companies and NGOs, designers and emerging-world governments.

However, the exciting thing about the emerging world at the moment is a prevailing belief that even the toughest problems can be solved. And a similar can-do moment, in the late 1940s, offers a striking historical precedent for the application of mass-production techniques to housing: as American servicemen flooded home after the second world war to start families, Levitt & Sons built Levittowns at the rate of 30 houses a day by mass-producing the components in factories, delivering them on lorries and using teams of specialists to assemble them.

Some emerging-world governments are beginning to realize that providing security of tenure is the only way to deal with the problem of ever-proliferating slums. And big companies that face stagnant markets in the West are increasingly fascinated by the "fortune at the bottom of the pyramid." Bill Gross of Idealab reckons the market for cheap houses could be worth at least $424 billion. But in reality it is worth far more than that: preventing the Earth from becoming what Mike Davis, a particularly gloomy follower of Marx and Engels, has termed a "planet of slums."

Other Invention Strategies

Great myths have grown up around writers who can supposedly sit down, put pen to paper, and write a masterpiece. If these myths had developed about any other type of artist—a musician or a painter—we would scoff about them and ask about the years of study and practice those artists had spent before they created their masterpieces. Since all of us can write to some degree, perhaps it seems more feasible that great authors simply appear magically amongst us. Alas, it is not so; like all talented artists, good writers must learn their craft through consistent and continuous practice. Similar to how the ancient Greeks used **topoi** (a strategy or heuristic made up of questions about a topic which allows a rhetor to construe an argument) to generate raw material for their compositions, many writers today use the following invention strategies as prewriting activities.

Freewriting

One practice method developed in the 1970s and often attributed to Peter Elbow, author of *Writing without Teachers*, is called freewriting. This method is just what it sounds like—writing that is free of any content restrictions. You simply write what is on your mind. This method is freeform, but there is some structure—you must set a time limit before you begin, and once you begin, you must not stop. The time period is usually 10 to 20 minutes, and you must keep your pen or pencil moving on the page—no hesitations, no corrections, no rereading. Don't worry about spelling, or punctuation, or grammar—just download onto the paper whatever comes to mind. It will seem awkward at best; some have said it is downright painful. But after a few weeks practice, you will realize it is effective and a wonderful individual method of getting at your thoughts on a subject.

Invisible Freewriting

If you just cannot stop paying attention to your spelling and grammar, or if you find yourself always stopping to read what you have written, you can freewrite invisibly. To do this, you will need carbon paper and a pen that is retracted or out of ink. You sandwich the carbon paper, carbon side down, between two sheets of paper and write on the top sheet with your empty pen. You cannot see what you are writing, but it will be recorded on the bottom sheet of paper. If you prefer to work on the computer, you can easily modify this technique by taping a blank sheet of paper over the monitor while you type.

Focused Freewriting

When freewriting, you are writing without sticking to any particular topic. You are exploring many ideas and your sentences may roam from your day at work, the letter you just got from your sister, or a story you read in the paper about a man who tracks the nighttime migrations of songbirds. With focused freewriting, you are trying to concentrate on one particular subject. You can write the name of that subject at the top of the page to remind you of your topic as you write. The rules are the same as the other types of freewriting, but you are focusing on one question or idea and exploring it in depth.

One drawback of focused freewriting is that students sometimes confuse it with a different step in the writing process, drafting. Remember that freewriting is "invention" work, intended only to help you explore ideas on paper. Drafting takes place only after you have explored, analyzed, and organized those ideas. Freewriting helps you think and write critically about a topic while drafting occurs once you have done the critical thinking necessary to come up with a unified, cohesive, and organized plan for an essay.

Listing/Brainstorming

This method of mapping is the least visual and the most straightforward. Unlike freewriting, where you write continuously, with listing you write down words and/or phrases that provide a shorthand for the ideas you might use in your essay, much as you would a grocery or "to-do" list. Brainstorming is a bit looser. Lists usually follow line after line on the page; brainstorming consists of words and phrases placed anywhere you want to write them on the page.

Clustering

When you think of a cluster, you think of several like things grouped together, often with something holding them together. Peanut clusters, a type of candy, are peanuts joined together with milk chocolate. Star clusters are groupings of stars, like the Pleiades or the Big Dipper, connected by their relative positions to each other in space. You can create clusters of like ideas by grouping your ideas around a central topic on a blank sheet of paper.

Organizing or Arranging

The "invention" process is intended to get our ideas out of our heads and onto a piece of paper, but rarely do these ideas arrive in the most logical or effective order. Take some time (an hour or so for a short essay) to analyze your inventions. Place all the ideas in a logical order, and join similar ideas. Next, look for your most significant point, the most important thing you want to say about your subject. This may become your tentative thesis. Then identify which of the other items on your list will help you communicate your point and delete items that are irrelevant to your thesis.

Reading 4.5

When I was working at Berkeley's College Academic Support Center, I often tutored second-language learners who struggled with sentences that had awkward constructions. Sometimes, I would say to a student, "What is it you're trying to say here?" The student inevitably could state the point orally with accuracy and clarity. I would then say to the student, "Write down what you just said." The student would write it down with pen and paper. Then I'd say, "Okay, pretend you're the professor. Which do you think is the easier sentence to understand: what you wrote or what you typed?" The student would say, "What I wrote. Whenever I type, I'm always afraid of what the professor will say."

Take a Leap into Writing

by Craig Wynne

Craig Wynne says, "When jumping out of an airplane, you don't have time to think about consequences. You just have to do it....The same principle applies to writing."

Around that time, I read an article in *Writer* magazine entitled "Forget the Rules and Take a Leap," by an author named Deanna Roy. In this article, Roy had been suffering from writer's block, and she found that skydiving was a way for her to release her thoughts without fear of saying the "wrong thing." So I decided to put this idea into practice myself for the purposes of teaching my students about overcoming their inhibitions when it came to writing.

When jumping out of an airplane, you don't have time to think about consequences. You just have to do it. You can see from the photo, jumping wasn't an easy thing for me to do, but afterwards I was glad I had gone through with taking that leap.

The same principle applies to writing. You need to find a way to write without thinking about whether your words are spelled correctly or whether the professor won't like the idea. Those thoughts get in the way with your writing process. Some students can write with that kind of freedom on a computer, but others find that with the computer comes an uninvited editor who looks over their shoulder and criticizes. Yet, they can escape that editor by talking out their thoughts and then writing with pen and paper. Whatever works. This doesn't mean that writing is ever going to be easy. It's just easier if you can get your thoughts down on a piece of paper before that internal editor starts looking for errors.

A professor named Peter Elbow developed a process called freewriting, which helps writers take that leap from thoughts into words. To freewrite, you put your pen to paper and just write. You don't want to think about whether something is spelled incorrectly or whether the professor will like an idea. Freewriting is the chance for you to get your ideas down on paper (or on the computer). When you freewrite, you don't stop. You just write. Even if you have an idea you think sounds completely stupid or off-the-wall, just write it down. You never know. Sometimes, those "silly" ideas could contain something you might be able to use for your assignment. When I start a project, I begin by letting all my ideas out in words in a row, even if they don't sound quite right. Professor Elbow remarked that freewriting results in a lot of words that are garbage. That's true. However, eventually, I come to words that express an idea I like. In order to get to the point of liking my words, I have to take that leap onto the page. Eventually, I have to worry about grammar, structure, and the end product, but not while I'm freewriting.

Activity 4.6 Consider "Take a Leap into Writing"

1. How do you write most easily? On a computer? With pen and paper? Share your experience getting words onto a page.

2. What do you think of Wynne's comparison of writing to skydiving? What do the two things have in common?

3. Do you have an internal editor that keeps you from writing freely? Can you describe your editor? What does it do?

Activity 4.7 Focused Freewriting

1. Write your topic at the top of a blank sheet of paper.

2. Write a list of at least 10 aspects or characteristics of your topic.

3. Choose two or three items from your list and do a focused freewriting on each item for five to eight minutes.

4. Add more items to your list if you have discovered new ideas during your freewriting.

Activity 4.8 Begin with What You Know

In your small group, make a list of controversial topics that you already have some knowledge about because of personal experience or course work. For example, one of you may be among the millions of Americans without health insurance or you may know someone else in this position. If so, you probably know about some of the failings of the American health care system. Alternatively, you may have lost a job during the 2009 recession or been unable to find a job when you needed one. If so, you probably have some thoughts about the efforts of the federal government to deal with the economic crisis. These personal connections with controversial issues give you a starting point for research on a topic. Share your group's list with the class.

Expand Your Personal Knowledge through Observation

Close observation for descriptive detail can enhance almost any topic. If you are writing a paper on the effectiveness of recycling in your community, you might take a trip to your community's processing area for recycled glass. There you could gather information through observing the glass recycling process. You also might be able to conduct short, informal interviews with the employees about the process.

You may need to call to get permission to visit certain places. You'll need to identify yourself and your topic. Usually you can get permission to visit and observe. However, if you cannot get permission to visit an area, you can ask your contact if there is a similar area nearby. Again, look at your research questions before you visit to decide which questions might be answered by your observations. For example, if you have read about recycling centers in other communities, during your visit to the local center, you could observe the similarities and differences in their procedures. Good writers always gather more detail than they actually use so they have choices about what to include.

The key to successful observation is tuning the senses. Can you remember what your room smelled like when you woke up this morning, the first thing you saw when you opened your eyes, the way your sheets or blanket felt against your skin, the sounds in the room after you turned off your alarm, or the taste of the orange juice or coffee you had with breakfast? Our minds are trained to ignore seemingly unimportant information, so if you can't remember any sensory details from your morning, you're not alone. When conducting an observation, however, those sensory responses are an important part of your research. Sitting in the place you're observing, freewrite for at least five minutes on each of the senses: touch, taste, smell, sight, and sound. You might even freewrite on each of the senses from several different vantage points, depending on the size of the place or the event you're observing. Take notes on the responses given by those you speak with.

Within fifteen minutes of leaving the place you have been observing, take a few minutes to read over your notes and write a few overall impressions or add details you missed in your description. Look again at your research questions and decide which ones have been answered by your visit.

Activity 4.9 Observation Exercise

In this exercise, describe your classroom. Alternatively, go to another setting such as a museum, restaurant, or library and describe that space and the people in it.

- How large is the space, approximately? Describe the shape of the room, and the color and texture of the walls, the ceiling, and the floor.

- How is the space furnished? Describe the color, shape, and style of the furnishings.

- What about representing the other senses? Is the room silent or noisy? Does it have a characteristic smell? Describe.

- How many people are in the room? What are they doing? Describe their ages, general style of dress, and possessions such as computers, backpacks, or purses.

- Pick two or three people that stand out in some way from the other occupants and write a sentence or two about each, describing what it is about each person that caught your attention.

Reading 4.6

Typically, car makers will choose a special color for the introduction of a special vehicle, known in the biz as the "launch color." In the case of the 1M Coupe—the Motorsports division variant of BMW's beastly looking 135i—the launch color is a sort of burnt tangerine, a phrase that also describes my own mental citrus after a weekend behind the wheel.

BMW 1M: Miniature, Mighty and Miles of Fun
by Dan Neil

Dan Neil, auto columnist for *The Wall Street Journal*, reviewed the new BMW Coupe in his weekly column "Rumble Seat."

As you read the article that follows, pay attention to how the author uses details from both personal knowledge and close observation to enrich his writing.

A bratty little barrel-racer of a car, with a spirit that seems to want to bite through the bit, the 1M Coupe is quick, playful, aggressive and laugh-out-loud fun to drive; indeed, it's as much fun as the law will allow. For BMW fanboys, I gather, that's just the problem.

A little history is in order: The M division began in the 1970s building highly tuned versions of the Werks' production cars, with more powerful engines, bigger brakes, more athletic legs and edgier electronics. Some of these cars have been, simply, epic. The M3 that I imprinted on was a '96 Euro-spec yellow coupe. That car is, to this day, the best handling five-seater I've ever driven.

Bratty Little Barrel Racer

(Note to Bavaria: Bring back the narrow-section steering wheel. And stop hogging all the good scenery.)

To describe the pleasures of that M3—known to the geek squad as the E36 model—is to define a kind of atavism that the Bimmerphiles pine for. Those cars were relatively simple (in-line six, manual transmission and spare amenities), with beautifully quick and sensitive steering and an easy progressiveness that meant you could let the rear end slide around without fear of losing it, catching the car with a dab of throttle and counter-steer. It wasn't the fastest car in the world but it was such a sheer limbic pleasure to drive, to wheel, to wield, to control. That's it: a sense of mastery. You got out of that car wearing a cape and a big S on your chest.

Most of all, that car was lightweight. That E36 coupe weighed about 3,200 pounds. By contrast, the current model-year M3 (E92) weighs fully 500 pounds more on a 2.4-inch-longer wheelbase. And while the current M3 has vastly more go-fast hardware—including a 414-horsepower V8, optional dual-clutch gearbox, cybernetic brakes and the M Variable Differential Lock (sounds like an outlawed wrestling hold, doesn't it?)—a certain something, call it a dynamic lucidity, has been lost.

And the fanboys feel betrayed. They whine, they fume, they wear black. You'd think Rudolph Valentino had just died or something. Why does the M3 have to be so heavy? What part of Ultimate Driving Machine does BMW itself not understand?

But everyone's favorite M3 of yore didn't have to have a monster stereo, navi, power seats, umpteen airbags or five-star crash structure. The M3 so fondly remembered has been essentially optioned up and regulated out of existence. Unless BMW discovers the formula for Flubber, that car isn't coming back.

And the bloat isn't confined to the weight scales. The current M3 is also punitively pricey, starting at $61,075 (with gas-guzzler tax) and luxed-out to nearly $70,000. More fanboy despair. Oh, Rudy!

To these disconsolate few, the news last year that the M division was going to hot up the 135i coupe (the E82 platform, in nerd-speak) must have sounded like salvation. The numbers were there. Not quite 3,400 pounds, with a twin-turbo 3.0-liter in-line six delivering 335 hp and 332 pound-feet of torque—with brief computer-summoned overboost of 369 pound-feet—and the sole choice of a six-speed manual transmission, the 1M Coupe sounded like more than just a cool car. It promised a return to form, an end to a kind of despised lavishness, a cure for what ails the BMW brand.

2012 BMW 1M Coupe

Base price: $47,010

Price as tested: $49,000 (est.)

Powertrain: Twin-turbo 3.0-liter in-line six cylinder with variable valve timing; six-speed manual transmission; rear wheel drive with variable differential lock

Horsepower/torque: 335 hp at 5,900 rpm/332 pound-feet at 1,500–4,500 rpm (369 pound-feet at overboost)

Length/weight: 172.4 inches/3,362 pounds

Wheelbase: 104.7 inches

EPA fuel economy: 19/26 mpg, city/highway

Cargo capacity: 8 cubic feet

Now that the car is here, is it? You know, it is, sort of.

To boil it down a bit, the 1M Coupe is the smaller car with the mighty M3's dirty bits, less 400 pounds. The same highly evolved suspension componentry, the same massive brakes behind the same stick-with-a-grip 35-series, 19-inch tires and wheels, the same electronically controlled rear differential, and the same M-tuned dynamics control, which allows drivers to color outside the lines safely at the track. And yes, you can turn the electronic interventions off. But once the nannies are dismissed, be advised, the car has a measure of the old-school, free-gimbaling character of the early M's. In other words, it can get away from you. Me? Oh, please. You'd like that, wouldn't you?

The 1M is certainly track-day ready, with a dry-sump engine-lubrication system with its own heat exchanger as well as a radiator for the heavy-duty six-speed transmission. The car I drove had a brake warning light come on—I think the 14-inch cross-drilled brakes got a little too warm after being lapped at Laguna Seca for a half-hour or so—but they never failed to haul the car down with a precise and determined yank rearward.

Here, at last, is a man's clutch—heavily weighted, with a smooth, precise uptake—and slick-shifting gearshift to go with it. Pedal position is just about perfect for heel-and-toe footwork.

Serene and smooth at low speeds, but with an increasingly impatient growl from the quad exhaust as the revs build, the 1M does several dynamic things particularly well. First, at corner exits, it pulls like hell, like it has deployed some magical torque spinnaker. BMW gives the 0–60 acceleration at 4.7 seconds, but the way this thing gets on the cam in second and third gear will bring a tear to your eye. Like my favorite M3 of olden days, the car is not unnervingly fast but it's hugely willing. This thing hits redline faster than one of the Real Housewives of Atlanta.

Second, it has splendid cornering grip, and the corner-to-corner transitions happen without a lot of heaving, rolling or rebound to unsettle the car or cause you to correct your line. The 1M Coupe has impeccable cornering manners, and the M Sport Seats lock you in driving position.

Third, it trail-brakes like a dream. Turn in to a corner with the brakes on and ease off the binders. The car's rear end slides gracefully to the outside, the world swivels and now you're looking at corner exit. Dig in the spurs, up come the revs. Hi-yo, Silbern, away!

So what could possibly be wrong? Well, for one thing, the 1M Coupe is a total buttaface, one of the ugliest, most disturbingly wrong car designs in modern history. The addition of all the massive wheel arches, lip spoilers, aero mods and the so-called Air Curtain front spoiler helps not at all. This car is the last revenge of former BMW styling head Chris Bangle. Jeez, put a flag over its head and drive for glory.

Second—at least to the fanboys—it's still too heavy, despite the fact it's actually 77 pounds lighter than the standard 135i. But I checked the trunk for lead bars and found none, and I found very little in the way of depleted uranium in the cabin.

I can only conclude that, for some old-schoolers, nothing BMW makes will ever be light enough again. That's too bad. This thing's a tangerine dream.

Activity 4.10 **Find Artistic and Inartistic Proofs in a Reading**

Much of Dan Neil's column, "BMW 1M: Miniature, Mighty and Miles of Fun," comes from his own personal experience and observation. For example, his description of the car as a, "bratty little barrel-racer of a car, with a spirit that seems to want to bite through the bit," is his own evaluation or thought and, thus, an artistic proof. So is the first sentence, "Typically, car makers will choose a special color for the introduction of a special vehicle, known in the biz as the 'launch color.'" That information comes from his long experience with reviewing cars. Also, his remark that the brake light came on in the car he drove is his observation.

However, the information that the car has "a dry-sump engine-lubrication system with its own heat exchanger as well as a radiator for the heavy-duty six-speed transmission" may have come from the manufacturer's promotional literature.

For this activity, go through the reading and highlight (or underline) the parts that you think come from Dan Neil's own knowledge or observation. These are the artistic proofs. Information he has obtained from other sources (such as the car company) would be inartistic proofs. If you aren't sure whether or not a sentence is his own knowledge or observation, make a note of that in the margin. Discuss this as a class.

Activity 4.11   Write a Product Review

Choose a new product in a category you know well, such as a computer or an MP3 player, and write a review as if you were a columnist for a newspaper, magazine, or blog. Using the techniques explained in this chapter, do prewriting to elicit what you know about the product and the product category. Then, observe the product and try it out, so that you can review its positives and negatives. If you need specific information that you do not know, consult the product advertising, packaging, or instruction manual.

Like Dan Neil's auto product review, you can use vivid language and insider slang in order to provide an enjoyable experience for your reader. Remember, however, that this is an argument. You need to evaluate whether the product is a good or bad selection for its target audience and why.

Activity 4.12   Write on Your Blog

Choose a controversial topic and speculate in your blog whether or not that topic is at a stasis point for any of the stasis questions.

Activity 4.13   Write in Your Commonplace Book

In your commonplace book, freewrite about how you do invention. What methods do you use to extract from your mind what you already know about a subject (what Aristotle would call artistic proofs)?

5
WRITING RHETORICALLY

Praxis in Action

How I Write by Matthew Harding

Writing can seem very daunting at times, especially when you have a major writing assignment that's worth as much as a test. It should be easy since you know about the assignment way ahead of time, but somehow the time ends up getting away from you because it's hard to get started. You end up both stressing about the paper and trying to write it at the last minute. One way that I reduce the pressure of a writing assignment is to start writing long before the paper is due, giving myself enough time to work on it.

If I tell myself that I am only going to write a certain amount at a time, say a page a day, it is less intimidating to write. While this method may seem drawn out, it works. Whenever I come back to the paper the next day, I always review what I have already written, so I can be sure I keep the topic in mind. This way, I avoid burning myself out, getting my ideas confused, or losing track of the topic and, ultimately, rushing to finish by the end. This allows me to come to my paper with a fresh perspective and new ideas with every installment I write. Once I finish that day's work I feel good because I am getting the paper done while also giving it my best effort, which also greatly reduces the stress of having to write it.

Matthew Harding points out that writing can be daunting even for experienced writers.

Through Writing, Enter the Conversation

Cicero's famous work, *On the Ideal Orator*, is not a treatise or handbook about how to be an effective rhetorician. Instead, it is a dialogue, a conversation. The setting is a villa outside Rome belonging to Lucius Licinius Crassus, and the time is 91 CE, an era of dangerous unrest in the Roman Empire. Prominent and respected citizens gather with Crassus to escape, for a while, the political crisis developing in the city. Crassus and his guests settle at leisure under a wide, spreading plane tree, not only to enjoy its shade but also to pay homage to Plato's *Phaedrus*, which similarly took place under a plane tree, though in Greece. They take time this day to dialogue about the attributes of an ideal orator. The purpose of the arguments they present to each other is not to win out over the others but, conversing together, to come to knowledge. It is not a trivial pursuit. Cicero reveals what his characters do not know—soon they will all die horribly as part of the civil unrest in Rome, violence traceable to the failure of leaders to resolve their differences in nonviolent dialogue.

Throughout ancient times, dialogue appears alongside rhetoric. It was through dialogue that rhetoricians such as Aristotle, Isocrates, and Cicero taught their students rhetorical skills. Today, in the writing classroom, group discussion or pairs dialogue is also part of the teaching process. A rhetorical text, too, is a conversation with previous texts, responding to ideas they have presented. In addition, arguments include paraphrases and quotes from others' compositions, making them part of the conversation. Moreover, writers composing texts must anticipate their audiences' reactions—questions they might ask or objections they might raise—so responses to these questions and objects can be included in the argument. This process of responding to audiences in advance continues the conversation.

Organize Your Essay

All texts are conversational, a characteristic reflected in the format or organization. In ancient times, orators began a speech by attracting the audience's attention in what was called the *exordium*, which we would call the opening or introduction. Next, they provided background information in a *narratio* (narration), followed by an *explication* in which they defined terms and enumerated the issues. During the *partition* they would express the thesis or main issue to be discussed, and in the *confirmation* they would provide evidence to support the thesis. Opposition arguments would be addressed in the *refutatio*, and the composition would be wrapped up with a *peroratio* or conclusion. The order of these different elements was not rigid in ancient times, nor is it today. Sometimes one or more sections were eliminated if they were not needed, but then, as now, an effective text included most of these elements. For example, if your audience is very familiar with a particular subject, you may not need to define terms, as you would with an audience who was unfamiliar with the material.

As did the ancient Greeks and Romans, when you write an argument, you begin with an introduction that gains your audience's attention and presents your thesis; likewise, you end with a conclusion that ties together what you have said or presents a call to action. However, you have a choice of several formats for what happens between that introduction and conclusion. Following are three prominent alternatives; your choice of which to use depends on your purpose and the type of evidence you have.

■ Created by Stephen Toulmin, the **Toulmin model** for persuasion grew out of the 20th century emphasis upon empirical evidence and is *most effective for arguments that rely on evidence from scientific studies, surveys, or other data.* His model requires six elements. First, rhetors present a claim or statement that they want the audience to accept. Then, they back up the claim with data and facts, what Aristotle would have called inartistic proofs. A warrant links these data to the claim, explaining why the data make the claim valid. Backing provides additional support for the argument, while a counterclaim acknowledges any objections or weaknesses in the argument. And, finally, the rebuttal responds to any counterclaims, removing possible objections to the argument.

■ The **Rogerian** (or common ground) **argument** is named for psychologist Carl Rogers. It is *most effective for arguments that attempt to establish common ground between opponents* on an issue. Rogerian argument begins with an introduction that states the problem to be considered. Second, in a much different move than the Toulmin pattern, the rhetor states the opposing argument in neutral language to demonstrate that he or she understands the other side's position, as well as instances when it may be valid. The assumption is that, since the rhetor has been willing to pay attention to the other side's position, they will, in fairness, listen as the rhetor states his or her own position, as well as discusses the instances when it is preferable. The Rogerian argument ends on a positive note, describing how the rhetor's position could, at least in some instances, benefit the opposition.

- The **general modern format** for argument is one that will probably be familiar to you from previous English classes. It is a *format that you can use when your argument does not fit neatly into either the Toulmin or Rogerian patterns.* Moreover, you can adapt it to serve the needs of your argument. It is the standard five-paragraph essay modified for presenting an argument, and, like that pattern, it can be expanded to accommodate longer essays. Similar to the five-paragraph essay, you begin with an introduction that attracts your audience's attention and states your thesis. Then two or three sections each present major points that support your thesis. The next section presents a counterargument, which anticipates audience questions or objections and is followed by a rebuttal of the counterargument. Finally, a conclusion ties the argument together, perhaps by reflecting back to the introduction or issuing a call for action.

Notice that all of these formats include an attempt to dialogue with the audience. In the Toulmin model, the warrant, in particular, is designed to help the audience make the logical link between the claim and the data offered as evidence. In a Rogerian argument, the rhetor carefully and in emotionally-neutral language demonstrates that he or she has been listening to the opposition and can even restate their argument fairly. The arguments produced via these models, even if they do not immediately convince, will not worsen the situation. The aim of well-intentioned rhetors is not to convince at any cost but to continue the conversation until reasonable solutions can be found. For a comparison of the different argument formats, see table 5.1 presented on page 150–151.

Like the ancient Greeks, you will begin with an opening and end with a conclusion. However, in between the bookends of your essay, you have more flexibility to adapt the basic format than did the Romans.

Write a Thesis Statement

A **thesis** may be a sentence or a series of sentences, or in a few cases it may be implied rather than stated explicitly; but a thesis is at the heart of any piece of writing. If a reader cannot identify your thesis, the meaning of your text is not clear. How do you develop a thesis? First, you determine your occasion for writing—who is your audience, what is your purpose, and what special circumstances are there (if any)? Then you write a working thesis that makes an assertion or claim about your topic, something that will be affected by your audience and purpose. For example, if you are writing a research paper about the advantages and disadvantages of biodiesel fuel, your claim may be stated differently depending on whether your audience is an English class or a chemistry class. In the latter, you might need to use technical language that would be unfamiliar to your English professor.

Working theses are statements that develop and change as essays are written; they are basic frameworks that provide a connection for the ideas you have decided to convey to your reader. Later, after you have completed a draft of your text, examine your working thesis. If needed, rewrite your thesis so that it states the main idea of your essay in a clear and engaging fashion. Consider the following examples of thesis statements.

> The United States should implement a guest worker program as a way of reforming the illegal immigration problem.

> Nuclear power should be considered as part of a program to reduce the United States's dependence on foreign oil.

Compose an Introduction

Experienced writers have different methods of creating a good introduction. One writer who tends to discover his paper as he goes along swears the best way to write an introduction is to write the entire paper and then move the conclusion to the beginning of the essay and rewrite it as the introduction. Another writer lets the paper sit around for a few days before she writes her introduction. A third always writes two or three different introductions and tries them out on friends before deciding which to use. However you choose to write the introduction, make sure it is interesting enough to make your reader want to read on.

The introduction to your essay is an invitation to your reader. If you invite readers to come along with you on a boring journey, they won't want to follow. In magazine and newspaper writing, the introduction is

Essay Starters

If, after you have done extensive invention (prewriting and research), you still find it intimidating to face the blank computer screen, try one of the essay starters below. These are phrases to get the words flowing. Then, later, after you have written a rough draft, go back and revise the beginning. Delete the essay starter and, in its place, write a real introduction. As you probably know, you do not need to say, "In my opinion," because what you write in your essay, unless you attribute it to someone else, is your opinion. See the section in this chapter on writing introductions.

In my opinion . . .

I agree . . .

I disagree . . .

Studies show . . .

Experts say . . .

My paper is about . . .

I am writing this essay because . . .

In the beginning . . .

Argument Formats: A Comparison

Ancient Roman	General Modern Format
Standard pattern the ancients modified to suit the argument.	Good all-purpose format that can be adapted for the needs of the argument.
Introduction—Exordium Attracts the interest of the audience and identifies the argument.	**Introduction** Attracts the interest of the audience through its opening strategy and states the thesis.
Background or narration—Narratio Details the history or facts of the issue.	**First main point** Supports the thesis.
Definition—Explication Defines terms and outlines issues.	**Second main point** Supports the thesis.
Thesis—Partition States the particular issue that is to be argued.	**Third main point** Supports the thesis.
Proof—Confirmation Develops the thesis and provides supporting evidence.	**Counterargument** Acknowledges the opposing argument or arguments.
Refutation or opposition—Refutatio Addresses the arguments opposing the thesis.	**Rebuttal of counterargument** Refutes the opposing argument or arguments.
Conclusion—Peroratio Reiterates the thesis and may urge the audience to action.	**Conclusion** Ties together the elements of the composition and gives the reader closure. May summarize the essay and include a call to action.

table 5.1

Toulmin Model	Rogerian Argument
Good for an argument that relies on empirical evidence such as scientific studies or data collection.	Good when the object is consensus or compromise, so that opponents can work together while retaining their positions.
Claim Presents the overall thesis the writer will argue.	**Introduction** States the problem to be solved or the question to be answered. Often opponents will also agree there is a problem.
Data Supports the claim with evidence.	**Summary of opposing views** Describes the opposing side's arguments in a neutral and fair manner.
Warrant (also known as a bridge) Explains why or how the data support the claim. Connects the data to the claim.	**Statement of understanding** Concedes occasions when the opposing position might be valid.
Counterclaim Presents a claim that negates or disagrees with the thesis/claim.	**Statement of position** Avoids emotionally charged language, and identifies position.
Rebuttal Presents evidence that negates or disagrees with the counterclaim.	**Statement of contexts** Describes the specific contexts in which the rhetor's position applies/works well.
Conclusion Ties together the elements of the composition (if not included with the rebuttal).	**Statement of benefits** Presents benefits that may appeal to the self-interest of readers who may not yet agree with you; shows how your position benefits them. Ends on a positive note.
	Conclusion Ties together the elements of the composition (if not included in the statement of benefits).

sometimes called a *hook* because it hooks the reader into reading the text. If a magazine writer does not capture the reader's attention right away, the reader is not likely to continue. After all, there are other and possibly more interesting articles in the magazine. Why should readers suffer through a boring introduction? Depending on the topic and pattern of your essay, you might employ one of the following techniques to hook your readers and make them want to keep reading:

- An intriguing or provocative quotation

- A narrative or anecdote

- A question or series of questions

- A vivid sensory description

- A strongly stated opinion

Your introductory paragraph makes a commitment to your readers. This is where you identify the topic, state your thesis (implicitly or explicitly), and give your readers clues about the journey that will follow in the succeeding paragraphs. Be careful not to mislead the reader. Do not ask questions you will not answer in your paper (unless they are rhetorical questions). Do not introduce a topic in your introduction and then switch to another one in your paper.

Although the introduction is the first paragraph or so of the paper, it may not be the first paragraph the writer composes. If you have problems beginning your essay because you cannot immediately think of a good introduction, begin with the first point in your essay and come back to the introduction later.

If you have problems writing anything at all, consider the suggestions offered in the following essay.

Reading 5.1

The Truth about Writer's Block

by Judith Johnson

Judith Johnson suggests in this essay, first published in *Huffington Post Books*, that there is no such thing as writer's block. She suggests what writers experience is the ebb and flow of the writing process.

I don't choose to experience "writer's block" which I see as simply a matter of faulty perception. It is a mislabeling of a very natural part of the ebb and flow of the writing process. To say "I have writer's block" is to judge a temporary or permanent absence of writing momentum and productivity as wrong and therefore to see oneself as a failure in some way. The process of writing is an intricate interplay of conscious and unconscious dynamics and what actually lands on the page is a small part of it all. When we label and judge that process, we interfere with its natural flow and take a position of againstness with ourselves. It's all in how you look at it.

When a writer declares that he or she is experiencing writer's block, it is like grabbing hold of a fear (Fantasy Expectation Appearing Real) and fueling it with emotional distress. A way to reframe this is to simply trust that what appears to be a dry spell is a normal part of the process of being a writer and that either you need time to be away from the writing focus or that the process is largely unconscious at that time. Each writer has to make peace with this by finding their own particular rhythm and honoring that. For example, what works for me is not to have any rigid writing schedule, but rather to let the words come to me—and they always do—sooner or later. When working on a deadline, whether self-imposed or not, I never lose sight of the deadline, it is always there, but I don't beat myself up with it if time keeps passing and nothing is getting on paper. I'll notice that the topic is alive in me—turning this way and that finding its way to the paper. It takes a lot of trust to let this be. So far, it has never failed me.

I have lots of books and articles and projects on the back burner and no fear of running out of things to write about. I know that each piece of writing has a life of its own. For example, I have a poem that I started at the age of 16 that rumbles around in my head from time to time looking for its ending. I know it will end someday, but hasn't so far. That's not a problem to me—just a reality. I also keep what I call a "dump" file for each project and whether I am actively working on it or not, I capture ideas and information there.

In addition to building a strong bond of trust with yourself, here are some other keys to maintaining a good relationship with yourself as a writer:

Just Do It: There is a point at which every writer just has to sit down and write. Whether you write for five minutes or five hours straight doesn't matter, but if you are going to be a writer, you have to sit down and write.

Write with Freedom and Abandon, Then Edit Ruthlessly: It is important to give yourself permission to write whatever comes up without any judgment. Just focus on capturing your thoughts and ideas—forget about grammar, structure and eloquence. Just get a hold of whatever comes up. Then, just as Michelangelo described the sculpting process as discovering a statue inside every block of stone, each writer must ruthlessly revise and refine a piece of work until pleased with it.

Get Out of Your Own Way: If you get into a pattern of negativity and beating up on yourself when writing, find a way to be more loving with yourself and do not feed the negativity.

Patience: Writing takes enormous patience. As with any other art form, you are constantly revising and refining your work. For an artist the equation is never time is money, but rather "do I feel complete with this piece? Is it my best effort given the time I have available?"

Flexibility, Cooperation and Balance: There is always some level of agitation just under the surface that propels a writer forward giving momentum to the working process. But there are always other forces at work and writing is only one of many activities in an individual's life. Finding your own rhythm and being willing to cooperate with the other elements of life that often seem to intrude on the writer's solitary endeavor are like moving between shooting the rapids and gliding along on calm waters, never quite knowing which is going to present itself and when. Experience teaches us all to go with the flow and somehow that seems to yield maximum inner peace and outward productivity.

Keeping a Sense of Humor and Humility: I've learned never to take myself too seriously as a writer. I do my best and need to laugh at myself from time to time when I give too much importance to what I write. If people get value from what I write, that's great and positive feedback is extremely gratifying. However, while writing is ultimately about communication, I find it very funny that I don't write to communicate, but rather because I simply need to write—I am compelled to do so. If the end product of my endeavors is of value to others, that's great, but the solitary process of engaging in the art form itself is entirely for me and I think that is pretty funny.

Letting Go of the Illusion of Control: A really good writer is never in control of the writing process. You may find that having a rigid schedule works well for you or you might be someone who writes when the spirit moves you to do so. Either way, a good writer taps into the wellspring of human consciousness and like love, you can't make that happen on demand.

Is writing challenging? Absolutely! However, it is a great way to learn some profound lessons in life and to be of service to others.

Activity 5.1 Discuss "The Truth about Writer's Block"

1. How does Judith Johnson choose to reframe the concept of writer's block?

2. Johnson makes recommendations to deal with the "absence of writing momentum." Which of her suggestions makes the most sense to you? Which makes the least sense to you?

3. What do you think? Is there such a thing as "writer's block"?

Combine Your Ideas with Support from Source Materials

A research paper, by definition, makes use of source materials to make an argument. It is important to remember, however, that it is *your* paper, *not* what some professors may call a "research dump," meaning that it is constructed by stringing together research information with a few transitions. Rather, you, as the author of the paper, carry the argument in your own words and use quotes and paraphrases from source materials to support your argument. How do you do that? Here are some suggestions:

■ After you think you have completed enough research to construct a working thesis and begin writing your paper, collect all your materials in front of you (photocopies of articles, printouts of electronic sources, and books) and spend a few hours reading through the materials and making notes. Then, put all the notes and materials to the side and freewrite for a few minutes about what you can remember from your research that is important. Take this freewriting and make a rough outline of the main points you want to cover in your essay. Then you can go back to your notes and source materials to flesh out your outline.

■ Use quotes for the following three reasons:

1. You want to "borrow" the ethos or credibility of the source. For example, if you are writing about stem cell research, you may want to quote from an authority such as Dr. James A. Thomson, whose ground-breaking research led to the first use of stem cells for research. Alternatively, if your source materials include the *New England Journal of Medicine* or another prestigious publication, it may be worth crediting a quote to that source.

2. The material is so beautifully or succinctly written that it would lose its effectiveness if you reworded the material in your own words.

3. You want to create a point of emphasis by quoting rather than paraphrasing. Otherwise, you probably want to paraphrase material from your sources, as quotes should be used sparingly. Often, writers quote source material in a first draft and then rewrite some of the quotes into paraphrases during the revision process.

- Introduce quotes. You should never have a sentence or sentences in quotation marks just sitting in the middle of a paragraph, as it would puzzle a reader. If you quote, you should always introduce the quote by saying something like this: According to Dr. James A. Thomson, "Stem cell research. . . . "

- Avoid plagiarism by clearly indicating material that is quoted or paraphrased. See the appendix (at the end of the book) for more information about citing source material.

Support Your Thesis

After you have attracted the interest of your audience, established your thesis, and given any background information and definitions, you will next begin to give reasons for your position, which further develops your argument. These reasons are, in turn, supported by statistics, analogies, anecdotes, and quotes from authorities which you have discovered in your research or know from personal knowledge. Ideally, arrange your reasons so that the strongest ones come either at the beginning or at the end of this portion of the paper (points of emphasis) and the weaker ones fall in the middle.

Answer Opposing Arguments

If you are aware of a contradicting statistic or other possible objection to your argument, it may be tempting to ignore that complication, hoping your audience will not notice. However, that is exactly the worst thing you can do. It is much better to anticipate your audience's possible questions or objections and address them in your discussion. Doing so prevents you from losing credibility by either appearing to deceive your audience or being unaware of all the facts. Also, acknowledging possible refutations of your position actually strengthens your position by making you seem knowledgeable and fair-minded.

Vary Your Strategies or Patterns of Development

When composing your essay, you have many different strategies or **patterns of development** available to you. You may write entire essays whose sole strategy is argumentation or comparison and contrast, but more often, you will combine many of these different modes while writing a single essay. Consider the following strategies or patterns of development:

- *Analysis* entails a close examination of an issue, book, film, or other object, separating it into elements and examining each of the elements separately through other writing modes such as classification or comparison and contrast.

- *Argumentation* involves taking a strong stand on an issue supported by logical reasons and evidence intended to change a reader's mind on an issue or open a reader's eyes to a problem.

- *Cause and effect* is an explanation of the cause and subsequent effects or consequences of a specific action.

- *Classification* entails dividing and grouping things into logical categories.

- *Comparison and contrast* examines the similarities and differences between two or more things.

- *Definition* employs an explanation of the specific meaning of a word, phrase, or idea.

- *Description* uses vivid sensory details to present a picture or an image to the reader.

- *Exemplification* makes use of specific examples to explain, define, or analyze something.

- *Narration* uses a story or vignette to illustrate a specific point or examine an issue.

Write a Conclusion

After they have read the last paragraph of your essay, your readers should feel satisfied that you have covered everything you needed to and you have shared an insight. You may have heard the basic rules: A conclusion cannot address any new issues, and it should summarize the main points of the essay. Although these are valid and reliable rules, a summary is not always the best way to end an essay. The prohibition against new ideas in the final paragraph also might limit certain effective closures like a call to action or a question for the reader to ponder.

One effective technique for writing a conclusion is to refer back to your introduction. If you began with a narrative anecdote, a sensory description, or a question, you can tie a mention of it to your ending point. Or, if you are composing an argumentative essay, you might choose to summarize by using an expert quote to restate your thesis, giving the reader a final firm sense of ethos or credibility. You might also end with a single-sentence summary followed by a suggestion or a call to action for the reader. Another effective way to end an argument can be a paragraph that suggests further research.

A conclusion doesn't have to be long. As a matter of fact, it does not even need to be a separate paragraph, especially if your essay is short. If your closing comments are related to the final paragraph of the essay, one or two sentences can easily be added to the final body paragraph of the essay.

Consider Elements of Page Design

Professors now take it for granted that you word-process your paper using a professional looking typeface such as Times Roman. However, producing your text on a computer with Internet access gives you the option to do much more—including adding one or more images and other page design elements. Several of the assignments in this chapter offer you the opportunity to be creative with your project presentation. Even if you are required to submit your project in standard MLA or APA essay formats, however, you can still include one or more images, and it is important to consider where you place the images.

Some simple guidelines will help you design effective documents:

- Use space as a design element. Do not overcrowd your pages. Place material so that important parts are emphasized by the space around them.

- Rarely (if ever) use all capital letters. Words in all caps are hard to read, and on the Internet all caps is considered shouting.

- Use headings to group your information and make your pages easy to skim. Readers often like to skim pages before deciding what to read.

Indeed, many people will skim all the headlines, headings, and photo captions first, before reading the body text of any section.

■ Put important elements in the top left and lower right parts of the screen. English readers are trained to read from left to right, so our eyes naturally start at the upper left-hand corner of the screen. Our eyes, when skimming, don't flow line by line, but move in a Z pattern, as illustrated in the following diagram (see figure 5.1).

figure 5.1

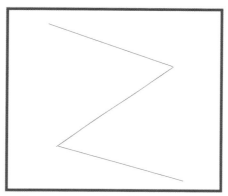

Eye movement when skimming a page

If you want to include a photo in your research paper, for example, you should put it either in the top left or the bottom right corner of the page, points of emphasis in the Z pattern. Today, with a sophisticated word processing program such as Microsoft Word, it is easy to import an image, size it, and move it to the desired place on a page. Once you have imported an image, you can click on it, hold your cursor at a corner, and enlarge or shrink the image by dragging the cursor. Also, by clicking on the image, you can activate the dialogue box that allows you to specify having the text run tightly around the image. Then you can easily move the image around on the page until you have placed it in a pleasing spot. Alternatively, Microsoft Word provides document templates that you can use for newsletters, brochures, and other types of projects.

If you look closely at figure 5.2 on the next page, you may notice that the text surrounding the image does not seem to make any sense (though it is actually Latin). That's because the text is Lorem ipsum text, sometimes called placeholder or dummy text, which designers use to create page layouts before they have the real text from writers. If you want to try using Lorem ipsum yourself, just do a search on the Internet for that name, and you will find sites that provide paragraphs of the nonsense words that you can utilize as placeholder text.

figure 5.2

Ullamcorper Suscipit Lobortis Nisl

Consectetuer Adipiscing Elit

Sed diam nonummy nibh euismod tincidunt ut laoreet dolore magna aliquam erat volutpat. Ut wisi enim ad minim veniam, quis nostrud exerci tation ullamcorper suscipit lobortis nisl ut aliquip ex ea commodo consequat. Duis autem vel eum iriure dolor in hendrerit in vulputate velit esse molestie consequat, vel illum dolore eu feugiat nulla facilisis at vero eros et accumsan et iusto odio dignissim qui blandit praesent luptatum zzril delenit augue duis dolore te feugait nulla facilisi.

Lorem ipsum dolor sit amet, consectetuer adipiscing elit, sed diam nonummy nibh euismod tincidunt ut laoreet dolore magna aliquam erat volutpat. Ut wisi enim ad minim veniam, quis nostrud exerci tation ullamcorper suscipit lobortis nisl ut aliquip ex ea commodo consequat. Duis autem vel eum iriure dolor in hendrerit in vulputate velit esse molestie consequat, vel illum dolore eu feugiat nulla facilisis at vero eros et accumsan et iusto odio dignissim qui blandit praesent luptatum zzril delenit augue duis dolore te feugait nulla facilisi.

Lorem Ipsum Dolor Sit

Amet, consectetuer adipiscing elit, sed diam nonummy nibh euismod tincidunt ut laoreet dolore magna aliquam erat volutpat. Ut wisi enim ad minim veniam, quis nostrud exerci tation ullamcorper suscipit lobortis nisl ut aliquip ex ea commodo consequat. Duis autem vel eum iriure dolor in hendrerit in vulputate velit esse molestie consequat, vel illum dolore eu feugiat nulla facilisis at vero eros et accumsan et iusto odio dignissim qui blandit praesent luptatum zzril delenit augue duis dolore te feugait nulla facilisi. Lorem ipsum dolor sit amet, consectetuer adipiscing

The image in this article has been effectively placed in the lower right corner, which is a point of emphasis.

Including Images in Your Projects: Copyright Implications

United States copyright law includes a provision called "fair use" that allows copyrighted images to be used for educational projects. However, copyright laws are complicated, and the implications of using digital images is still being determined in the courts. Clearly, if you take the photo yourself, you own the copyright. Many photographers post photos on websites such as Flikr.com and give permission for "fair use" of the images on the Internet, so long as their work is credited. Others, however, post their work for viewers to enjoy but do not allow it to be copied. Scanning a photo from a published work and using it once for a class project falls more clearly under the spirit of the "fair use" law than does putting such an image up on the Internet. If you are doing a web page or blog project that includes images, be sure to contact the copyright owner to obtain permission.

Activity 5.2 Write a Research-Based Argument Paper

The Purpose of the Assignment

Writing a research paper gives you the opportunity to practice key academic writing skills, including locating and utilizing research materials, prewriting, drafting, and revision. It also requires you to take a position on a topic, create an argument, and support it with quotes and paraphrases from authoritative sources.

Purpose as a Writer

Your purpose as a writer is to convince readers to consider your argument carefully, and, if possible, to persuade them to agree with your point of view. To do this, include appropriate background material and definitions, as well as a consideration of opposing arguments.

Topic

Your topic should address a current issue about which you can take and support a position in the paper length your instructor specifies. Choose your topic carefully, as it should be one that engages your interest and enthusiasm.

Audience

Unless your instructor specifies otherwise, you can assume that your audience has general awareness of your issue but is unfamiliar with scholarly sources on the topic.

Sources

To do your research, you will need to utilize recent and credible sources that include a mix of recent books, scholarly articles, public speeches, and news articles. You may also use interviews, observation, and personal experience, if they are relevant to your topic. Sources will need to be cited in the text and in a works cited page or references page, according to MLA or APA style.

Information that you gather from your sources should support the argument you have created. A research paper is not an assignment in which you take information from sources and simply reorganize it into a paper. The expectation for this course is that you will use your sources to create an argument that is distinctly your own.

Thesis

Your essay should have a clear thesis that takes a position on an issue that can be supported within the word limitations of the assignment.

Rough Draft

As directed by your instructor, bring two copies of your rough draft essay to class for peer editing. The draft should have your sources credited in the text and should have a works cited page or references page.

Final Draft

Submit your final draft in MLA or APA format in a folder with your rough draft and copies of all of your source materials with the location of quotes or paraphrased material highlighted. If you are using material from a book or books, copy enough of the text before and after your quotes or paraphrases so that your instructor can determine the context of the material being quoted.

Reading 5.2

Film Review: *The Hangover* (2009)
by Owen Gleiberman

This film review by Owen Gleiberman appeared in EW.com. As you read the review, decide what you think is the author's position. How does he support his argument?

Going to Las Vegas for a "wild" bachelor party is now the ultimate middle-class hedonist cliché. It's not just that the jaunt has been done so often, in the movies as well as in life. It's that there's a contradiction embedded in the lure of the Vegas bacchanal. Men—and women too, of course—go there to be as reckless as humanly possible. But the naughtiness is so *organized* that there's not much recklessness left in it. Sure, you can craps-table your way to financial ruin, but the lap dances, the glorified college drinking binges, the ritualized ordering of hookers: It's all about as spontaneous as a shuffleboard tournament on a cruise ship.

The fun of *The Hangover*—what makes it more than just one what-happens-in-Vegas romp too many—is that the film completely understands all this. The four comrades who drive from Los Angeles to the Nevada desert to prepare for the wedding of Doug (Justin Bartha) aren't daring or cool; they aren't born swingers. They're an unglamorous Everyguy quartet, doing what they all think they're supposed to do. They're probably imitating Vegas movies as much as those films imitated reality.

Phil (Bradley Cooper), the one who's good-looking enough to strut into a casino like he owns it, is a junior-high teacher devoted to his wife and kid; Stu (Ed Helms), the group dweeb, is an anxious-eyed dentist who's like the 21st-century version of *American Graffiti*'s Terry the Toad, with a fascist girlfriend (Rachael Harris) who treats him like a slave; and Alan (Zach Galifianakis), so brick-stupid he qualifies as more nutzoid than dorkish, is a pudgy, bearded runt who stands up in the group's cruising convertible and shouts "Road trip!" That's an inside nod to the fact that Todd Phillips, the movie's director, made *Road Trip* as well, though it also indicates that these four think they're living inside a stupid teen comedy.

They arrive at their hotel, and the film then cuts to the next day, when they wake up in their trashed villa. There's a tiger in the bathroom, and a baby in the cabinet. Stu is missing his top right incisor; the groom is nowhere to be seen. And the thing is, none of them remembers . . . anything. *The Hangover* is structured, basically, as one long morning-after *OMG what have I done?*, and the kick of the film is that the discovery of what the characters have, in fact, done becomes the perfect comeuppance to their tidy fantasy of Vegas bliss. A light-buttered comic nightmare, like Martin Scorsese's *After Hours* (or Peter Berg's scandalous, overlooked *Very Bad Things* with things not nearly so bad), *The Hangover* is a riff on what the stuff you do when you're *really* out of control says about you.

The surprises in this movie are everything, so without giving much away, I'll just say that a Vegas chapel figures into the mix. So does a crowbar-wielding Asian gangster (Ken Jeong) who might be the epicene brother of Long Duk Dong in *Sixteen Candles*. There's also a juicy run-in with Mike Tyson. *The Hangover* has scattered laughs (many in the cathartically funny end-credit montage), but overall it's more amusing than hilarious. The most deftly acted character is Stu, played by Helms with a realistic alternating current of horror and liberation. As Alan, Zach Galifianakis makes blinkered idiocy a cartoon rush, though a little of him goes a long way. I wish Phillips, working from a script by the knockabout team of Jon Lucas and Scott Moore (*Ghosts of Girlfriends Past*), had nudged the characters closer to being a true shaggy-dog Apatow-style ensemble. You're always a little too aware that they're types. But it's fun seeing each of them have the "fun" they deserve.

Activity 5.3 Discuss Review of *The Hangover*

1. Owen Gleiberman says that the "wild" bachelor party in Las Vegas has become a cliché. Is this true? What other films portray bachelor parties in Las Vegas?

2. What is different about the Vegas bachelor party in *The Hangover*, according to the review?

3. What is Gleiberman's thesis? What evidence does he offer to support his thesis?

4. Does the review make you want to see the movie, if you haven't? How so?

Activity 5.4 Write a Film Review

In this assignment, you are a film critic. Write a review that could appear in a newspaper, magazine, or blog. Your style and tone will be dictated by your audience, so identify the publication just under the title of your review by saying something like this: "Written for Undergroundfilms .com." Be sure to read several reviews published in your chosen media outlet.

1. Select a film you would like to review. Films that are social commentaries are particularly good for reviewing. It does not have to be a serious movie, but it should be one that makes you think about some social trend or historical event.

2. After you decide on a film, learn about its context. Who are the director, producer, and primary actors? What films have these individuals worked on before? Have they won awards? Are they known for a certain style? Read and annotate other reviews of the film, marking sections that you might paraphrase or quote to support your opinions.

3. What about the historical event or social context? Can you learn more about it to see if the film presents a reasonably accurate picture of that time and place (a kairos)? Is it based on a book? If so, what kind of a job does it do creating the world of the book?

4. Is the film persuasive? Does the film appeal to ethos, pathos, or logos? In what way?

5. Create a working thesis that makes an argument about the film. You can modify this thesis later, but it helps to identify early on what you want to argue.

6. Use some of the invention strategies in Chapter 4 to help you articulate what proofs you can use to support your argument.

7. Near the beginning of your draft, briefly summarize enough of the film that your review will be interesting to those who have not seen it. However, don't be a "spoiler." Don't ruin the film for potential viewers by giving away the ending.

8. Organize your essay into three main points that support your thesis and at least one counterargument that complicates or disagrees with your argument.

9. Write a compelling introduction that uses one of the approaches discussed in this chapter. You want your reader to be interested in what you have to say. For example, you might begin with a startling quote from the film or a vivid description of a pivotal scene.

10. Be sure to include specific examples and colorful details. These are essential to make your review interesting to the reader.

Activity 5.5: Write an Op-Ed Argument

The Op-Ed Project (www.theop-edproject.org) is an online initiative to "expand the range of voices" submitting op-ed essays to media outlets. According to its statistics, 80 to 90 percent of op-ed pieces are currently written by men, which is something it endeavors to change by helping women and members of other underrepresented groups develop the skills to get published in top media markets. Whether you are male or female, you may belong to an underrepresented group that is not having its voice heard as part of the national conversation about issues.

An op-ed is an opinion piece printed in a newspaper, magazine, blog, or other media outlet. The name derives from earlier times in print journalism when these opinion pieces would be printed on a page opposite the editorial page. Op-eds are written by individuals not affiliated with the publication, as opposed to editorials that are written by the publication's staff.

Tips for Op-Ed Writing from the Op-Ed Project

1. Own your expertise
Know what you are an expert in and why—but don't limit yourself. Consider the metaphors that your experience and knowledge suggest.

2. Stay current
Follow the news—both general and specific to your areas of specialty. If you write about Haiti, read the Haitian press. If you write about pop culture, read the media that cover it.

3. The perfect is the enemy of the good
In other words: write fast. You may have only a few hours to get your piece in before the moment is gone. But also . . .

4. Cultivate a flexible mind
Remember that a good idea may have more than one news hook; indeed, if the idea is important enough it can have many. So keep an eye out for surprising connections and new news hooks—the opportunity may come around again.

5. Use plain language
Jargon serves a purpose, but it is rarely useful in public debate, and can obfuscate—sorry, I mean cloud—your argument. Speak to your reader in straight talk.

6. Respect your reader
Never underestimate your reader's intelligence or overestimate her level of information. Recognize that your average reader is not an expert in your topic and that the onus is on you to capture her attention—and make the argument compel.

This assignment asks you to write an op-ed piece suitable for submission to a major newspaper or other media outlet. It does not require you to submit your text. That is up to you.

For this assignment, you need to do the following:

1. Read op-eds that appear in the major regional newspaper or other media outlet for your city, such as the *Chicago Tribune*, the *Washington Post*, or the *Arizona Republic*. The Op-Ed Project provides a list of the top 100 U.S. media outlets on its website. Read several op-eds to get a sense of the topics and style of the articles that the newspaper or other media outlet prints.

2. Notice that op-eds are not academic writing. They must be well-researched, but they also generally are written in a more casual and engaging style than traditional academic writing. You must first attract your audience's attention in order to present your case. Analyze how each op-ed you read captures the reader's interest.

3. Choose a topic that is timely and of interest to the readers of the publication that you choose. Research that topic using some of the tools in the research chapter of this textbook.

4. The length and structure of your op-ed should follow the pattern of pieces recently published in your publication.

5. Keep your audience in mind—the readers of the publication.

6. Follow the basic op-ed structure recommended by the Op-Ed Project, reprinted below.

7. Read the "Tips for Op-Ed Writing from the Op-Ed Project," in the sidebar.

(*Note*: A *lede* (or lead) is a journalism term that means the beginning of your article that catches your reader's attention and establishes your topic.)

Basic Op-Ed Structure from the Op-Ed Project
(*Note*: This is not a rule—just one way of approaching it.)

Lede (around a news hook)

Thesis (statement of argument—either explicit or implied)

Argument (based on evidence, such as stats, news, reports from credible organizations, expert quotes, scholarship, history, and first-hand experience)

- 1st Point
  - Evidence
  - Evidence
  - Conclusion
- 2nd Point
  - Evidence
  - Evidence
  - Conclusion
- 3rd Point
  - Evidence
  - Evidence
  - Conclusion

Note: In a simple, declarative op-ed ("policy X is bad; here's why"), this may be straightforward. In a more complex commentary, the 3rd point may expand on the bigger picture (historical context, global/geographic picture, mythological underpinnings, etc.) or may offer an explanation for a mystery that underpins the argument (e.g., why a bad policy continues, in spite of its failures).

"To Be Sure" paragraph (in which you preempt your potential critics by acknowledging any flaws in your argument and address any obvious counterarguments)

Conclusion (often circling back to your lede)

Activity 5.6 Write on Your Blog

Write an informal review of a film you have seen recently. What did you like and what did you dislike? Would you recommend the film to a friend?

Activity 5.7 Write in Your Commonplace Book

Find a piece from the Opinion/Editorial section of your local newspaper that interests you. If you were going to write a letter to the editor in response, what might you say?

The Casebook: In 2011, two professors launched a competition on the *Harvard Business Network* blog for designs to build $300 houses for the poor. Word of the competition spread quickly, and a wide variety of people began to write about the competition—in editorials in *The New York Times* and the *Economist* and in a companion blog, http://www.300house.com/blog.

Your Task: In Chapter 4 you read four articles about the $300 house competition. Read and discuss them in class and in small groups. Make a list of the different positions being argued in these texts and what evidence the writers offer to support their opinions. Then construct your own short research-based argument about the design competition or an op-ed essay (as your instructor specifies) agreeing with one of the positions or developing your own.

6
REVISING RHETORICALLY

Praxis in Action

How I Revise by Amber Lea Clark

Revising is an essential part of the writing process. One of the first things I do when I revise a paper is read with organization in mind. How is my introduction? Does my argument make sense? Did I transition well between points? Next, I look for words and phrases I have repeated too many times and look for other ways to say what I'm trying to say.

For me, a very necessary part of the revision process is reading the paper out loud to see how it flows. I look for any awkwardly worded sentences. It also helps me find typos and misused words. If I'm in a lab setting, I read very quietly, just mouthing the words. I might get a couple of funny looks but I don't care, it is a must when it comes to the revising process for me.

One of the best things to do in the revising process is set your paper aside and come back to it several hours or a day later. This requires some planning and an attempt not to procrastinate too much. Doing this allows me to look at my paper again with fresh eyes and see what I might have left out or want to say differently.

My mother always told me to have someone else give me feedback on my papers before I turn

them in. This is valuable advice. I always have someone look over my papers and try to help others when they need someone to look at their papers. I ask the person who is proofing my paper to look for typos but also any sentences that do not make sense as they are worded. Is my argument coming through clearly?

Also, I always run my paper through the computer's spell check and grammar check. The computer will flag things as grammatically wrong that aren't, so I don't follow everything it says; but the computer also finds errors I haven't. Oh, be sure to spell the proper names right!

Amber Lea Clark says that one important part of her revision is setting her paper aside for a few hours or overnight and then looking at it with fresh eyes.

Revision Is Part of the Writing Process

In ancient times, the focus of the rhetor was upon the presentation of oral arguments in the form of speeches and students trained to perform in pressured situations before a law court or assembly. Though a speaker might spend time in preparation, most speeches were one-time opportunities. If the words were not well-chosen and well-spoken the first time, there was no second chance to influence an audience.

With modern written documents, a composition does not have to be perfect when the words first appear on the page. A document is not truly finished until it is transmitted to an audience, and, even then, important documents are often circulated in draft stages to colleagues for comments before they are presented to an audience.

Many writers claim that revising is the most rewarding step in writing, the time when they have words on a page to work with and can manipulate them to create a composition that communicates effectively. Yet, many students feel that their first drafts should stay exactly the way they've written them because these writings are truest to their feelings and experience. They are sure they have made their point clearly. In reality, a first draft often leaves the reader scratching his or her head and wondering what it was the writer meant to say. To communicate effectively, a writer must learn to interact with his reader to ensure he has communicated his message clearly.

Begin Revision by Rereading

The first step of revising is rereading. This step can be simple, if you are reading something written by someone else. When it is your own writing, it becomes infinitely more difficult. After all, you know what you meant to say—you know the research behind the writing and why you chose certain words or phrases. You even know how every sentence is supposed to read—even though you may have left out a word or two or three—and your mind can trick you into seeing the missing words right where they belong. Unfortunately, the reader does not have your understanding, and communication can break down. You need to learn to read your own work critically, as if it were written by a stranger. One of the first aids in this process is to read your work aloud. You can often hear stumbling blocks quicker than you can see them.

You can also learn to read your own work more objectively by reading and commenting on other writers' work. Look at the structure of essays, at the way the writers use transitions and topic sentences, and at the sentence structure and choice of words. As you learn to see how good writers put ideas and words together, you will begin to think about the readings in a more thorough manner—thinking of alternative, perhaps even better, ways to express the message of each essay. You will also learn to read your own work with a more critical eye.

Qualities of Effective Writing

Reading the work of some professional writers, you may have developed the idea that the best writing is writing that is difficult to understand, writing that sends the reader to the dictionary with every sentence, or writing that uses many technical or specialized terms. Often, we think something difficult to read must be well written. Although it is sometimes difficult to read about topics that are new to us because we're learning new vocabulary and struggling with complex ideas, it simply is not true that the best writing is hard to read. Indeed, the most effective writing, the kind of writing you want to produce in your classes, is simple, concise, and direct.

William Safire's Rules for Writing

William Safire, long-time language enthusiast, political columnist, and contributor to "On Language" in the *New York Times Magazine,* has a little fun with grammar rules and myths.

- Remember to never split an infinitive.
- The passive voice should never be used.
- Do not put statements in the negative form.
- Verbs has to agree with their subjects.
- Proofread carefully to see if you words out.
- If you reread your work, you will find on rereading a great deal of repetition can be avoided by rereading and editing.
- A writer must not shift your point of view.
- And don't start a sentence with a conjunction. (Remember, too, a preposition is a terrible word to end a sentence with.)
- Don't overuse exclamation marks!!
- Place pronouns as close as possible, especially in long sentences, as of 10 or more words, to their antecedents.
- Writing carefully, dangling participles must be avoided.
- If any word is improper at the end of a sentence, a linking verb is.
- Take the bull by the hand and avoid mixing metaphors.
- Avoid trendy locutions that sound flaky.
- Everyone should be careful to use a singular pronoun with singular nouns in their writing.
- Always pick on the correct idiom.
- The adverb always follows the verb.
- Last but not least, avoid clichés like the plague; seek viable alternatives.

Keep It Simple

Simple means "unadorned" or "not ornate." *Writing simply* means saying something in common, concrete language without too much complication in the sentence structure. Writing simply doesn't mean you have to use only short or easy words. It doesn't mean that all your sentences will be simple sentences. It doesn't mean that you can't use figures of speech or intricate details. Simple writing means that you try to get your point across in a direct and interesting way. You aren't trying to hide your ideas. Instead, you are trying to amplify those ideas and begin an intelligible conversation with your reader.

Rely on Everyday Words

When writing about computers or other technical subjects, it's tempting to use **jargon** or specialized words you might use when talking to others with the same knowledge, interest, and background. When writing for a limited audience whose members are familiar with technical terms, a bit of jargon might be acceptable. However, most of the writing you will do in college and later in the workplace will address a larger audience. You will want to avoid the use of highly technical terms, acronyms, and abbreviations.

If it seems that the writers in this text use many big words or technical terms, stop for a minute to consider the original audience for each of the essays. Consider how your vocabulary grows each year as you read, discuss, and consider new ideas. The everyday words of a tenth grade student will probably be fewer in number than the everyday words of a junior in college. Similarly, the everyday words of a college freshman will be different from the everyday words of a computer professional with three years of work experience. Use words that are comfortable and familiar to you and your readers when you write, and you will write clear, effective essays.

Use Precise Words

We sometimes assume that the reader will know what we mean when we use adjectives like "beautiful," "quiet," or "slow." However, the reader has only his or her own ideas of those adjectives. You can make your writing more interesting and effective by adding concrete details to give the reader an image that uses at least two of the five senses.

You can use details from all of the senses to make your writing even more concrete and precise. What are some of the sensual qualities of the experience or thing? Can you compare it to another thing that your readers may be familiar with to help them understand it better? Can you compare it to something totally unlike it? Can you compare it to a different sense to surprise readers and help them understand the image you are trying to create?

A good way to practice your ability to write original concrete images is to expand on a cliché. A **cliché** is an overused saying or expression. Often, clichés begin as similes that help make images more concrete. They become clichéd or overused because they lose their originality or they don't contain enough detail to give us the entire picture. Choose a cliché and write a sentence that expands the cliché and uses the senses to create a clear picture of the thing described. You might try some of the following clichés:

> She is as pretty as a picture.
>
> It smelled heavenly.
>
> It was as soft as a baby's bottom.
>
> His heart is as hard as stone.
>
> It tastes as sour as a pickle.
>
> We stared at the roaring campfire.
>
> We listened to the babbling brook.

Precise details allow us to experience the world of the writer. We leave our own views and perceptions and learn how someone else sees the world. We learn what "quiet" is like for one writer and what "beautiful" means to another. Fill in the gaps between your words and ideas with vivid images and your writing will become more interesting and more effective.

Be Concise

Rid your writing of excess words and leave only that which makes your meaning clear and concrete. Becoming aware of several common problems can help you make your writing more concise. When you begin a sentence with either "it is" or "there is," you transfer all the meaning of the sentence to the end of the sentence. This is known as a **delayed construction**. You have delayed the meaning. The reader must read on to find out what "it" or "there" refer to. They don't get anything important from the beginning of the sentence.

> Examine the following sentences:

> > It is important to change the oil in older gasoline engines.
> >
> > There is an apple on the table.
> >
> > There isn't anything we need to fear except our own fear.

We can rewrite these sentences, making them more concise, by deleting the "there is" or the "it is" and restructuring the sentence.

Changing the oil in older gasoline engines is important.

An apple is on the table.

We have nothing to fear but fear itself.

Notice that the second group of sentences is shorter and the important information is no longer buried in the middle. Revising this type of sentence can make your writing more concise and get information to the reader more effectively.

If you think you may be guilty of using "it is" and "there is" (or "it's" and "there's") too often, you can use most word processing programs to seek these constructions out. Use the "search" or "find and replace" tool that's found in the Edit portion of your pull-down menu. Type "it is" and ask your computer to find every place you use this construction in your document. When you find a sentence that begins with "it is," revise the sentence to make it more concise. Do the same with "there is," "it's," and "there's." After you become more aware of these errors by correcting them, you'll find that you notice the errors before or as you make them. You will begin to write more concisely, and you'll have fewer delayed constructions to revise.

You can also make your writing more concise by avoiding common wordy expressions. Sometimes when we're nervous about writing or insecure about our knowledge of a topic, we try to hide that insecurity behind a wall of meaningless words, such as in the following sentence:

At this point in time, you may not have the ability to create a web page due to the fact that you've avoided using computers for anything other than playing Solitaire.

This sentence is full of deadwood phrases that add no meaning to the sentence. If we take out the unneeded words, we have this sentence:

You may not be able to create a web page because you've only used your computer to play Solitaire.

Your computer may have a grammar checker that will identify some commonly used wordy expressions. If your computer doesn't have a grammar checker, or if your instructor has asked you not to use the grammar checker in your computer, you can still learn to revise the wordiness out of your paragraphs. Use the computer to separate a paragraph of your writing into sentences. As you scroll through the paragraph, hit the hard return or "Enter" key on your keyboard twice every time you find a period. Once you have separated the sentences, look at each sentence. What is the important idea in the sentence? What words are used to convey that idea? What words don't add any meaning to the sentence? Delete words that don't convey meaning, and revise the sentence to make it more concise.

Use Action Verbs

Action verbs are words that convey the action of a sentence. They carry much of our language's nuance and meaning. Many inexperienced writers use only "to be" verbs: *am, is, are, was, were, be, been,* and *being.* If you use too many of these verbs, you risk losing much of the power of language. If I say someone is coming through the door, I've created a picture of a body and a doorway. If I say someone marches or slinks through the door, I've added information not only about movement but also about the quality of that movement. I've given my subject the attitude of a soldier or a cat. For example, consider this sentence written by Howard Rheingold:

> Thirty thousand years ago, outside a deceptively small hole in a limestone formation in the area now known as southern France, several adolescents shivered in the dark, awaiting initiation into the cult of toolmakers.

By using the verb "shivered," especially when accompanied by the words "in the dark," Rheingold paints a word picture much more vivid than he would have conveyed with the use of a "to be" verb. Using interesting verbs can enliven your writing.

If you want to focus upon using more action verbs, skim through your essay and circle all the "to be" verbs. Read the sentences with circled "to be" verbs more closely, and choose several to rewrite using active verbs in place of the "to be" verbs. You won't be able to do this for every sentence, but replace them where you can and your writing will become more lively, more concise, and more effective.

Fill in the Gaps

When we write, we sometimes forget that we are writing to an audience other than ourselves. We expect that our readers are people just like us, with our experiences, memories, and tastes. Because we have assumed they're so much like us, we expect our readers to be able to read more than what we've written on the page. We expect them to read our minds. We may leave large gaps in our essays, hoping the reader will fill in exactly the information we would have included.

If I'm writing an essay about my childhood in the South and I say it was always so hot in the summer that I hated to go outside, I might think my reader knows what I mean by hot. However, there are many different ways to be "hot." In east Texas where I grew up, the hot was a sticky hot. Eighty degrees made me long for a big glass of sweetened iced tea with lots of ice. The heat made my clothes cling. Sweating didn't help because the sweat didn't dry. I spent the day feeling as if I'd never dried off after my morning shower. In New Mexico, I never really felt hot unless the temperature got above 110 degrees. At that point, the heat would rush at me, making it difficult to breathe. I would open the door to leave the house, and it felt as if I had opened the oven door to check on a cake. If I say I was hot in the summer without describing how heat felt to me, my reader may not get the message I'm trying to convey. Don't expect your reader to know what you mean by "hot" or by any other general description. Instead, take a minute to add details that will fill in the gaps for the reader.

Speak Directly

To *speak directly* is to say, up front, who is doing what. Sometimes we don't tell the reader who is completing the action or we tell them too late. Let's look at the following sentences:

> The steak was stolen from the grill.
>
> The decisive battle was fought between the Confederate and the Union armies in Vicksburg, Mississippi.
>
> The red truck has been driven into the side of the green car.

Although we might be able to guess who the actors are in each of the sentences, the first and last sentences don't tell us directly. Even if the reader can guess that it was a dog who stole the steak from the grill or my neighbor who drove the red truck into the side of the green car, the reader has to stop and figure out who is doing what before he or she can read on. This slows the reader down and diminishes the effectiveness of your writing.

Language professionals call this **passive voice**. The action comes before the actor. Note that sometimes, as in the first and last sentences above, the writer doesn't mention the actor at all. To identify passive verbs in your writing, look for verbs coupled with another action word that ends in "-ed" or "-en" such as "was stolen" or "was forgotten."

Find the action and the actor in the sentence to make sure that they are in the most effective order. The most effective sentence order is actor first, then action. If the sentence does not specify the actor but leaves it implied, chances are that it is a passive sentence. For example, read this sentence: "The red truck was driven into the green car." It does not say who the driver was, and thus it is a passive sentence.

Rewriting some of your sentences to eliminate use of the passive voice will make your writing stronger and more interesting.

© Don Wright (2009)

President Barack Obama has won high marks for his verbal eloquence, as illustrated by this cartoon published in the *International Herald Tribune*. His 2004 Keynote Speech at the Democratic National Convention and his best-selling book, *The Audacity of Hope,* helped propel him to national prominence.

Activity 6.1 When You Reeeaaallly Want to Describe Something

This activity requires a thesaurus or access to the Visual Thesaurus website (http://www.visualthesaurus.com).

1. Strunk and White's *The Elements of Style,* in an entry on "Misused Words and Expressions," says,

    "*Very.* Use this word sparingly. Where emphasis is necessary, use words strong in themselves."

    With a partner, paraphrase and discuss this Strunk and White writing tip.

2. To demonstrate Strunk and White's advice in (1) above, revise the following sentence, getting rid of the adverb "very."

    Julie is very pretty.

    No, don't say, "Julie is beautiful." Make a list of more precise and vivid words that could be used instead. Refer to a thesaurus (or the Visual Thesaurus website) to find words such as "stunning" and so on.

3. As a class, brainstorm other intensifying adverbs such as "awfully" or "extremely" that you tend to use as words of emphasis (in writing or in everyday speech) and list those words on the board.

4. In pairs again, compose a short paragraph of two or three sentences about a subject or event (e.g., a tornado, a celebrity sighting, a sports event, a news event, a concert, etc.) and intentionally use as many common or trite intensifying words as possible.

5. Exchange the short paragraph you composed in (4) above with another pair of classmates. Revise the other partnership's dialogue with the use of a thesaurus. The revised dialogue should not contain any "intensifiers" or trite words of emphasis. Replace such words and phrases with more powerful and concise language. For example, "I was really happy to see the Hornets win. They totally beat the Giants," could be revised to read (with the help of more concise and powerful words): "I was euphoric to see the Hornets thrash the Giants."

6. Read your "before" and "after" dialogues to the class. Afterward, discuss which words were eliminated and how the words that replaced those intensifiers changed the tone and/or meaning of the dialogue.

Source: Adapted from a lesson plan, "When You Reeeaaallly Want to Say Something," from the Visual Thesaurus website, http://www.visualthesaurus .com/cm/lessons/1450.

Remember to Proofread

It is understandably difficult to find the errors in an essay you have been working on for days. A few tricks used by professional writers might help you see errors in your essay more clearly.

1. With pencil in hand, read the essay aloud, slowly—and preferably to an audience. When you are reading aloud, it is more difficult to add or change words, so you tend to catch errors you would not see reading silently to yourself. Plus the reactions of your audience may point out areas where future readers may become confused or lose interest.

2. Another trick is to read the essay backwards, sentence by sentence. This forces you to look at sentence structure and not at the overall content of the essay. If you are working on a computer, another way to accomplish this is to create a final edit file in which you hit the hard return twice at the end of every question or statement. You might even go so far as to number the sentences so they look more like grammar exercises. Then look at each sentence individually.

Reading 6.1

Grammar Girl's Top Ten Grammar Myths
by Mignon Fogarty, quickanddirtytips.com

In this blog entry by Mignon Fogarty, she offers her top-ten list of grammar mistakes and misunderstandings.

10. **A run-on sentence is a really long sentence.** Wrong! They can actually be quite short. In a run-on sentence, independent clauses are squished together without the help of punctuation or a conjunction. If you write "I am short he is tall," as one sentence without a semicolon, colon, or dash between the two independent clauses, it's a run-on sentence even though it only has six words.

9. **You shouldn't start a sentence with the word "however."** Wrong! It's fine to start a sentence with "however" so long as you use a comma after it when it means "nevertheless."

8. **"Irregardless" is not a word. Wrong!** "Irregardless" is a bad word and a word you shouldn't use, but it is a word. "Floogetyflop" isn't a word—I just made it up and you have no idea what it means. "Irregardless," on the other hand, is in almost every dictionary labeled as nonstandard. You shouldn't use it if you want to be taken seriously, but it has gained wide enough use to qualify as a word.

7. **There is only one way to write the possessive form of a word that ends in "s." Wrong!** It's a style choice. For example, in the phrase "Kansas's statute," you can put just an apostrophe at the end of "Kansas" or you can put an apostrophe "s" at the end of "Kansas." Both ways are acceptable.

6. **Passive voice is always wrong. Wrong!** Passive voice is when you don't name the person who's responsible for the action. An example is the sentence "Mistakes were made," because it doesn't say who made the mistakes. If you don't know who is responsible for an action, passive voice can be the best choice.

5. **"i.e." and "e.g." mean the same thing. Wrong!** "e.g." means "for example," and "i.e." means roughly "in other words." You use "e.g." to provide a list of incomplete examples, and you use "i.e." to provide a complete clarifying list or statement.

4. **You use "a" before words that start with consonants and "an" before words that start with vowels. Wrong!** You use "a" before words that start with consonant sounds and "an" before words that start with vowel sounds. So, you'd write that someone has an MBA instead of a MBA, because even though "MBA" starts with "m," which is a consonant, it starts with the sound of the vowel "e"—MBA.

3. **It's incorrect to answer the question "How are you?" with the statement "I'm good." Wrong!** "Am" is a linking verb and linking verbs should be modified by adjectives such as "good." Because "well" can also act as an adjective, it's also fine to answer "I'm well," but some grammarians believe "I'm well" should be used to talk about your health and not your general disposition.

2. **You shouldn't split infinitives. Wrong!** Nearly all grammarians want to boldly tell you it's OK to split infinitives. An infinitive is a two-word form of a verb. An example is "to tell." In a split infinitive, another word separates the two parts of the verb. "To boldly tell" is a split infinitive because "boldly" separates "to" from "tell."

1. **You shouldn't end a sentence with a preposition. Wrong!** You shouldn't end a sentence with a preposition when the sentence would mean the same thing if you left off the preposition. That means "Where are you at?" is wrong because "Where are you?" means the same thing. But there are many sentences where the final preposition is part of a phrasal verb or is necessary to keep from making stuffy, stilted sentences: "I'm going to throw up," "Let's kiss and make up," and "What are you waiting for" are just a few examples.

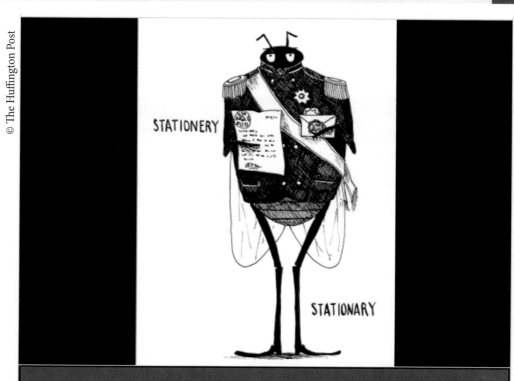

Stationary means "fixed in place, unable to move;" **stationery** is letterhead or other special writing paper. (Hint: **Station_e_ry** with an **e** comes with an **_e_nvelope.**) Examples: Evan worked out on his **stationary** bike. The duke's initials and crest appeared atop his personal **stationery**.

Eminent means "distinguished or superior"; **imminent** means "impending, sure to happen." Also, **eminent** domain is the right of a government to take over private property for public use. Examples: The rain was **imminent**; it would arrive soon, soaking the **eminent** dignitaries on the stage. (Think of **imminent** and **impending**, which both begin with the same letters.)

Reading 6.2

Top Ten Distractions for Writers, or Any Job Really

by Sam Scham

The following list, "Top Ten Distractions for Writers, or Any Job Really," by Sam Scham, was published in the Yahoo Contributor Network.

When you have a set goal in mind, whether it is for personal or work reasons, so many other things can become easy distractions. For writers in particular, life seems to get in the way. There are other pressing matters that we have to worry about.

1. The Internet

The Internet is a very huge distraction these days. For writers who do research online for their great idea, it is easy to stumble upon different links and steer away from the main point in focus. If you find yourself doing this, try to limit the time you do research therefore getting off the Internet earlier and allow more time for writing.

2. The Radio

Music can help a writer generate ideas and feelings. Listening to the radio can be a distraction if you leave it on for too long. If you are like me, you are able to write the best in silence. You need to be able to hear yourself think. If you are listening to the radio and it is hard to turn away from it, listen to it in segments. Listen to some music and when a commercial comes on, mute the radio and start writing. Maybe, before you know it, you will forget that you were ever listening to the radio.

3. The Television

The television and the radio are similar in many ways. For one, it is hard to turn off, especially if you are in the middle of a show that you want to finish. But then, you see a commercial for what is coming up next and you are intrigued to watch it. At the end of the current show, turn off the TV and get writing. Soon, you will not notice the absence of the picture box.

4. Own Procrastination

You want to sit down and write, but at the same time you don't, you have no motivation. The solution is to take a day off, do not think of it at all. Work on any other pressing matters like home chores or calling up an old friend that you've been meaning to catch up with. On the next day, wake up and get writing. Just jump right into it and it will be like you never took a break.

5. Other People

Especially if you live with family or friends other people always being around can be a huge distraction. In order to solve this, find out when everyone will be out and fit in time to write while they are gone. If that just doesn't work with your everyday schedule, find a nice place outside or at the local library where you can work in peace without other people bugging you.

6. Other Responsibilities

Work, chores, walking the dog; these everyday responsibilities are tiring and at the end of the day you just cannot get the energy to write. Try writing in the morning, even if it is just for a few minutes. Get the best out of what you got and do not get discouraged.

7. Telephones

With cell phones these days, you can be getting texts at every minute either from friends or social networks. When you are writing, the best way to refrain from your cell phone is by turning it completely off and leaving it somewhere out of sight so that you are not tempted to check it.

8. Outdoor Activities

Especially on a really nice day, you may want to forget the writing and spend some time outdoors. That is completely fine. Enjoy life to the fullest. If you end up not writing for the day, remember that there is always tomorrow. But be careful not to put it off for too long and too often. If you really want to spend time outside, take the writing with you and kill two birds with one stone.

9. Everyday Needs

You need to eat sometime and when you work and do everything else, cooking can really tire you out and make you not want to write. On those days, try to make simple meals if you absolutely do not want to order out. There is nothing wrong with having a bowl of cereal for dinner.

10. Being Bored

We all get bored sometimes, even of our own writing. Take a break. Do not work on writing your big project, but work on something else. A day or two later go back to that big project and start working on writing it again and if you are still bored, put it to the side again. At least you cannot say that you did not try.

Activity 6.2 Write a List of Your Writing Habits

As you write an essay assigned by your instructor, keep notes about your writing process. What distracts or keeps you from writing? What works well when you write? What kind of prewriting do you do? What are the best (or worst) conditions for you when you write?

Organize your notes about your writing process into a theme such as "Best Places to Write" or "Ways to Avoid Procrastinating." As Sam Scham does, write two or three sentences about each of your writing habits.

Gain Feedback by Peer Editing

Your instructor may schedule class periods for peer workshops. These workshops are opportunities for you to get responses from your readers. Often, you will be divided into groups of three or four students and you will be given a list of questions to answer about your peers' essays. Your peers will get copies of your essay, and they will give you comments as well. The first peer workshop can be a difficult experience. It is never easy to take criticism, constructive or not. Taking criticism in a small group is even more difficult. There are several things you can do to make your peer groups more productive.

When Your Essay Is Being Reviewed

1. Write down everything the reviewers say. You think you will remember it later, but often you will forget just that piece of advice you need. More importantly, writing while the reviewers speak is an effective way to keep the channels of communication open. It is hard to come up with a defense for your paper if you are busy writing.

2. Save your comments until all the reviewers are done. If you have specific questions, write them in the margins of your notes. If they ask you questions, make a note to answer them when everyone is done. If you allow yourself to speak, you will be tempted to start defending your essay. Once you start defending your essay, two things happen. First, you stop listening to the comments. Second, you offend your reviewers, making it less likely that they will give you honest criticism in the future.

3. The first comment you should make to your reviewers is "Thank you." The second comment can be anything but a defense. Your readers are only telling you how they have interpreted your essay. They are giving you their opinions; you do not have to make the changes they suggest.

4. Save all the comments you get on your essay. Set them aside for a day or so. Then make the changes that you think will make your essay better.

When You Are the Reviewer

1. Read an essay through, at least one time, just to browse the content of the essay. Appreciate the essay for what it does well. Try to ignore any problems for now. You will get back to them the second time you read and begin your comments in the margins. Every essay will have at least one thing about it that is good.

2. Always begin your comments with a sincere discussion of what you like about the essay.

3. Be specific in your comments. Your peers will probably understand you better if you say, "The topic sentence in paragraph four really sets the reader up for what the essay accomplishes in paragraph four. But I can't really find a topic sentence for paragraph six, and the topic sentences in paragraphs two and three could be improved." Note how this statement gives a positive response and then identifies specific places where the author can improve the essay. This works much better than a generalized statement like, "Topic sentences need work."

4. Be descriptive in your comments. It is often helpful for students to hear how you are reading their essays. "Paragraph five seems to be telling me . . . " or "I got the feeling the essay's overall message is . . . " are good ways to start descriptive sentences.

5. Realize that you are analyzing a paper and not a person. Directing your comments toward the essay, "Paragraph nine doesn't really have anything new to add, does the paper need it?" sounds better to the listener than "You repeat yourself in paragraph nine. Do you really need it?"

Independent Reviewing

If your instructor does not require peer editing, you can ask someone to review your essay. Choose someone you trust to give you an honest opinion. It might not be effective to ask a parent, spouse, or girlfriend/boyfriend to give you a critique if you know they are going to like anything you write, just because you wrote it. It might be better to ask another student who has recently had an English class or one of your current classmates. In exchange, you might offer to look over their work. Remember, you learn to read your own essays better by reading other peoples' essays more critically.

Sample Questions for Peer Review

When you have revised your paper several times, have someone answer these questions regarding its overall content, paragraph development, and word choice and sentence structure.

Overall Content

1. What is the thesis or main point of the essay? Where does the writer state this main point? If the main point is implied rather than stated, express it in a sentence. Does the main point give a subject and an opinion about the subject? How might the writer improve his/her thesis?

2. What is the purpose of this essay? What are the characteristics of the audience the writer seems to be addressing (formal, fun-loving, serious, cynical, laid-back, etc.)?

Paragraph Development

1. Do each of the paragraphs in the essay work to support the main point of the essay? Which paragraphs seem to wander from that main point? What other information needs to be added to develop the main point?

2. List two places in the essay where the writer uses vivid sensory details. How effective are those details? Are they used to support the thesis of the essay? Identify two places in the essay where the writer needs more effective details. What kind of details might he or she include?

3. What grade would you give the introduction? How does it draw the reader into the essay? What specific things can the writer do to make the introduction more inviting?

4. Which paragraph do you like the best? Why? Which paragraph in the essay do you like the least? Why? What can the writer do to improve his/her paragraphs?

5. What grade would you give the conclusion? How does it provide closure for the essay? What specific things can the writer do to make the conclusion more effective?

Word Choice and Sentence Structure

1. Are adequate transitions used between the paragraphs? Find an effective paragraph transition and identify it. Why does it work? Find two places between paragraphs that need more or better transitions. What can the writer do to improve these transitions?

2. Are a variety of sentences used? Where might the writer vary the sentence structure for better effect? What two sentences in the essay did you find most effective? Why?

3. Are there any words that seem misused or out of place? What positive or negative trigger words are used? Do they enhance the message of the essay or detract from it?

Activity 6.3 Peer Editing of Sample Student Essay

As your instructor directs, either individually or in groups, peer edit one of the following sample student papers and then answer the questions regarding overall content, paragraph development, and word choice and sentence structure listed in the above section, Sample Questions for Peer Review. Then discuss your peer editing in your small groups, comparing your answers to those of others in your group.

Sample Student Essay for Peer Editing, Profile Assignment

Longing for Better Days

As she sits in her cramped room in Amman, Jordan, watching the recent news, Aysha Mustafa, 92, is saddened by the world she lives in today. As she places her wrinkled hands on her lap and begins to recall a time when things were pleasant, tears begin to flow down her cheeks. Those times are long gone she says. Aysha moved from Palestine to Jordan after the sudden death of her husband in 1995. Moving here was tough she says, "It was hard to leave my country." Aysha's story goes back 60 years ago, where she lived in her homeland Palestine. She recalls her childhood as being peaceful and joyous. She smiles as she describes memories of her and her brother riding in the back of her father's wagon. "Life was good," she says. Although her family had very little to live on, she was still happy.

Like many Palestinians, Aysha still dreams to one day return back and live in her homeland Palestine, where she longs to rekindle sweet memories there. "Jordan is fine she says but I rather live on the land that is mine." As we sit in the living room watching the crisis in Gaza in January 2009, Aysha begins to wipe the tears from her sad yet hopeful eyes, and reiterates with a sigh in her voice, "May God be with them." The appalling images of young children being killed by Israeli rockets leave 92 year old Aysha in distress. How many more men, women and children will die before both sides reach an agreement she questions? As her grandson flips through the channels, he crosses upon the Al-Jazeera news that announces that the number killed in Gaza has reached the disturbing number of 781. She suddenly lowers her head and gazes into space. . "It kills me to see my people getting killed like this," she stutters trying to hold back tears. The Israeli and Palestinian conflict has been going on for more than 60 years now. Many innocent civilians of both sides have been killed due to this grotesque war.

Despite all of this, it is people like Aysha that still carry hope that one day they will return back to their homeland and live in peace and harmony. Aysha's wish like many others is for all Palestinians to live a life of security and freedom, freedom to make their own choices and decisions on their own land. Aysha struggles to explain how as a child she used to run around in the fields freely, fearing no one or anything. "The feeling of freedom is indescribable," she says. "I was free to walk and go as I pleased, with no blockades to hold me back."

Today however, boys and girls in Palestine do not share the same luxury that Aysha experienced before the occupation. It is heart breaking watching this old yet strong willed woman recalling her childhood memories. Suddenly, Aysha begins to hold her chest and breathe heavily; her grandson approaches her and gives her her heart medicine. He explains that talking about such a personal and stressful topic leaves his grandmother feeling tired and overwhelmed. She has a weak heart, "My days are getting shorter," she says. Aysha is an inspiration, throughout this interview she kept calm and never wavered or seemed weak. One would think she would be vulnerable to everything surrounding her, but on the contrary she was full of wisdom. When asked what she hoped for, she said with a confident tone, "My people will see better days than this; I know this for a fact. They will be happy again; mothers will no longer be forced to bury their children. The day of justice and freedom is near, I can feel it." As she said this, Aysha seemed certain that this war will not last very long. Many Palestinians have the same hopes as Aysha, they too are confident that the day will come when their people will believe in security again.

Aysha is one of many Palestinians who shares the same dream as millions, which is a liberated and a prosperous Palestine. As she stands up and leans on her cane she says, "We want our rights, we want justice, we want freedom on our land, and we want Palestine."

Aysha's final words were that she prays that once her soul rests, she hopes to be buried next to her husband's grave on the holy land of Palestine.

Sample Student Essay for Peer Editing, Rhetorical Analysis Assignment

Rhetorical Analysis of President Reagan's "Challenger Speech"

FIVE, FOUR, THREE, TWO, ONE, WE HAVE LIFT OFF! THE SPACE SHUTTLE CHALLENGER HAS CLEARED THE LAUNCH PAD. This was supposed to be a glorious day in American history, a mile stone in the United States Space Program. Instead this day quickly turned into one of the most horrific scenes witnessed live by the American public, which included thousands of school children, who watched from the comfort and safety of their classrooms.

On January 28, 1986, the space shuttle Challenger was scheduled for launch in Florida. It would mark the second flight by the United States Space program and it was the first educational launch program. On this particular flight there was to be a teacher on board, she was the first teacher on a space shuttle as a result of a special program from NASA. Although there were some clear concerns regarding whether the shuttle should launch, NASA officials gave the green light and the mission moved forward. Within seconds of lift off, the space shuttle Challenger burst into flames and disintegrated in mid flight, instantly killing all seven passengers aboard. The nation was shocked, especially thousands of young children who eagerly watched the live coverage on television. Within hours of the explosion President Ronald Reagan went on live television and addressed the nation from the White House. President Reagan was scheduled to address the nation on that particular day to report on the state of the Union, instead he went on television and paid tribute to the Challenger Seven. President Reagan delivered one of the most inspirational, and motivational speeches of his tenure as the President of the United States. It is a speech, like all great speeches, that would out live his presidency, and be regarded as one of the great speeches of our time.

The nation stood still, not knowing what to make of the days events. In such times of sorrow people tend to need support, guidance, and reassurance. The American people needed someone to follow, a shoulder to lean on, a vision of the future, a leader. President Reagan went on live television and paid tribute to the "Challenger Seven" in a speech from the White House. President Reagan sat alone behind a large desk surrounded in the background by family pictures. President Reagan used his ethos as a credible individual; he was the leader of the free Nation. He gave the speech from the White House, which is clearly recognized by the American public as a symbol of power and security. The image of him sitting behind a great desk flanked by pictures of family and loved ones borrowing once again from their ethos. This was a not only the President of the United States delivering this speech, this was a husband, a father, and a son too.

The occasion for the speech was obvious: The Nation had just witnessed seven brave individuals perish before their very eyes. These brave souls were, husbands, sons, daughters, fathers, and they had paid the ultimate sacrifice for mankind. President Reagan portrayed all of these different roles played by each of the "Challenger Seven" from behind that desk. As the speech proceeded, President Reagan was careful to not down play the Challenger incident, but he appealed to logos, or logic, by saying "But we have never lost an astronaut in flight. We've never had a tragedy like this one." Here he used pathos to emphasize the severity of the incident while at the same time letting the nation know that there have been other brave astronauts who have also paid the ultimate price for the visions and progress of mankind. President Reagan throughout his speech used his words very carefully and with great insight. His words and the double meaning or relation to the events of the day made a huge impact on the delivery and acceptance of his speech by the American public. As he stated "Your loved ones were daring and brave, and they had that special grace, that spirit that says, Give me a challenge, and I'll meet it with joy." As one can see, President Reagan is using the word challenge here, this is a direct reference to the space shuttle Challenger.

President Reagan goes on to address the thousands of children who also witnessed the event, addressing the emotion or pathos of the occasion. He states, "And I want to say something to the schoolchildren of America who were watching the live coverage of the shuttle's take-off. I know it's hard to understand, but sometimes painful things like this happen. It's all part of the process of exploration and discovery. It is all part of taking a chance and expanding man's horizons. The future doesn't belong to the fainthearted; it belongs to the brave. The Challenger crew was pulling us into the future, and we'll continue to follow them." Here President Reagan's audience is the children, who in turn are the future of the nation. By saying that the Challenger was taking them towards the future, he is saying what everybody already knows. The children are the future of the nation and he is telling them that they must continue to move forward, for one day they will be the leaders of the country.

President Reagan's message is very clear: This was a tragedy, yet we as a nation must continue to move forward in order to honor the memory of the "Challenger Seven." President Reagan, utilizing logos, then mentions the

NASA employees in his speech. Here he does not blame or degrade the space program or its employees. Instead he praises there hard work and dedication to the American people and the space program. He does not speculate on the cause of the explosion nor does he address any issues related to who is to blame. He completely omits any negative or accusatory comments in his speech. This was a very tactful and extremely intelligent move by Reagan. He knew the American public had many questions regarding the explosion. He also knew that those questions needed to be answered and that it was his responsibility to provide those answers to the nation. Yet on this day, and in this speech, it was not the right time to do so.

President Reagan in closing his speech borrows from the ethos of the past when he stated "There's a coincidence today. On this day three hundred and ninety years ago, the great explorer Sir Francis Drake died aboard ship off the coast of Panama… a historian later said, He lived by the sea, died on it, and was buried in it. Well, today, we can say of the Challenger crew: their dedication was, like Drake's complete."

President Reagan's speech on the space shuttle Challenger served several purposes. First, it paid tribute to the seven astronauts who lost their lives in the explosion. Second, it provided the nation with a much needed reassurance that everything was going to be all right. And although this was terrible accident and set back for our country, he also left no doubt that the Nations commitment to NASA and the space program would not only survive, but continue to advance forward into the future.

Sample Student Essay for Peer Editing, Short Op-Ed Argument

Women in Combat

It is without a doubt that most of us have seen, read, or even heard about women in foreign countries, specifically the Middle East, being victims of sexual discrimination in male dominated work. But, would anyone possibly imagine, that even at a smaller scale, it occurs right here right now. This op-ed piece focuses on women in combat. While some countries do allow women to fight in combat, it seems archaic that the leader of the free world and by many referred as the #1 nation in the world, that we still bar women from certain roles in the military.

The most common fallacies believed by many include, women's enervated strength. Or, there psychological structure is so that they are considered nurturers not murderers. The most archaic mentality yet is that women are a distraction to men. The list can go on, but the above seems to be the most common misconceptions.

The case against the strength of a woman seems irrefutable. No one can argue that in general men are stronger than women. But there are many factors to be considered in arguing the rebuttal. For instance, the double standards set by our military. The annual Physical fitness test clearly subordinates the female's potential physical ability. A study conducted in Great Britain by the Ministry of Defense concluded that "women can be built to the same levels of physical fitness as men of the same size and build" (Shepard, 2007). How can we expect a woman to perform closer to a man's standards when we delude her understanding of what it really takes to achieve physical fitness? Would it be any different if we took a male chef and only taught him how to cook appetizers, then graded him for the entire meal including entre and desert?

Psychological structure is also a hot topic. Women are nurturers, not murderers. Kingsley Browne, author of Co-Ed Combat, The New Evidence Why Women shouldn't Fight the Nation's Wars, made a diluted attempt to answer this question by stating "There are large differences in men and women and willingness to take Physical risks. For example something like 93% of work place deaths are men" (Traders Nation, 2007). While men seem quite capable to murdering, Browne failed to cite that women are also capable of committing heinous crimes, as evidenced by the 2.1 million women serving sentences in American Prisons for violent crimes (Shepard, 2007).

Psychological Structure is an important factor in wars, as Browne reiterates. "Women's greater fear of death and injury and greater aversion to physical risks are likely to affect their combat performance negatively" (Arron, 2007). Clearly not all women are cut out for combat. But if we use this formula, it is also evidenced that not all men are cut out for combat. It is said that over 100,000 men panicked at the thought of going to the Vietnam War and fled the country to avoid the draft (Shepard, 2007). Surely any veteran of any War would consider this a perfect paradigm of a coward?

Another myth is that, women are a distraction to men. While the idea may rain ring true one could also conclude that any soldier, male or female, that is so easily distracted may be a danger not only to themselves but also to the unit they serve. While this conclusion does not rectify that argument, it does show the weak rationales that women face. Furthermore this mentality sends society the message that it's acceptable to punish/exclude women from full participation due to men's personal failings. Since World War One female nurses have served on the front line, and it has never been documented that women distract men (Jericho, 2008, p. 8).

This topic clearly incites emotions from opponents and proponents of women in combat. Women deserve attention to the matter starting with the Pentagon ensuring our women are properly trained and given the tools to succeed. But the story doesn't begin there, it begins at home. If we cannot treat a boy and a girl the same when growing up, why should we expect anyone to treat them any different as adults. How many times do we see a girl with a dole while the father teaches the son to hunt? Or watch a father rough house with his son, while the mother teaches her daughter how to apply makeup? Give your sister the tools and she will build you a bridge.

References

Arron. (2007) The Clock Stopped. Retrieved from: http://thestoppedclock. blogspot.com/2007/12/cowardly-untrustworthy-women.html

Jericho, J. (2008) Effectiveness of the Sex Discrimination Act. Retrieved from: http://www.aph.gov.au/Senate/committee/legcon_ctte/sex_ discrim/submissions/sub02.pdf

Sheppard, c. (2007) Women in Combat. Strategy Research Project. Retrieved from: http://www.carlisle.army.mil/usawc/Registar/ policies.cfm

Traders Nation. (2007) Retrieved from: http://www.youtube.com/ watch?v=1VgAd3WdaD0

Activity 6.4 Write on Your Blog

Choose one of your previous blog postings, and revise it using the suggestions provided in this chapter.

Activity 6.5 Write in Your Commonplace Book

Choose one of the readings in this chapter that you think could be improved, and write in your commonplace book about how it could be changed. Give specific examples.

Mitchell, Alexandar Thomas. *GSU.*

RESEARCH AND DOCUMENTATION

INTRODUCTION TO RESEARCH

In college writing, you will be expected to think critically; to offer strong, compelling, and appropriate research to advance your arguments; to discern between scholarly and non-scholarly sources in your research; and to write directly and clearly.

Academic writing has conventional practices, like any other endeavor. For example, scholars writing in their fields routinely include a "Literature Review" in academic papers, showing that they are familiar with the works of scholars who've gone before. Conventions of academic research can be easily learned, and your research skills will expand and improve with practice.

You engage in research every day. If you're in the market for a car, you may research online or talk to a knowledgeable family member about which model best fits your needs. If your car requires repair, you may consult online reviews to find a trustworthy mechanic near you. Perhaps you've read the nutritional information on a can or box to find the sugar content of your favorite foods or consulted an online medical article to learn more about artificial sweeteners. The information-gathering you will do for college research simply builds on these informal research skills.

By the end of ENGL 1101, and throughout ENGL 1102, you will be expected to write a *researched argument paper*. In this paper, you will make an argument—a *claim*. Your claim may be an opinion, an interpretation, a policy proposal, or a cause-and-effect statement. In your paper, you will be expected to:

1. Make a concise, compelling claim (your argument), and

2. Support your argument with evidence gathered from your research.

MLA DOCUMENTATION STYLE

In college writing, you must *document* all of the sources you use. Each discipline uses a particular style according to the priorities and nature of their written discourse. The American Psychological Association (APA) style, for example, is followed in business, social sciences, and education, and journalism usually follows the Chicago Style guidelines. In the humanities, including English Studies, scholars use the documentation style of the Modern Language Association (MLA).

The MLA Handbook for Writers of Research Papers, Seventh Edition provides guidelines for the MLA style of documentation. For links to resources on MLA citation, please visit the *Guide to First-Year Writing* companion Website at www.guidetowriting.gsu.edu.

Reviewing the "MLA Documentation" section of this chapter serves as a great introduction to the style guide, but the best way—by far—to get the hang of documentation is to read the model research essays included here and on our Website.

Note how authors:

1) smoothly incorporate and synthesize research sources into their texts;

2) create in-text parenthetical citations; and

3) format Works Cited pages.

If you are like many first-year writing students, you may be intimidated by the prospect of thorough scholarly documentation, not only because of the multiplicity of documentation styles that each have detailed rules to follow, but also because of the looming spectre of plagiarism. First-Year students frequently, and rightfully, worry about using the undocumented words or ideas of others.

Your instructor is here to help you learn modes of documentation. So stop, ask questions, be sure you understand the documentation rules so that you learn how to responsibly acknowledge the work of others while maintaining your credibility as an author.

EVALUATING SOURCES

In researching and writing rhetorically, you boost your *ethos*, or credibility as a writer, by synthesizing your personal knowledge with expert knowledge in a field. As you begin the research process, ask, "How will this source strengthen my argument? Is the source truly relevant and timely?" The goal is to find sources that are appropriate, compelling, complete, and expert. For any source, key factors to consider include *academic credibility, argument, accuracy, and currency.* Scholarly journals and books published by university presses usually carry the most credibility in academic writing. Some popular sources (popular = written by journalists, not by experts in the field) are credible, depending on context; a news item from *The New York Times*, for example, may be a source of accurate, up-to-the-minute data on a topic. Many popular sources that are meant for entertainment— glossy magazines like *Glamour*—are usually not credible as sources in academic writing (depending upon your topic, of course). In addition, most instructors discourage citing Wikipedia as a source because entries are written by volunteers; readers cannot always evaluate the accuracy of entries. Wikipedia articles on your topic, however, can provide excellent bibliographies and links as starting points for your research.

Supreme, James. *Reach for More.*

To succeed in academic writing, you must develop a practiced eye for the difference between scholarly and popular sources, and commit to using scholarly sources.

Scholarly Journals

In general scholarly journals:

- Are written for an audience of professors and students in an academic field

- Are published usually by a university press

- Include few, if any, advertisements within the articles

- Make use of highly specialized vocabulary

- Include articles, graphics, tables, charts

- Append an extensive bibliography at the end of each journal article or book

Examples:

JAMA: The Journal of the American Medical Association
(Written by experts in the field of medicine for others in the field.)

The Journal of Economic Theory
(Writer/audience of economics PhDs, researchers, and students.)

American Literature
(Published by Duke University Press for an academic audience.)

Popular Publications

Popular publications generally:

- Are written by journalists or other contributing writers

- Are published by a news or popular press

- Include glossy or eye-catching color, many photos

- Rely upon non-technical vocabulary

- Do not include bibliographies

Examples:

The Wall Street Journal (Despite "journal" in the title, it is a popular source—a newspaper written by journalists for a wide audience)

The Economist (Written by journalists, full color, with many ads)

PCWorld (Full color, many ads. Written by journalists for a wide audience)

Primary and Secondary Sources

You also need to learn to distinguish between primary and secondary research tools.

Primary research involves first-hand interaction with your subject, including interviewing people and analyzing/working with primary sources like diaries, novels and films (rather than working with second-hand *analyses* of these primary sources). Primary sources stand alone in that they are not overtly analyzing other source materials. *The Diary of a Young Girl* by Anne Frank is a primary source.

Secondary research materials, on the other hand, interpret and analyze primary sources. Secondary sources include scholarly journal articles, analyses, and biographies, such as *Anne Frank: The Biography* by Melissa Müller.

Walsh, William. *Books.*

A LIBRARY SEARCH; OR, WHY YOU CAN'T "JUST GOOGLE IT"

Google searching returns a world of information—but often not a world of credible sources. Suppose you are researching the history behind Dr. Martin Luther King's "Letter from Birmingham Jail." You Google "Martin Luther King," and you click on the link for "www. martinlutherking.org."

As a "dot-org," the source seems credible. The site is visually pleasing, in terms of neatness and layout. At first glance, you think the site might be sponsored by the Martin Luther King Center or a memorial foundation, or serve as a reputable archive of King's speeches. You read the plausible website heading: "Martin Luther King Jr: A True Historical Examination. A Valuable Resource for Teachers and Students Alike."

Unfortunately, this page is indeed the work of an organization—a supremacist hate group offering their take on King's life and on the accomplishments of African Americans in general. The site includes numerous hateful statements about African Americans and other groups.

A good rule of thumb:

To be used in an academic paper, a Web source:

1) must list an author (the above source does not);

2) must cite its sources, and

3) should not exist to advertise and sell products.

Of note, GoogleScholar—not just Google—provides an excellent search engine for finding online scholarly articles. What is the downside of GoogleScholar? Unlike a library database search, this site doesn't always give the full text of an article; often, you must pay for the article. The good news: most scholarly articles are available free of charge through a GSU Library search.

http:www.library.gsu.edu/

QUICK-START: SEARCHING THE GSU PULLEN LIBRARY WEBSITE

You can search the Georgia State University Pullen Library website and numerous scholarly databases from your personal computer. Go to http://www.library.gsu.edu/ and click "Libraries" and then "University Library." Last year, the library's website was visited 1.7 million times. If you're searching for books, the library houses 1.5 million volumes. Whether you are accessing the library from home or from a library computer, use the following steps to complete a simple and quick search.

For Academic Search Complete, click on "A" in Discover's "Databases A to Z" field. Then, click "Academic Search Complete."

Finding Articles in Scholarly Journals

To establish credibility in your academic writing, research and include peer-reviewed scholarly journal articles in your work. "Peer-reviewed" means that articles have been screened and vetted by experts in the field for reliability and relevance before being published and used by other scholars.

Go to the library webpage http://www.library.gsu.edu/ and view the Discover field.

You can use Discover for your search, as it searches many other databases. The results, however, are often cumbersome, and many will be irrelevant to your topic.

For a more efficient search, go to the bottom of the Discover search box and click "Databases By Name A-Z." Click "A," and then choose the database "EBSCO Host/Academic Search Complete." You will then be asked for your campus ID and password.

Academic Search Complete is a comprehensive, multi-disciplinary source of more than 10,000 scholarly publications. Once you're in Academic Search Complete, conduct a basic search using keywords from your topic (for example, *water quality*), a title, or an author. Academic Search Complete also will limit the results to scholarly journals if you click "Search Options" and then "Scholarly Journals Only." You may choose to see only articles with full-texts available, and you also can earmark desired articles to an electronic folder.

Use Boolean operators to tailor your search. Use quotation marks to search for *phrases*, like "bipolar disorder" or "a midsummer night's dream." Use *AND, OR and NOT* in ALL CAPS, as in biomedical AND engineering NOT nuclear. Use an asterisk* for *wild card searches*; cinema* will return "cinematic" and "cinematography." Use multiple search terms to narrow the results; keep in mind that a search for a term like "environment" will yield millions of hits.

Note: EBSCO Host/Academic Search Complete is one of more than 100 databases available through the library, serving a wide range of disciplines. For discipline-specific databases, seek out the Subject Librarian for your field (art, for example), or browse "Databases A-Z" in Discover. You'll find everything from NASA's database to MedLine to ARTstor to Rock'N'Roll and Counterculture.

Here are some suggested databases for different disciplines:

- Humanities, including Languages and Literatures—EBSCO Host/Academic Search Complete, JSTOR, MLA International Bibliography, Project Muse

- Social Sciences—ERIC, Government Document Catalog Services, PsychInfo

- Business—ProQuest, LexisNexis Academic
- Sciences—Academic Search Complete, Web of Science, General Science Index
- News, Legal Cases—LexisNexis Academic

Finding Library Books

Scholarly books usually treat academic topics with in-depth discussion and careful documentation of evidence. Scholarly books are often published by university presses, such as Oxford University Press or the University of California Press. However, keep in mind that a well-researched popular book with a thorough bibliography is also a good research find; the bibliography can point you toward scholarly books/articles on your topic. Remember: In academic writing, we build on the work of scholars who have come before us.

It is easy to search for library books. Go to the Discover window and click "Catalog"; under "All Fields," search by title, subject, or author. At the bottom of the catalog entry for each book, you will find the location of the book in the Pullen Library:

"Library North 3"—and the call number by which you can find the book on the shelves: "RC516 .B526." Proceed to third floor north and find the RCs on the shelves.

Using Internet Sources Wisely

Earlier we cautioned you to not "just Google it"; however, the World Wide Web is an extremely useful resource for legitimate research when following scholarly research practices. Through the Web, you can find full texts of pending legislation, searchable online editions of Shakespeare's plays, scholarly articles, environmental impact statements, stock quotes, and much more. Finding credible sites for research through a Google search, however, is not that easy. Sites range, in terms of credibility and usefulness, from the spectacularly good (like Google Books, with millions of searchable titles) to the spectacularly bad. When evaluating a web site, your job as a scholar is to learn to recognize the difference between legitimate resources, and those that are not credible. Remember, you are trying to build ethos: Which is more credible, a paper citing nothing but unexamined Web sources or, one that cites statistics from published studies, articles from peer-reviewed journals, and news reports providing historical and social context?

A rule of thumb – just like a scholarly journal, a reliable internet source:

1) lists an author,

2) lists its sources, and

3) isn't selling a product or service.

Researchers, in general, evaluate web sites for *relevance, reliability, accuracy and currency.* In addition to asking *"How does this information fit my research purpose?"* they ask questions such as:

Who is the author of the site? Is he or she a legitimate expert? What organization or entity does the writer represent? Think of the credibility gap—and the gap between the writer's rhetorical stance and tone—between the American Medical Association

Deljou, Nadia. *Colored Bricks of Wisdom.*

website (ama-assn.org) and "The Anti-Liberal Page" (a .com site). Researchers view .com sites, short for "commercial," with a healthy dose of skepticism. The .edu suffix, indicating a college or university, indicates credibility, as does .gov, which indicates a government agency or search engine like www.searchusa.gov.

What is the purpose of the site? What is its agenda? Compare the purpose of a recognized informational website (like the United Nations web site, at http://www.un.org/en/), to the purpose of the www.MartinLutherKing.org. site mentioned earlier. One seeks to provide accurate information; one is a supremacist-group smear campaign that seeks to destroy reputations.

To help you in your Internet research, two specialized search engines yield only results that have been vetted by university librarians for accuracy and credibility. They are: Information You Can Trust, http://www.ipl.org, and Infomine: Scholarly Internet Resource Collections @ http://infomine.ucr.edu.

THE THESIS STATEMENT AND RESEARCH PROPOSAL

To review, an *argumentative* paper makes a claim, which is supported with specific evidence gleaned from your research.

Early in the research process, your argument—the main claim of your research paper—will begin to take shape, and you will form ideas of how you will incorporate resources. In the research proposal, you specify the argument and sources for your research project. The proposal is not a contract, and you are not locked into the topic at this point. In fact, your proposal most likely will be refined, narrowed, or changed based on conversations with your instructor and peers, as part of the writing process. As your research proposal develops, think of it as a guide to help you keep your writing and research focused on your primary claims.

The art of crafting a research statement (or question) requires study and practice; consult your writing textbook for techniques and examples. As for the research proposal, requirements vary among instructors; your teacher may ask for a bare-bones outline (see example below) or a multiple-page written document.

Here is an outline-form proposal with some typical required elements, as assigned by one instructor:

SAMPLE RESEARCH PROPOSAL

My Classical Argument Proposal: Why Writing Teachers Should Study Depression and Bipolar Disorder in Student Writers

My Audience: Writing teachers, including my writing instructor, and my 1102 class members

My Thesis/Argument: Composition teachers should study how depression and bipolar disorder affect student writing.

Three Reasons Why:

1. Depression and bipolar illness have long been associated with writing creativity.

   I knew this, and will find more examples in research.

2. Seven percent of undergraduates nationwide currently take antidepressants; a full one in four say depression has hurt their academic performance.

   I knew this generally, but didn't know the numbers until I researched. Wow!

3. Depression can cause writer's block; perhaps not all late papers are due to laziness.

   I didn't know this; I found more data to illustrate it.

Possible Counter-Arguments

THEY SAY: Writing teachers don't need to study this. They're not therapists.

I SAY: True, but this affects the writing of many, many students. It's relevant for the study of composition.

Preliminary Research Sources:

At this point, I have found three main sources:

1. A website (The National College Health Association's major mental health study of 200 colleges nationwide). *I will use data from this study to illustrate the breadth of depression and bipolar illness in the student population.*

2. An article (from the academic journal *Comprehensive Psychiatry*) *I will use this article for Reason No. 3, that depression can cause writer's block, which may affect students' academic performance.*

3. A library book (published by Columbia University Press) *I will use this book for background on depression and mania in writers in English.*

PLAGIARISM

Before discussing how to quote, paraphrase, and summarize sources, we want to define and explain what constitutes plagiarism.

Plagiarism means handing in someone else's words, thoughts, or artifacts as your own. Intentional plagiarism is forbidden in academic writing, and the stigma of a plagiarism charge follows students throughout their academic careers. The basic concepts of plagiarism are straightforward.

At Georgia State, "*The student is responsible for understanding the legitimate use of sources . . . and the consequences of violating this responsibility.*" In other words, the burden rests upon you as the writer to give credit where credit is due.

Common types of plagiarism include:

1. Turning in a paper that was written by someone else as your own, including papers obtained from online paper banks and papers that your purchase.

2. Copying from a source without acknowledging that source in the proper format (in English courses, you must follow MLA documentation guidelines, which includes an in-text

parenthetical citation and a source entry on the Works Cited page).

3. Paraphrasing materials from a source without attributing the information to that source.

4. Copying materials from a text but treating them as your own, leaving out quotation marks and acknowledgements.

All instances of plagiarism are reported to the College of Arts & Sciences. Please be sure you understand your instructor's policy for plagiarism as stated on the course syllabus.

To learn how to avoid plagiarism and properly cite sources, talk to your instructor, closely read the MLA guidelines, make an appointment with a tutor at the GSU Writing Studio, and visit comprehensive web sites like The Purdue Online Writing Lab (owl.english.purdue.edu/).

Internet searches, anti-plagiarism software like turnitin.com, and instructors' in-depth knowledge of students' writing make it easy to catch plagiarism among composition students. The "easy way," paradoxically, is simply to do the work.

From the GSU Policy on Academic Honesty (Section 409 of GSU Faculty Handbook)

"The University expects students and faculty to be academically honest, and it expects faculty members to communicate expectations to students in their syllabi. That said, it is the student's final responsibility to understand plagiarism and avoid it. See the definitions below.

GSU's Definitions of Academic Honesty

The examples and definitions given below are intended to clarify the standards by which academic honesty and academically honorable conduct are to be judged. The list is merely illustrative of the kinds of infractions that may occur, and it is not intended to be exhaustive. Moreover, the definitions and examples suggest conditions under which unacceptable behavior of the indicated types normally occurs; however, there may be unusual cases that fall outside these conditions which also will be judged unacceptable by the academic community.

Plagiarism: Plagiarism is presenting another person's work as one's own. Plagiarism includes any paraphrasing or summarizing of the works of another person without acknowledgment, including the submitting of another student's work as one's own. Plagiarism frequently involves a failure to acknowledge in the text, notes, or footnotes the quotation of the paragraphs, sentences, or even a few phrases written or spoken by someone else. The submission of research or completed papers or projects by someone else is plagiarism, as is the unacknowledged use of research sources gathered by someone else when that use is specifically forbidden by the faculty member. Failure to indicate the extent and nature of one's reliance on other sources is also a form of plagiarism. Any work, in whole or in part, taken from the Internet or other computer-based resource without properly referencing the source (for example, the URL) is considered plagiarism. A complete reference is required in order that all parties may locate and view the original source. Finally, there may be forms of plagiarism that are unique to an individual discipline or course, examples of which should be provided in advance by the faculty member. The student is responsible for understanding the legitimate use of sources, the appropriate ways of acknowledging academic, scholarly or creative indebtedness, and the consequences of violating this responsibility.

Cheating on Examinations: Cheating on examinations involves giving or receiving unauthorized help before, during, or after an examination. Examples of unauthorized help include the use of notes, computer based resources, texts, or "crib sheets" during an examination (unless specifically approved by the faculty member), or sharing information with another student during an examination (unless specifically approved by the faculty member). Other examples include intentionally allowing another student to view one's own examination and collaboration before or after an examination if such collaboration is specifically forbidden by the faculty member.

Unauthorized Collaboration: Submission for academic credit of a work product, or a part thereof, represented as its being one's own effort, which has been developed in substantial collaboration with another person or source, or computer-based resource, is a violation of academic honesty. It is also a violation of academic honesty knowingly to provide such assistance. Collaborative work specifically authorized by a faculty member is allowed.

Falsification: It is a violation of academic honesty to misrepresent material or fabricate information in an academic exercise, assignment, or proceeding (e.g., false or misleading citation of sources, the falsification of the results of experiments or of computer data, false or misleading information in an academic context in order to gain an unfair advantage).

Multiple Submissions: It is a violation of academic honesty to submit substantial portions of the same work for credit more than once without the explicit consent of the faculty member(s) to whom the material is submitted for additional credit. In cases in which there is a natural development of research or knowledge in a sequence of courses, use of prior work may be desirable, even required; however the student is responsible for indicating in writing, as a part of such use, that the current work submitted for credit is cumulative in nature."

Two Examples of Plagiarism

Plagiarism takes many forms; two definitive examples follow. Examine the following original passages and student use of them. Determine which one is:

1.) Word-for-Word Plagiarism

2.) Too-Close Paraphrasing/Lack of Acknowledgement of Sources

Original Passage #1:

"As you read the book, you really do feel for Ender. He's used like a tool, honed and shaped against his will, with no one to turn to, which is pretty much the point. If he's in the midst of battle, there won't be a grownup there to turn to. His childhood is ripped from him, bit by bit, and perhaps that's why you feel sorry for him. By the time the book comes to its climax, he's only eleven years old. He's very smart, and very talented, but he's still only eleven." (From www.10brinkster. com/MShades/books/e/ender.html)

A Student's Use #1:

As you read the book, you really do feel for Ender. The idea of a child being used like a tool, having their childhood bypassed and eliminated, is a harsh thing, and perhaps that's the lesson of this book.

Ender is used like a tool, honed and shaped against his will, with no one to turn to. If he's in the midst of battle, there won't be a grownup there to turn to. Ender's childhood is ripped from him, bit by bit, and perhaps that's why you feel sorry for him. By the time the book comes to its climax, he's only eleven years old. He's very smart, but he's still only eleven.

CITATION STRATEGIES YOU WOULD USE FOR THIS EXAMPLE #1: Review and practice what it means to summarize and/or paraphrase the piece.

Review how to quote the author. Use a page number if available. Here is how: According to Smith, Ender "is used like a tool, honed and shaped against his will" (1).

Use parenthetical citation at the end of sentences both quoted AND paraphrased. If you paraphrase, be sure to introduce the paraphrased material in a way that illustrates the difference between your words and ideas and those you summarize from your source.

Original Passage #2:

"At about 1:01 p.m. on March 18, 1925, trees began to snap north-northwest of Ellington, Missouri, and for the next three and a half hours more people would die, more schools would be destroyed, more students and farmers would be killed, and more deaths would occur in a single city than from any other tornado in U.S. history. Records would be set for speed, path length, and probably for other categories that can't be measured so far in the past. The tornado maintained an exact heading, N 69 degrees E, for 183 of the 219 miles, at an average of 62 mph, following a slight topographic ridge on which a series of mining towns were built. These towns were the main targets of the devastating winds. No distinct funnel was visible through much of its path, yet for over 100 miles, the path width held uniformly at about three-quarters of a mile." (http://www.carolyar.com/Illinois/Misc/Tornado.htm)

A Student's Use #2:

A terrible tornado passed through north-northwest of Ellington, Missouri at about 1:01 p.m. on March 18, 1925. The trees began to snap, and for the next approximately three hours, many people died, many schools were destroyed, and the U.S. record was set for deaths occurring in a single city. Records also would be set for path length and speed. The tornado maintained the heading of N 69 degrees E, and traveled at an average of 62 mph for the length of its path. You couldn't see a funnel, but for more than 100 miles, the monster left a destruction path three-quarters of a mile wide. Big tornadoes like this are the reason that towns and cities should install more tornado warning sirens.

Graziano, Marissa. *Awakening.*

Determine which is word-for-word plagiarism and which is too-close-paraphrase/didn't cite sources plagiarism. Then, let's revisit the idea of common and uncommon knowledge:

Common Knowledge: Every year, tornadoes kill people in an area of the central U.S. known as Tornado Alley. (You do not have to name a source for this).

***NOT* Common Knowledge:** "The 1925 Missouri tornado maintained an exact heading, N 69 degrees E, at an average of 62 mph." You did not know this as you came into your research. In MLA format, you must name the source of this data, both in 1) parentheses at the end of the sentence, and 2) in the Works Cited page.

In the second example, the student did not *credit a source* when he/she directly quoted and paraphrased facts that are *NOT common knowledge.*

Remember the important rule of thumb: *If a fact wasn't in your head when you began your research, assume it is NOT common knowledge.*

By the same token, if a fact is new to you but common knowledge to your audience, you may not need to cite it.

Citation strategies you would use for this example:

1. Put quotation marks around all direct quotes (whole sentences AND phrases).

2. Use a looser, more contextual paraphrase (combine it with text above and below).

3. Use parenthetical citation at the end of fact-laden sentences, both quoted AND paraphrased (Smith 1).

For more on researching and note-taking, understanding plagiarism, and plagiarism examples, consult the "Is It Plagiarism?" and "Safe Practices" sections of the Purdue OWL at http://owl.english.purdue. edu/owl/resource/589/03/. The OWL is an excellent source across the board for research paper writing. These two sections cover reading, note-taking, summarizing, paraphrasing, quoting, and safely writing about the ideas of others.

Plagiarism: Easy to Commit, Hard to Live Down

In 2006, Harvard undergraduate Kaavya Viswanathan wrote the best-selling novel *How Opal Mehta Got Kissed, Got Wild, and Got A Life.* The novel was subsequently recalled by the publisher—who took the unprecedented step of destroying all copies—because Viswanathan plagiarized throughout.

Here is an example of how the writer followed sources much too closely:

From Salman Rushdie's 1990 novel *Haroun and the Sea of Stories*: "If from speed you get your thrill, take precaution, make your will."

From Viswanathan's novel: "If from drink you get your thrill, take precaution—write your will."

Taking Notes From Sources

As you take notes, ALWAYS indicate which words are YOURS and which are quotes from sources. Find a way that works for you—large quotation marks, highlighting for "mine," etc.

Careful note-taking is the best defense against plagiarism. Note-taking strategies differ among researchers. Whether you are jotting down notes on paper, typing up notes on your computer (using a different page or file for each topic), or on a program like Zotero (a Firefox plugin available through the library), be sure to keep neat and organized notes. Here is the basic note card format, for paper or computer:

Google's Data-
Gathering Practices (subject heading)
Stallworth, "Googling for Principles in
Online Advertising," p. 470
"Google's enormous data-crunching
machine is able to make calculated
assumptions about consumers based
on their searches, or on information
consumers reveal when registering for
Google's free services."
Direct quote.

Write a subject heading at the top—a category that makes sense to you. Then, carefully enter either 1) *a direct quote of the source, with quote marks* 2) your *summary* of the source, or 3) your *paraphrase* of the source. Write which of the three formats you have created at the bottom of the card or file.

Common and Uncommon Knowledge

Once again, to avoid plagiarism, *you must credit a source* when you quote, paraphrase, or summarize *any facts that are not common knowledge* (see below for instructions on how to quote, paraphrase and summarize). For example, the following facts, none of which are common knowledge, must be cited: "In March of 2012, the population of the United States was estimated at 313,232,882." Or, "The *RMS Titanic* sank on April 15, 1912." Or, "The University of Texas has seven museums and 17 libraries."

You don't have to credit a source for facts that *are* common knowledge, such as: "The United States government is divided into three branches: executive, legislative and judicial." "The University of Texas is in Austin."

Two rules of thumb:

> *If a fact wasn't in your head when you began your research, assume it is NOT common knowledge.*

Preparing Sources for Your Paper

If you've copied words directly from a source without changing them, these copied words must be enclosed in quotation marks. Failure to put quotation marks around copied material constitutes plagiarism, since the reader will believe the words are yours.

Always introduce the quotation with a signal phrase of your own (see below, "For William Styron"), and insert an ellipsis if you take words out of the quote (Use "insert, symbol," in Word, then click on Ellipsis). End the sentence by crediting the source of the quote. Here are the original sentences from William Styron's memoir *Darkness Visible*:

(Original) "The madness of depression is, generally speaking, the antithesis of violence. It is a storm indeed, but a storm of murk. Soon evident are the slowed-down responses, near paralysis, psychic energy throttled back close to zero."

Here is an example, using an ellipsis (…) to mark excised words:

(Student Example) For William Styron, the experience of severe depression is "a storm of murk … of slowed-down responses, near paralysis, psychic energy throttled back to zero" (47).

When you summarize and paraphrase, you still must credit the original author. The preceding example cites through the use of a signal phrase-- "For William Styron"-- and by listing the page number in parenthesis at the end of the sentence-- (47).

IMPORTANT: Never copy words verbatim to your paper unless you use *direct, essentially unchanged quotes in quotation marks*. Changing only a word or two here or there is plagiarism, and is easy for instructors and readers to catch. To guard against plagiarism, use the following read-think-write strategies.

Directly Quoting a Source

When using a direct quote, use the source's exact language, and always set off the quote in quotation marks. If you take words out of the source's exact language, always replace them with an ellipsis (...) Always end a quote with a parenthetical citation (often, a page number).

IMPORTANT: Never just drop quotes into your paper. The effect on your audience is jarring, and meaning is often lost. Always use an introductory "signal" verb or phrase.

Examples:

> *According to Smith, "Quote" (21).*
>
> *Smith argues, "Quote" (21).*

Refer to your writing handbook or a rhetoric text for a list of these "signal" verbs that add smoothness and sophistication to your writing.

Indirect Quoting of a Source (Paraphrasing)

Sometimes, you will want to paraphrase a quote—to put it simply, in your own words, rather than use it verbatim. Paraphrasing is fine as long as you 1) get the source's meaning exactly right and 2) include all the main issues in the order you encounter them in the original sources, and 3) cite the source at the end of the sentence.

Be sure, too, to make it clear where your own thoughts begin and end. Simply putting a parenthetical citation at the end of a paragraph is not sufficient (is the entire paragraph the restating of the source's ideas?). You must introduce the source and discuss the source's relevancy to your topic.

Example:

Job creation is heavy on the minds of the American public. In response to this public concern, at a July 15 press conference, President Obama said he would launch a new job creation program (20). Many of these jobs will be in the environmental and sustainability sector, which means a degree in these two areas will be more advantageous than ever before.

The Rhetorical Précis

The rhetorical précis (pronounced "pray-see") is a highly specialized, brief and useful summary you may be asked to write; writing a précis is an excellent way to summarize sources (as opposed to the simple summary outlined below). The précis places emphasis on the rhetorical aspects of the work, like author, purpose, and audience, and is based on four very specific sentences, which are highlighted in the example below:

1. The first sentence provides the author's name, the genre (article, book), the title, and the date of the work in parentheses. Then, it uses a concise verb (like "claims" or "argues") followed by a "that" phrase stating the thesis of the work. The thesis can be either quoted or paraphrased.

2. The next sentence explains how the author supports his/her thesis. Stay general here; avoid details.

3. The third sentence uses an "in order to" phrase to state the purpose of the piece. Why is the author writing this piece?

4. The last sentence names the author's intended audience.

Durland, Stephen. "Witness: The Guerrilla Theater of Greenpeace." *High Performance* 40 (Winter 1987). *Community Arts Network Reading Room Archives.* Community Arts Network. 1999. 15 February 2009. Web.

In his article "Witness: The Guerrilla Theater of Greenpeace" (1987), writer Stephen Durland _argues that the performative environmental rhetoric of Greenpeace should be considered art_ and should not be overlooked by the world of performance art. _In order to make his argument,_ Durland traces the beginnings of Greenpeace's brand of theater to the "guerrilla theater" of the Yippie movement of Abbie Hoffman and Jerry Rubin in the 1960s, narrates the major symbolic acts of the organization, and interviews Action Director Steve Loper about the group's philosophy and purpose. The purpose of Durland's article is to call attention to the need for an expansion of the sort of activism through art that Greenpeace practices. _The audience for Durland's article_ includes primarily the readers of *High Performance*, a (now-defunct) magazine for the subgenre of performance art.

Taking Notes: Summarizing a Source

A *summary*, as opposed to a précis, simply condenses the original material, presenting its core ideas *in your own words*. Summarize to condense long passages that emphasize your point, and when details are not critical. Don't use "I," or evaluate the piece. Just condense.

1. In the first sentence, state the article's main claim, or thesis; begin with the author's full name, the title of the article (in quotation marks), and page numbers.

2. State the major supporting points in their original order. Omit details and examples.

3. End with the author's conclusions or recommendations.

Taking Notes: Paraphrasing a Source

A *paraphrase*, on the other hand, reflects *your* understanding of the source. A paraphrase includes *all* points and ideas in the same order as originally written by the author. You should paraphrase when direct quoting is not permitted. Paraphrasing represents a by-product of your learning process, and as such communicates the ideas in your own words without condensing the material. Use your own language and structure, and always differentiate your ideas from those ideas published by others.

Rule of Thumb:

> *If you are using information to support a claim you make in your paper, it is best to use direct quotes. If you paraphrase, remember you must indicate (in writing) where your thoughts begin and end; paraphrased material must be introduced, explained, and properly cited in your writing*

Paraphrasing with The Look-Away Method—Read one or two sentences over several times. Then set the article aside and paraphrase the meaning of the sentences without looking back at the article. When you are finished, review the article and make sure your paraphrase is accurate and that you didn't the same words as the author.

Consider this original text from page 141 of Nicholas Carr's *The Shallows: What the Internet is Doing To Our Brains* (2010):

Original: "Given our brain's plasticity, we know that our online habits continue to reverberate in the workings of our synapses when we're not online. We can assume that the neural circuits devoted to scanning, skimming, and multitasking are expanding and strengthening, while those used for reading and thinking deeply, with sustained concentration, are weakening or eroding. In 2009, researchers from Stanford University found signs that this shift may already be well underway. They gave a battery of cognitive tests to a group of heavy media multitaskers as well as a group of relatively light multitaskers. They found that the heavy multitaskers were much more easily distracted by "irrelevant environmental stimuli," had less control over the contents of their working memory, and were in general much less able to maintain their concentration on a particular task."

Student Paraphrase: Carr makes the assumption that heavy use of brain pathways involved in scanning and skimming information online has a strengthening effect on those circuits, while pathways used for deep reading and concentration atrophy. He cites a 2009 Stanford study suggesting that multitaskers were more distractable and less in control of memory and concentration. (141)

Note: For each summary or paraphrase, always record the relevant page numbers for the article in parentheses. This practice will save you a great deal of hunting and work toward the end of your paper, when you prepare the Works Cited list.

Taking Notes: The Annotated Bibliography

At some point in the research project, you may be asked to create an Annotated Bibliography. For each entry, annotate the source (write a brief summary or paraphrase), and include a few sentences on how the source is relevant to your research project. An annotated bibliography, written as you research, is an ideal reference for you to use as your prepare your final paper. Here is a sample annotation:

Ehrenreich, Barbara. "Nickel and Dimed." *Mothering.* 2001. *Academic Search Complete.* Web. 10 May 2011.

Waxelbaum, Teal. *Whitman's 'Song of Myself.'*

In this article, Ehrenreich discusses welfare assistance in America as it applies to single parents, as well as how minimum wage affects these households. She argues against the idea that putting single mothers on welfare increases the likelihood that they will keep having children they cannot take care of. She uses statistics to prove that most people who go on welfare are hardworking individuals who just do not make enough on their own to support themselves, much less their children. This article will help me to show that while the government does offer assistance to single parents, it does not offer enough, and it offers assistance in a way that makes the general public scoff at and belittle those who accept it. This also will help me highlight what individuals who received welfare really do with the money, to build the credibility of hardworking single parents who do not abuse the system.

Remember, You Have Resources Available to Help You

Correctly documenting the information you cite in your writing is a way to develop strong ethos. Aside from the penalties a student can incur by flagrantly plagiarizing the work of others, research is a key element in argumentation. Using research appropriately will make your writing stronger. Your composition instructor is here to help you learn the proper way to collect, integrate, and cite the information you find during your research process. If you are ever in doubt, ask him or her to explain the formatting and integration rules again. The *Guide to First-Year Writing* and its companion website offer examples to help you work through citation difficulties. In addition to these resources, the English Department also houses the Writing Studio. The Studio, as it is commonly called, provides a space for in-person and on-line tutoring and writing help. In Chapter Eight, you will learn what services the Studio offers all Georgia State students, and how these services can be specifically geared toward students in composition classes.

MLA Documentation

When you do research to find supporting evidence for your ideas or arguments, you need to credit your outside sources. Depending on what type of essay you are writing or which type of course you are writing for, you will need to choose a documentation style and continue with that style for the entire essay. Two of the most common styles, especially for freshman and sophomore students, are MLA (Modern Language Association) and APA (American Psychological Association).

If you write in composition, language, linguistics, and literature courses, you will often be asked to use documentation guidelines created by the Modern Language Association (MLA). The *MLA Handbook for Writers of Research Papers*, in its seventh edition, provides a full description of the conventions used by this particular community of writers; updates to the *MLA Handbook* can be found at <www.mla.org>.

MLA guidelines require that you give both an in-text citation and a Works Cited entry for any and all sources you use. Using accurate in-text citations helps guide your reader to the appropriate entry on the Works Cited. For example, the in-text citation given below in parentheses directs the reader to the correct page of the book given in the Works Cited.

> In-text citation➔ When a teenager sleeps more than 10 hours per night, it is time to question whether she is having significant problems (Jones 63).

Entry in Works Cited➔
Jones, Stephanie. *The Signs of Trouble.* Boston: Dilemma

    Publishing, 2010. Print.

This chapter provides a general overview of MLA documentation style and an explanation of the most commonly used MLA documentation formats, including a few significant revisions since the previous edition.

Did You Know?

The Modern Language Association was founded in 1883 at The John Hopkins University as a group that discussed literature and modern languages, such as Spanish, French, Chinese, and English. The MLA, now with over 30,000 members in over 100 countries, is the primary professional association for literature and language scholars.

37a   Using MLA in-text citations

In-text citations (also called *parenthetical citations*) point readers to where they can find more information about your researched supporting materials. When you use MLA documentation style, you need to indicate the author's last name and the location of the source material (page or paragraph number). Where this in-text information is placed depends on how you want to phrase the sentence that is summarized, paraphrased, or quoted. Be sure that the in-text citation guides the reader clearly to the source in the Works Cited, where complete information about the source is given.

The following are some of the most common examples of parenthetical citations.

1. Author's name in text

When using a parenthetical reference to a single source that is already named in the sentence, use this form: (Page number). Note that the period goes after the parentheses.

➔ Stephanie Jones, author of *The Signs of Trouble*, describes "excessive sleeping, refraining from eating, and lying about simple things" as signs to look for when parents are concerned about their children (63).

2. Author's name in reference

When the author's name is not included in the preceding sentence, use this form for the parenthetical information at the end of the sentence: (Author's Last Name Page number). Note that there is no comma between the name and page in an MLA parenthetical reference, and also note that the period comes at the end of the sentence after the parentheses.

➔ When a teenager sleeps more than 10 hours per night, it is time to question whether she is having significant problems (Jones 63).

3. No author given

When a work has no credited author, use a clipped version of the work's title.

➔ In a recent *Time* article, a list of 30 common signs of teenage trouble cites lack of sleep as the most common sign ("Thirty" 3).

4. Two or three authors given

When you use a source that was written by two or three authors, use all the names in the text of the sentence or in the citation.

➔ The idea that "complexity is a constant in biology" is not an innovative one (Sole and Goodwin 2).

➔ Most signs in English that the authors encountered on the road had "grammar mistakes, misspellings, or just odd pictures" (Smith, Jones, and Best 55).

5. Four or more authors given

MLA documentation style allows a choice when there are four authors or more of an item to be cited. You can either name all the authors or include only the first author's name followed by *et al.* (Latin for "and others").

→ In Hong Kong, most signs are in Chinese and English; however, once you are in mainland China, English is rarely found on signs, except in tourist areas (Li, Smith, Jones, and Franz 49).

→ In Hong Kong, most signs are in Chinese and English; however, once you are in mainland China, English is rarely found on signs, except in tourist areas (Li, et al. 49).

6. Authors with the same last names

If your source material includes items by authors who happen to have the same last name, be sure to use each author's first name or initial in the parentheses.

→ When a teenager sleeps more than 10 hours per night, it is time to question whether she is having significant problems (S. Jones 63).

→ Another sign of trouble can be when you do not see your child for meals (B. Jones 114).

7. Encyclopedia or dictionary unsigned entry

When you use an encyclopedia or dictionary to look up a word or entry, be sure to include the word or entry title in the parenthetical entry.

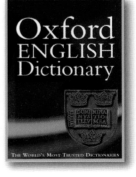

→ The word *thing* has more definitions than any other entry in the *Oxford English Dictionary* ("thing").

8. Lines of verse (plays, poetry or song lyrics)

For plays, give the act, scene, and line numbers that are located in any edition of the play. Separate the act, scene, and line numbers with periods. For example, the quotation below comes from *Romeo and Juliet*, Act II, Scene 2, lines 43 and 44. The MLA also advises using this method with biblical chapters and verses. Be sure, though, that the sequence goes from largest unit to smallest unit.

> → Juliet grapples with how names can influence feelings as she questions, "What's in a name? That which we call a rose/By any other name would smell as sweet" (2.2.43-44).

Use a slash (/) to signify line breaks when you quote poetry or song lyrics, and put line numbers in the in-text citation instead of page numbers.

> → An early song by Will Smith shows the frustration of children as he sings, "You know parents are the same/No matter time nor place/They don't understand that us kids/Are going to make some mistakes" (1-4).

9. Indirect quotation

When you use a quotation of a quotation—that is, a quotation that quotes from another source—use *qtd. in* to designate the source.

> → Smith has said, "My parents really didn't understand me" (qtd. in Jones, par. 8).

37b Using long or block quotations

Long or block quotations have special formatting requirements of their own.

1. Block quote of prose

If you quote a chunk of prose that is longer than four typed lines, you are using what is called a *block quotation*. Follow these MLA guidelines for block quotations:

1. If introducing the block quotation with a sentence, use a colon at the end of the sentence.

2. Begin the quotation on a new line.

3. Do not use quotation marks to enclose the block quote.

4. Indent the quote one inch from the left margin, and extend the right margin to the end of the line.

5. Double space the entire quotation.

6. Put a period at the end of the quotation, and then add the parenthetical citation.

➔ However, Lansky states:

> Despite the statement on <www.signspotting.com> that we don't accept signs with the intention of being funny, people like sending them in. I've opted not to use these as it could encourage people to start making them, sticking them up in their driveway, and snapping a picture. Plus, funny signs are so much more amusing when the humor is accidental. (72)

2. Block quote of poetry, drama, or song lyrics

For songs and poems, be sure to give line numbers rather than page numbers and to use the original line breaks.

➔ The Fresh Prince, an early Will Smith character, sings about parents not understanding:

> You know parents are the same
>
> No matter time or place
>
> They don't understand that us kids
>
> Are going to make some mistakes
>
> So to you other kids all across the land
>
> There's no need to argue
>
> Parents just don't understand. (4-7)

37c   Adding or omitting words in a quotation

1. Adding words to a quotation

Use square brackets ([ ]) to point out words or phrases that are not part of the original text.

→   Original quotation: "When we entered the People's Republic of China, we noticed that the signage began dropping English translations."

→   Quotation with added word: She said, "When we entered the People's Republic of China, [Dunkirk and I] noticed that the signage began dropping English translations" (Donelson 141).

You can also add your own comments inside a quotation by using square brackets. For example, you can add the word *sic* to a quotation when you know that there is an error.

→   Original quotation: "When we entered the People's Repulic of China, we noticed that the signage began dropping English translations."

→   Quotation with added comment: She said, "When we entered the People's Repulic [sic] of China, we noticed that the signage began dropping English translations" (Donelson 141).

2. Omitting words in a quotation

Use an ellipsis (. . .) to represent words that you delete from a quotation. The ellipsis begins with a space, then has three periods with spaces between them, and then ends with a space.

Original quotation→ "The Great Wall is something that can be seen from space. When we reach a time when advertisements can be seen from space, we have probably gone too far."

Quotation with words omitted in middle of sentence➔ Frank Donelson, author of *Signs in Space*, remarks, "The Great Wall . . . can be seen from space. When we reach a time when advertisements can be seen from space, we have probably gone too far" (178).

If you omit words at the end of a quotation, and that is also the end of your sentence, use an ellipsis plus a period with no space before the ellipsis or after the period.

Original quotation➔ "The Great Wall is something that can be seen from space. When we reach a time when advertisements can be seen from space, we have probably gone too far with our advertising and signage."

Quotation with words omitted at end of sentence➔ Frank Donelson, author of *Signs in Space*, remarks, "The Great Wall is something that can be seen from space. When we reach a time when advertisements can be seen from space, we have probably gone too far. . ." (178).

Helpful hint

MLA guidelines can change with a new edition. Sometimes, class textbooks can use an older MLA documentation style. Always check with your instructor if rules seem to be in conflict.

37d   Citing online sources

In the MLA documentation style, online or electronic sources have their own formatting guidelines since these types of sources rarely give specific page numbers.

The MLA recommends that you include in the text, rather than in an in-text citation, the name(s) of the person (e.g., author, editor, director, performer) that begins the matching Works Cited entry. For instance, the following is the recommended way to begin an in-text citation for an online source:

➔ Roger Ebert says that Shyamalan "plays the audience like a piano" in the film *Signs* (par. 8).

If the author or creator of the Web site uses paragraph or page numbers, use these numbers in the parenthetical citation. If no numbering is used, do not use or add numbers to the paragraphs, pages, or parenthetical citation.

> When Web site does not number paragraphs➔ In his review of the film *Signs*, Roger Ebert says that Shyamalan "does what Hitchcock said he wanted to do, and plays the audience like a piano."

> When Web site numbers paragraphs➔ In his review of the film *Signs*, Roger Ebert says that Shyamalan "does what Hitchcock said he wanted to do, and plays the audience like a piano" (par. 8).

37e General formatting guidelines for the MLA Works Cited

If you cite any sources within a paper, be sure to include a Works Cited at the end of the paper. Here are some general formatting guidelines to follow when setting up a Works Cited.

1. Put the Works Cited at the end of your paper as a separate page.

2. Use one-inch margins on all sides.

3. Include any header used for the paper on the Works Cited.

4. Center the title Works Cited at the top of the page, using no underlining, quotation marks, or italics.

5. Place the first line of each entry flush left with the margin. Indent any additional lines of the entry one-half inch (or one tab).

6. Double space the entries in the Works Cited, not adding any extra spaces between entries.

7. Alphabetize the Works Cited. Use the first major word in each entry, not including articles such as *a, an,* or *the,* to determine the alphabetical order. If the cited source does not have an author, alphabetize by using the first word of the title of the source.

8. Put author's last name first (e.g., Ebert, Roger). Only reverse the first author's name. If more than one author, follow the first author's name with a comma, and add the other author names in the order of first then last names (e.g., Ebert, Roger, and Gene Siskel).

9. Use hyphens when you use more than one source from the same author. Alphabetize the titles, use the author's full name for the first entry, and then use three hyphens to replace the author's name in all entries after the first (see 37f3).

10. Capitalize all words in titles except for articles, conjunctions, and short prepositions. Always capitalize the first word of a subtitle.

11. Use quotation marks for titles of shorter works, including articles, book chapters, episodes on television or radio, poems, and short stories.

12. Italicize the titles of longer works, including album or CD titles, art pieces, books, films, journals, magazines, newspapers, and television shows.

13. Give the edition number for works with more than one edition (e.g., *MLA Handbook for Writers of Research Papers*, 7th edition).

14. Use the word *Print* after print sources and *Web* for Internet or Web sources.

37f   Formats for print sources

1. Books (includes brochures, pamphlets, and graphic novels)

Author's Name. *Title of Book*. Place of publication: Publisher, date of publication. Print.

> → Lansky, Doug. *Signspotting*. Oakland, CA: Lonely Planet, 2005. Print.

Helpful hint   Only use the state after the city if the city is not a place that would be commonly known or if there may be more than one commonly known city by that name.

2. Books with two or more authors

A comma is used between the author names, even if there are only two authors.

First Author's Name, and second Author's Name. *Title of Book*. Place
    of publication: Publisher, date of publication. Print.

> ➜ Maasik, Sonia, and Jack Soloman. *Signs of Life in the
>   USA: Readings on Popular Culture for Writers.* 6th
>   edition. Boston: Bedford/St. Martin's, 2008. Print.

3. Two books by the same author

Use three hyphens and a period in place of the author name(s) in the
consecutive entries. Be sure the entries are in alphabetical order.

> ➜ Maasik, Sonia, and Jack Soloman. *California Dreams and
>   Realities: Readings for Critical Thinkers and Writers.*
>   3rd edition. Boston: Bedford/St. Martin's, 2004. Print.

> ➜ ---. *Signs of Life in the USA: Readings on Popular Culture
>   for Writers.* 6th edition. Boston: Bedford/St. Martin's,
>   2008. Print.

4. Anthology or collection

Editor's Name(s), ed. *Title of Book*. Place of publication: Publisher,
    date. Print.

> ➜ Smith, Allison D., Trixie G. Smith, and Karen Wright,
>   eds. *COMPbiblio: Leaders and Influences in Composi-
>   tion Theory and Practice.* Southlake, TX: Fountain-
>   head Press, 2007. Print.

5. Work within an anthology

Author's Name. "Title of Work." *Title of Anthology*. Ed. Editor's Name(s). Place of publication: Publisher, date. Pages. Print.

→ Tan, Amy. "Mother Tongue." *The Norton Field Guide to Writing*. Ed. Richard Bullock, et al. New York: Norton, 2010. 564-70. Print.

6. Article in a scholarly journal

Author's Name. "Title of the Article." *Journal Title* vol. number (date of publication): pages. Print.

→ Holbrook, Teri. "An Ability Traitor at Work: A Treasonous Call to Subvert Writing from Within." *Qualitative Inquiry* 16.3 (2010): 171-83. Print.

7. Article in a scholarly journal that uses only issue numbers

Author's Name. "Title of the Article." *Journal Title* issue number (date of publication): pages. Print.

→ Franks, Lola. "The Play in Language." *Child Signs* 73 (2006): 3-17. Print.

8. Article in a newspaper

Author's Name. "Title of Article." *Newspaper Title* Day Month Year: pages. Print.

→ Genzlinger, Neil. "Autism is Another Thing that Families Share." *New York Times* 6 Apr. 2010: A4. Print.

Note: when citing English language newspapers, use the name on the masthead but be sure to omit any introductory article (*New York Times*, not *The New York Times*).

9. Article in a magazine

Author's Name. "Title of Article." *Magazine Title* Day Month Year: pages. Print.

Note: only use day if magazine is published on a weekly or bi-weekly basis.

➜ Musico, Christopher. "Sign 'Em Up!" *CRM Magazine* Nov. 2009: 49. Print.

10. Review

Reviewer's Name. "Title of Review." Rev. of *Title of Work*, by name of author (editor, director, etc.). *Journal or Newspaper Title* Day Month Year: pages. Print.

➜ Ebert, Roger. "A Monosyllabic Superhero Who Wouldn't Pass the Turing Test." Rev. of *X-Men Origins: Wolverine*, by Dir. Gavin Hood. *Chicago Sun-Times* 29 Apr. 2009: E4. Print.

11. Article in a reference book

Author's Name. "Title of Article." *Title of Reference Book*. Ed. Editor's Name. Location: Publisher, date. Pages. Print.

➜ Jones, Amber. "Semiotics." *Encyclopedia of Signs*. Ed. Jeffrey Haines and Maria Smith. Boston: Brown, 2003. 199-202. Print.

12. Religious works

Title of Work. Ed. Editor's Name. Place of publication: Publisher, date. Print.

➜ *Zondervan NIV Study Bible*. Fully rev. ed. Ed. Kenneth L. Barker. Grand Rapids, MI: Zondervan, 2002. Print.

37g Formats for online sources

> **Helpful hint**
>
> Including the URL is optional under the 7th edition of the *MLA Handbook for Writers of Research Papers*, so only include it after the "Date of Access" **in angle brackets** (<, >) if your source cannot be easily found by typing the author and title into a search engine or if your professor requires it.

1. Web site

Author's Name (if author given). *Name of Page.* Name of institution or organization associated with the Web site. Date of posting/revision. Web. Date of access.

→ *Services Locator.* United States Post Office. 2010. Web. 9 Feb. 2010.

2. Article on a Web site (including blogs and wikis)

Author's Name. "Article Title." *Name of Web site.* Name of institution or organization associated with the Web site. Date of posting/revision. Web. Date of access.

Note: If there is no author given, begin the citation with the article title.

→ "China's Traditional Dress: Qipao." *China Today.* Oct. 2001. Web. 9 Feb. 2010.

→ Ebert, Roger. "Signs." *rogerebert.com Movie Reviews. Chicago Sun-Times.* 2 Aug. 2002. Web. 9 Feb. 2010.

3. Online newspaper or magazine

Author's Name. "Title of Article." *Newspaper Title* Day Month Year: pages. Web. Date of access.

→ Bailey, Holly. "The Sign of the Red Truck." *Newsweek* 2007: 1. Web. 9 Feb. 2010.

4. Online journal article

Helpful hint If the online journal does not include page numbers, use *n. pag.* to indicate this.

Author's Name. "Title of Article." *Title of Journal* Vol. Issue (Year): pages. Web. Date of access.

➔ Austen, Veronica. "Writing Spaces: Performances of the Word." *Kairos* 8.1 (2003): n. pag. Web. 9 Feb. 2010.

5. Article from an online service, such as General One-File or LexisNexis

Author's Name. "Title of the Article." *Journal Title* vol. issue (Date of publication): pages. Name of database or other relevant information. Access Provider. Web. Date of access.

Franks, Elizabeth. "Signing Up for Trouble." *Semiotics and Signs* 13.4 (2009): 112-7. *InfoTrac OneFile.* Thomson Gale. Middle Tennessee State University. Web. 9 Feb. 2010.

6. Article from an online reference work

Author's (or editor's) Name. "Title of Article." *Title of Reference Work.* Location, Date of publication (Day Month Year). Web. Date of access (Day Month Year).

Jones, Amber. "Semiotics." *Encyclopedia of Signs.* U of AK, 20 Mar. 2009. Web. 21 Sept. 2010.

37h Formats for other commonly used sources

1. Television or radio program

"Title of Episode or Segment." *Title of Program or Series*. Name of network. Call letters and city of the local station (if applicable). Broadcast date. Medium of reception (e.g., Radio, Television). Supplemental information (e.g., Transcript).

➜ "Signs and Wonders." *The X Files*. FOX. 23 Jan. 2000. Television.

2. Sound recording

Artist/Band. "Song Title." *Title of Album*. Manufacturer, year of issue. Medium (e.g., Audiocassette, CD, Audiotape, LP, Digital download).

➜ Five Man Electrical Band. "Signs." *Good-byes and Butterflies*. Lionel Records, 1970. LP.

➜ Tesla. "Signs." *Five Man Acoustical Jam*. Geffen, 1990. CD.

3. Film

Title. Dir. Director's Name. Perf. Actor's Name(s) (if relevant). Distributor, year of release. Medium.

➜ *Signs*. Dir. M. Night Shyamalan. Perf. Mel Gibson. Touchstone, 2002. Film.

You may also include other information about the film, such as the names of the writers, performers, and producers, after the director's name.

➜ *Signs*. Dir. M. Night Shyamalan. Perf. Mel Gibson. Ex. Prod. Kathleen Kennedy. Touchstone, 2002. Film.

If you would like to highlight the specific contribution of one actor, director, or writer, you may begin the entry with that person's name, as you do with an author for a book.

➔ Phoenix, Joaquin, perf. *Signs*. Dir. M. Night Shyamalan. Touchstone, 2002. Film.

4. Advertisement

Name of product, company, or institution. Advertisement. Publisher date of publication. Medium of publication.

➔ SunChips. Advertisement. *Newsweek* 15 Jan. 2010: 33. Print.

➔ SunChips. Advertisement. NBC. 15 Jan. 2010. Television.

Note the difference in how the citations for print and television advertisements are formatted.

5. Painting, sculpture, or photograph

Artist's Name. *Title*. Creation date (if known). Medium of Composition. Name of institution that houses the work or the individual who owns the work, City.

➔ da Vinci, Leonardo. *Mona Lisa*. c. 1503-6. Oil on Poplar. Louvre, Paris.

6. Interview

Interviewee's Name. Descriptive Title of Interview (e.g., Personal, Telephone, Webcam). Date of interview.

➔ Elbow, Peter. Personal Interview. 1 Jan. 2009.

7. Lecture, speech, address, or reading

Author's Name. "Title of Speech." Relevant information of where
speech was given. Date of presentation. Descriptive label (e.g.,
Lecture, Speech, Address, Reading).

→ Stephens, Liberty. "The Signs of the Times." MLA
    Annual Convention. Hilton Downtown, New York.
    28 Dec. 2009. Address.

37i   Sample Works Cited using MLA

Following is an example of how a completed Works Cited would look
at the end of your paper.

Your Last name 14

Works Cited

Ebert, Roger. "Signs." *rogerebert.com Movie Reviews. Chicago*

Sun-Times. 2 Aug. 2002. Web. 9 Feb. 2010.

Five Man Electrical Band. "Signs." *Good-byes and Butterflies.*

Lionel Records, 1970. LP.

Signs. Dir. M. Night Shyamalan. Perf. Mel Gibson. Touchstone,

2002. Film.

Stephens, Liberty. "The Signs of the Times." MLA Annual

Convention. Hilton Downtown, New York. 28 Dec. 2009.

Address.

APA Documentation

When you do research to find supporting evidence for your ideas or arguments, you need to credit your outside sources. Depending on what type of essay you are writing or which type of course you are writing for, you will need to choose a type of documentation style and continue with that style for the entire essay. Two of the most common styles, especially for freshman and sophomore students, are MLA (Modern Language Association) and APA (American Psychological Association).

If you write an essay in the social sciences, you will usually be asked to use documentation guidelines created by the American Psychological Association. The *Publication Manual of the American Psychological Association*, in its sixth edition, provides a full description of the conventions used by this particular community of writers; updates to the APA manual can be found at <www.apastyle.org>.

Did You Know?

The American Psychological Association was founded in 1892 at Clark University. The APA, now with over 152,000 members, is the primary professional association for social science scholars in the United States.

This chapter provides a general overview of APA documentation style and an explanation of the most commonly used APA documentation formats.

38a   Using APA in-text citations

In-text citations (also called *parenthetical citations*) point readers to where they can find more information about your researched supporting materials. In APA documentation style, the author's last name (or the title of the work, if no author is listed) and the date of publication must appear in the body text of your paper. The author's name can appear either in the sentence itself or in parentheses following the quotation or paraphrase. The date of publication can appear either in the sentence itself, surrounded by parentheses, or in the parentheses that follow the quotation or paraphrase. The page number(s) always appears in the parentheses following a quotation or close paraphrase.

Your parenthetical citation should give enough information to identify the source that was used for the research material as the same source that is listed in your References list. Where this in-text information is placed depends on how you want to phrase the sentence that is summarized, paraphrased, or quoted. Be sure that the in-text citation guides the reader clearly to the source in the References list, where complete information about the source is given.

The following are some of the most common examples of in-text citations.

1. Author's name and date in reference

When using a parenthetical reference to a single source by a single author, use this form: (Author's Last name, Year of publication). Note that the period is placed after the parenthetical element ends.

→   When a teenager sleeps more than 10 hours per night, it is time to question whether she is having significant problems (Jones, 1999).

2. Author's name and date in text

In APA, you can also give the author's name and date within the sentence, using this form: Author's Full Name (Year of publication)

→ Stephanie Jones (1999) describes the signs to look for and when to be concerned.

3. Using a partial quotation in text

When you cite a specific part of a source, give the page number, using *p.* (for one page) and *pp.* (for two or more pages).

→ Stephanie Jones (1999) describes the signs parents should look for when concerned about their children: "excessive sleeping, refraining from eating, and lying about simple things" (p. 63).

4. No author given

When a work has no credited author, use the first two or three words of the work's title or the name that begins the entry in the References list. The title of an article or chapter should be in quotation marks, and the title of a book or periodical should be in italics. Inside the parenthetical citation, place a comma between the title and year.

→ In a recent *Time* article, a list of 30 common signs of teenage trouble cites lack of sleep as the most common sign ("Thirty," 2010).

5. Two to five authors given

When you use a source that was written by two to five authors, you must use all the names in the citation. For the in-text citation, when a work has two authors, use both names each time the reference occurs in the text. When a work has three to five authors, give all authors the first time the reference occurs in the text, and then, in subsequent citations, use only the surname of the first author followed by *et al.* (Latin for "and others") and the year for the first citation of the reference in a paragraph.

→ The idea that "complexity is a constant in biology" is not an innovative one (Sole & Goodwin, 1997, p. 63).

The last two authors' names in a string of three to five authors are separated by a comma and an ampersand (e.g., Jones, Smith, Black, & White).

→ Most signs in English that the authors encountered on the road had "grammar mistakes, misspellings, or just odd pictures" (Smith, Jones, & Best, 1999, p. 55). The most common mistake was an "incorrect or misplaced apostrophe" (Smith, et al., p. 56).

6. Six or more authors given

When there are six authors or more of an item to be cited, include only the first author's name followed by *et al.* (Latin for "and others"). Use this form for the first reference of this text and all references of this text after that. Note: be sure, though, to list all six or more of the authors in your References list.

→ In Hong Kong, most signs are in Chinese and English; however, once you are in mainland China, English is rarely found on signs, except in tourist areas (Li, et al., 2007).

7. Authors with the same last names

If your source material includes items by authors who happen to have the same last name, be sure to use each author's initials in all text citations.

→ When a teenager sleeps more than 10 hours per night, it is time to question whether she is having significant problems (S. Jones, 1999, p. 63).

→ Another sign of trouble can be when you do not see your child for meals (B. Jones, 2003, p. 114).

8. Encyclopedia or dictionary unsigned entry

When you use an encyclopedia or dictionary to look up a word or entry, be sure to include the word or entry title in the parenthetical entry.

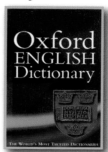

→ The word *thing* has more definitions than any other entry in the *Oxford English Dictionary* ("thing," 2001).

9. Indirect quotation

When you use a quotation of a quotation—that is, a quotation that quotes from another source—use "as cited in" to designate the secondary source.

→ Smith has said, "My parents really didn't understand me" (as cited in Jones, 1990, p. 64).

10. Personal communication

Personal communications—private letters, memos, non-archived emails, interviews—are usually considered unrecoverable information and, as such, are not included in the References list. However, you do include them in parenthetical form in the text, giving the initials and surname of the communicator and providing as exact a date as possible.

→ A. D. Smith (personal communication, February 2, 2010)

→ J. Elbow (personal interview, January 6, 2009)

38b   Using long or block quotations

Long or block quotations have special formatting requirements of their own. If your quotation is prose and longer than 40 words, this is called a *block quotation*. Follow these APA guidelines for block quotations.

1. If introducing the block quotation with a sentence, use a colon at the end of the sentence.

2. Begin the quotation on a new line.

3. Do not use quotation marks to enclose the block quote.

4. Indent the quote five spaces from the left margin, and extend the right margin to the end of the line.

5. Double space the entire quotation.

6. Indent the first line of any additional paragraph.

7. Put a period at the end of the quotation, and then add the parenthetical citation.

➜ However, Lansky (1999) states:

> Despite the statement on <www.signspotting.com> that we don't accept signs with the intention of being funny, people like sending them in. I've opted not to use these as it could encourage people to start making them, sticking them up in their driveway, and snapping a picture. Plus, funny signs are so much more amusing when the humor is accidental. (p. 72)

38c   Adding or omitting words in a quotation

1. Adding words in a quotation

Use square brackets ([ ]) to point out words or phrases that are not part of the original text.

➜ Original quotation: "When we entered the People's Republic of China, we noticed that the signage began dropping English translations" (Donelson, 2001, p. 141).

➜ Quotation with added word: She said, "When we entered the People's Republic of China, [Dunkirk and I] noticed that the signage began dropping English translations" (Donelson, 2001, p. 141).

You can also add your own comments inside a quotation by using square brackets. For example, you can add the word *sic* to a quotation when you know that there is an error.

➜ Original quotation: "When we entered the People's Repulic of China, we noticed that the signage began dropping English translations" (Donelson, 2001, p. 141).

➜ Quotation with added comment: She said, "When we entered the People's Repulic [sic] of China, we noticed that the signage began dropping English translations" (Donelson, 2001, p. 141).

2. Omitting words in a quotation

Use an ellipsis (. . .) to represent words that you delete from a quotation. The ellipsis begins with a space, then has three periods with spaces between them, and then ends with a space.

Original quotation➜ "The Great Wall is something that can be seen from space. When we reach a time when advertisements can be seen from space, we have probably gone too far" (Jones, 1993, p. 101).

Quotation with words omitted in middle of sentence➜ Frank Jones, author of *Signs in Space*, remarks, "The Great Wall . . . can be seen from space. When we reach a time when advertisements can be seen from space, we have probably gone too far" (1993, p. 101).

If you omit words at the end of a quotation, and that is also the end of your sentence, you should use an ellipsis plus a period with no space before the ellipsis or after the period. Only use an ellipsis if words have been omitted.

Original quotation➜ "The Great Wall is something that can be seen from space. When we reach a time when advertisements can be seen from space, we have probably gone too far with our advertising and signage" (Jones, 1993, p. 45).

Quotation with words omitted at end of sentence➜ Frank Jones, author of *Signs in Space*, remarks, "The Great Wall is something that can be seen from space. When we reach a time when advertisements can be seen from space, we have probably gone too far . . ." (1993, p. 45).

Helpful hint

APA guidelines can change with a new edition. Sometimes, class textbooks can use an older APA documentation style. Always check with your instructor if rules seem to be in conflict.

38d   Citing online sources

In the APA documentation style, online or electronic sources have their own formatting guidelines since these types of sources rarely give specific page numbers.

The APA recommends that you include in the text, rather than in an in-text citation, the name(s) of the person that begins the matching References list entry. If the author or creator of the Web site uses paragraph or page numbers, use these numbers in the parenthetical citation. If no numbering is used, do not use or add numbers to the paragraphs, pages, or parenthetical citation.

When Web site does not number paragraphs➜ In his review of the film *Signs*, Roger Ebert says that Shyamalan "does what Hitchcock said he wanted to do, and plays the audience like a piano."

When Web site numbers paragraphs➜ In his review of the file *Signs*, Roger Ebert says that Shyamalan "does what Hitchcock said he wanted to do, and plays the audience like a piano" (para. 8).

38e   General formatting guidelines for the APA References list

If you cite any sources within a paper, be sure to include a References list at the end of the paper. Here are some general formatting guidelines to follow when setting up a References list.

1. Put the References list at the end of your paper as a separate page.

2. Use one-inch margins on all sides.

3. Include any header used for the paper on the References page.

4. Center the title **References** at the top of the page, using no underlining, quotation marks, or italics.

5. Place the first line of each entry flush left with the margin. Indent any additional lines of the entry one-half inch (or one tab) to form a hanging indent.

6. Double space the entries in the References list, not adding any extra spaces between entries.

7. Alphabetize the References list. Use the first major word in each entry, not including articles such as *a, an,* or *the,* to determine the alphabetical order. If the cited source does not have an author, alphabetize by using the first word of the title of the source.

8. Put author's last name first and then the initial representing the author's first name and the initial for the author's middle name, if given (e.g., Ebert, R.). If a work has more than one author, invert all the authors' names, follow each with a comma, and then continue listing all the authors, putting a comma and ampersand (,&) before the final name (e.g., Ebert, R., & Siskel, G.).

9. Arrange two or more works by the same author(s) in the same name order by year of publication.

10. Capitalize only the first word in a title and a subtitle unless the title or subtitle includes a proper noun, which would also be capitalized.

11. Do not use quotation marks for titles of shorter works, including articles, book chapters, episodes on television or radio, poems, and short stories.

12. Italicize the titles of longer works, including album or CD titles, art pieces, books, films, journals, magazines, newspapers, and television shows.

13. Give the edition number for works with more than one edition [e.g., *Publication manual of the American Psychological Association* (6th ed.)].

14. Include the DOI (digital object identifier), a unique alpha-numeric string assigned by a registration agency that helps identify content and provides a link to the source online. All DOI numbers begin with a *10* and contain a prefix and suffix separated by a slash (for example, 10.11037/0278-6133.27.3.379). The DOI is usually found in the citation detail or on the first page of an electronic journal article near the copyright notice.

CITATION DETAIL WITH DOI

stet Detail

Title:

An Ability Traitor at Work: A Treasonous Call to Subvert *Writing* From Within.

Authors:

Holbrook, Teri[1] *tholbrook@gsu.edu*

Source:

Qualitative Inquiry; Mar2010, Vol. 16 Issue 3, p171-183, 13p

Document Type:

Article

Subject Terms:

*DISABILITIES

*QUALITATIVE research

*MANAGEMENT science

*SIGN language

*WRITING

Author-Supplied Keywords:

assemblage

disability

multigenre

multimodal writing

NAICS/Industry Codes:

541930 Translation and Interpretation Services

Abstract:

In questioning conventional qualitative research methods, St. Pierre asked, "What else might *writing* do except mean?" The author answers, it oppresses. Co-opting the race traitor figurative, she calls on qualitative researchers to become "ability traitors" who interrogate how a valuable coinage of their trade—the written word—is used to rank and categorize individuals with troubling effects. In this article, she commits three betrayals: (a) multigenre *writing* that undermines the authoritative text; (b) assemblage as a method of analysis that deprivileges the written word; and (c) a gesture toward a dis/comfort text intended to take up Lather's example of challenging the "usual ways of making sense." In committing these betrayals, the author articulates her "traitorous agenda" designed to interrogate assumptions about inquiry, power, equity, and *writing* as practice-as-usual. [ABSTRACT FROM AUTHOR]

Author Affiliations:
    [1]Georgia State University
ISSN:
    10778004
DOI:
    10.1177/1077800409351973
Accession Number:
    47934623
Database:
    Academic Search Premier
View Links:
    Find Fulltext

38f   Formats for print sources

1. Books (includes brochures, pamphlets, and graphic novels)

Author's Last name, Author's Initial of first name. (Year of publication). *Title of book*. Place of publication: Publisher.

➔ Lansky, D. (2005). *Signspotting*. Oakland, CA: Lonely Planet.

Helpful hint

Only use the state after the city if the city is not a place that would be commonly known or if there may be more than one commonly known city by that name.

2. Books with two or more authors

A comma is used between the author names, even if there are only two authors.

First Author's Last name, First author's Initial of first name, & Second author's Last name, Second author's Initial of first name. (year of publication). *Title of book*. Place of publication: Publisher.

➔ Maasik, S., & Soloman, J. (2008). *Signs of life in the USA: Readings on popular culture for writers*. Boston, MA: Bedford/St. Martin's.

3. Two books by the same author

Be sure the entries are in sequential time order with earliest date first.

➔ Maasik, S., & Soloman, J. (2004). *California dreams and realities: Readings for critical thinkers and writers* (3rd ed.). Boston, MA: Bedford/St. Martin's.

➔ Maasik, S., & Soloman, J. (2008). *Signs of life in the USA: Readings on popular culture for writers*. Boston, MA: Bedford/St. Martin's.

4. Anthology or collection

Editor's Last name, Editor's Initial of first name. (Ed). (Year of publication). *Title of book*. Place of publication: Publisher.

➔ Smith, A. D., Smith, T. G., & Wright, K. (Eds.). (2007). *COMPbiblio: Leaders and influences in composition theory and practice*. Southlake, TX: Fountainhead.

5. Work within an anthology or collection

Author's Last name, Author's Initial of first name. (Year of publication). Title of work. In Editor's Name(s) (Ed.) *Title of anthology* (page numbers). Place of publication: Publisher.

➔ Tan, A. (2010). Mother tongue. In R. Bullock, M. D. Goggin, & F. Weinberg (Eds.). *The Norton field guide to writing* (pp. 564-70). New York, NY: Norton.

6. Article in a scholarly journal without DOI (digital object identifier)

Include the issue number if the journal is paginated by issue. If there is not a DOI available and the article was found online, give the URL of the journal home page.

Author's Last name, Author's Initial of first name. (Year of publication). Title of the article. *Journal Title, volume number* (issue number), pages. URL (if retrieved online).

➔ Holbrook, T. (2010). An ability traitor at work: A treasonous call to subvert writing from within. *Qualitative Inquiry, 16* (3), 171-183. Retrieved from E-Journals database.

7. Article in a scholarly journal with DOI (digital object identifier)

Author's Last name, Author's Initial of first name. (Year of publication). Title of the article. *Journal Title, volume number* (issue number), pages. doi:

➔ Franks, L. (2006). The play in language. *Child Signs, 73*(1), 3-17. doi:10.1770/69873629

8. Article in a newspaper

Use *p.* or *pp.* before the page numbers in references of newspapers.

Note: if the newspaper article appears on discontinuous pages, be sure to give all the page numbers, separating them with a comma (e.g., pp. A4, A10, A13-14).

Author's Last name, Author's Initial of first name. (Year of publication, Month and Date of publication). Title of article. *Newspaper Title*, pp. page numbers.

➔ Genzlinger, N. (2010, April 6). Autism is another thing that families share. *The New York Times*, p. A4.

9. Article in a magazine

Author's Last name, Author's Initial of first name. (Year of publication, Month of publication). Title of article. *Magazine Title, volume number* (issue number), pages.

Note: only use day if magazine is published on a weekly or bi-weekly basis.

➔ Musico, C. (2009, November). Sign 'em up! *CRM Magazine, 13*(11), 49.

10. Review

Be sure to identify the type of work being reviewed by noting if it is a book, film, television program, painting, song, or other creative work. If the work is a book, include the author name(s) after the book title, separated by a comma. If the work is a film, song, or other media, be sure to include the year of release after the title of the work, separated by a comma.

Reviewer's Last name, Reviewer's Initial of first name. (Year of publication, Month and Date of Publication). Title of review [Review of the work *Title of work*, by Author's Name]. *Magazine or Journal Title, volume number* (issue number), pp. page numbers. doi number (if available).

➜ Turken, R. (2008, May 5). Life outside of the box. [Review of the film *Signs*, 2002]. *Leisure Times*, pp. A12.

11. Article in a reference book

Author's Last name, Author's Initial of first name. (Year of publication). Title of chapter or entry. In A. Editor (Ed). *Title of book* (pp. xx-xx). Location: Publisher.

➜ Jones, A. (2003). Semiotics. In B. Smith, R. Lore, and T. Rex (Eds.). *Encyclopedia of signs* (pp. 199-202). Boston, MA: Rutledge.

12. Religious and classical works

In APA, classical religious works, such as the Bible and the Qur'an, and major classical works that originated in Latin or Greek, are not required to have entries in the References list but should include reference to the text within the sentence in the essay. Note: it is always a good idea to check with your instructor on this type of entry since there can be some variety across instructors and schools.

38g Formats for online sources

1. Web site

The documentation form for a Web site can also be used for online message, blog, or video posts.

Author's Last name, Author's Initial of first name (if author given). (Year, Month Day). *Title of page* [Description of form]. Retrieved from http://www.xxxx

➜ United States Post Office (2010). *United States Post Office Services Locator* [search engine]. Retrieved from http://usps.whitepages.com/post_office

2. Article from a Web site, online newspaper, blog, or wiki (with author given)

Author's Last name, Author's Initial of first name. (Year, Month Day of publication). Title of article. *Name of Webpage/Journal/Newspaper*. Retrieved from http://www.xxxxxxx

➔ Ebert, R. (2002, August 2). Signs. *Chicago Sun-Times*. Retrieved from http://rogerebert.suntimes.com/

3. Article from a Web site, online newspaper, blog, or wiki (with no author given)

Title of article. (Year, Month Day of publication). *Name of Webpage/Journal/Newspaper*. Retrieved from http://www.xxxxxxx

➔ China's traditional dress: Qipao. (2001, October). *China Today*. Retrieved from http://chinatoday.com

4. Online journal article

The reference for an online journal article is set up the same way as for a print one, including the DOI.

Author's Last name, Author's Initial of first name. (Year of publication). Title of the article. *Journal Title, volume number* (issue number), pages. doi:xxxxxxxxxxx

➔ Franks, L. (2006). The play in language. *Child Signs, 73*(1), 3-17. doi:10.1770/69873629

If a DOI is not assigned to content you have retrieved online, use the home page URL for the journal or magazine in the reference (e.g., Retrieved from http://www.xxxxxx).

➔ Austen, V. (2003). Writing spaces: Performance of the word. *Kairos*. Retrieved from http://kairos.com

5. Article from an online service, such as General One-File, LexisNexis, JSTOR, ERIC

When using APA, it is not necessary to include database information as long as you can include the publishing information required in a normal citation. Note: this is quite different from using MLA documentation, which requires full information about the database.

6. Article in an online reference work

Author's Last name, Author's Initial of first name. (Year of publication). Title of chapter or entry. In A. Editor (Ed). *Title of book.* Retrieved from http://xxxxxxxxxx

➜ Jones, A. (2003). Semiotics. In B. Smith, R. Lore, and T. Rex (Eds.). *Encyclopedia of signs.* Retrieved from http://brown.edu/signs

38h Formats for other commonly used sources

1. Television or radio program (single episode)

Writer' Last name, Writer's Initial of first name. (Writer), & Director's Last name, Director's Initial of first name. (Director). (Year). Title of episode [Television/Radio series episode]. In Executive Producer's name (Executive Producer), *Title of show.* Place: Network.

➜ Bell, J. (Writer), Carter, C. (Creator), & Manners, K. (Director). (2000). Signs and wonders [Television series episode]. In C. Carter (Executive Producer), *The X files.* New York, NY: FOX.

2. Sound recording

Writer's Last name, Writer's Initial of first name. (Copyright year). Title of song. [Recorded by Artist's name if different from writer]. On *Title of album* [Medium of recording]. Location: Label. (Date of recording if different from song copyright date).

➜ Emmerson, L. (1970). Signs. [Recorded by Five Man Electrical Band]. On *Good-byes and butterflies* [LP]. New York, NY: Lionel Records.

➜ Emmerson, L. (1970). Signs. [Recorded by Tesla]. On *Five man acoustical jam* [CD]. New York, NY: Geffen. 1990.

3. Film

Producer's Last name, Producer's Initial of first name. (Producer), & Director's Last name, Director's Initial of first name. (Director). (Year). *Title of film* [Motion picture]. Country of Origin: Studio.

➔ Kennedy, K. (Producer), & Shyamalan, M. N. (Director). (2002). *Signs* [film]. USA: Touchstone.

4. Painting, sculpture, or photograph

Artist's Last name, Artist's Initial of first name. (Year, Month Day). *Title of material*. [Description of material]. Name of collection (if available). Name of Repository, Location.

➔ Gainsborough, T. (1745). *Conversation in a park*. [Oil painting on canvas]. Louvre, Paris, France.

5. Personal interview

Unlike MLA documentation, personal interviews and other types of personal communication are not included in APA References lists. Be sure to cite personal communications in the text only.

6. Lecture, speech, address, or reading

Speaker's Last name, Speaker's Initial of first name. (Year, Month). Title of speech. *Event name*. Lecture conducted from Sponsor, Location.

➔ Stephens, L. (2009, December). The signs of the times. *MLA annual convention*. Lecture conducted from Hilton Hotel Downtown, New York, NY.

38i   Sample References list using APA

Following is an example of how a completed References list would look
at the end of your ≥paper.

Your Last name 14

References

Emmerson, L. (1970). Signs. [Recorded by Five Man Electrical

Band]. On *Good-byes and butterflies* [LP]. New York,

NY: Lionel Records.

Franks, L. (2006). The play in language. *Child Signs*, 73(1), 3-17.

doi:10.1770/69873629

Jones, A. (2003). Semiotics. In B. Smith, R. Lore, and T. Rex

(Eds.). *Encyclopedia of signs*. Retrieved from

http://brown.edu/signs

Kennedy, K. (Producer), & Shyamalan, M. N. (Director). (2002).

Signs [film]. USA: Touchstone.

Lansky, D. (2005). *Signspotting*. Oakland, CA: Lonely Planet.

Stephens, L. (2009, December). The signs of the times. *MLA*

annual convention. Lecture conducted from Hilton Hotel

Downtown, New York, NY.

Tan, A. (2010). Mother tongue. In R. Bullock, M. D. Goggin, &

F. Weinberg (Eds.). *The Norton field guide to writing* (pp.

564-70). New York, NY: Norton.

Clark, Moira Catherine. *Hustle and Bustle.*

8

WRITING IN THE
WRITING STUDIO

Calm, Coffee, and Conversation

Transitioning from high school or workplace writing to college writing can feel daunting. Despite everything this textbook offers to help construct cohesive, rhetorically-sound essays and other texts, the chapters herein can't fully address the anxiety you feel when faced with the dreaded flashing cursor at the beginning of a blank document. Truthfully, all writers face roadblocks prior to or during the writing process; a distracting environment, lack of confidence, and a shortage of resources constitute just a few. That's why Georgia State University offers students free, one-on-one writing assistance at the GSU Writing Studio.

Perched high on the 24th floor of the 25 Park Place building (which is located at the corner of Park Place and Edgewood Avenue, overlooking Woodruff Park), the Georgia State University Writing Studio is an open, airy place featuring floor-to-ceiling windows which provide its patrons an inspiring opportunity to pause and reflect

The GSU Writing Studio is located on the 24th floor of 25 Park Place in Room 2420.

while looking out at the city from the midst of Atlanta's towering skyline. It's also a place that offers free coffee and tea each time you visit. Though personal assistance is the Writing Studio's main function, students can also borrow laptops (in exchange for their Panther ID) and work freely within this quiet, productive space. You might see a game like Scrabble™ open on the coffee table in the waiting area, and you'll definitely find various writing resources filling the bookshelves throughout the room. Essentially, the Writing Studio is just what its name denotes—a Studio, a place where the lighting, temperature, aroma, and soft hum of conversation unite so that each writer can feel inspired and create.

To assist with that creative process, the Writing Studio is staffed with approximately 35 writing experts prepared to help answer any of your writing inquiries. Our staff primarily consists of graduate students, some of whom teach English at Georgia State, as well as undergraduate English majors who have taken GSU's peer-tutoring class. While you have the luxury of selecting your tutor by reviewing profiles online, you can also benefit from choosing those who have actually taken the courses you're in, are teaching them, or simply have years of experience tutoring college writing. And, no matter who ends up tutoring you, that person will certainly embody the calm, competent, and above all, confident Writing Studio environment, as explained by KaTerra Smith, a first-year student majoring in psychology:

> Our tutors are a diverse group, and our experiences help us serve you better. Many of us have degrees and work experience in areas outside of English, including film studies, biology, public health, history, and art. Some of us have even written extensively in the areas in which you are writing. While all tutors could successfully help you with any writing project, you might find someone with just the skills and experience you need by accessing the tutor profiles at the writing center website.
>
> Pam Logan, Tutor, M.A. in Literature

"Although the Writing Studio is an academic environment, it does not feel like one. The tutors do not make you feel any less than a student who simply needs some extra help developing a strong piece of writing."

Beyond the environment and assistance, the Writing Studio also provides an approach to teaching that is different than what you will find in a classroom setting. Similar to students' instructors, tutors at the Studio are trained to assist students by appealing to a strong understanding of rhetoric and years of writing experience. However, because writing tutors do not grade students' papers, students who visit the Studio can benefit from speaking to a peer, rather than a traditional authority figure. Also, while we always encourage students to visit their instructors during office hours, tutors are able to offer more timeslots during the week for which students can meet. This dynamic allows students to make the agenda of each session, choosing what they want to work on and when, and asking questions that are most pertinent to them.

To help you learn more about the ways in which the GSU Writing Studio can help you improve as a writer, let's take a look at all the various options one-on-one tutoring allows for students.

Six Reasons to Visit the Writing Studio

We Welcome Any Stage of the Writing Process

Earlier in the book, you read about "Inventing," "Writing," and "Revising Rhetorically." These stages are what many researchers consider the main components of the writing process, despite the misconception that the process only begins once initial drafting has commenced. So, what do these stages look like in the Writing

Studio? And, what priorities should each be assigned given the mandatory time limits for each tutoring session? A pioneer in the field of composition, Donald Murray, suggests invention, or pre-writing, "takes about 85% of the writer's time" (4). While there is no definitive answer as to how much time one should give to pre-writing, Murray's claim does align with what most writing experts know: the quality of ideas tend to be worthy of more attention than the correction of spelling, grammar, and punctuation. Therefore, no matter where you find yourself in the writing process, it is useful to consider dividing questions you have for your tutor into Higher-Order Concerns (HOCs) and Lower-Order Concerns (LOCs).

> In great writing, what happens on the page always begins long before a single word is written.
>
> Randall Harrell, Tutor
> M.A. in Literature

Identifying specific topics you need to address empowers both you and the tutor to make the best use of your time together, regardless of whether or not you approach the session with a blank page or a complete draft. Understanding the difference between HOCs and LOCs, or what often carries more weight within your rhetorical situation, eases this process considerably. Higher-Order Concerns require you to look at your paper macroscopically, questioning the structure of your paragraphs and asking yourself if they refer cohesively back to your thesis statement; reviewing your purpose and audience and double-checking how well you have addressed each; and finally, leveling with yourself about whether or not you have done everything in your power to form and develop strong ideas. Further down the priority list, Lower-Order Concerns ask writers to approach their paper microscopically, verifying solid sentence structure, auditing word choice, and ensuring

> After I got back my first essay in my English 1101 class, I knew I needed major help with my writing. I took the paper I had done so poorly on into the writing studio and quickly got the help I needed. Once I got my next essay assignment, I quickly made appointments at the writing studio and got the help I needed from the outline of my paper through the final revisions. The writing studio has helped me turn my writing around, and I can bet I will be using this resource as I progress at Georgia State.
>
> Nicole Berne, Freshman
> Early Childhood Education

that spelling, grammar, and punctuation are as polished as one can make them (see tutor Randall Harrell's elaboration on writing priorities below). Both sets of writing concerns are important and can help you determine exactly where you are in the writing process. Finding and understanding your location in this process and what you would like to work on makes for the most productive sessions. If, however, you are not quite sure what your priorities should be, the Writing Studio's tutors can work with you to figure them out.

Tutor Randall Harrall on Writing Priorities

Writing that is out of focus is not convincing. Because of this, tutors at the Writing Studio tend to favor focused and organized writing over writing free of grammatical errors. Though grammar is an important concern, we are most concerned with helping the student develop a cohesive paper (as are most professors). A cohesive paper is one with a controlling idea (whether implicit or explicit), content that supports that central claim, and a structure that is organized with intentional paragraph breaks and transitions. These are what we refer to as global issues. In my own writing, I like to ask myself if the paper works. Do my paragraphs follow a convincing and logical order? Do I actually follow through and fulfill the expectations of the reader? These are questions that we might ask a student during a session. We might question the paper's intention, effectiveness, tone, voice, rhetorical moves, etc. We will also ask general questions: how do you feel about your paper so far; where do you feel like your paper needs the most attention; where do you feel your paper is strongest; and what would you like to work on today. There is a line that separates the writer's expectations and the writing's needs. At the Writing Studio, we attempt to blur that line as much as possible.

Activity 8.1 Editing for Lower-Order Concerns

1. On a blank sheet of paper, draw three columns.

2. Begin reading the paper without regard for its content. Observe the sentence structure, the use of punctuation, spelling, subject-verb agreement, and other grammatical concerns.

3. If you notice a concern, stop, and write it down in the first column.

4. In the second column, draft the correct form of the word, phrase, or sentence in question.

5. Finally, in the last column, write the rule you used to correct the error.

For a peer review exercise, we recommend identifying no more than three different writing concerns. That way, writers can use the columns and practice those rules with their current essay. For the next paper, they can add three more rules to the list. This exercise helps facilitate long-term improvement.

We Provide One-on-One Feedback

Though offering one-on-one feedback might be an obvious advantage of the Writing Studio, the change in dynamic from the classroom that this represents is too significant not to discuss. In many high schools, various circumstances like standardized testing and district requirements construct a narrow view of the writing process—one that happens in relative isolation. Teachers teach material, asking students to draft a response to an assignment and submit that assignment for a grade. While this approach might still be common in some classrooms, most composition theorists maintain the notion that "writing and learning to write" are naturally collaborative activities (Gillespie and Lerner). Whether the text has one or two names in the byline, writers always speak

"The best part about such a relaxed environment is that it breaks down the "teacher/ student" barrier and allows you to be completely interactive."

KaTerra Smith

with others about their ideas and get feedback before committing those ideas to a page. Even prior to being given an assignment, most writers go through life developing their ideas based off previous interactions and experiences. In other words, talking with someone about your work is just as much a part of the writing process as the act of writing itself.

At the Writing Studio, you have access to those important conversations. Regardless of how strong or weak of a writer you are, speaking with others about your writing provides some degree of insight into the minds of your audience and affords a perspective distanced from your personal biases. Writing tutors stand particularly equipped to recognize areas of concern, not just because of their expertise in composition, but also because their eyes are simply fresher than the writer's when it comes to the subject and the ideas at hand. Finally, seeking one-on-one feedback from a Writing Studio tutor allows your writing instruction to be personalized; you have thirty minutes to ask only the questions you need answered with a tutor committed to helping you achieve your personal writing goals.

"With the help of another person guiding me through the brainstorming process, my ideas seem to naturally fall onto the paper. I benefitted from the Studio by having a second or third eye read my paper. The tutors take my work seriously and make me feel more confident turning in my paper."

Justin Jones, Freshman
Psychology

We Welcome Any Genre of Writing

Today, people are publishing more than ever before. Bloggers are redefining what it means to be an "expert" and journalists are relaying information by the second. The world is shrinking with the help of innovative, real-time translation software. Every field, from engineering to biology, is increasing its demand for employees with strong communication

skills. In response to these expectations, universities have developed programs that require the inclusion of writing assignments in core classes outside of the humanities. Science, Technology, Engineering, and Math (STEM) students, for example, are no longer exempt from communication-focused tasks.

Fortunately, as you have learned in this book, writing is a rhetorical act; the writer must consider audience, purpose, and context when considering how to communicate a message effectively. This applies to any and all writing tasks that you will ever encounter—not just those assigned in English 1101 and 1102.

Consequently, understanding rhetoric allows both writers and tutors to work toward any writing goal, including but not limited to papers for other subjects in the humanities, reports involving the sciences, memos for business writing, and personal statements for graduate school, résumés, and even emails to professors. And don't forget that the writing skills you work on for one assignment (general things like concision or idea development) can easily be taken with you as you approach a new task in a completely different genre. Pam Logan, another tutor at the Writing Studio, elaborates on this by explaining:

"Techniques that are useful to create good writing in English are still useful when writing about the sciences or technology. The transfer-ability of writing skills and practices makes your tutor able to help with projects in economics, philosophy, or any other subject."

Therefore, the Writing Studio encourages students to visit through-out their college careers whenever they begin to navigate the specific writing conventions of their chosen major.

Tutor Pam Logan on Writing Genres

Everyone, including people who love to write and those who are just writing because they have to, should feel free to stop by. Students come to the studio with a variety of writing projects. On a single morning, I have worked on a research paper about planets, an economics cost analysis, a personal narrative on a grandparent's lifestyle in the 1930's, and a study of students' opinions about a slow elevator in a residence hall. As you can see, we work on all genres of writing in the studio. While it can be challenging to work on topics in which we are not experts, tutors enjoy learning new things from students. I think most tutors will agree that the most exciting part of our job is the challenge to continually learn.

Activity 8.2 For Organization

Exercise #1: Read the introduction and conclusion. Both should function, on their own, to tell the reader what the paper is about. If they do not, note whether they address two different topics or if they need more development.

Exercise #2: Read each body paragraph and, on a separate sheet of paper, write down the one topic addressed in each paragraph. Then, read the thesis statement. Ask yourself these questions:

1. Is there more than one topic being written about in a single paragraph? If so, recommend separating the paragraph into two paragraphs.

2. Are all topics necessary in order to support the thesis?

3. Are the paragraphs in an order that makes sense to you, the reader?

4. Is there anything that should still be discussed to support the thesis?

We Offer Online Appointments

The student population at GSU is one of the most diverse in the country: commuters sit alongside athletes, veterans next to working parents, and sorority presidents beside international scholars. The Writing Studio is proud to reflect such diversity in its staff of tutors as well as its practices. To help support the variety of lifestyles within the GSU community, the Studio offers online tutoring appointments. This allows any student who has an account with the Writing Studio to sign up for WriteChat, the web-based audio/visual communication interface that gives both writer and tutor the ability to chat and work simultaneously on the same document.

How to meet your tutor online:

1. Ensure your computer has audio and visual capabilities.

2. Login to the Writing Studio schedule.

3. Click on your appointment in yellow.

4. Press "Start or Join Online Consultation."

We Work with International Students

As mentioned earlier, identifying the main points of concern for a paper can lead to a very productive discussion for both writer and tutor. However, for many students whose primary language is not English or who did not grow up in an American school system, numerous other factors can complicate the writing process. In some cultures, for example, a circular essay structure is valued more than a linear structure, which can cause a student to have a different definition of "organization" than his or her

"When my English 1102 teacher first introduced me to the idea of going to the Writing Studio, I felt like it would be a waste of time. I didn't feel like it would be necessary for me to revise my writing with a tutor when I could do it myself in the comfort of my own home. I was wrong. The Writing Studio is extremely helpful in more than one way. Aside from potentially getting a better grade after having your paper looked over by a certified tutor, you walk away with new knowledge that you may not have had before your session."

KaTerra Smith

teacher. Additionally, each language possesses its own colloquial terms, idioms, and dialect-specific features, causing the writing process to take two or three times longer than for a native speaker of English. As an institution that values the many rich cultures represented in its student population, GSU offers a number of resources for scholars working to develop a mastery of the English language.

One valuable resource is the Writing Studio, where tutors are familiar with ESL-related writing concerns and are trained to address those concerns in a way that leads to long-term language improvement. Beyond training however, most of our tutors have experienced learning a new language themselves, and the Writing Studio has consistently hired a handful of tutors whose primary language is not English. Therefore, ESL students can feel confident that tutors will understand the unique challenges they face and offer effective strategies to overcome them.

*Another valuable resource is the Intensive English Program (IEP), which offers a non-degree-seeking English program, ESL courses that can fulfill degree-seeking requirements, and tutoring services for reading and writing in English, as well as listening and speaking. For more information, visit iep.gsu.edu.

We Improve Writers, Not Just Writing

"I can't write." This phrase is repeated year after in year in the college writing classroom. Despite hearing teachers' light-hearted responses, which might include "Yes you can," "Writing is just talking on paper," and "But, you write all the time," student writers across the country still lack confidence. One reason that might contribute to this lack of confidence is the widely accepted notion that there is only one way to correctly write academic prose. Because most people grow up writing only for an academic audience, one that will pass judgment on their work, students begin to associate writing with a great amount of pressure.

At the GSU Writing Studio, tutors are devoted to assisting students with their assignments. They want students to achieve the greatest level of success they can with whatever document they bring in. However, tutors will still approach each writing assignment with long-term improvement in mind. They will not only tell you which of your current ideas to expand, but they will also show you how to fully explicate your thoughts on a subject more generally. For example, Writing Studio tutors won't just point out a comma splice in your third paragraph; they will teach you how to recognize and prevent comma splices in the future. By the end of a typical session, most tutors have gone further than merely addressing students' original concerns; they have helped the student develop more concrete, long-term writing skills—skills that will build the confidence necessary to reduce anxiety associated with future writing assignments.

Tutor Randall Harrall on Better Writers

As a tutor in the Writing Studio, I have the opportunity to work with students at every stage of the writing process. Every session is different. There are no requirements, and there is no preset agenda. There is only one tutor expectation: the student leaves the studio a better writer. Having no predetermined agenda nurtures a dynamic environment, always changing and never static. This freedom keeps the space exciting for the tutor and the tutee. We allow the students to express their concerns, then we facilitate a discussion based on their needs and the aforementioned expectation. As trained and passionate tutors, we attempt to discern the major issues of a student's writing quickly. The student's expectations and the tutor's expertise always shape the session and lead to better writing.

How to Make an Appointment

Now that you have a better idea about what the Writing Studio offers, we encourage you to make an appointment. While the Studio does accept walk-ins, the best way to ensure that you're able to schedule a session at a convenient time is to book it through our online scheduling system. The Writing Studio often becomes very busy, so if you don't book at least two days in advance, a good chance exists that no appointment times will be available. Fortunately, scheduling is easy. Use the steps below to help get started.

Step One

Visit https://gsu.mywconline.net/ and log into the scheduling system. If you have never made an appointment with us before, you will need to click the link, "Click here to register." We encourage you to use your GSU Campus ID username and password so that they will be easy to remember.

Step Two

Once you login, you will see a box labeled with the current day of the week. On the left side of this box is a list of tutors' names, and on the right side, white and blue squares. The white squares are available appointments and the blue squares represent appointments that are already booked. As you scroll down, you will see the schedules for the remaining days of that week. At the top of the screen, you also have the option to advance to another week. If you need to pick a specific day and time, scroll to that day and click on the appropriate white squares that aligns with the time you prefer.

If you are more flexible with your time, it may be advantageous to book your appointment based on a tutor's profile. By clicking on a tutor's name, you can review a brief description of his or her academic specialties.

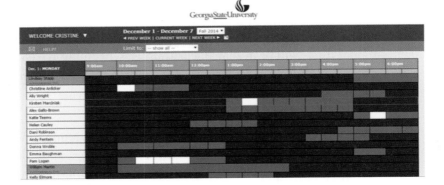

Step Three

Once you click on a white box to make your appointment, you will see a pop-up box that will ask you to list the "Course," "Instructor," and what you plan to work on for that session. It is tremendously important to be specific, especially in the last text field, so your tutor can better prepare for your session. After everything is entered, click on the "Save Appointment" button at the bottom of the pop-up box.

Time:	Monday, December 01: 10:00am ▾ to 10:30am ▾
Course:	
Instructor:	
What would you like to work on today?	

SAVE APPOINTMENT   CLOSE WINDOW

Please note that the "Instructor" box is only for Writing Studio use. Your appointments at the Writing Studio will always remain confidential and the instructor of your course will not be notified; GSU Writing Studio policy prevents tutors and all other Writing Studio personnel from discussing tutoring sessions with anyone other than the tutee.

Step Four

After you have saved your appointment, the only thing left to do is show up on your chosen date at the appointed time. If for any reason you cannot make your appointment, please log into the system again, click the yellow box that signifies your appointment, and then click "Cancel This Appointment."

IMPORTANT: The Writing Studio staff strongly recommends that you show up at least five minutes early for your appointment in order to sign in. You will need your Panther ID card.

Advice from the Studio's staff on how to make the most out of a session:

Draft a list of three specific questions you would like the tutor to answer.

Show up 5-10 minutes early in order to sign-in before your session begins.

Bring a copy of your assignment sheet.

Bring at least one copy of you draft. (If your draft is in a digital format, have the document open on a laptop computer prior to the session.)

Bring a previously-graded paper with feedback so your tutor can see what suggestions have already been made about your writing.

Expect the unexpected: Your tutor might point out areas of concern you had not considered.

Overcoming Writer's Anxiety

As mentioned in the beginning of this chapter, one of the main obstacles writers face is anxiety. Writing, unlike other academic enterprises, forces us to slow down and seek answers within ourselves. It challenges us to confront what we know and what we don't, and constantly forces us to make changes, whether they constitute crossing words out, moving paragraphs around, or altering our perspective. For college students, this process can often seem too intensive since jobs, other classes, and extra-curricular activities often make the act of purposefully slowing down feel nearly impossible. To overcome writer's anxiety, we encourage you to read the essay below by Ryan Ocampo, a dually-enrolled high school student who faced his own struggles with balance during his first semester at Georgia State. Ryan's essay responds to a prompt which asked students to write a narrative detailing their experience within a GSU-specific place. The essay provides a detailed depiction of the Writing Studio's unique environment. As you read through it, consider your own anxieties and to-do lists. Ask yourself how a change in scenery might affect your writing process.

More than a Writing Studio

BY RYAN OCAMPO

There's an old saying that, "it is not the place itself but the journey there that makes it all worthwhile." This is exactly what happens as I walk into the Georgia State University writing studio. However, my experience didn't start there. As I said, the journey there was a gift in itself, for my past endeavors of woe and anxiety made me appreciate the place more than for what it was worth. This was to become my sanctuary.

In the 10 minutes before I got to the writing studio, my nerves and anxiousness were getting to me as my professors threw assignments at me one by one. I was on a mental track and field, running through laps as to how I could finish all these assignments accordingly. I thought, "Okay I have astronomy homework due Monday, the same day as the 30 question quiz.... but wait...I have an exam for calculus on Wednesday, and now that I'm done with English I realized that I was supposed to complete the Reader's response discussion post on my teacher's website, so I can't start on the homework yet! Also, the draft for my first essay is due that Friday, along with my government essay due the following Monday! Did I leave my phone? No, thank goodness! My headphones? In my pocket. Do I have everything? Can I still attend my club meetings?" But what I didn't ask myself was where my mind was. It appeared to be all over the place! While at the same time, I saw my physical-self careening through the masses of students located in the University Courtyard. Amidst the aroma of chlorine from the water fountain and cigar smoke from almost everywhere else, I almost forgot where I was going. I knew one word that perfectly fitted my predicament: Stressful. I needed a sanctuary. That was where I needed to go.

The Writing Studio is located in the SunTrust corporate building. For my second time coming here, I never really got to know the place in depth. As long as I survived my expedition across the courtyard, and then across the street between Hurt Plaza and Peachtree Center Avenue, it was only five minutes away from all the chaos. My mind kept running mental laps around the track that was my brain. Repeatedly I would recite these thoughts so that I wouldn't forget why I was working so hard, for when I worked hard, I thought hard. Not only did I hear my thoughts, but I couldn't help but listen to the random chatter of passers by and by as they went on about their daily lives and creating small-talk. Listening to so many voices caused me to stagger mentally once again, but luckily I managed as I was almost there.

"Homework due Monday, quiz Monday, English essay draft due Friday, government essay due Monday, calculus exam Wednesday, reader's response due today. Club meeting Thursday, read for astronomy, read for government, read for calculus.... repeat." The mental to do list was put on repeat as long as I was outside in the heat of Atlanta. As I entered the SunTrust building, the rush of long awaited air conditioning bursted right through me as if the building was greeting me a symbolic welcome for my relief. Ever since the rush of cold air, I began to feel my mental to do list, my thoughts, slipping away, fading into the depths of my mind that I could not recall: "Quiz Monday... Homework... Calculus... Readers..." The elevator, the metallic guide to my destination, waited for my urgent request. It welcomed me as I went to press the number 24. Then it obliged.

With each metallic ring of assurance, I started to relax little by little, feeling lighter and lighter despite that the forces of gravity kept weighing me down heavier and heavier. "21, 22..." I almost did not realize the silence in this building in comparison to the busy streets of Atlanta. It was bliss. "23..." I was almost there, but at the same time I was not sure if I was supposed to be there because I needed a place to be productive in other aspects than writing. "24th floor". With the little remnants of my to-do list in mind, I resumed reciting it as I exited the elevator. Through the hallway: "Quiz Monday, homework Monday, calculus exam, readers response...". Even as I latched open the large, unusually heavy door at the end of the hall way I keep in mind: "Quiz Monday, homework Monday, calculus exam Wednesday, readers response today..."but as I drew closer to my destination, the pleasant and casual feel of carpet threw off my thoughts as it reminded me of home; and then as I turned left I saw an entranceway to my right, into the place I believed to be the solution to all my problems.

"Hello, How may I help you?"

The only thought that remained of my to-do list was: "response". But my actual response to the lady behind the desk was, "Whoa!!".

Signaling her that I didn't need help, I was drawn towards the almost completely transparent wall that made up the windows spanning the side of the building. It looked almost invisible, for the view was breathtaking and clear as day. The view has awoken me. I was in the heart of Atlanta, the heart of innovation, industry, inspiration, and motivation. Not only did I tower over the industrially inclined streets and the distinguishingly large giants of skyscrapers across from me, but the grandeur silhouette of greenery amongst the outskirts of the city made me realize that God has given me a beautiful world to live in. This view made me believe that God wanted me to make the world mine, by expanding my horizons and exceeding my potential in productivity. The skyscrapers are my inspiration, the rural silhouette my motivation, the sky my limit, and the busy streets my reminder that I should contribute something to this world as all other people did. This is where I will start.

With new eyes, I start to absorb myself into the space of the writing studio. Long brown tables span the walls, while the open ends act as homes to chairs in the hopes of being extended by a body. Several people find these homes to channel their productivity. Carpet floor engulfs the studio in a nature-like green that seems to represent order, for order is the basis of production. Productive: The word by which everybody complied to in such a soothing space. Asian, White, Black, Young, Old, formal, informal, quiet, loud. It mattered not who inhabited this place. There was no trace of intimidation, discrimination, arrogance, or even ignorance in the air. We were all here to help one another, and there are some like me who need it dearly. I needed help in terms of knowing how to relieve my overwhelming anxiety. A sitting area against the windows consisted of light blue couches and lounge chairs that emitted an air of relief. Sitting in those chairs made me feel lighter, as if my mind cleared of all the chaos that was my mental to-do list. Then I decided to act.

The first thought that came to mind was, "A Rubik's cube". Sitting on the wooden center table of the lounging area, I was tempted to make the scrambled unscrambled. Algorithms started coming to mind. How do I solve it? Then I grabbed it. I started to feel homesick, for forty miles north of Atlanta lies a scrambled Rubik's cube awaiting me at home. I always wanted to solve my own problems, and this was merely an understatement of my dilemma. Therefore, successfully solving the Rubik's cube will get me started, and hopefully it should lead me to get things done as quick too.

Like the Rubik's cube, my life was full of colors, a rainbow-esque mess of feelings: Blue for sadness, red for urgency, orange for nervousness, Yellow for anxiety… these were all feelings that I had to put into the right place at the right time. Such disorganization had to become organized again, so I took care of what was messing me up inside and took it out on this puzzling cluster of color. Then after I solved the Rubik's cube, within less than a minute, I ignored the awe and smirks of the several people that were here. I didn't feel so stressed anymore. I felt lighter again, like in the elevator, but for a longer duration. Was this the pride of accomplishment? It was relieving to feel that again. White is the color of pride.

Then I noticed the Laptop cart sitting in the left-most corner of the Studio. "Perfect," I thought. My one and true friend since middle school, the one who told me what I did not know, was a computer, the most reliable friend I could trust. To produce work, I needed my friend. So I asked the lady behind the desk for a laptop, but she said, "To rent a Laptop, you need to trade in your Panther ID".

I felt a hole forming at the base of my stomach. It wasn't hunger. But as I walked back to my work station, that emptiness turned into satisfaction. I was proud to give up my identity… my ego… to gradually produce work in order to resolve my problems. I came into college as insecure as I was in high school. I didn't know anybody, but I cared what people thought of me. I judged myself, thinking for other people and what they thought was normal even though my thoughts weren't theirs, like "Kid in the corner must think I don't care about class because I don't have a class to go to at this time, thus making me look delinquent" or "College professors are merciless, so I must get assignments done quietly without question". Random thoughts of criticism towards me kept wandering in my mind as I grew more anxious about how my experience here will turn out. But none of that matters because this was my ego, and I chose to put it away symbolically into the one true thing that identified me at this school: the Panther ID. My ego, which contained all my self-criticism and anxieties, was put aside so that my mind could clear of all the mental stresses that strained me. I would finally come to focus on one problem I had at a time.

I'm glad I got to know this place beyond its purpose. It was more than some lodge to sit down and write a paper. I felt like I found a second home, and home was where I could organize myself and my thoughts. With those values, I believed that no one could negate me, especially if the pessimist was me, for I was my own self-destruction, bound to self-criticize and draw into a whirlpool of chaotic anxieties and stress. However I couldn't feel that way in such a safe-haven from my inner chaos… because the view of the world as it was, the different people that were around me here, my Panther card of an ego, and even the colors on the Rubik's cube that awaited resolution… made me feel like I was above all my stress so that I could overlook the higher potential in myself… especially since I am 24 floors above it all.

Conclusion

When you receive your first essay assignment of the semester, the most important thing to understand is that you are not alone. The tutors at the Writing Studio understand how unpredictable and overwhelming the writing process can be; that is why we are here. We encourage you to take the first step in understanding your personal writing process and identifying the strategies that help you succeed by visiting us for a one-on-one session. Foundational to the Writing Studio's philosophy is that students decide how they want to use their time, whether that means reviewing a completed draft with a tutor or staying in the Studio to write while the tutor remains available for assistance. Regardless of what brings you in, know that the best and most long-lasting learning comes from simply "talking it out." We are happy to speak with you about any writing concern and encourage you to talk out your ideas with others as much as you can. In the meantime, happy writing and see you soon!

Young, Eun Kyoung. *Freeze.*

9

WRITING ABOUT VISUAL IMAGES

"There can be no words without images" ~ Aristotle

Images in Everyday Life

We are immersed in a visual culture. In our digital age, we continually process the multitude of images meeting our eyes—photographs, illustrations, videos, and other graphic elements. In order to be effective critical thinkers, we must learn not only how to read alphabetic texts, but also visual ones, as well as texts that combine images and words. We think about, discuss, and describe images with language. Even though we can never completely replicate the meaning of an image in words, it is important to develop a vocabulary so that we can understand and evaluate visuals more skillfully. Because we use language to understand sensory information, in this chapter we will use words like "read" and "text" that are typically applied to written texts. Seeing images and other forms of our lived experience (such as fashions, buildings, and spaces) as "texts" helps us to understand how *rhetoric* pervades our lives. This chapter offers ways to look at images rhetorically—in other words, to perceive what messages visual "texts" get across and how (and how effectively) these messages are delivered. We will look at some familiar terms like *ethos, logos,* and *pathos,* but in new ways, as they are applied to the study and creation of visual images.

As just one example of the pervasiveness of visual images, think for a moment about how many advertising images you see in a given day. They could be posters, murals, signs, package labels, billboards, print ads in magazines, commercials on TV or the Internet, or vehicle wraps. Because to some degree we can now control the commercials we watch on TV or the Internet (by watching them on ad-free venues or by skipping the ads), the ad agencies on Madison Avenue have devised more creative ways to get visual and alphabetic texts in front of our eyes, a phenomenon known as "ad clutter." Now, ads appear on

Osborne, Steve. *Have a Coke and a Smile.*

every available surface, including spaces such as vehicles, mobile billboards, physicians' examination tables, restroom stalls, dining trays on airlines, turnstiles in public transit stations, video screens in taxis, blimps and planes over stadiums, eggs in cartons, floors, parking stripes, and postage stamps (Johnson; Story). Researchers estimate that most people in the industrialized world are exposed to over 5,000 advertisements per day (Johnson). Though some ads consist of written texts or audio, most of these advertisements have some visual components, and some of them are entirely visual in nature. In this ad-saturated environment, we experience a kind of sensory overload.

The only way for us to cope effectively with this reality is to know how to process and evaluate the images we see. Because of the emergence of Web 2.0, we not only consume images, but we also now produce them on social media, blogs, and other forms of web presence. By studying ways to analyze and evaluate images, we are able not only to think critically about the visual data coming into our consciousness, but we can also learn ways to create our own visual arguments. This chapter provides a rationale for studying visual rhetoric, a *lexicon*[1] of relevant terms, connections to concepts from the analysis and argument chapters, activities that will help you try out the strategies of analysis you will learn in the chapter, and an example of rhetorical analysis. Whether visual texts work on their own or in conjunction with written/alphabetic texts, they work to move specific audiences to think or act differently. This effort is called *visual rhetoric,* and a number of scholars study and practice this form of rhetoric.

Coca-Cola's neon sign has long served as a landmark at Atlanta's Five Points intersection. In what ways does the sign symbolize both the city and the company?

---

1 A *lexicon* is a collection of words and their definitions or the vocabulary of a particular field.

Images in Context

People construct visual arguments in particular historical moments. This context of place and time is influenced by and in turn influences the nature and reception of visual texts. In other words, the time and place in which an image is created has an impact on what kind of an image it is, the way that it is produced, who sees it, and what they think of it. Sometimes, the image is ahead of its time, and it teaches the audience a new way to see images and to create their own images. Thus, if enough people see an image and it changes the way that they think, it can change what they do, leading to a new cultural environment with new practices. In this process, an image becomes *iconic*[2]—that is, it takes on a range of meanings and it influences work produced in later historical periods.

FOR THOUGHT AND DISCUSSION

The masterpiece *Girl with a Pearl Earring* (1665) by Dutch painter Johannes Vermeer has remained iconic for centuries, inspiring not only countless imitations and tributes, but also a novel and a movie imagining the story behind the painting. Depicted below are the original painting and four appropriations of it. *Appropriations* recreate the image but change certain aspects of it. Study each re-imagining and jot down ideas about how each one changes the original image. What effect does each one have on you? What thoughts or emotions does each painting evoke? What messages does each convey about

Girl with a Pearl Earring. Left: Johannes Vermeer, 1665. Right: Dutch Renaissance Self-Shot. Anonymous.

Vermeer's historical context and our current historical moment?

---

2 An icon is a person or thing (usually an image) that is used to represent something else.

Girl with a Pearl Earring. Dorothee Golz.

Left: *Girl with a Pearl Earring.* David Barton. Right: *Girl with a Pearl Earring.* Jetoy Choo-Choo.

Three historical realities play into the visual rhetoric made in an historical moment: technology, literacy, and values. These three elements influence the production, distribution, consumption, and reception of visual texts. Technological innovations influence the options available for creators of texts. *Medium* refers to the material or the technical means through which something is made.[3] The particular technology used to produce an image is called *media specificity.* These media arise from the technology that makes them

---

3 Media is the plural of medium.

possible. For example, before the advent of the printing press, books had to copied out by hand; in the decades before the invention of the motion picture camera, people took photographs. Now, people can choose to make books by hand or reproduce them mechanically on presses; they can make videos or take photographs with the film or digital camera of their choice. Technology has expanded to make more media possible.

To some degree, the kinds of literacies that people achieve and practice connect to the kinds of technologies available in societies. In the Middle Ages, only highly educated people could read and write. After Johannes Gutenberg invented the printing press in 1451, books gradually became more widely available, but it was not until the invention of steam presses and the discovery of cheaper materials for paper in the 1800s that books became affordable enough to be available to common people (Faigley et al. 4). The combination of these developments and the social reform of compulsory primary school education led to an expansion of *alphabetic literacy,* or the ability to read and write texts needed in personal and professional life. Similarly, the development of the personal computer[4] made it necessary for the general population to become proficient in *digital literacy,* which involves not only ways to navigate digital spaces, but also codes and commands for receiving and producing messages by using digital technology. These highly refined skills have become not only possible but obligatory in our current historical moment.

Thus, literacies arise from the economies and technologies of the societies in which people live. In a *pre-literate* or oral culture, images and symbols provide ways to convey information. Today, in our *hyperliterate* culture, images act as a kind of shorthand—conveying a great deal of information in a flash for an information-saturated populace. Hyperliterate people are exceptionally literate in a variety of environments such as written texts, symbolic languages, and digital spaces. However, remember that digital literacy does not replace alphabetic literacy; one builds upon the other. So, reading and writing avidly and actively remain as important as always in terms of building proficiencies in other areas such as digital technologies.

---

4 IBM put the first personal computer, or PC, on the market in 1981. This machine, the 5150 or IBM-PC, was the first computer intended for individual home use.

In the early Roman Empire, most people could not read and write the Roman alphabet, but they understood symbolic inscriptions. These inscriptions on the Marble Road in the Roman Imperial city of Ephesus (in modern-day Turkey) give travelers directions to the local brothel. Notice the broken heart (indicating loneliness), cross (indicating a crossroad), left foot (indicating the left side of road), and female form (indicating who awaited the weary traveler) (Lewandowski).

Which literacies are taught and practiced in a society has to do with what that society *values*. Cultural values, also known as mores or conventions, determine the nature of visual images produced within that culture. United States society values individual freedom, competition, and private property, so these notions are at work in the media used, in the subject matter of visual images, and in the ways that images are perceived by audiences. Photographs, for instance, are often copy-protected on websites such as *Flickr* to prevent unauthorized use. And while the freedom to take photographs is valued, so also is the privacy that enables someone to refuse to have their photograph made, or, if it is made, restricts it from being distributed online. Of course, these rules of copyright and privacy are broken often, but practices related to the production, distribution, and consumption of photographic images certainly indicate the values important in a society. This inherent cultural bias in the creating and reading of texts is known as *cultural specificity*.

Form Follows Function: The Architecture of Images

How exactly does cultural specificity work in visual images? Both the form and content of an image can be influenced by the culture in which it is produced. Painters, to use just one example, use the materials available to them. They may use oil paint on canvas, or they may use acrylic on wood, depending on what they can procure, who taught them to paint, and the final form the painting might take. It might be a painting to hang on a wall in a gallery, or it might be a painted functional object that a family could use or display in their home. These structures of the painting constitute the *form* that it takes. In the production of visual images, form has to do with how the image is produced. Its mode of production influences what it can do, and that mode is also part of the culture in which it was created.

Content refers to the narrative or the subject matter portrayed in images. Every culture has its own store of folklore, stories, legends, and icons that provide much of the material seen in images produced in that culture. Each culture's buildings, statuary, clothing, decorative objects, and other forms of art depict the people, places, and events important in that culture. The Hagia Sophia (Ayasofya or "Divine Wisdom") in Istanbul, Turkey provides a glimpse into two very different cultures. Initially, this building was a Byzantine basilica, a place of Christian worship. When the Ottoman Turks took over the Christian city of Constantinople and transformed it into Istanbul, they also transformed the basilica into a Muslim mosque, plastering over the Byzantine art. In the twentieth century, the Turkish government restored much of the Byzantine splendor and turned the Hagia Sophia into a national museum. To this day, the beautiful structure is adorned with the artwork of two magnificent cultures. The Christians depicted Jesus, Mary, saints, and other human figures, but the Muslims do not depict human or animal images in their mosques, so they used plants, inscriptions in Arabic, and other decorative designs. The Byzantine Empire and the Ottoman Empire used different forms (basilica, mosque) and different content (people, plants) that reflected their beliefs and values.

Two major factors that have transformed the form and content of the visual images we produce today are reproducibility and malleability. *Reproducibility* refers to the capability of reproducing a work of art. Lithographs, photographs, posters, magazines, and digital downloads are all examples of ways in which artists can rep-

The Hagia Sophia in Istanbul, Turkey. Notice the Arabic inscription on the circular surface to the left and a depiction of Mary and Jesus in the center of the photo.

The Hagia Sophia in Istanbul, Turkey. The man seated on the throne is the Holy Emperor Leo. The silver decorations along the bottom of the frame are Ottoman designs added when the Turks overtook the Byzantine city of Constantinople.

licate works for mass distribution. The reproducibility of much of the visual work created today expands tremendously the reach and accessibility of the image, but it also increases the ubiquity of images, contributing to sensory overload.[5] Seeing so many images in so many places means that we pay less and less attention to any one image. They all vie for the limited amount of attention we can give.

Many images produced today also possess *malleability,* which means that they can be manipulated or altered. When you use Instagram to post photos, you might alter the color, lighting effects, of other as-

Osborne, Steve. *Reproducibility: fliers wheat pasted onto a particle board wall* (Decatur, Georgia).

---

5 Ubiquity means presence everywhere or in many places at the same time.

pects of the image. The fact that an image can be changed means not only that is malleable, but that its objectivity could be challenged. Photos are often used as evidence in court hearings and in reports of research studies, but if these images are manipulated, the soundness of the verdict may be compromised. Sometimes we see a photograph and wonder whether the phenomenon or event really happened or whether the person or animal really has that appearance. The reality of the reproducibility and malleability of images opens up limitless possibilities for broadening audiences, but it also means that we have to remain especially alert and thoughtful about what we see.

Osborne, Steve. "*Malleability:* Corey smokestack, downtown Atlanta" Pre-Photo Shop Photo.

Osborne, Steve. "*Malleability:* Corey smokestack in downtown Atlanta" Post-Photo Shop Photo.

Images Are Appealing

In the Practicing Rhetoric chapter of this book, you read about three rhetorical appeals—ethos, logos, and pathos—and you learned how these appeals work in written texts. In this section of the visual chapter, we will apply each of those terms to visual rhetoric.

From previous study, you may know that an author establishes *ethos* or credibility with an audience by gaining their respect and good will through covert and overt methods. Demonstrating common sense and decorum, for instance, instills confidence in the author's rational mind and the author's identification with the audience's needs and desires. In visual texts, authors can establish ethos in a number of ways, including proximity, objectivity, and research. Proximity refers to how close the author is positioned to the story. First-hand eyewitness accounts with valid evidence count for more that second-hand hearsay. We tend to believe news photography, but we do not always account for its limitations such as malleability (digitally altering the image) or composition (which might leave key information outside the frame of the image). Editing the image in one or both of these ways will shape our interpretation of it. Thus, we give more ethos to the author who seems objective, using facts and other forms of quantitative, verifiable evidence. For this reason, we value someone who does a great deal of research. Understanding the issue, getting the details right, and fact-checking all build more confidence in the author.

The results of first-hand experience, research, and fact-checking can enable the artist to offer *logos*-based appeals in a visual argument. Visual texts provide data and organized arguments just as written texts do, but they do so in different ways. A documentary film might offer statistics, expert opinions, charts, and text flashing on the screen with facts related to the issue it explores. A painter might do historical research to get the details just right for a period piece. A sculptor uses a model to make sure that the contours of the sculpture are lifelike. Design elements like line, balance, shading, and perspective lend the "logic" of reality to the artist's representation of it. Most of us are visual learners, and images offer an educational shorthand in which substantive information is condensed into one graphic. Therefore, visual texts have the potential of delivering powerful logos appeals, either standing alone or in tandem with written text.

Using *pathos* directs the appeal to the audience's emotion or imaginations. Because visual images activate a part of the brain that handles emotional responses, and because people act on their emotions (rather than their reason), visual texts offer some of the most effective pathos appeals. For this reason, advertisers incorporate images in ads, and you will likely recall many movies that remain vivid in your memory and that even changed your thinking. Dreams and memories play in our minds primarily as visuals, so authors find innovative ways of appealing to our imagination and helping us to envision an alternate reality. When you look at apartments, you probably imagine your belongings in the space in order to see if the apartment is feasible and desirable. A photograph of a needy child causes us to want to help more than a written message about the child's plight. Arguably, pathos is the dominant appeal in visual texts.

Eisenstaedt, Alfred. *Times Square Kiss,* August 14, 1945.

When your professor assigns you a rhetorical analysis or another assignment in which you examine a visual text and write about it, consider using the three appeals as criteria for your analysis. Additional criteria follow, including ways in which texts are reimagined and recreated, as well as how images address rhetorical situations.

FOR THOUGHT AND DISCUSSION

One of these images is an iconic photograph taken by Alfred Eisenstaedt on VJ Day, August 14, 1945. It's commonly called *Times Square Kiss.* The illustration that follows it appeared on the cover of the *New Yorker* in 1996. Write a brief comparison of these images, taking into consideration their historical contexts, their form and content, and their rhetorical appeals. In particular, think about how the photo and the illustration establish ethos and make logos- and pathos-based arguments.

Re-Mixing Images

Through the continual creation of new images, we have built up an incredibly large collection of visual texts across various cultures; many of these images continue to be reproduced and altered. Because images can be

Blitt, Barry. Cover of *The New Yorker,* June 17, 1996.

endlessly reproduced and altered and because they can serve as a powerful symbolic shorthand to convey ideas, images can become *icons* that are appropriated, or used, to create new images. The new references the old and helps us understand the historical context of the old image, how the images are connected, and how the allusion to the icon enhances the meaning of the re-mix. Furthermore, recognizing the old image (icon) in the new (re-mix)—that is, recognizing the *appropriation,* helps us to understand embedded messages the author conveys to the audience. Visual texts relate not only to the historical context(s) in which they were created and in which we view them, but manufactured and also to other images they reference. Just like composers and DJs sample music from other composers, visual artists "sample" from other artists. There are several forms such appropriations typically take, including parody, pastiche, memes, and mashups.

Culture-jamming ad spoof/parody by Adbusters, a Canadian organization.

First, let's look at parody and pastiche. A *parody* replicates aspects of the original that make the reference recognizable while creating a satirical or humorous effect. Sometimes the humor is gentle, and sometimes it is biting. The humor derives from distorting the image or adding incongruent content to the original image. See the example of parody on the opposite page. Adbusters, a culturejamming[6] organization with a website and journal, created this image to mock the misleading ads of the tobacco industry.

Pastiche is similar to parody, but the re-mix merely uses some of the formal elements or content of the original. The purpose of pastiche is to make an allusion to or homage to the original—that is, a reference of admiration rather than mockery. In this example, the artist incorporates some of the objects and features of the landscape, and he imitates the style. What similarities do you see? His work pays tribute to Salvador Dali's *The Persistence of Memory* without replicating fully its formal elements and content matter. The artist also makes an allusion to a hero from pop culture. Do you recognize the reference?

Dali, Salvador. *The Persistence of Memory,* 1931.

Rivera, Paolo. *The Self-Absorbing Man,* 2009.

---

[6] Culture jamming refers to a practice in which an individual or group critiques the logos, brands, and values of consumerist, capitalist culture by refiguring or appropriating corporate images and words to challenge the values that underpin them.

Apasun. *Pulp Fiction* vs. *Star Wars.*

Contemporary forms of parody and pastiche include *mashups* and *memes.* Most mashups come from the worlds of music and web design, but there are mashups that create new still and moving visual texts. A *mashup* in music, also known as a mesh or blend, combines and synchronizes one or more vocal and instrumental tracks, creating a new sound. Mashups in visual art juxtapose or combine two cultural icons, creating a new image. The artist combines disparate and sometimes seemingly dissonant elements to give the audience a new way of looking at something. In this rendering, the Storm Troopers from the *Star Wars* movies are "mashed up" with Vincent Vega and Jules Winnfield, the two main characters from the film *Pulp Fiction.* This juxtaposition is both unsettling and darkly humorous, giving new meaning to the characters in both films.

For Thought and Discussion

The first image mashes up two images: the BP logo and a silhouette from a Pulitzer Prize-winning iconic photo (*Vietnam Execution,* Saigan, 1968 by Eddie Adams). Study these two images and research the historical context of the photo. How does the history of the iconic photograph affect the message in the parody? Based on the form and content of the mashup, how do you interpret the message? What do the two figures represent? Articulate the message in two or three sentences and discuss your conclusions with a partner. Did you come to the same conclusion regarding the author's intended message?

BP-Vietnam Spoof, Adbusters.org website.

Adams, Eddie. Vietnam Execution, Saigon, 1968.

Richard Dawkins, an evolutionary biologist, coined the word *meme* in his 1979 book *The Selfish Gene.* He desired "a word that sounded like gene" and would convey the notion of "cultural transmission" (Dawkins). As Dawkins explains, examples of memes include "tunes, ideas, catch-phrases, clothes fashions, ways of making pots or of building arches. Just as genes propagate themselves in the gene pool by leaping from body to body via sperms or eggs, so memes propagate themselves in the meme pool by leaping from brain to brain via a process which, in the broad sense, can be called imitation" ("What Is a Meme?"). Memes "leap from brain to brain" because they resonate with us. They resonate with us because we perceive the truth behind the humor. Using *macros* (the images from which memes are generated) found on a meme generator website, anyone can create memes. Using the image macro, users can add captions. The juxtaposition of the image and the words contributes to the meanings of both. Memes are in visual art what variations on a theme are in musical art—they take the artistic foundation and change it for an unprecedented effect on the audience.

One popular meme on the Internet right now is "Keep Calm and Carry On." This meme emerged from the 2000 discovery of a 1939 poster created by the Ministry of Information in the United Kingdom. A couple found the poster at the bottom of an old box of books they bought at an auction. They framed it and began selling prints ("Keep Calm and Carry On: About"). This image has leaped into many brains, and now we see it all over the place—not only in memes, but in thousands of products such as t-shirts, school supplies, and coffee mugs. As the examples below

"Keep Calm and Carry On" Memes. *Know Your Memes website.*

show, not only do meme creators alter the text, they also alter the image itself. This example demonstrates the reproducibility and malleability of memes as well as the way that users parody the original propaganda from which the macro derived. All of these forms of appropriation—parody, pastiche, mashup, and meme—illustrate ways that visual texts recall and revise earlier texts in order to create new meanings. Both authors and audiences participate in this *intertextuality*, or "conversation" among visual texts.

FOR THOUGHT AND DISCUSSION

This meme memes a meme for a darkly humorous effect. The unnamed author changes both the icon and all but three words of the text, yet the appropriation maintains enough of the meme it echoes for us to understand that the appropriation references "Keep Calm and Carry On." What do the hammer and sickle signify, and how are the images and the text connected? Discuss with your partner or as a class.

"Keep Quiet and Continue Working" Meme. *Know Your Memes* website.

For Thought and Discussion

Visit the *Know Your Memes* website. Look up "Haters Gonna Hate." In this meme, the caption is the macro—it remains stable, but the images in the meme change. In what ways does the user's authorship of pictures differ from the authorship of text? In other words, how does creating new images for the static text of "Haters Gonna Hate" change the standard meme-making experience of changing the caption?

Addressing Rhetorical Situations with Visual Texts

Just as written texts address particular rhetorical situations, so do visual texts. Think about what you have learned regarding the *rhetorical situation* already in your writing classes. If we simplify the rhetorical situation into its most basic components, we have these three: text, author, and audience. These three elements influence and inform each other—in other words, by knowing more about one, you can understand more about the others. In this section of the chapter, we will apply some of the concepts covered thus far in this chapter to a discussion of how they apply to aspects of the rhetorical situation.

The Text

The nature of the *text* connects to the purpose and subject of the message. If you are asked to analyze a text, you could start by asking what kind of visual text you are viewing, what it is doing, and why. Take notes, answering the following questions:

- What is the text's *genre?* Is it a painting, a photograph, a sculpture, a film, a print ad, a TV commercial, a flier?

- What is the purpose of the text? How does the author convey his or her purpose?

- If the purpose is to persuade, what is the audience being persuaded to think or do? What is the thesis or argument of the text?

- How is the "so what" question addressed? Why should the audience pay attention to this text?

- What effect does this text have on me?

In order to explore some of these questions more deeply, think back to the section of this chapter called "Form Follows Function: The Architecture of Images." Remember that this section dealt with the form and content of visual arguments. Let's expand on that discussion by looking at how words and images work together to enhance each other. In the most effective texts, form and content merge into a unified work that addresses the rhetorical situation well. Think of the mixing of form and content as being similar to the mixing of iconic and linguistic elements. Many if not most of the visual arguments we see mix images and words. Think of a photograph and a caption. The caption helps to contextualize the photograph so that we understand the significance of the narrative that is being depicted in the image.

Look at this photograph. Do you know the story behind it?

Thornell, Jack. *James Meredith Shot,* June 6, 1966.

The man is lying prone on a road, and he is the only figure in the photo. We can read from his face that he is in pain, or perhaps he is angry or sad, but we might not know why without words to explain the meaning of what we are seeing. You may recognize that this is a famous photograph; in fact, it won a Pulitzer Prize in 1967. If you do not recognize this photo, this caption gives its context: "Civil rights activist James Meredith grimaces in pain as he pulls himself across Highway 51 after being shot in Hernando, Miss., June 6, 1966. Meredith, who defied segregation to enroll at the University of Mississippi in 1962 completed the march from Memphis, Tenn., to Jackson, Miss., after treatment of his wounds (AP Photo/Jack Thornell)" ("James Meredith Shot Pulitzer 1967"). With the words, we now know who this man is and what has happened to him. The caption provides *anchorage* for the viewer because it pins down and narrows the many meanings this photo could possibly convey. Without the image, however, the words would not give us a sense of his physical and emotional pain. The image conveys the pathos that the words, with their objective, journalistic tone, do not.

At the beginning of this chapter, the following epigraph appears: "There can be no words without images." This sentence comes from one of Aristotle's lectures about how words carry meanings through rhetorical devices that create images in the mind's eye such as metaphor and narrative. The best writing brings images to the minds of audiences, but words, like visual art, can only imitate reality. We can never fully capture all of the meanings of a scene or an experience. When writing about visual texts, though, remember that the iconic and the linguistic work in tandem to create meaning. Examine these elements carefully to gather as much meaning as possible.

In some ways, words and images are not all that far removed from one another. Words, after all, are made up of letters—shapes formed by lines. These shapes have particular meanings as letters or when they are grouped into words. In Nathaniel Hawthorne's novel *The Scarlet Letter*, a character named Hester Prynne is forced by her community to wear an "A" as a mark of shame for committing adultery. This scarlet-red "A" possesses an altogether different meaning from the red "A" that signifies the Atlanta Braves baseball team. The field of typography discovers the artistic/rhetorical possibilities of alphabetic texts such as the capital "A" that Prynne and the Braves wear. Also, as we have seen in this chapter, artists who create images use a visual vocabulary, grammar, and syntax—a set of design principles such as line, space, shape, texture, and color ("Visual Language"). Because of this visual "language," visual texts are *poly-*

semous, which means that they are able to carry multiple meanings to address rhetorical situations.

Gun by ~mou5e. An example of typography, in which words become art. Here, the words and the images complete each other (Torbjornsen).

FOR THOUGHT AND DISCUSSION
"Ordeal by Cheque" by Wuther Crue, 1932

This piece, which appeared in *Vanity Fair* magazine in 1982, uses checks to tell a story. It provides a notable example of the interplay between iconic and linguistic elements. The checks themselves are images, but the handwriting forms images as well that give clues to the plot. Look carefully at each check in chronological order, and pay careful attention to who writes the check, the date it is made out, the recipient, and the amount. This story contains a large amount of *subtext*, which requires a great deal of reading between the lines to perceive possible meanings.

After you read the story, list the main characters and their relationships. Then, write a brief summary of the story, including the major events in the characters' lives.

Once you have finished writing, discuss the following as a class or in small groups.

Ordeal by cheque

BY WUTHER CRUE

LOS ANGELES, CALIF. Aug. 30th 19 03 No. ____
HOLLYWOOD STATE BANK 90-984
6801 SANTA MONICA BOULEVARD
PAY TO THE ORDER OF Goosie Gander Baby Shoppe $148.50
One hundred + forty-eight ——— 50/ DOLLARS
Lawrence Exeter

LOS ANGELES, CALIF. Apr. 18th 19 10 No. ____
HOLLYWOOD STATE BANK 90-984
6801 SANTA MONICA BOULEVARD
PAY TO THE ORDER OF City Bicycle Co. $52.50
Fifty two ——— 50/ DOLLARS
Lawrence Exeter Jr.

LOS ANGELES, CALIF. Sept 2nd 19 03 No. ____
HOLLYWOOD STATE BANK 90-984
6801 SANTA MONICA BOULEVARD
PAY TO THE ORDER OF Hollywood Hospital $100.00
One hundred ——— XX DOLLARS
Lawrence Exeter

LOS ANGELES, CALIF. Aug. 26th 19 15 No. ____
HOLLYWOOD STATE BANK 90-984
6801 SANTA MONICA BOULEVARD
PAY TO THE ORDER OF Columbia Military Acad. $2,150.00
Twenty-one hundred + fifty ——— XX DOLLARS
Lawrence Exeter Jr.

LOS ANGELES, CALIF. Oct. 3rd 19 03 No. ____
HOLLYWOOD STATE BANK 90-984
6801 SANTA MONICA BOULEVARD
PAY TO THE ORDER OF Dr. David M. McCoy $476.00
Four hundred + seventy-five ——— XX DOLLARS
Lawrence Exeter Sr.

LOS ANGELES, CALIF. Sept 3rd 19 21 No. ____
HOLLYWOOD STATE BANK 90-984
6801 SANTA MONICA BOULEVARD
PAY TO THE ORDER OF Hollywood Cadillac Co. $3,885.00
Thirty eight hundred + eighty five XX DOLLARS
Lawrence Exeter Sr.

LOS ANGELES, CALIF. Dec 19th 19 03 No. ____
HOLLYWOOD STATE BANK 90-984
6801 SANTA MONICA BOULEVARD
PAY TO THE ORDER OF California Toyland Co. $83.20
Eighty Three ——— 20/ DOLLARS
Lawrence Exeter Jr.

LOS ANGELES, CALIF. Sept. 7th 19 21 No. ____
HOLLYWOOD STATE BANK 90-984
6801 SANTA MONICA BOULEVARD
PAY TO THE ORDER OF Wilshire Auto Repair Service $288.76
Two hundred + eighty-eight ——— 76/ DOLLARS
Lawrence Exeter Sr.

LOS ANGELES, CALIF. Oct. 6th 19 09 No. ____
HOLLYWOOD STATE BANK 90-984
6801 SANTA MONICA BOULEVARD
PAY TO THE ORDER OF Palisades School for Boys $1,250.00
Twelve hundred + fifty ——— XX DOLLARS
Lawrence Exeter Jr.

LOS ANGELES, CALIF. Oct. 15th 19 21 No. ____
HOLLYWOOD STATE BANK 90-984
6801 SANTA MONICA BOULEVARD
PAY TO THE ORDER OF Stanford University $339.00
Three hundred + thirty-nine ——— XX DOLLARS
Lawrence Exeter Sr.

LOS ANGELES, CALIF. June 1st 19 23 No. ____
HOLLYWOOD STATE BANK 90-984
6801 SANTA MONICA BOULEVARD
PAY TO THE ORDER OF Miss Daisy Windsor $25,000.00
Twenty-five thousand ——— XX DOLLARS
Lawrence Exeter Sr.

Crue, W. (1932 [renewed 1960, 1988]). Ordeal by Cheque. *Vanity Fair*. Cited in Vacca, R. T., & Vacca, J. L. (1999). Content area reading: Literacy and learning across the curriculum (6th ed.). New York: Longman.

Crue, W. (1932 [renewed 1960, 1988]). Ordeal by Cheque. *Vanity Fair*. Cited in Vacca, R. T., & Vacca, J. L. (1999). Content area reading: Literacy and learning across the curriculum (6th ed.). New York: Longman.

LOS ANGELES, CALIF. July 16 19 27 No. ____
HOLLYWOOD STATE BANK 90-984
6801 SANTA MONICA BOULEVARD
PAY TO THE ORDER OF *Parisian Gown Shoppe* $25.00
Nine hundred, twenty five DOLLARS
Lawrence Epeter, Jr.

LOS ANGELES, CALIF. Aug. 30, 19 29 No. ____
HOLLYWOOD STATE BANK 90-984
6801 SANTA MONICA BOULEVARD
PAY TO THE ORDER OF *Tony Spagoni* $126.00
One hundred, twenty six DOLLARS
Lawrence Epeter, Jr.

LOS ANGELES, CALIF. Dec. 1, 19 27 No. ____
HOLLYWOOD STATE BANK 90-984
6801 SANTA MONICA BOULEVARD
PAY TO THE ORDER OF *Anita Lingerie Salon* $750.00
Seven hundred, fifty DOLLARS
Lawrence Epeter, Jr.

LOS ANGELES, CALIF. May 25, 30 No. ____
HOLLYWOOD STATE BANK 90-984
6801 SANTA MONICA BOULEVARD
PAY TO THE ORDER OF *University Club Florists* $87.00
Eighty seven DOLLARS
Lawrence Epeter, Jr.

LOS ANGELES, CALIF. April 1, 19 28 No. ____
HOLLYWOOD STATE BANK 90-984
6801 SANTA MONICA BOULEVARD
PAY TO THE ORDER OF *Parisian Gown Shoppe* $1,150.00
Eleven hundred fifty DOLLARS
Lawrence Epeter, Jr.

LOS ANGELES, CALIF. May 28, 19 30 No. ____
HOLLYWOOD STATE BANK 90-984
6801 SANTA MONICA BOULEVARD
PAY TO THE ORDER OF *Broadway Diamond Co.* $575.00
Five hundred, seventy five DOLLARS
Lawrence Epeter, Jr.

LOS ANGELES, CALIF. Nov. 1, 19 28 No. ____
HOLLYWOOD STATE BANK 90-984
6801 SANTA MONICA BOULEVARD
PAY TO THE ORDER OF *Moderne Sportte Shoppe* $562.00
Five hundred, sixty two DOLLARS
Lawrence Epeter, Jr.

LOS ANGELES, CALIF. Nov. 13, 19 30 No. ____
HOLLYWOOD STATE BANK 90-984
6801 SANTA MONICA BOULEVARD
PAY TO THE ORDER OF *Miss Flossie Wentworth* $50,000.00
Fifty thousand DOLLARS
Lawrence Epeter, Jr.

LOS ANGELES, CALIF. July 1, 19 29 No. ____
HOLLYWOOD STATE BANK 90-984
6801 SANTA MONICA BOULEVARD
PAY TO THE ORDER OF *The Bootery* $145.25
One hundred, forty-five 25/100 DOLLARS
Lawrence Epeter, Jr.

LOS ANGELES, CALIF. Nov. 14, 19 30 No. ____
HOLLYWOOD STATE BANK 90-984
6801 SANTA MONICA BOULEVARD
PAY TO THE ORDER OF *Wall & Smith, attys. at Law* $525.00
Five hundred twenty five DOLLARS
Lawrence Epeter, Jr.

LOS ANGELES, CALIF. Aug 23, 19 29 No. ____
HOLLYWOOD STATE BANK 90-984
6801 SANTA MONICA BOULEVARD
PAY TO THE ORDER OF *Tony Spagoni* $126.00
One hundred, twenty six DOLLARS
Lawrence Epeter, Jr.

LOS ANGELES, CALIF. Nov. 15, 19 30 No. ____
HOLLYWOOD STATE BANK 90-984
6801 SANTA MONICA BOULEVARD
PAY TO THE ORDER OF *Mrs. Lawrence Epeter, Jr.* $5000.00
Five thousand DOLLARS
Lawrence Epeter, Jr.

Crue, W. (1932 [renewed 1960, 1988]). Ordeal by Cheque. *Vanity Fair.* Cited in Vacca, R. T., & Vacca, J. L. (1999). Content area reading: Literacy and learning across the curriculum (6th ed.). New York: Longman.

LOS ANGELES, CALIF. June 20, 19 31   No. ____
HOLLYWOOD STATE BANK 90-984
6801 SANTA MONICA BOULEVARD
PAY TO THE ORDER OF _Clerk, Reno Municipal Court_ $52 00
Fifty-two ——————— DOLLARS
Lawrence Exeter, Jr.

LOS ANGELES, CALIF. July 2, 19 31   No. ____
HOLLYWOOD STATE BANK 90-984
6801 SANTA MONICA BOULEVARD
PAY TO THE ORDER OF _Tony Spagoni_ $100 00
One hundred ——————— DOLLARS
Lawrence Exeter, Jr.

LOS ANGELES, CALIF. June 20, 19 31   No. ____
HOLLYWOOD STATE BANK 90-984
6801 SANTA MONICA BOULEVARD
PAY TO THE ORDER OF _Marie Wharton Exeter_ $75,000 00
One hundred seventy five thousand ——— DOLLARS
Lawrence Exeter, Jr.

LOS ANGELES, CALIF. July 3, 19 31   No. ____
HOLLYWOOD STATE BANK 90-984
6801 SANTA MONICA BOULEVARD
PAY TO THE ORDER OF _Peter Ventizzi_ $25 00
Twenty-five ——————— DOLLARS
Lawrence Exeter

LOS ANGELES, CALIF. June 20, 19 31   No. ____
HOLLYWOOD STATE BANK 90-984
6801 SANTA MONICA BOULEVARD
PAY TO THE ORDER OF _Walker + Walker_ $700 00
Seven hundred ——————— DOLLARS
Lawrence Exeter, Jr.

LOS ANGELES, CALIF. July 5th, 19 31   No. ____
HOLLYWOOD STATE BANK 90-984
6801 SANTA MONICA BOULEVARD
PAY TO THE ORDER OF _Hollywood Hospital_ $100 00
One hundred ——————— xx DOLLARS
Lawrence Exeter, Sr.

LOS ANGELES, CALIF. June 20, 19 31   No. ____
HOLLYWOOD STATE BANK 90-984
6801 SANTA MONICA BOULEVARD
PAY TO THE ORDER OF _Wall + Smith_ $450 00
Four hundred fifty ——————— DOLLARS
Lawrence Exeter, Jr.

LOS ANGELES, CALIF. July 15th, 19 31   No. ____
HOLLYWOOD STATE BANK 90-984
6801 SANTA MONICA BOULEVARD
PAY TO THE ORDER OF _Dr. David M. McCoy_ $175 00
One hundred + seventy-five ——— xx DOLLARS
Lawrence Exeter, Sr.

LOS ANGELES, CALIF. July 1, 19 31   No. ____
HOLLYWOOD STATE BANK 90-984
6801 SANTA MONICA BOULEVARD
PAY TO THE ORDER OF _Tony Spagoni_ $100 00
One hundred ——————— DOLLARS
Lawrence Exeter, Jr.

LOS ANGELES, CALIF. July 16th, 19 31   No. ____
HOLLYWOOD STATE BANK 90-984
6801 SANTA MONICA BOULEVARD
PAY TO THE ORDER OF _Hollywood Mortuary_ $1,280 00
Twelve hundred + eighty ——— xx DOLLARS
Lawrence Exeter

Crue, W. (1932 [renewed 1960, 1988]). Ordeal by Cheque. *Vanity Fair*. Cited in Vacca, R. T., & Vacca, J. L. (1999). Content area reading: Literacy and learning across the curriculum (6th ed.). New York: Longman.

- Think about the historical context of the story and its publication. What was going on in American society at this time? What might have sparked the writing of the story? (What was its exigence or origin?)

- How would you characterize this text? What, if any, genre does it fit into?

- Why might Crue have written the story in the form of checks? How would it be different if it had been written as a prose narrative with words only?

- What is the "so what" of the story? What does Crue want us to take away from our reading of it?

The Author(s)

With written texts, we can generally ascertain authorship. We know who wrote the text because the author's name often appears in the text, unless the author is anonymous or the text was written by a corporate author (generally a team of people or one person who writes without attribution for an organization). However, the same clear authorship does not hold true as frequently for visual texts. After the advent of *Web 2.0* (a term coined in 1999), the notion of authorship changed dramatically for texts composed of alphabetic and/or graphic elements. User-generated content meant that everyone could potentially create written and visual texts. Nevertheless, whether or not we have the author(s)' name(s), we can often determine a great deal about authorial intention by examining clues from other aspects of the rhetorical situation.

The following questions will provide the groundwork for you to analyze a text's authorship:

- Who is the author?

- What aspects of the author's *background* give him or her ethos (credibility)?

- What does the author *do* to establish ethos with the audience?

- What kind of impression does the author want to make about himself/herself??

- In what ways does the author create common ground or consensus with the audience?

By asking these five questions, you can establish the author's role and ethos. This credibility, as you remember from the section dealing with *ethos,* arises from the wisdom, good will, and common sense of the author.

In order to see how visual artists, designers, and filmmakers build their ethos through their work, we will look at a phenomenon that started right here in Atlanta. Living Walls, a local not-for-profit group, started a few years ago in Atlanta to make the city more aesthetically pleasing through a grassroots effort to make street art into public art (Rojo and Harrington). The organization put on its first street art festival in 2010, inviting artists to select walls and create murals in Atlanta inner city neighborhoods such as Cabbagetown, the Old Fourth Ward, and Summer Hill. The conference, called "Living Walls, the City Speaks," seeks not only to showcase exceptional street art but also to start a dialogue about some of Atlanta's problems. In its fifth year, Living Walls[7] has recently partnered with the Google Street Art Project[8] to preserve images of the typically ephemeral art form of street murals and to bring these incredible images to a wider audience.

The authors of these huge pieces submit their proposals to a committee, so the show is vetted by the festival organizers. Typically, art shows are juried, which means that artworks undergo a form of peer review. Artists have come from more than seventeen countries, competing to put their work up on everyday buildings such as warehouses, restaurants, and hotels. Let's look at three pieces created by one artist from Paris. He goes by the name of JR, and he won the TED Prize[9] in 2011 for his innovative work. For these pieces, JR performed research in the SCLC (Southern Christian Leadership Conference) collection at Emory University's MARBL (Manuscript, Archives, and Rare Book Library).[10] The 50th anniversary of the

---

7 For more on the organization's initiatives, visit http://livingwallsatl.com/
8 For more on this project, visit https://streetart.withgoogle.com/en/#home
9 TED is an international organization highlighting the work of thinkers with ideas to change the world. The acronym stands for Technology, Entertainment, Design. For more on TED, visit www.ted.com.
10 For more on Emory's outstanding archive and rare book collection, visit https://marbl.library.emory.edu/.

March on Washington inspired JR to create these murals for Living Walls 2013.

FOR THOUGHT AND DISCUSSION

Examine the following three photographs of murals carefully. Write down answers to these questions and discuss with your classmates.

■ How does JR challenge the preconceptions of street art through establishing his ethos?

■ How does he create common ground with his audience by using this genre in this context?

■ Research the images with which he does his pastiches, and research his method of wheatpasting the images on the wall. How are the form (wheatpasted photos) and content (archival artifacts of the civil rights movement) of these pieces related to JR's overall vision and purpose?

Photo by Jaime Rojo and Steve Harrington *March on Washington.* 2013 Living Walls Mural by JR.

Photo by Jaime Rojo and Steve Harrington. *No More Hunger. 2013 Living Walls Mural by JR.*

Photo by Jaime Rojo and Steve Harrington. *I Am a Man. 2013 Living Walls Mural by JR.*

By exhibiting their art on the walls of buildings in the city, Living Walls artists bring art to everyday, mass audiences. People who cannot afford the expensive tickets of a museum or a film festival can still enjoy this artwork.

The Audience

Many of the artists who create Living Walls installations started their careers as graffiti artists, and the genre of graffiti provides an intriguing opportunity to discuss audience.

When you analyze a visual text, think about the following elements of audience:

- Who is the intended or target audience?

- What kind of text (genre) might appeal to audience members? What does the audience expect regarding the form and content of the text? Does the author use the most effective genre for the intended audience?

- What background knowledge does the audience already have? What bias or prejudice might influence their reception of the message?

- How might an ethical appeal (ethos) influence the intended audience? An emotional appeal (pathos)? A rational appeal (logos)?

- What does the audience expect from the author?

As we look at how graffiti affects audiences, think about these questions as they relate to the intended audiences of graffiti artists.

The word *graffiti* comes from the Greek word *graphein*, meaning "to write," and in actuality, graffiti artists prefer to be called "writers" ("Graffiti History"). The first instances of "modern style" graffiti include inscriptions such as the directions to the brothel in Ephesus, a city in the Eastern Roman Empire. However, the "tagging" that contemporary writers do emerged from an artist named "Taki 183" in 1960s New York City. Taki wrote his name in marker on the interiors and exteriors of subway trains, and he became (in)famous among young people and city officials ("Birth and Evolution"). Now, taggers generally use cans of spray paint instead of markers. Although the

Osborne, Steve. *Diablos.*

term is more widely used to describe different forms of vandalism or highly stylized typography, we will use the tagging-with-spray-paint sense of the word in this section. Let's look at the rhetorical situation of graffiti—that is, its text, author, and audience.

The *text* of graffiti—acrylic paint sprayed on walls, bridges, billboards, and other outdoor surfaces—is ephemeral in nature. That is, it may only last a little while. Someone might sand blast it off or paint over it. It might fade in the sun. No matter how fleeting the message might prove to be, writers create highly stylized letters, symbols, words, and decorative elements, crafting a unique ethos for themselves. They use pseudonyms or false names to provide anonymity for their guerrilla art. Because graffiti is illegal, its very existence makes a statement: "I climbed up here. I left my mark. I didn't get caught." Graffiti combines aesthetic and athletic skill, and those who practice it appreciate its subversiveness and defiance of cultural norms.

The *author* of graffiti is generally unknown, though many artists such as Taki 183, Banksy, Shepard Fairey, and Keith Haring have gained a following. Writers use assumed names or pseudonyms, but they do seek attention for their art. If tags become ubiquitous, they gain a cult following and create a more substantive ethos for the writer. While writers want audiences to notice what they are doing, they do not necessarily want audiences to know their identities. For this reason, the author's identity or self comes out only in the form and content of their art. The art has to speak for itself.

Although the nature of putting up illegal art entails that the artist remain all but invisible to his or her *audience*, writers intend for their tags to be pervasive and visible. Potentially, the audience for graffiti could be global in scope, if viewers take and post photos. A tremendous repetition of tags and the viral nature of social media provide the possibility of fame for the text and the artist's reputation. Graffiti treads on the edges of society, provoking discussion and creating tension among its audiences. Its allure comes from the pairing of criminal behavior and artistic creation: violation without violence. This tension explains graffiti's tremendous influence on rock and hip-hop, and their influence on graffiti in turn. Graffiti demonstrates the importance of understanding the meanings embedded in the text, audience, and author, as well as their interrelationships.

Osborne, Steve. *Crazy Train.*

Osborne, Steve. *Graffiti Bus.*

For Thought and Discussion

The City of Atlanta has an ordinance (law) against graffiti. Under Nuisances, Article V, graffiti is defined as "any inscriptions, words, figures, paintings, or other defacements that are written, marked, etched, scratched, sprayed, drawn, painted, or engraved on or otherwise affixed to any surface of real property or improvements thereon without prior authorization of the owner or occupant of the property. …" Graffiti's illegality makes it more appealing to graffiti artists. Its existence makes an anti-authoritarian, rebellious argument. You are in a perfect environment to spot graffiti because GSU is embedded in an urban infrastructure. If graffiti is anything from a small sticker affixed to a light post all the way up to a large mural, the range of possibilities for the nature and scope of texts is virtually limitless.

Take photos of examples of graffiti on or near the GSU campus. Write an essay describing, analyzing, and/or evaluating your photo collection. Post the photos and the essay to your personal or class blog. In what ways is your curation (collection) and description of the images a form of appropriation? What about intertextuality? What are you contributing to the ongoing conversation about this relatively new cultural practice?

For Thought and Discussion

Shepard Fairey's first major tagging project was to post stickers depicting a stenciled bust of wrestler Andre the Giant with the word "OBEY" below the face. He posted variations of this image all over the world, gaining followers and notoriety. Later, he became more famous for creating the "HOPE" image that became iconic (and since that time, widely appropriated) during President Obama's 2008 campaign.

In 1990, Fairey wrote this "Manifesto" explaining the intent behind his "Obey Giant" image. Use this manifesto as an example to use when writing about an image from your own collection.

Fairey, Shepard. *Obey the Giant.* 1989.

MANIFESTO by Shepard Fairey

The OBEY sticker campaign can be explained as an experiment in Phenomenology. Heidegger describes Phenomenology as "the process of letting things manifest themselves." Phenomenology attempts to enable people to see clearly something that is right before their eyes but obscured; things that are so taken for granted that they are muted by abstract observation.

The FIRST AIM OF PHENOMENOLOGY is to reawaken a sense of wonder about one's environment. The OBEY sticker attempts to stimulate curiosity and bring people to question both the sticker and their relationship with their surroundings. Because people are not used to seeing advertisements or propaganda for which the product or motive is not obvious, frequent and novel encounters with the sticker provoke thought and possible frustration, nevertheless revitalizing the viewer's perception and attention to detail. The sticker has no meaning but exists only to cause people to react, to contemplate and search for meaning in the sticker. Because OBEY has no actual meaning, the various reactions and interpretations of those who view it reflect their personality and the nature of their sensibilities.

Many people who are familiar with the sticker find the image itself amusing, recognizing it as nonsensical, and are able to derive straightforward visual pleasure without burdening themselves with an explanation. The PARANOID OR CONSERVATIVE VIEWER however may be confused by the sticker's persistent presence and condemn it as an underground cult with subversive intentions. Many stickers have been peeled down by people who were annoyed by them, considering them an eye sore and an act of petty vandalism, which is ironic considering the number of commercial graphic images everyone in American society is assaulted with daily.

Another phenomenon the sticker has brought to light is the trendy and CONSPICUOUSLY CONSUMPTIVE nature of many members of society. For those who have been surrounded by the sticker, its familiarity and cultural resonance is comforting and owning a sticker provides a souvenir or keepsake, a memento. People have often demanded the sticker merely because they have seen it everywhere and possessing a sticker provides a sense of belonging. The Giant sticker seems mostly to be embraced by those who are (or at least want to seem to be) rebellious. Even though these people may not know the meaning of the sticker, they enjoy its slightly disruptive underground quality and wish to contribute to the furthering of its humorous and absurd presence which seems to somehow be antiestablishment/ societal convention. Giant stickers are both embraced and rejected, the reason behind which, upon examination reflects the psyche of the viewer. Whether the reaction be positive or negative, the stickers existence is worthy as long as it causes people to consider the details and meanings of their surroundings. In the name of fun and observation.

Looking Back, Looking Forward

This chapter has given a brief overview of some of the major considerations artists and scholars make when creating and evaluating visual texts. We have only scratched the surface of the prolific body of work on visual rhetoric, but we hope that this chapter has provided you with a foundation on which you can build your knowledge base and your skills in this area. Whether you are critiquing visual texts or creating them, we hope that you will look at images with new eyes.

We have explored how images pervade our everyday lives, how they fit within historical contexts (or break free of contexts), the form and content of images, the three rhetorical appeals (ethos, logos, and pathos), re-mixes (parodies, pastiches, mashups, and memes), aspects of the rhetorical situation (text, author and audience), and we have provided you with an example rhetorical analysis assignment and a model student essay. Going forward, you will want to explore more about visual rhetoric, such as design considerations, new media and technologies for working with images, and theoretical models dealing with visual arguments. This area of study continues to be dynamic and relevant to our lives, and we encourage you to read widely and write deeply about images in your college and professional future.

Rhetorical Analysis Assignment and Student Essay

Dr. Oriana Gatta's scholarship and teaching often deal with visual rhetoric. She developed this assignment for her 1102 classes. In what follows, you will see Dr. Gatta's assignment as well as the essay one of her students, Joe Beard, wrote for the class. These materials will provide you with a useful example of a rhetorical analysis of a visual text: a TV commercial.

Rhetorical Analysis Assignment by Oriana Gatta

Rhetorical Analysis (10%, 100 pts)

Due: *No later than 11:59 9.m., Sunday, September 15, 2013*

Submission Instructions: *Email* (as a .doc or .docx file) oriana.gatta@gmail.com

INTRODUCTION

In class we have been discussing the ways in which all texts, not just formal written arguments, are designed to send messages by appealing to an audience's emotions. These appeals are constructed using formal design elements, and identifying a text's message(s) requires us to understand the relationship between a text's rhetorical situation and its formal design elements. The primary purpose of the rhetorical analysis essay, then, is to help familiarize you with this relationship. Secondarily, as rhetorical analyses are a form of argumentation, this assignment also functions as preparation for your final project, in which you will make a research-based argument regarding a design-related topic of your choice.

DETAILS

In a 3–4 page (not including Works Cited) essay, make and support a unique claim regarding the message of an advertisement (or advertising campaign). More specifically, this essay should include:

- An introduction that clearly describes the advertisement (or advertising campaign) you have chosen to analyze, along with the advertisement's rhetorical situation (i.e. purpose, audience, and context).

- A thesis statement that identifies the claim you are making regarding the message of the advertisement (or advertising campaign) of your choice, as well as the criteria you are using to analyze the advertisement (or advertising campaign).

- Evidence in support of your thesis, i.e. clear and detailed explanations of how the advertisement (or advertising campaign) you have chosen fits into your analytical criteria and therefore supports your claim regarding the advertisement's (or advertising campaign's) message.

- A conclusion that reiterates your thesis statement (in different words) and broadens its (your thesis statement's) scope by placing the advertisement (or advertising campaign) in the context of other, similar advertisements, campaigns, and/or messages.

- A Works Cited page that cites the advertisement or advertising campaign you chose to analyze.

- MLA format.

EVALUATION

Your rhetorical analysis essay will be evaluated based on the following criteria:

10 points: Introduction

10 points: Thesis statement

40 points: Evidence

10 points: Conclusion

10 points: Formal tone and linguistic clarity

10 points: Length – at least 3 full pages, not including Works Cited.

5 points: Works Cited

5 points: MLA format

Joe Beard

Professor Oriana Gatta

English Composition 1102

15 September 2013

Rhetorical Analysis Essay

The public service advertisement, or PSA, has always been a reliable medium for communicating messages about potential dangers through television. The 1987 anti-drug public service advertisement, "This is Your Brain on Drugs," was very popular in its time, and its simple yet effective imagery and slogan remain recognizable in 2013. Anti-drug PSAs have continued to use minimalistic imagery to make their point in recent years, as exemplified in the Georgia Meth Project's PSA "Just Once." The ad shows five sequences involving a teenage girl and the street drug known as meth. Throughout these sequences, the ad narrates the girl's downward spiral after she becomes addicted to the drug, although she had initially planned on using it "just once." The ad's use of repetition, sequence, and mood asserts that meth will ruin your life if you try it, as well as the lives of those you care about.

This ad primarily utilizes the formal design element of repetition, specifically of the phrase "Just once," to communicate to viewers that it is nearly impossible to try meth without becoming immediately addicted to it. The phrase is uttered five times in the ad's 31-second airtime, four times by the older girl who is the main focus of the ad, and once by her younger sister at the end. The use of this phrase is clearly meant to be ironic: although the girl initially claims that she is only going to try meth once, we are shown how her life spirals out of control from continued use of the drug throughout the commercial. Ironically, she continues to use the phrase to justify her worsening behavior. For example, she states "I'm going to sleep with him for meth just once" as she is led out of a party by a total stranger, as if having sex with someone for drugs is fine as long as it is a one-time experience. At the end of the ad, the girl's sister repeats her line from its first scene, stating, "I'm going to try meth just once." The viewer is left with the ominous suggestion that the younger sister has been negatively influenced by the older sister's careless attitude towards meth use. Viewers are meant to understand by this point that "just once" loses its meaning when applied to meth use.

The ad also utilizes the element of sequence to make the point that, once one tries meth, only addiction and worse follows. In the ad's five sequences, viewers are shown how the girl's life begins falling apart after trying the drug, until it ultimately affects someone close to her. The girl addresses the camera with thoughts all ending with the phrase "just once" at the end of the first four sequences, describing increasingly self-destructive meth-related activities (such as trying meth with her friends, stealing from her family, and sleeping with a stranger for the drug) in each. Her appearance worsens in each sequence, showing her looking exhausted and gaining a number of strange scars on her face. In the final sequence, her little sister is shown about to try meth "just once," clearly having been influenced by her older sister's actions. The ad uses these sequences to communicate that one's life will spiral out of control very quickly after trying meth, due to its incredibly addictive qualities. Viewers are meant to realize how quickly the girl's life was ruined by meth, even though she had her mind set on only trying the drug once in the ad's first sequence. The final sequence is meant to appeal to viewers emotionally; even after the girl has obviously hit rock bottom (passed out in bed with strange scars and bruises all over her face), it is suggested that her younger sister is about to become addicted to meth as well, falling victim to the same "just once" mentality that her sister did.

Finally, the ad incorporates the element of mood to make

its point. The mood of the ad is very dark and gets darker throughout. One way this is accomplished is through the absence of background music, which gives the ad an unsettling and realistic atmosphere. The mood is also established through the lack of any bright or vibrant colors in its imagery, as well as the lack of enthusiasm in either character's voice. This is well-exemplified by the ad's fourth sequence, the last one in which the older girl addresses the camera. The scene is almost completely dark, and the dead, joyless tone of the girl suggests to viewers that she does not believe her own words, or even feel in control of her own actions. The last two sequences both take place at night, which gives them a dark and bleak atmosphere. The final sequence feels ominous and foreboding, as viewers know that the girl's younger sister is most likely doomed to become addicted to meth as well. The overall mood of the ad accurately reflects what a horrible and unpleasant topic meth addiction truly is.

This ad is similar to other anti-drug PSAs in that it presents a cautionary tale to viewers about the effects of drug addiction on one's life, a common theme in advertisements by the Georgia Meth Project. While other anti-drug ad campaigns are more vague and rely on metaphors (such as the "This is Your Brain on Drugs" ad), this ad is realistic and to the point, exposing viewers to the realities of how meth addiction can be destructive to one's family life, morals, and physical appearance. This ad stands out from other anti-drug ads by also addressing how drug use negatively influences those who look up to the user, instead of simply focusing on the user as an individual. Through the three elements of repetition, sequence, and mood, this ad asserts to viewers that meth is a dangerous drug that will ultimately only hurt you and those close to you.

Works Cited

GaMethProject. "Just Once – Georgia Meth Project." Online video clip. *YouTube. YouTube.* 16 Jun. 2010. Web. 4 Sept. 2013.

Criteria	Total Points	Earned Points
An introduction that clearly describes the advertisement (or advertising campaign) you have chosen to analyze, along with the advertisement's rhetorical situation (i.e. purpose, audience, and context). Well done.	10	10
A thesis statement that identifies the claim you are making regarding the message of the advertisement (or advertising campaign) of your choice, as well as the criteria you are using to analyze the advertisement (or advertising campaign). Well done.	10	10
Evidence in support of your thesis, i.e. clear and detailed explanations of how the advertisement (or advertising campaign) you have chosen fits into your analytical criteria and therefore supports your claim regarding the advertisement's (or advertising campaign's) message. Well done.	40	40
A conclusion that reiterates your thesis statement (in different words) and broadens its (your thesis statement's) scope by placing the advertisement (or advertising campaign) in the context of other, similar advertisements, campaigns, and/or messages. Well done.	10	10
Formal tone and linguistic clarity A couple of instances of redundancy. An unnecessary comma. Overall, a clearly written essay employing an appropriately formal tone.	10	8
Length – at least 3 full pages, not including the Works Cited page. Well done.	10	10
A Works Cited page that cites the advertisement or advertising campaign you chose to analyze. Well done.	5	5
MLA format Unnecessary additional spacing. Unnecessary underlining. Missing hanging indent.	5	2
Grade		95/100 A

Works Cited

TEXTS

"ARTICLE V. NUISANCES." *ARTICLE V. NUISANCES.* Municode. Web. 17 June 2014.

Crue, Wuther. "Ordeal by Cheque." *Pbworks.com.* n.d. Web. 17 June 2014.

Dawkins, Richard. "What Is a Meme?" *What Is a Meme?* University of Cambridge. Web. 17 June 2014.

Faigley, Lester, Diana George, Anna Palchik, and Cynthia Selfe. *Picturing Texts.* New York: W.W. Norton, 2004. Print.

Fairey, Shepard. "MANIFESTO." *Obey Giant.* Obey, 1990. Web. 17 June 2014.

"James Meredith Shot Pulitzer 1967." *The Big Story.* Associated Press. Web. 17 June 2014.

Johnson, Caitlin. "Cutting Through Advertising Clutter." *CBSNews.* CBS Interactive, 17 Sept. 2006. Web. 17 June 2014.

"Keep Calm and Carry On: About." *Know Your Meme News. Cheezburger, Inc.* Web. 17 June 2014.

Rojo, Jaime, and Steven Harrington. "20 New Murals From Atlanta Living Walls 2013." *The Huffington Post. TheHuffingtonPost. com,* 21 Aug. 2013. Web. 17 June 2014.

Story, Louise. "Anywhere the Eye Can See, It's Now Likely to See an Ad." *The New York Times.* The New York Times, 15 Jan. 2007. Web. 17 June 2014.

IMAGES

Adams, Eddie. *Vietnam Execution.* Photo. 1968. *Stevenkasher.com.* 2014. Web. 17 June 2014.

Black, Nancy. "Welcome to Marlboro Country." 11 February 2011. *Adbusters.org,* Web. 17 June 2014.

Blitt, Barry. "Times Square Kiss." 17 June 1996. *Canonblogger.com,* n.d. Web. 17 June 2014.

"BP-Vietnam Spoof." Spoof Ad. *Adbusters.org.* 11 Feb. 2011. Web. 17 June 2014.

Dali, Salvador. *The Persistence of Memory.* 1931. *Tufts.edu,* n.d. Web. 17 June 2014.

Dutch Renaissance Self-Shot. "Great Art Parodies: 25 Iconic Paintings Recreated by Funny and Clever Contemporary Artists." *Blog of Francesco Mugnai,* n.d. Web. 17 June 2014.

Eisenstaedt, Alfred. *Times Square Kiss.* 14 August 1945. *Canonblogger. com,* n.d. Web. 17June 2014.

Golz, Dorothee. *Girl with a Pearl Earring.* "Great Art Parodies: 25 Iconic Paintings Recreated by Funny and Clever Contemporary Artists." *Blog of Francesco Mugnai,* n.d. Web. 17 June 2014.

"Hagia Sophia." *Milliyet.tr.com.* n.d. Web. 17 June 2014.

"Istanbul: Hagia Sophia (Imperial Gate Mosaics)." *Flickr.com,* 26 July 2011. Web. 17 June 2014.

"Keep Calm and Carry On: Part of a Series on Propaganda Parodies." *Knowyourmeme.com.* n.d. Web. 17 June 2014.

"Keep Quiet and Continue Working." *Knowyourmeme.com.* n.d. Web. 17 June 2014.

Lewandowski, Kim. "Photo Friday: Symbols." *Lemony Zest: Kim Lewandowski,* 8 May 2010. Web. 17 June 2014.

Marshall, Julian. "Obey the Giant – The Shepard Fairey Story." *Posca-life-custom.com.* 23 April 2013. Web. 17 June 2014.

"Pulp Fiction vs. Star Wars." *Nyuisva.wordpress.com.* "Commons II." 23 Nov. 2011. Web. 17 June 2014.

Rivera, Paolo. "The Self-Absorbing Man." *Acardona574.wordpress. com.* "Pastiche-Exercise-1-and-2," 2014. Web. 17 June 2014.

Rojo, Jaime and Steve Harrington. "20 New Murals From Atlanta Living Walls 2013." *Huffingtonpost.com.* 21 August 2013. Web. 17 June 2014.

Thornell, Jack. *James Meredith Shot*. Photo. 1966. *Bigstory.ap.org.* "James Meredith Shot Pulitzer 1967." n.d. Web. 17 June 2014.

Torbjornsen, Hilde. "50 Great Examples of Extremely Awesome Typography." *1stwebdesigner.com. 2010.* Web. 17 June 2014.

Vermeer, Johannes. *Girl with a Pearl Earring*. 1665. *Essential Vermeer. com.* n.d. Web. 17 June 2014.

10

INTO CULTURE: RESEARCH AND WRITING BEYOND THE CLASSROOM

In the first-year writing program, instructors recommend researching and writing about culture as a means of exploring different genres of writing. Cultural writing also invites experimentation with language as we adapt to the needs of an audience of academic peers. The *Oxford English Dictionary* defines *culture* as "the distinctive ideas, customs, social behavior, products, or way of life of a particular nation, society, people, or period." The ideas that organize culture serve as a promising topic in the first-year writing classroom because the connections between writing and culture are changeable and open to influence on both the individual and group level. In other words, writing about culture can result in a measurable impact on local, national, and even global arenas.

Student writers frequently find they are expected to develop their own topics for writing and research in English 1101 and English 1102 classes. Choosing to write about culture offers unique opportunities in that writers can explore their relationships with surrounding communities, and they can exercise their freedom to write with authority based on personal experiences and observations. Directly engaging culture provides writers the opportunity to realize *praxis,* that is, writing in the optimum rhetorical situation. Praxis is achieved when the right *writer* delivers the right *message* to the right *audience* in the right *place* (*context*) at the right *time* (*kairos*).

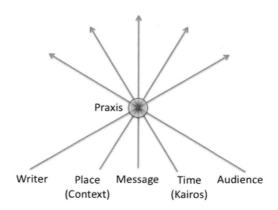

figure 10.1

The Axis of Praxis

Praxis

Writer Place Message Time Audience
(Context) (Kairos)

Praxis goes beyond just "good writing" or effective communication: it is a practice and therefore an action that capitalizes on a rhetorical situation to produce change. In this mode, cultural writers write with a purpose, often to either change or preserve what they see. Ideally, writing about culture can lead to the realization that topics of scholarship are all around us, woven into the everyday people, places, and artifacts we encounter.

Entering a discussion about culture can be disorienting at first. Where does culture exist? How do we find our way in? While many cultural markers are more obvious—whether protests and demonstrations, political debates and legislation, religious and spiritual gatherings, or even the flicker of news broadcasts from cable networks—culture also travels up and down our streets in less conspicuous ways. For example, consider the places you access attending college here in the urban core of Atlanta. Just by standing in the middle of Woodruff Park, you are likely to see locals playing oversize chess, artists displaying their work, musicians improvising new riffs, construction workers improving the streets, and a steady stream of students, business women and men, and other city dwellers passing by. Each of these scenes reveals a small glimpse into a rich cultural story.

Anderson, Courtney. *GSU's Dragon.*

Believe it or not, everyday culture in these everyday places can be used to produce academic writing. This type of writing intersects with *Cultural Studies* in that it investigates the beliefs, values, and traditions of a society in order to better understand the lived experience of that society's members. In order to access that lived experience, a cultural writer has three main access points to the culture: the *people* who are part of the culture, the *place* where the culture resides, and the *artifacts* made by members within the culture.

Doing the Right Thing: Ethics and Cultural Writing

When writing about culture, it is important to remember that you are working with the beliefs, values, and traditions that shape a group's entire way of life. Writing about something as sacred as others' beliefs can be fraught with ethical dilemmas: Have I represented these beliefs accurately? Have I portrayed them in a way that demonstrates respect for those who hold these beliefs? Has my writing done only good, and not harm, to the members of the culture? Remember that *a cultural writer is NOT an investigative reporter.* Your goal is never to *expose* a culture but rather to *understand* that culture and to help your readers do the same.

For this reason, we recommend that you choose to write about a culture to which you already belong. Doing so ensures that you already have a strong sense of the culture's fundamental beliefs before you research more nuanced issues.

In addition to selecting a culture to which you already belong, the following are a few general reminders about our responsibilities as cultural writers and researchers. Writers of culture:

- appreciate values/traditions that are not their own

- work for the benefit of the people and places they study

- seek opportunities to give back to the community

- try to understand the community, not exploit it with "exposé" techniques

- avoid objectifying research subjects

Entry Point: Culture and People

When writers investigate culture, they grapple with questions about their personal experiences and those of other people within a community (their own or another). Responding to questions about culture encourages us to reflect on our own position within our community and even the world at large. The questions themselves may relate to our feelings about a particular community (does participation in the community's gatherings and rituals feel freeing or restrictive?), our habits or behaviors, including the roles we play (for example, are we leaders or followers within the community?), and most importantly, our relationships with other people within the community (how well do we know and get along with members of the community?). This section discusses our responsibility to ethically establish and respectfully maintain our relationships with people within the cultures we are studying.

Simply put, culture cannot exist without people. Ultimately, we are the agents of creation, transmission, and change in our culture. As we begin to write about culture, a logical starting point is to locate our position within culture. This is often referred to as establishing our *positionality*. We construct our relationship to the topic at hand by considering our personal data: gender, age, nationality, race, and ethnicity. To this information, we add notes about our background: where we grew up, our education, our religious/spiritual affiliations, and the economic factors that are relevant to us. As we review this material, we may come to find it connects us, in sometimes surprising ways, to multiple communities. In other words, we might find that our high school education in a suburb of Atlanta connects us to one community, while our membership at a local synagogue includes us in a different community. Sometimes these communities overlap, and sometimes we find ourselves participating in ever-widening circles of community. A study of positionality can also reveal our proximity to communities of which we are not members. All in all, clarifying our positionality results in a clearer idea of the places where we are "insiders" and the places where we clearly exist on the outside of a given community. Consciously and honestly acknowledging our position as either an insider or an outsider is an important first step in cultural research and writing.

Collaborate

Activity 10.1

Envision what it would be like to perform cultural research in a community to which you already belong. With a partner, take turns with the following activity. Select a community of which you are already a member and take a brief moment to describe that community to your partner. Next, describe your positionality within that community.

Below are some sample questions you can ask to help determine your positionality:

What personal data influences your position (gender, age, nationality, race, ethnicity, etc.)?

What is your personal background and how does that influence the way you approach the community (where did you grow up, what is your education experience, etc.)?

What kinds of events prompt your engagement with this community (sports practice, monthly meetings, weekly service, etc.)?

What role do you play when you engage with this community (leader, observer, facilitator, entertainer, etc.)?

When you do speak up during community gatherings, what are you likely to say (ask questions, gossip, play devil's advocate, solve problems, share personal experience, etc.)?

What kind of relationship do you prefer to have with other members of your community? Why?

Big Picture

Once you and your partner have worked through the questions above, take a step back and think about how you each might research and write about your chosen community in light of your positionality:

1. **What question would you want to ask about this community to initiate your research and writing?** *For example, what elements contribute to the community's success?*

2. **What features of your positionality lead you to ask this question?** *For example, perhaps you are a leader interested in growing the membership base because you are an ambitious person.*

3. **If you were to proceed with a cultural research project on this community and question, what personal bias might influence your writing, and what steps could you take to ensure you write responsibly?** *For example, is your desire to grow the membership base for personal gain? If so, you may need to step back and consider what is right for the community as a whole.*

Sample Assignment

The following is an example of student Angell Green's response to a typical first-year writing prompt from instructor Sara Sunderland's English 1101 course. Green successfully composed an essay titled "A-Part of the Whole" wherein he describes his positionality within and without the Woodward Academy community. Take a moment to read the excerpt below and consider how Green's open acknowledgement of his positionality strengthens his ethos as a writer.

Going to an institution like Woodward, you get placed into a group: the private school kid. Now what is the typical private school kid? The stereotype is that you are a preppy, snobbish, very wealthy white kid who has no respect and does not know the value of a dollar. You are intent upon being bourgeoisie, with a name like Master Benjamin Mastercard IV, Esquire. You probably live in Buckhead, Alpharetta, or Gwinnett in a massive five-story house with a butler and maids. At least, that's what I would have thought before I ever attended private school. The misconception, to me, is quite entertaining. Yes, there are students of this description who attend private institutions, yet most students are nothing similar to this. I could not have broken the mold any better; I was the complete opposite. I was not the typical private school kid because I grew up in a poorer part of inner city Atlanta in a single-parent household. I lived in a simple two-story house where I held the positions of butler, maid, cook, and dishwasher among others. To be truthful, I had the intelligence of a private school kid, just not the funds. Woodward

Here, Green clarifies that these stereotypes are what he "would have thought" while he was still an outsider to the Woodward community.

Here, Green situates his identity within the Woodward community as a result of his demographic and life experiences.

exposed me to new groups of people. I had always grown up with middle class to below the poverty line blacks; Woodward, however, was a microcosm of the world. For example, there were whites, blacks, Asians, Indians, Christians, Jews, Hindus, agnostics, smart kids, regular kids, athletes, musicians, artists, rich kids, poor kids, middle class kids, and so on all going to school together. I found myself becoming friends with others who were completely different than me.

Woodward, as Green describes it, is a complex social space, encompassing students from a variety of different places and backgrounds—not the homogeneous private school that he anticipated, and he highlights these demographics to characterize the diverse relationship that evolved within that community.

Entry Point: Culture and Places

What do you see when you look at your surroundings? Your home, whether it's your GSU dorm room or a house shared with your nuclear family, is simultaneously the site of your everyday life and an expression of culture. Home is, after all, a place you have marked as your own, and as a physical location, it also represents a particular space within a large metropolitan area. Homes are culturally-dynamic places that we can read as texts which contribute considerably to academic discourse.

As will be discussed in Chapter 11, online spaces are proliferating rapidly in our society, and our presence in those spaces consumes more and more of our attention, whether by preference or necessity. These online spaces offer entirely different opportunities for cultural study. For example, we might explore the GSU English Major Facebook page to get a glimpse of the activities of our peers, or follow hashtag discussions through the Department's Twitter feed. In either of these activities, we might discover how our digital traces both affect online spaces and influence the physical places we inhabit.

Tran, Lillia. *Stranger.*

Activity 10.2

When was the last time that you mentioned an online interaction (a Tumblr post, an Instagram picture, a Tweet) in a face-to-face conversation?

Try this: Using the hashtag #GSUCulture, compose a tweet or Instagram about something you observe on campus today or about an element of GSU's culture, in general. Peruse this hashtag discussion and think about how your digital trace might follow you when you return to the physical classroom. Have you represented yourself in the way that you want your classmates to see you? How does your online persona compare to your classroom personality? How could your online interactions influence face-to-face discussions? How would you compare and contrast online spaces and physical places?

https://www.facebook.com/EnglishDepartmentGSU

Whether digital or physical, places familiar to GSU students can generate research and writing about culture. For example, pause for a moment to reflect on your most recent visit to the Panthers Club food court located in the

Presley, Shedaria. *My 1st Apartment.*

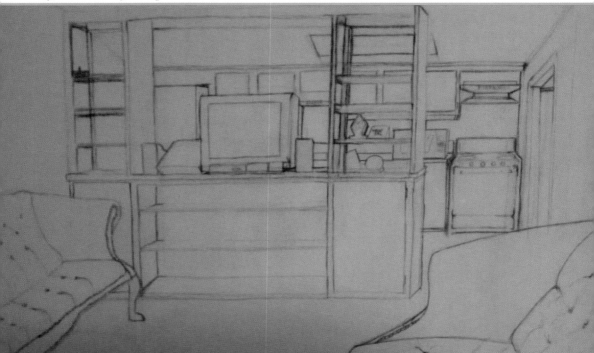

GSU University Center. Do you remember feeling satisfied with the appearance and layout of the food stations available to you? Were the prices reasonable, the locations hygienic, the food nutritious or appetizing? Analyzing and comparing the layout and appearance of the various food stations allows you to draw inferences about how members of the GSU community select and purchase food in that space. Such inferences can lead to hypotheses about values within GSU's culture. For example, long lines at the salad station might indicate a strong, health-conscious value, whereas easy-to-grab snacks disappearing from the shelves might indicate an "on-the-go" mentality. We are not just concerned with how the shoppers purchase food, but with what their purchasing processes say about values within their community. Once we take the time to make these observations, it is important to record them.

The practice of *mapping* is a visual approach to recording observations and initial hypotheses about a place. The researcher begins by drawing a rough map of the space and proceeds to identify important features of the space for reference during the writing process. Below is an easy step-by-step approach to mapping.

Steps for effective mapping:

1) Once you have selected a place to study (perhaps a place that you visit often, such as GSU's library, shuttle system, or your place of employment), determine when you will perform your research. Remember that some places experience different levels of activity on different days and/or times, so consider how busy you want the place to be when you go. For example, the researcher in the sample below has selected the Panthers Club for her project. She decided to visit around lunchtime during a weekday to witness the peak of the dining hall's activity.

2) Upon arrival, spend some time observing the physical space around you. Determine how you will define this cultural place. What boundaries will you use to limit the scope of your field observation? Look at the example of a mapping exercise below. Our researcher decided only to observe the area that is visible to the general public (excluding "employee only" spaces), and she has also decided to use the turnstiles in the entryway and the cash registers at the back as boundaries. The researcher uses physical features to limit the space and consciously control the scope of her study. It allows her to stay focused on food selection and purchase, not on consumption, conversation, trash disposal, etc.

3) Once you have defined the boundaries of your cultural place, use them to sketch a map. Include significant objects and spaces that exist within that place. Try to record as many of the non-human objects as you can before beginning to observe the people there.
4) Now, observe the *activity* within the place you have defined. How do people move and interact in this location? Mark the spaces where interactions occur and add arrows to indicate movement through these spaces. Then add notes describing what you see in the margins of your map.
5) Before you leave, take one last look around you. Consider what details you might forget when you are no longer in this place. Note those last few details on your map, as well.

Example of Mapping Exercise

The map in figure 10.2 was drawn from first-hand observation at Panthers Club on Wednesday, May 21, 2014 at 12:14pm.

figure 10.2

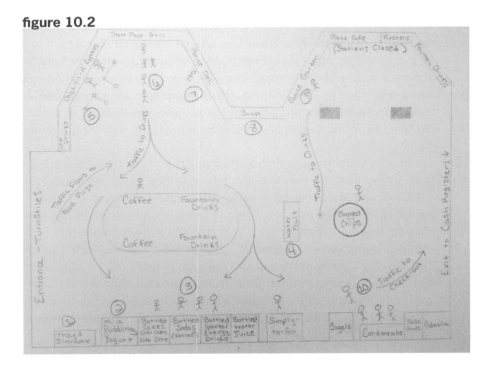

figure 10.3

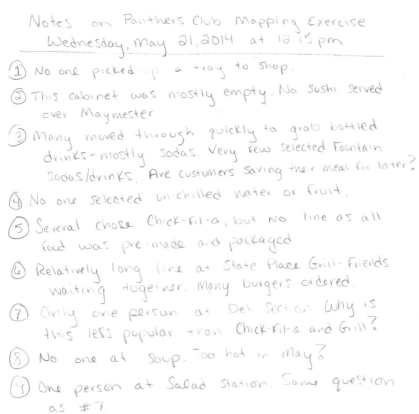

Notes on Panthers Club Mapping Exercise
Wednesday, May 21, 2014 at 12:15 pm

1. No one picked up a tray to shop.

2. This cabinet was mostly empty. No Sushi served over Maymester

3. Many moved through quickly to grab bottled drinks - mostly sodas. Very few selected Fountain sodas/drinks. Are customers saving their meal for later?

4. No one selected un-chilled water or fruit.

5. Several chose Chick-fil-a, but no line as all food was pre-made and packaged

6. Relatively long line at State Place Grill- Friends waiting together. Many burgers ordered.

7. Only one person at Deli Section. Why is this less popular than Chick-Fil-a and Grill?

8. No one at Soup. Too hot in May?

9. One person at Salad Station. Same question as #7.

10. Long back-up at Condiments. There is another station after check-out. Do these customers not know about it? If so, are they visitors?

In addition to mapping, *field notes* can help you capture and respond to your own observations before you move on to outlining and drafting your ideas. Composing a detailed set of field notes can help you separate your direct, empirical observations from how you feel about what you see. Although this may seem like an easy distinction to make, we all carry biases that influence the way we interpret the world around us.

Steps for writing effective field notes:

1) Divide a notebook page in half by drawing a line from top to bottom, creating two equal columns.
2) Take note of the date, time, location, and subject of your notes.
3) Label one column "Direct Observations." This column is the place for concrete, measurable, objective observations.
4) Label the other column "Personal Responses." This column is the place for your own thoughts, feelings, and questions that arise during note-taking.
5) After you finish your field notes, take a step back and re-read what you have written. Field notes are most useful when you take the time not only to write them but also to write *about* them. Review both columns of notes, and comment on what you see there. Pay special attention to patterns, repetitions, questions, and opportunities for further study.

Supreme, James. *Go.*

Ultimately, the information you gather and the inferences you make from that information can then be shaped into writing that takes action. Writing inspired by observations and research on culture is purposeful and dynamic; it works to accomplish something, and it changes over time. Your writing could develop into a research project in your first-year writing class, or an informative blog post intended to advise other first-year writing students in your class about how to make the most of campus resources. As you can see, writing about culture can take any number of forms.

QUICK REMINDER:

Be mindful about your choice of place and ask yourself the following questions: Does this place require special permission for entry? Is admission free and safe? Your selection process should include a quick set of notes on your assumptions about the location and the people who frequent it before you undertake the mapping activity.

Activity 10.4

Using the Panthers Club example above, try experimenting with mapping and writing field notes at an off-campus location. Grab a notebook and pen and walk over to the Sweet Auburn Municipal Market to examine the extensive food and dining options this popular neighborhood spot offers. Consider the languages and aromas around you. As you take everything in, pay attention to small details like how the quinoa looks next to other grains and herbal medicine sticks. If you can, sample something that's new for you. Take the time to carefully record what you see in a set of field notes and then draw a meticulous map. Ask yourself the following questions:

How do these cultural markers compare to the Panthers Club?

What do your observations lead you to believe about food in the area surrounding the GSU campus?

What do the restaurants, food stands, and markets communicate about the culture of the neighborhood?

The results of this investigation could easily lead to writing a culture-based essay for your English Composition class, or it might lead to writing beyond the classroom. For example, you could write an op-ed piece for *The Signal* urging readers to patronize this market to keep the community's food culture vibrant, or you could craft a proposal to the SGA to lobby for new food stations in the dining halls that would more accurately represent GSU's multicultural population.

Entry Point: Culture and Artifacts

Working with *artifacts,* or material objects made by human beings (rather than those produced by nature), means employing evidence of *material culture.* Artifacts might take the form of clothes, jewelry, furniture, sports equipment, workplace, or any other material item. These items often bear a rich cultural history available for exploration through writing. Using artifacts as an entry point to study culture may seem, at the outset, like an easier task than researching cultural places,

Marden, Lorelei Crystalilly. *Celebrating Life.*

but the challenges these types of writing projects present simply test writers in different ways. When writing about artifacts, we are frequently prompted to scan these objects for deeper meanings.

In first-year writing, instructors may require students to stretch their writing skills to include *sensory description*; writing about cultural artifacts offers ways to accomplish this task from a variety of angles. First, keep in mind that when instructors request "more details," or they say, "make this paragraph more descriptive," they often are looking for you to engage one or more of the five senses. When you have a concrete object in front of you, this task becomes more manageable. Simply begin with one of your five senses and use it as a *lens* (or mode of seeing). For example, imagine you were holding the object depicted in *Celebrating Life* in your hands. How would it feel to the touch? After experiencing this sensation first-hand, you would list your findings (perhaps it would be lightweight, delicate, dry, rough around the edges) and then move on to one of the four remaining senses. Alternatively, you could return to your field notes on your previous trip to the Sweet Auburn Municipal Market. Did the smell or appearance of an unfamiliar food lead you to purchase and try it? What did you learn from your transaction with the vendor? How did you describe the taste of the food? Collecting this type of data builds a bank of details from which you can draw in order to generate descriptive language for your writing.

Sample Assignment

Below is an example of a way one student writer at GSU approached an instructor's prompt through a cultural artifact. The following writing prompt from instructor Jessica Temple's English 1102 course is an example of a typical first-year writing assignment. After the prompt, you will find first-year GSU student Amanda Tice's essay, "A Culture of Words," which Amanda successfully composed in response to this prompt. Amanda's essay enters a discussion of her family's culture through a group of common, everyday artifacts found throughout their home: books.

Instructor Temple's Prompt:

Essay 1: Writing about an Artifact

Select an artifact that tells a story about your cultural background that you can share with the class. This artifact can be a picture, a coat of arms, or an object (a piece of clothing, jewelry, a tool, etc.). If possible, choose an item that illustrates something about your cultural background that is not obvious. If you cannot find a "hidden" part of your background, teach us something we may not have known about your culture. Turn to your family members to learn more about your background. If that is not possible, do research so that you have something significant to share with the rest of the class about your cultural heritage.

Once you have selected your cultural artifact, write an essay that describes what the cultural artifact reveals about a culture and analyzes the ways in which it does so. Your essay should have a clear thesis and organized evidence to support that thesis. The thesis should state what the artifact is and which culture it comes from. It should then make an argument about how it illuminates that culture.

In the body of your paper, first describe the artifact in more detail. If it's an object, describe it physically (using your five senses). If your artifact represents an event or ritual, describe what it involves, even if your audience is already familiar with the object. Show your audience, in detail, how and what the artifact conveys about the culture. Include lots of details, examples, and specifics.

Your essay should be in MLA format (which includes double spacing and 12-pt. Times New Roman font – see Purdue's OWL website for detailed instructions). Your paper will be graded on its thesis, supporting evidence, organization, and mechanical correctness.

Your analysis should shed new light on the meanings of your artifact. In other words, you are being asked to select a cultural artifact and consider:

How does the artifact illuminate the culture? What aspects of this culture does it bring to light? How does it do so?

What ideas are embedded in this artifact?

How are these messages conveyed? Through what rhetorical means are they conveyed?

What ideas, beliefs, or stereotypes are being represented through the rhetoric of the artifact?

Who is the target audience? What is the context? What is the purpose? Does the artifact succeed in fulfilling this purpose? (Keep in mind that there can be more than one target audience or purpose.)

Are there appeals to ethos, pathos, and/or logos exuded by the artifact? If so, describe the different ways that you see these appeals working by using details, specifics, and examples.

What (or who) is being left out of the artifact or the culture it represents?

Lastly, your paper should include some evaluation on your part: Is the rhetoric of the message effective? What is its impact? How, if at all, do you think the artifact affects its audience?

Note that you do not need to answer all of these questions. You may want to pick and choose the ones that work best to support your central purpose (your thesis).

Amanda Tice

Instructor Jessica Temple

ENGL 1102

29 Jan 2014

A Culture of Words

Every room in my house contained books. The kitchen had its shelves for the cookbooks; the living room held three bookcases; and even the bathroom had its share of reading material. Some rooms didn't even have walls anymore, just shelves from floor to ceiling covered as much as three rows deep in literature--hundreds of authors spanning thousands of years across the world offering all they know of science, math, history, and art. It's hard to grow up in a place like that without developing some fancy ideas about everything being well within reach. With so much knowledge available to peruse at your fingertips, it's hard to imagine that you can't do anything you want. These books are the center of my family's culture, a culture of self-education.

I want you to think deeply about the implications of the book. Think of the possibility and potential that the book represents. Think of the power and safety that books can bring to you through their inherent education, and you will get a glimpse into my culture.

Before the irreplaceable Johannes Gutenberg changed the world irrevocably with the invention of the printing press, the power and prestige of books was more keenly felt. The knowledge held inside was for but a privileged few. Most couldn't read what they found inside even if they had a book to hold and call their own, and so their education was in the hands of another. The knowledge was kept by the nobility and the clergy. With no way to learn for themselves, people were held down in the dark ages for centuries, unable to free themselves from the fear of the unknown that surrounded them. The printing press changed all that by reducing the process time of making a book from half a lifetime to days. It brought forth an age of middle class wisdom and literacy. It gave rise to a generation of people able to learn for themselves, people capable of even interpreting their own bibles. They were free to know God personally again and seek their own salvation. Books removed the shackles of spiritual slavery and reshaped the future of the western world. This is the force of the written word.

This force has grown exponentially over the last decade with the invention of the internet. No longer is a book bound to the physical world. The overwhelming power inherent in the written word transcended its physical bonds and leaped into subatomic realms of electric transfer.

Our family members are people of education. Not in the traditional sense most people imagine, but we are self-educated. We consider nothing to be beyond our abilities. We do not resign ourselves to failure because a thing is too complicated, or we don't know where to begin. We know that someone has this knowledge. Someone stood in our novice shoes before and walked this path. All we need to do is find their story and learn from that experience.

My family is full of these people, including myself. My grandfather was a classically-educated man. He earned three degrees from various institutions in theology. While this formal education was valuable to him to be sure, it was not where he learned to fly a plane. Nor did he invent an electrical device that earned his living for two lucrative decades with any of this knowledge. Formal education did not teach him improved farming techniques that helped maximize the output of his acres while running his company A/B Electronics. These were skills he taught himself through a life of avid literacy. These are things that books gave to him, and in turn he gave that drive to the next generation.

My father is another beacon of our culture. He earns his living as an electrical engineer and professional photographer, although he has never earned a degree in either area. He never attended classes to learn how to use AutoCAD, build sophisticated robotics, or streamline thousand part automation processes, but these are the kinds of books you find on our bookshelves. *AutoCAD 2007, The Viscosity of Honey,* and *Absolute Zero* are the sources of his education. Not once did a professional teach him the secrets of albumin and overcast, shutter speeds and film grain. For that information, he consulted *The Art of Photography* and *An Everyday Guide to Meteorology.* His award winning work has been published in *National Geographic* and captured the most significant moments of many people's lives. Books brought him those accolades.

Those same titles brought my sisters art to life through the lens, but other tomes in the house bear the brunt of my usage. *Chemistry, The Joy of Cooking,* and *The Mad Italian* are the educators behind my bakery, Better Than Sex Cheesecakes. By reading the dozens of ways that an egg can change shape on the molecular level to vary in consistency from the fluff of meringue to the divinity that is pasta, I learned my craft.

This knowledge didn't happen by coincidence, though. The books didn't jump off the shelves and demand to be read. It was a shared experience like most cultures, a taught experience. The sharing began long before I actually remember, but my memory picks up with *Where the Sidewalk Ends* by Shel Silverstein, read to me until I was able to read it for myself. My sister now reads those same poems to her children. I still remember many of the lines. They pop into my head from time to time reminding me of my culture. "Oh I'm being eaten by a boa constrictor," and I am eternally grateful for it.

Graziano, Marissa. *Nostalgia.*

Activity 10.5 Questions for Reflection

1. How do books function in Amanda's essay? How would you describe her critical approach to the book archive? To the individual books as artifacts?

2. Amanda references a wide variety of books from *The Joy of Cooking* to Shel Silverstein's children's poetry. How does her critical approach to these books allow her to talk about something distinct from the actual content of the books?

3. How do these inanimate objects come to contain cultural meaning, revealing values that the family holds both as a group and as individuals?

4. How are these artifacts employed as teaching tools beyond what Amanda might call a classical education? How does her family's engagement with these artifacts reveal her family's beliefs about classical education?

5. Thinking of the objects that you encounter in your everyday life, how can these objects become cultural artifacts? How might you look at these items as not merely tied to their primary purpose, but simultaneously as artifacts that document the culture(s) to which you belong?

Artifacts and Primary Research

While most college essays require research that begins in scholarly texts found in libraries or online, research and writing about culture can also begin with action. Depending on the location you decide to write about, research on that site may not even exist yet. Don't be discouraged if this is what you find; you have actually discovered a tremendous opportunity! The absence of research about a topic gives you the chance to identify or even create a ***primary source.***

As introduced in the chapter on Research and Documentation, research is considered ***primary*** when it discovers information first-hand. For example, a scientist who performs an experiment on the health effects of e-cigarettes performs ***primary research*** because the effects of these devices are not yet defined *until the researcher performs her study.* Furthermore, her lab report would be considered a ***primary source*** because it details information obtained through her first-hand experimentation.

Examples of ways to create primary sources:
1) Conduct interviews
2) Write and distribute surveys
3) Record your own observations and experiments
4) Start a Twitter exchange based on a hashtag of your choice or start a blog on a topic of your choice and invite others to contribute
5) Build your own archive of images or artifacts

KROG STREET TUNNEL: A CASE STUDY

Vala Jr., Jiri. *Krog Street Tunnel*

One Atlanta place that could produce a rich cultural study of primary sources is the Krog Street Tunnel. Located just a few miles from GSU's campus, this tunnel has been the focus of much local speculation, controversy, and conversation. Built in 1912, the tunnel provides a route beneath railroad tracks and leads into a small neighborhood called Cabbagetown. The origin of the neighborhood's unique name, a neighborhood that once housed the workers in a local cotton plant, continues to be a source of speculation. Atlanta's *Creative Loafing* boasts of the tunnel as "the original social networking site" for its collection of posters, messages, and graffiti art (you can follow the tunnel's daily transformations at http://thedailyk-rog.tumblr.com/). This cultural place lends itself to multiple research projects supported by primary sources in the form of art, text, architecture, newspaper coverage, exchanges over social media, even conversations on the neighborhood's email listserv.

Additionally, you are not bound to engage solely with existing primary sources. The option always exists to generate your own primary sources, especially if you find existing sources do not open a course of investigation that interests you. For example, if you were intrigued by the Krog Street Tunnel but had the sense more could be learned from researching the residents' real feelings about the graffiti on their neighborhood walls, then you have reached a productive point in your research process. From here you have any number of options for creating primary sources that will reveal the information you seek. You might write a set of questions and request to interview members of the neighborhood association (often a place where community-minded individuals donate their time). You might also write a survey and distribute it throughout the neighborhood in order to get a broader perspective from a larger number of residents. As you can see, either using already existing primary sources or creating your own can lead to engaging, innovative research allowing you to explore your interests while producing new knowledge about local cultural places.

Interested in supplemental information about this case study? Visit guidetowriting.gsu.edu for companion readings about recent controversies surrounding the Krog Street Tunnel.

Political Modes of Inquiry

Once a writer establishes who, where, and what she wants to research, she must then decide *how* she will approach the research. Because the cultural writer values the beliefs of a society in her writing, the argument she produces about this society will always be *political*. The term *politics* is frequently used in popular culture to describe activities that relate to formal government operations, such as campaigning for elections and deliberating legislation.

However, the term *politics* itself extends beyond just government. Its etymology stems from the Greek word "polis," meaning city or society. In the most basic sense, *politics* refers to *any purpose that a person (or persons) endorses within a society.* In this context, when a writer explores how a social trend (like "selfies") influences or expresses culture, she engages politics in her argument because she writes about that social activity for a particular purpose. The cultural researcher would ask what that selfie says about the author's identity (i.e. the author values documenting personal experience) and what selfies as a social trend communicate about politics in that culture (i.e. the culture is fascinated by the private lives of others).

Investigating how selfies reveal individual identity in a social context is a kind of inquiry that engages *identity politics* by asking how those persons are identified, whether by themselves or by society as a whole. Identity politics are evident across nearly all forms of rhetoric, particularly in pop culture, government campaigns, and advertising. The cultural researcher explores how an individual's identity shapes his culture and how his culture shapes him in return.

The chart in table 10.1 outlines three common *political modes of inquiry* that can help shape your exploration of culture and further narrow the scope of your writing. This chart *is by no means a comprehensive list of all possible ways to inquire about a culture's politics.* This chart also includes brainstorming questions and sample research questions to help you apply these political modes of inquiry to your own writing topic.

table 10.1
Political Modes of Inquiry

Political Modes of Inquiry	OED Definition	Potential Brainstorming Questions	Sample Research Questions
Race	"A group of people belonging to the same family and descended from a common ancestor; a house, family, kindred"	How does race inform social dynamics in a culture? How does a culture define or generate behavioral expectations for members of a particular race? How does that particular race define itself as conforming with or in opposition to a dominant culture?	How do race-based GSU student organizations interact with each other? What does their collaboration (or lack thereof) say about cultural beliefs about race among GSU undergraduate students today?
Gender	"Males or females viewed as a group; also: the characteristic of belonging to one of these groups"	How do gender roles within this society shape broader social issues? How does this culture define and uphold gender roles? In response, how does an individual's expressed gender influence the culture at large?	Considering how college students dance at social gatherings, do the moves performed reveal anything about cultural expectations of gender? How might particular dance moves "perform" (or refuse to conform to) "acceptable" femininity or masculinity? How do they reveal what the culture expects from men and women?
Class	"A division or stratum of society consisting of people at the same economic level or having the same social status"	How does class organize social interactions? How does culture define or produce class distinctions among members of the culture?	Does the class status of one's parents (low-income, middle-class, or affluent) influence a student's selection of a major? What might this influence say about how different classes define a "successful career?"

Notice that in the chart above, each brainstorming question actually includes *two* questions. One asks how that particular identity category influences culture, and the other asks how culture defines and produces each identity category. This two-way exchange of meaning between individual identity and culture demonstrates a **reciprocity** that is important to keep in mind when writing about culture. Individuals influence culture at the same time that culture influences individuals. Race, gender, and class do not simply "exist" without social context; if they did, then people across all cultures throughout the world would believe and act the same way.

Because we know expressions and expectations of identity are not the same in every culture, the responsible cultural writer always keeps in mind that she is investigating a dynamic, reciprocal relationship between identity and culture, not a simple cause-and-effect dynamic.

Creating a Culture-Based Research Question

When writing about culture, placing your attention on people, places, and artifacts is the best way to establish a research question that will focus your project. A **research question** is a way of turning a hypothesis or "hunch" about a given topic into a form that a writer can address with research. The research question is a refined version of the broader topic. For example, a writer might choose to research Martin Luther King, Jr. for her essay on a social issue, but when she types in "Martin Luther King, Jr." in to the GSU Library's "Discover" search engine, the search returns 236,143 results! She will need to narrow her topic in order to sort through this overwhelming volume of available sources.

Scope: Breadth and Depth

In order to focus her research question on Dr. King, our writer will need to narrow the **scope**, or focus, of her topic. A research scope can be measured in two ways:

- breadth, or "how much material you can cover"
- depth, or "how thoroughly you can cover it"

As a rule of thumb, most college courses expect a writer to favor depth over breadth in research, and just like scientific research, a cultural researcher must "control" for differences in variables to obtain a specific, supportable conclusion. In cultural work, the researcher understands that, for example, the way a community in Capetown, South Africa remembers Dr. King is different than the way a community in Atlanta, Georgia remembers him. By the same token, residents in Dr. King's childhood Atlanta neighborhood of the Old Fourth Ward experience his memory still differently than, say, residents in the metro-Atlanta suburb of Marietta.

To "control" for the differences in these geographic "variables," a cultural researcher will need to select the narrowest researchable scope possible so that she can go deeper into the topic than just the surface level. Recall that cultural writing engages the "ideas, customs, social behaviour, products, [and] way of life" for a community. Research about the ideas of a community compels the responsible researcher to discover how individual members in that culture think and behave relative to the chosen topic. In order to research these thoughts thoroughly within the constraints of an assigned essay (typically, five or more pages in length), a researcher will need to narrow her scope.

Returning to the example given above, the original research topic of "Martin Luther King, Jr." was simply too broad; it returns *every topic* about Dr. King, in *every place* he influenced, in *every time period*. This scope is far too broad to provide deep, thorough research in a first-year writing course. In cultural writing, asking brainstorming questions about the people, places, and artifacts related to your topic is a great way to narrow the scope and establish a research question. In the Dr. King example, the researcher could ask herself the following questions:

1. ARTIFACT(S): *What kind of cultural artifacts* can produce the most useful information about Dr. King?

Possible Brainstorming Answers:

Interviews with people who knew Dr. King

Documented observation of a place where he lived or worked

Objects that Dr. King created/wrote or that he owned

Martin Luther King, Jr. National Park: exhibit and monuments

Our researcher must consider accessibility when considering what materials she can use for her research. While interviews with people who knew Dr. King or objects he owned would provide great artifacts for this study, they may not be easily attainable. However, the Martin Luther King, Jr. National Park already provides a convenient collection of artifacts memorializing Dr. King, and because it is safe, close to GSU's campus, and can be surveyed within the time constraints of her assignment, it provides a promising source of artifacts appropriate for her study.

2. PLACE: Because my paper is about culture, *where* is the culture that Dr. King influenced?

Possible Brainstorming Answers:

Throughout the World

In the United States

In the U.S. South

In his hometown of Atlanta

In the neighborhood he was born and reared: Old Fourth Ward

While it is true that Dr. King influenced lives worldwide and throughout the U.S., these places are too large to presume that all of the residents within them are part of the same culture, and there are too many people involved to allow for truly exhaustive research. Turning to the South and Atlanta, while these are narrower than the first two options, they still include such a diversity of cultures that it would be difficult to cover all of them thoroughly within the page- or word-length requirements of most college essays. Because the National Park is located in the neighborhood where Dr. King was born and raised, and because this neighborhood offers the narrowest researchable scope possible: our researcher will likely choose the Old Fourth Ward neighborhood.

3. PEOPLE: Although my paper is about a person (Dr. King), it is a cultural project. And because a single person is not an entire culture, *who* am I interested in writing about?

Possible Brainstorming Answers:

Politicians and/or activists during the Civil Rights Era

International diplomats who were influenced by King

Famous rhetoricians since King

Pop Icons

Writers (novelists, poets, screenwriters, playwrights)

His family

Residents of the Old Fourth Ward neighborhood

Visitors/Tourists who come to the Martin Luther King, Jr., National Park

While all of the answers above might generate an intriguing essay, because cultural writing privileges the everyday lived experience of members in a society–not only the political or popular figures in the media–our researcher might decide to explore Dr. King through the eyes of the visitors and tourists who remember him through the National Park.

4. POLITICAL MODE OF INQUIRY: Given the people, place, and artifacts selected, which political perspective is most relevant to this writing project? Because King dedicated his life to activism in racial equality, and particularly because his greatest legacy in the American memory is as a champion of civil liberties, our researcher is likely to select "race" as a productive mode of inquiry.

Now our writer has a narrower scope: "What can the exhibits and monuments at the Martin Luther King, Jr. National Park tell us about how Dr. King's legacy and how he is remembered by visitors Atlanta's Old Fourth Ward neighborhood?" With a more focused research question, our writer is now ready to get to work on her project.

Funnel Exercise

Narrowing down a topic to a research question is much like running sand through a funnel: it limits the volume that passes through while simultaneously directing its flow in a neater, more organized fashion. Take a moment to review the "funnel" diagrams below. Figure 10.4 has been completed using

figure 10.4

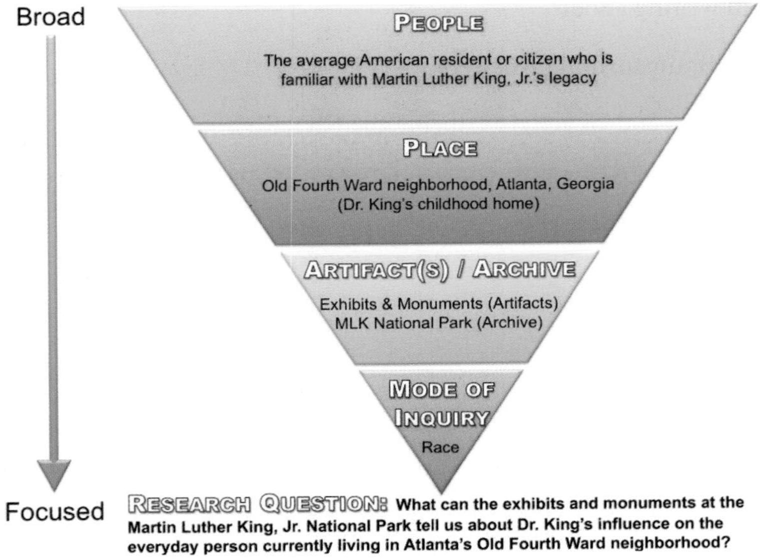

Broad

PEOPLE
The average American resident or citizen who is familiar with Martin Luther King, Jr.'s legacy

PLACE
Old Fourth Ward neighborhood, Atlanta, Georgia (Dr. King's childhood home)

ARTIFACT(S) / ARCHIVE
Exhibits & Monuments (Artifacts)
MLK National Park (Archive)

MODE OF INQUIRY
Race

Focused   RESEARCH QUESTION: What can the exhibits and monuments at the Martin Luther King, Jr. National Park tell us about Dr. King's influence on the everyday person currently living in Atlanta's Old Fourth Ward neighborhood?

figure 10.5

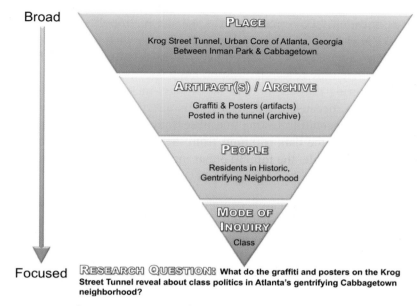

Broad

PLACE
Krog Street Tunnel, Urban Core of Atlanta, Georgia
Between Inman Park & Cabbagetown

ARTIFACT(S) / ARCHIVE
Graffiti & Posters (artifacts)
Posted in the tunnel (archive)

PEOPLE
Residents in Historic,
Gentrifying Neighborhood

MODE OF
INQUIRY
Class

Focused   RESEARCH QUESTION: What do the graffiti and posters on the Krog
Street Tunnel reveal about class politics in Atlanta's gentrifying Cabbagetown
neighborhood?

the Martin Luther King, Jr. example detailed above, and figure 10.5 considers
new topics. Notice that each one starts with a different "entry point" (People,
Place, or Artifact). When generating ideas for cultural writing, any of these
categories may inspire your topic.

What's at Stake: Empirical vs. Interpretive Research

A cultural researcher employs both empirical and interpretive research
techniques, though the final product, a piece of culture-based writing, typically aims to produce answers that are more *interpretive* than *empirical*.
Interpretive answers are speculative; they are shaped by the researcher's
personal perspective, and they are valuable because they reveal a multiplicity of perspectives. In contrast, **empirical** conclusions are measurable, and
they can be supported through experimentation. Nothing written in culture-
based writing is ever purely empirical, even though empirical data may be
used to produce interpretive results.

Consider the following example of a scientific experiment that produces
empirical results but could also lead a cultural researcher to generate interpretive conclusions. In 2013, Jeremy Diem, an associate professor in
GSU's Department of Geosciences published his research on the effects of
the Clean Air Act of 1970 in Atlanta, Georgia (for more information, see

GSU's News webpage at http://news.gsu.edu/2013/06/05/research-clean-air-act-increased-atlanta-rainfall/). For Diem's scientific study, he asked the research question, "Has rainfall in the Atlanta metropolitan area changed since the Clean Air Act was implemented? If so, in what way?" Notice that, in much the same way as we encourage you to do with culture-based writing, Diem's scientific research question has a specifically-limited scope: he is only measuring rainfall, only in the Atlanta metro area, and only since 1970. However, because the answer to this question can be unequivocally proven through scientific testing and observation, the answer he produces will be empirical; the data resulting from the research provides an answer that is indeed provable: the rainfall either increased, decreased, or remained the same.

In contrast, a cultural researcher might use empirical evidence to contextualize and support her studies, but such empirical data would not be the intended result of her research question. Instead, she could ask, "How has the increase in rainfall caused by the Clean Air Act influenced the emergence of an urban gardening culture?" Notice that the scope of this cultural-based research question is just as focused as its scientific sibling: she is only researching urban gardening as a cultural phenomenon, only in the Atlanta urban core, and only since the Clean Air Act went into effect. However, this culture-based research question differs in the kind of conclusion it generates. Rather than discovering concrete, empirical facts, the cultural researcher interprets the set of beliefs, or ideology, that shapes the way members of a society interact with one another.

Ideology in Culture:

Another feature that distinguishes cultural research from other forms of research is the interest cultural research has in uncovering a culture's ideology, or the system of beliefs that characterizes a culture. Ideology exists in the thoughts and opinions of members within that culture, and because thoughts and opinions cannot be scientifically tested, we can see how research questions about a culture's ideology can lead to interpretive conclusions.

A Reminder about Ethics in Cultural Writing

Because cultural researchers are responsible for interpreting the opinions and experiences of others, they must approach their work with the utmost respect for the members of the studied culture and their beliefs. Recall the discussion of positionality earlier in this chapter. Ethical cultural writing acknowledges the researcher's positionality and subjective opinions, attempting always to minimize bias. For this reason, we recommend that you consider writing about a culture to which you already belong. (See the "Doing the Right Thing" text box earlier in this chapter for more on the ethical considerations of cultural writing.)

Conclusion

No matter which entry point or political mode of inquiry you choose, researching culture presents the opportunity for you to generate meaningful, compelling, and socially-conscious writing. It is writing that takes political action in a public sphere with the goal of increasing understanding of a culture's values, beliefs, and behaviors. Furthermore, writing through culture has the potential to tap into fresh topics and new ideas, as is the case in Carla Bazemore-Colclough's essay included at the end of this chapter. Bazemore-Colclough composed her research essay "Universality of Nonaggression" to fulfill a social issue research assignment in Stephanie Rountree's English 1102 course. Her essay was so impressive that it received GSU's annual Bert H. Flanders Freshman Award for the most outstanding nominated essay written in any 1000-level class university-wide. Please take a moment to read through her essay, noting how she employs the skills discussed in this chapter. Think about what kinds of questions she asks and how she approaches her research. How could you ask similar (or very different) questions about the everyday culture you encounter here at GSU? Chances are, a locally-based cultural research and writing project will allow you to impact the world beyond the limits of your classroom.

Carla Marie Bazemore-Colclough

Professor Rountree

English 1102

9 November 2012

Universality of Nonaggression

I sit a few seats down from a girl sitting quietly alone in the

dining hall. Her only concentration appears to be the huge plate

of food in front of her that seems to overwhelm her slight, fragile

looking frame. She appears to be one of the most unobtrusive

people in the hall, at least physically, but is obviously conscious of

her position in relationship to others. She scoots her chair in a little

closer to the bar, bundles herself a little tighter, as fellow students

crowd in. I think she is quite adorable and the personification of

nonaggression. However, I fear for her the bustle and tumble of

the masses, shoving their way through the doors of the hall. I can

imagine her being washed away in an ocean of busy, absorbed

people, oblivious to the small, but important people they engulf

on their way. No one advocates for nonaggression. No one fights

for nonaggression. A nonaggressive movement is practically an

oxymoron because, to many of us, a nonaggressive society is an

unrealistic ambition. Although we idealize peaceful demonstration,

we cast aside the ideology that fuels such protests in our daily lives.

The ideology of nonaggression is confirmed by venerated peace activists and leaders like Dr. Martin Luther King, Jr. as a powerful form of reserve that embodies the spirit of revolution (Zimmerman et al. 84). Nonaggression is not a naiveté to scoff, but a principle to embrace in the battle for equality. A nonaggressive ideology serves several purposes for the advancement to a liberated, equal, and fair society by encouraging inclusion and discouraging hierarchies, allowing us to fulfill our altruistic ideals on a personal and global level.

In "Boys' and Girls' Relational" study, Lansford et al. define aggression as "the defining characteristic of aggressive behavior is the aggressor's intent to cause harm" (299). An important aspect that connects the willingness to shoot someone and to shove oneself into an elevator is this "intent to cause harm." Shooting someone is obvious, but less obvious is the idea or threat of harm expressed by someone who unapologetically shoves his or her way into an elevator. The assertion of one's being is characteristic in all forms of aggressive behavior. Society commonly observes this in men (i.e. a young man stretching widely and yawning loudly). When women display similar behavior, it is attributed to feminist progression, a celebration of flexible gender roles.

However, as the feminist movement orients itself less around women, and moves more centrally to all participants in the "gender-social construction," the question that arises is how men find a place

The author argues that American culture is aggressive, and to support this claim she offers evidence from a secondary source in the form of a definition of the term "aggressive."

in the war on oppression. Using the individualistic-collectivistic

paradigm, Gordon Forbes et al. examine the connection between

aggression and the extent of individualism and collectivism in

several nations in their article "Relationships between Individualism-

Collectivism, Gender, and Direct or Indirect Aggression: A Study

in China, Poland, and the US." The results of the study conclude

that societies that are more individualistic and self-minded are also

more aggressive than collectivistic societies, which are community

and socially directed (Forbes et al. 24). The study made a significant

observation on the consistent levels of aggression from males in

a nation to females in the same nation, showing that the greatest

indicator for aggressive behavior is not the sex of the individual, but

the society or culture from which the person originates (Forbes et

al.). Thus, aggressive behaviors are manifestations of an individual's

society. The problem of excessive aggression in America does

not exclusively lay on the men in our society. Studies like that of

Forbes' show that we are culturally aggressive, men and women,

children and adults. Aggression is a pervasive characteristic of

American society and should be treated as such. We have to ask why

aggression is so common, so Americans can determine how it should

be perceived and handled.

Supporters of aggression in the feminist movement answer

that this condition of our society is responsive to the capitalistic

---

Notice how the author considers both the individual within a culture and the broader culture, or society, as a whole. She also highlights how personal beliefs shape social dynamics, and she supports her claim with reliable secondary research.

The author questions whether gender – one of the Political Modes of Inquiry – influences an individual's level of aggression. The study she cites here demonstrates that other factors are working on individuals, not just gender. Here, she recognizes the reciprocity between gender and culture; rather than simply assuming that men are more aggressive because of their gender, she explores how an individualistic, aggressive culture influences both men and women.

environment in which we work. Not only does aggression spur political movement, it encourages economic growth and financial independence. Competitiveness and aggression in the marketplace are fundamental to any capitalist system, any free enterprise. Aside from businesses and corporations, women repeatedly find that as individual job-seekers they must assertively market their assets and skills in order to participate effectively. In a study on gender stereotypes, researchers analyze the effect expectations have on males' and females' propensity for ambition, or "entrepreneurial intentions" (Gupta, Turban, Bhawe 1053). The study concludes that "gender stereotype activation" does occur with both men and women in business and workplace settings. It observes that the decidedly masculine and aggressive character of entrepreneurship discourages female participation and affirmation in these competition-based fields. Although no solution is explicitly endorsed by Gupta, Turban, and Bhawe's study, to overcome exclusion in this bustling marketplace women need to aggressively defend, promote, and advance their acumen, ability, and professional selves.

Here again, the author employs gender as her Political Mode of Inquiry to more thoroughly consider aggression in American culture.

The chief assertion in the above argument is that women must act as capitalists to survive capitalism. I agree that many women face obscurity in the workforce, in the form of lower paying jobs and lack of professional opportunity primarily because they do not aggressively approach their livelihood as a fierce competition. Within

Additionally, the author acknowledges that gender is not the only defining feature of aggression in American culture. Here, she acknowledges that gender and class both influence the lived-experience of individuals within an aggressive American culture.

capitalism, indeed, aggression and force will advance your career, profits, and status, but in what way does this personal advancement change the unfair structures that make it so? The conclusion is understandable, given the position some women are left in when they do not act as the big actors do. In the long term though, the solution to undermining the "dog eat dog" career model is to discourage it. Finding ways to effectively participate in a frequently inequitable and unequal model only substitutes the players in the game and encourages its operation.

Notice how the author uses the first person plural ("our" and "us"). By doing so, she acknowledges her positionality as both an insider and member of American society and as a woman within that culture. This technique is a subtle, yet effective, way of acknowledging your positionality as the author. However, be careful to use this technique only to express academic claims that can be supported with research. Avoid using first person as a personal soap box.

However, this cycle is insufferable. One of the greatest challenges to women is that our society judges us as incapable, specifically, less so than men. Supporters argue, again, that aggression is important for our *perception* as capable and deserving human beings. Another aspect of women's battle with professional audiences is the presumptuous notion that women are professionally incapable. The reason for this has been debated, but it still holds that women are wrongly perceived as less able than men. In our search for level ground, some argue, women must be aggressive in order to be perceived as competent as men (Rudman et al.). For example, in a status disparity study, Rudman et al. finds that although women in power positions are frequently disliked and rated as unapproachable, these "agentic" women are perceived as equally competent, effective, and qualified as men in the workplace (174). Both studies agree that to achieve status as proficient and able in professional environments women have needed to be aggressive by performing assertive, commanding behavior. We find in this argument for aggression that its greatest benefit is the perception of capability, the impression of respectability.

Again, we must ask why these findings are the case. Why are women perceived as more capable when they are commanding, even domineering? Aggressive behavior certainly does not give one a higher understanding of operations. It does not add any technical skills, resolution, or even legitimacy to a person's resume. Aggressive behavior only grants the perception of these things. The reason for this phenomenon is that aggressive males are the power bearers in our society. We are socialized to accept aggressiveness as desirable and respectable, while nonaggression is rejected as weak and ineffective. To adopt or encourage aggressive personalities for the perception of capability is to meet the standards of what an unjust society idealizes as an effective and successful person. To fulfill society's unjust and vain expectations does not advance feminism, and does not defeat injustice.

Notice how the author pays attention to both genders within the essay's scope. A cultural project that employs gender as its Political Mode of Inquiry does not need to isolate just one gender (for example, only men or only women). Instead, it can consider how social beliefs about all genders can create a particular cultural dynamic.

A connected though deeper level of the argument for aggressive agency is the fear of losing or never obtaining status within society. This includes women in educational, professional, and political environments. When women exhibit aggressive executive behavior,

they command respect and status in professional environments.
For example in "Teaching to Spite Your Body," LeBlanc proposes
that women need to be aggressive to earn respect in professional
careers even in spite of some of their less harsh, less forceful natures.
LeBlanc narrates her experience as a female university professor
having to project a more than assertive demeanor to command
respect from both her pupils and peers. She comments, "knowing
that I have pulled off power plays like the mid-class period seat
switch has lent me useful confidence in less contentious situations"
(51). LeBlanc's narrative essay addresses an essential aspect of the
necessity for aggression in the feminist movement: gaining the status
of capability.

Another study gives example of how the society we rebel against
has influenced us personally. In "The Duality of Individualism:
Attitudes toward Women, Generation Me, and the Method of
Cross-Temporal Meta-Analysis," Jean M. Twenge addresses the
issue of high and rising aggression in the United States relative
to the increasingly liberal and feminist views regarding women's
equality. She observes from extensive research that as attitudes
towards women have improved, "narcissism" and self-involvement
have risen to excess (Twenge 194). Because American feminism
developed in an individualist society, the attitude of its offspring has

transformed accordingly. The respect achieved in the second wave feminist movement has evolved into entitlement and self-absorption that mutes the advances that have been achieved (Twenge 194). Too often in American society, those who earn or obtain respect mutilate it into a commanding title, becoming possessive and vain of it, as if everyone and everything were a threat to it. This individualistic approach invests too much into the self and is contrary to feminist principles. If we instead thought of concepts like respect and equality as shared and a part of community, we could respect ourselves and everyone around us. Ideas of self-absorption and narcissism have no place in any civil movement, certainly not a global feminist one.

The author rightly recognizes that culture changes over time. Here, she compares gender beliefs from the second wave of feminism (1960s-1980s) to how those beliefs exist today. This historical comparison allows her to question the causes behind cultural change.

The unfortunate consequence of meeting an unjust society's expectations is that we embody its negative and at times oppressive characteristics. LeBlanc's essay describes the power she experienced from dominating her critical students, but it also observed the doubt and the regret she endured to experience this power. She doubted if this was the "right" way to maintain order and regretted that she was forced to be aggressive, even domineering in order to do so. Many feminist writers find it ironic and confusing that they must embrace fundamentally patriarchal tricks of authority to either teach feminism or teach as feminists. I believe that our discomfort is intuitive. So engulfed in defeating the patriarchy, recalibrating "the system," we forget that there are other ways to be empowered.

In this paragraph, the author names some of the key elements of American culture and compares them to the feminist movement. Doing so, she questions: (1) How does American culture influence the feminist movement, (2) Are the values of the feminist movement aligned with American values, and (3) If not, how can the feminist movement change American culture for the better? By looking critically at American culture, she is able to make an argument for social change. In the following paragraphs, she will describe what that change might look like.

Revisiting the point earlier about our embodiment of the society we attempt to reform, feminism in the United States suffers because patriarchy, capitalism, and American individualism are so incorporated into the movement. Originating from American culture, it is logical that feminism would be influenced by it. However, some of the structures in our culture are the obstacles to equality we wish to eliminate. Thus, nonaggression is not only the more ideal approach to feminism; it is also the more effective. Nonaggression looks outside of the limits of one culture, one nation and sees progression globally and collectively, with power in the hands of many.

This benefit of nonaggression for the progression of the feminist movement addresses a fundamental aspect of the feminist ideology, which is the eradication of discriminatory power structures (Zimmerman et al 78). Nonaggression in the feminist movement discourages hierarchies because it eliminates the rivalry for domination or the "upper hand" that aggressive feminism and aggression of all kinds encourage. By doing so, nonaggression offers diverse, non-dominating ways to be empowered. The feminist movement has embraced this concept most evidently in its teaching methods. We find that a non-hierarchical system of teaching encouraged by dialogue and nonaggression effectively aid progress on many stages. In a "curriculum development" study provides excellent opportunities to find and influence culture.

As a GSU student, the author recognizes that the classroom is an excellent location to search for a culture's belief systems. It is a site where teachers and students can consider new ideas that have the power to change a culture's ideology for the better.

Looking to your classroom or the GSU campus more broadly provides excellent opportunities to find and influence culture.

titled "Teaching Public Health through a Pedagogy of Collegiality," Chávez et al. discusses an alternative approach to teaching medicinal health through a community of students and teachers who effectively "learn from each other." This "community-based" pedagogy supports the idea of a level-playing field and the necessity of a collectivistic paradigm for effective social change of all kinds (Chávez et al. 1176). The purpose is to create a more inclusive, diverse group of medical professionals who are "culturally competent" (Chávez et al. 1176) Derived from feminist thought, this article supports the idea that civil success is best driven through nonaggressive, communal strategies.

This thinking underscores why nonaggression is such an important aspect of civil progression and introduces the reasoning for a microcosmic approach to nonviolence in the feminist movement. Zimmerman et al. approach this peace building in a systematic way, suggesting that our idolization of peace movements should be incorporated into feminist thought and practice (Zimmerman et al. 80). Nonaggressive behaviors allow us to embody nonviolence and peacemaking in our daily lives. Zimmerman et al. states that mutuality amongst people originates from our decisions to embody our individual power as a tool for universal benefit (80).

The inspiration for the experimental public health pedagogy, feminist pedagogy, approaches instruction in a communal, mutuality-

The author makes several strong rhetorical moves here. First, she recognizes and acknowledges a potential objection to her argument. Doing so, she establishes ethos because she does not ignore objections but welcomes them, as she believes her argument is strong enough to handle the challenge. Second, she explains how her claim overcomes the objection, strengthening the logos of her argument with sound academic reason.

Third, she takes the opportunity to do more than just overcome an objection, she further clarifies her argument. These three steps – (1) admitting potential objections, (2) overcoming objections, and (3) further clarifying her argument – produce a sense of trust between the author and reader. She has created a strong rhetorical argument.

driven way. It encourages academically educated and advanced teachers to maintain a level-playing field in the classroom. This collective, community-based learning must be fundamentally nonaggressive to be truly effective. It eliminates the competition in education, the credential war that patriarchal teaching embodies. Despite contrary belief, everyone will not fight or speak up when confronted or threatened. A very close-minded attitude suggests that women who refuse to be confrontational or assertive are being influenced, controlled, and dominated by misogyny, and are frankly not feminists. However, the appropriate approach should encourage women to understand and embrace their autonomy. The idea should not be to coerce women into performing in a way that we deem acceptable, or using any form of intimidation to yield the results we desire.

Reflective of principles in American individualistic culture, the perspective that accepts the aggression predominant in our society as vital to sustaining equality, individuality, and independence maintains that the solution to oppression is assertive guarding of the individual's rights. The opposing perspective rejects the prevalent aggression in our society, looks to collectivistic cultures for a less-violent approach to liberation, and urges that the answer to oppression may be found beyond our individualistic culture. The controversy is a question of whether the basis of an important

ideology in America, feminism, is best considered through a
masculine-centered, individualistic lens or a communal, collectivistic
one. As Twenge concludes in her reflective article, if we are to take a
global approach to the feminist philosophy, as third-wave feminists
profess, we must consider our behavior beyond the "American"
context and how this behavior affects women's response globally
and in future generations (195). Therefore, I suggest that we are led
by multi-cultural guidance. In the later development of feminism,
we heard and embraced the voices of feminists from all backgrounds
of color and class as leaders of the movement. This development
expanded feminisms reach, and I feel its effectiveness and sincerity.
If we really mean to eliminate injustice and create a platform for
the voice of all women and underprivileged members of the world,
should not their diverse influence, values, and beliefs take stage in
the movement?

Here, the author uses the Twenge article to transition from problems in American culture to an example from beyond U.S. borders.

In his article "War AND Peace?: An Agenda for Peace Research
and Practice in Geography," Megoran retells a story of a reporter's
account of a village in India's choice to withhold from violence in
a situation where "retaliatory violence" was expected. An obstacle
in the region which borders Pakistan is high tensions that result in
violence. Essentially, the community chose not to act violently on a
large, political scale, because they embraced humility and hospitality

The author cites a factual event in Pakistan's history and develops the cited information thoroughly. Rather than simply leaving the facts to stand alone, she explains to the reader exactly how this cited event connects to and supports her argument. This allows her to read a historical event critically to uncover cultural beliefs about social change. In doing so, she also practices responsible academic writing by incorporating her citation into her argument.

in their daily affairs with the opposing group (Megoran 184). This example imparts to us several things. First, to defeat violence, injustice, and to progress on a large scale, we have to embody our values on a microscopic level. Also, the retaliatory nature of political movement tends to be destructive because of the "fight fire with fire" approach. The people here did not retaliate by fulfilling their oppressors' expectations of violence. Intuitive though not commonly practiced, the most definitive way to establish disapproval of another's actions is to do the opposite.

Universality of progression supports the necessity of inclusion and hierarchy elimination through nonaggressive means in the feminist movement. I reiterate that the most modern forms of feminism wish to create a movement that involves every member of society, from all genders, ethnicities, religions, etc. One of the principle reasons that nonaggression is necessary for the feminist movement is that it is a positive ideology that operates universally. The quote from Zimmerman et al.'s article on third- wave feminism's goals for the future precisely expresses the reason nonaggression is so vital and appropriate for the feminist movement's efforts against subjugation:

The reward addresses a concept Gandhi advanced, that of himsa. Himsa, in reductive terms means "intent to harm," whereby even the thought of wanting another's harm tears at our human connection, is a violence (Nagler, 1997). Moving through the world with deep consideration of how responsibility and choice is proffered is an "intent to heal." (Zimmerman et al. 81)

This quote logically and compassionately delivers the most essential solution to the issue of feminist progression. If we proceed with the ideal of healing what has been torn by discrimination, hegemony and misogyny, then we can expand our success globally. Instead of reiterating our strength and our argument, we should seek those without strength or voice, discover what will heal them, and do so. A combination of embodying our beliefs, thinking as a community, and going with the intent to heal is the way forward. I see the urge to continue with an aggressive approach, to take our turn for power and authority in feminism. We have made great strides with just that as its slogan; "Take back the power." However, following this, we should supplement "And redistribute equally." Right now, a great deal of power is in our hands, but the current direction involves taking the power away from those in our community; it is becoming a battle to see who can obtain the loudest voice, the biggest bite, the most power. The solution, then, is to restructure the system in which we work. I have faith that collectively we have enough power and certainly enough initiative to do more than refurbish but recreate the spaces in which feminism lives. In universities, corporations, organizations, communities,

Here, the author consolidates her argument to assert that American culture should not be focused on aggressively taking "power," but on returning that power to those who have been disenfranchised. To support her ultimate goal of influencing American culture for the better, she concludes by explaining the tangible ways that the reader can apply a nonaggressive ideology to his or her everyday life.

and families, feminists should consider the intent in all of our actions. Perhaps, small businesses can proceed with the intent of providing a service to the community, not beating competitors. In feminist pedagogy, more chances should be offered to collaborate with other scholars, to synthesize ideas, not disprove them. Of course, though, in nonaggression, it is the small mannerisms and offerings of kindness that are the easiest and the most structure-changing. Noticing others, acknowledging them welcomingly, can be the greatest chance to offer the ones who need it most a bit of empowerment.

Works Cited

Chávez, Vivian, Ruby-Asuncion N. Turalba, and Savita Malik.

"Teaching Public Health through a Pedagogy of Collegiality."

American Journal Of Public Health 96.7 (2006): 1175-1180.

MEDLINE with Full Text. Web. 24 Oct. 2012.

Cole, E.R., and N.J. Sabik. "Associations Between Femininity and

Women's Political Behavior During Midlife." *Psychology Of

Women Quarterly* 34.4 (2010): 508-520. *CINAHL Plus with Full

Text.* Web. 24 Oct. 2012.

Forbes, Gordon, Xiaoying Zhang, Krystyna Doroszewicz, and Kelly

Haas. "Relationships between Individualism-Collectivism, Gender,

and Direct or Indirect Aggression: A Study in China, Poland, and

the US." *Aggressive Behavior* 35.1 (2009): 24-30. Print.

Gupta, Vishal K., Daniel B. Turban, and Nachiket M. Bhawe. "The

Effect of Gender Stereotype Activation on Entrepreneurial

Intentions." *Journal Of Applied Psychology* 93.5 (2008): 1053-

1061. *PsycARTICLES.* Web. 8 Oct. 2012.

Lansford, Jennifer E. Skinner, Ann T. Sorbring, Emma Giunta, Laura

DiDeater-Deckard, Kirby Dodge, Kenneth A. Malone, Patrick

S. Oburu, Paul Pastorelli, Concetta Tapanya, Sombat Uribe

Tirado, Liliana Maria Zelli, Arnaldo Al-Hassan, Suha M. Peña

Alampay, Liane Bacchini, Dario Bombi, Anna Silvia Bornstein,

Marc H. Chang, Lei. "Boys' And Girls' Relational And Physical

Aggression In Nine Countries." *Aggressive Behavior* 38.4 (2012):

298. *Advanced Placement Source*. Web. 19 Sept. 2012.

LeBlanc, Maria. "Teaching to Spite Your Body" *Feminist Activism in Academia: Essays on Personal, Political and Professional Change*. Ed. Ellen C. Mayock and Domnica Radulescu. Jefferson, NC: McFarland, 2010. 36-51. Print.

Megoran, Nick. "War And Peace? An Agenda For Peace Research and Practice in Geography." *Political Geography* 30.4 (May 2011): 178-189. *ScienceDirect*. Web. 24 Oct. 2012.

Rowbotham, Sheila. *Women in Movement: Feminism and Social Action*. New York: Routledge, 1992. Print.

Rudman, Laurie A., Corinne A. Moss-Racusin, Julie E. Phelan, and Sanne Nauts. "Status Incongruity and Backlash Effects: Defending the Gender Hierarchy Motivates Prejudice Against Female Leaders." *Journal Of Experimental Social Psychology* 48.1 (Jan 2012): 165-179. ScienceDirect. Web. 8 Oct. 2012.

Twenge, Jean M. "The Duality of Individualism: Attitudes toward Women, Generation Me, and the Method of Cross-Temporal Meta-Analysis." *Psychology Of Women Quarterly* 35.1 (2011): 193-196. *ERIC*. Web. 19 Sept. 2012.

Zimmerman, Amber Lynn, M. Joan McDermott, and Christina M. Gould. "The Local Is Global: Third Wave Feminism, Peace, and Social Justice." *Contemporary Justice Review* 12.1 (2009): 77-90. *Academic Search Complete*. Web. 24 Oct. 2012.

11
NEW MEDIA LITERACY

How do digital practices—mostly, the things that we do when we interact with the Internet—affect our lives? We can look to our economic activity and observe how frequently people shop, pay their bills, and manage investments online. We choose restaurants, concerts, and films based on feedback that we receive digitally from both advertisers who don't know us and friends who do. Most of the work that you did to apply to this university probably happened online. Our culture is no longer fascinated by the existence of the Internet; in fact, we often take it for granted. However, the last decade of collaborative, social activity on the Internet is a subject of intense academic study right now. As the Internet shifted from a location where one could *receive* information to a place where one could *participate* in information, a new model of activity developed. This transformation is commonly called Web 2.0, a term that describes how online users have moved from consumption to production of content. This chapter will address how that consumption and production relates to the act of composing in your ENGL 1101 and 1102 courses at Georgia State University.

We should define an important term. "New media," we can loosely assert, are the host of programs, apps, and collectives that enable and produce participatory digital culture. Television and radio do not count as new media, but as soon as we say that, we see the boundaries of these concepts dissolving. Maybe you watch a program on NBC (a TV broadcasting network that started as RCA in 1926), but you watch over an ATT connection that is also your pipeline to the Internet. You might watch it on a television that, with one click, can enable browsing on the Web. More to the point, you might watch that NBC content on Hulu, the website that streams NBC's television content on the Web. Movies are technically not "new media," but they are certainly embedded in the culture

Black-Akert, Michael. *Usage Error*

of the Internet, considering the millions of people who stream movies from Netflix or watch movie trailers on YouTube every day. New media certainly interacts with and cross-pollinates with "old media" (as silly as that sounds), but the defining quality of new media forms is engagement. Pre-Internet media produced static content; new media invite and depend on *user content*.

FOR THOUGHT AND DISCUSSION:
Consider how the Internet delivers new media to users who may or may not have the digital experience to interpret those media.

This section will address how three terms in digital culture have an impact on our work as critical thinkers and composers. We will examine *attention*, *participation*, and *audience* in the context of new media and the composition classroom.

Attention

Early computer users sat down to their boxy towers with specific tasks in mind—"I will write an email," for instance. Increasingly, the phrase "sitting down at a computer" seems antiquated, as many of us carry the functionality of a small computer around in our pockets. Our cellphones can quickly gain and delete new programs (apps), connect us to instantaneous live conversation (Twitter or chat programs), and sometimes serve as one of our main sources of media consumption. Whether you consider your cellphone or tablet, your laptop or the desktop computer in the library's digital commons, you are rarely removed from the constant stream of multimedia content that the Internet provides. How does this stream, sometimes a flood, affect our academic work, our theory of knowledge, or our control over our activities? In short, how does being five seconds away from the Web impact our attention?

You might not find it surprising that interest in the field of neuroscience has increased parallel to our digital activity. After all, the more we learn about the world through our computers, the more we have to think about how we manage that learning and how it impacts our future learning. For example, you may think that the Internet automatically provides you with a wider lens on world events than citizens had before the Internet. Back then, radio, television, and newspaper media held control over what most people could realistically "know" outside of their own experience. With the Internet—blogs, Twitter, online newspapers, YouTube, etc.—you might be tempted to say that that control has been transformed. Now, you can learn anything that you want. However, consider what happens when we decide to follow someone on Twitter or friend them on Facebook, when we add a blog to our RSS reader account or subscribe to a YouTube channel. We are selecting or curating our own list of regularly updated media. However, if we collect that list according to our pre-existing and unexamined tastes, we are essentially avoiding Web content that we feel is irrelevant. Our curation, if not reflective, can put a boundary around our learning.

Therefore, attention involves what media we attend to. It also involves *how* we pay attention. A variety of studies over the last several years have attempted to understand whether we learn differently when we use digital technologies. Consider the iPad or the Kindle, even the laptop; are these items ideal for reading specific kinds of material and not for others? Given that many of us work these days with several Internet browser windows up at the same time, we toggle back and forth among several sites: email, social media (like Facebook or Twitter), research, and writing. We chat with our collaborative partner who posts a link to a *New York Times* story, which links to an academic study, which in turn includes a graph that we want to drop into our presentation. That process entails several steps, but we move through them without much effort and without thinking about the implications of all of those windows, all of those platforms.

In *Net Smart: How To Thrive Online*, Howard Rheingold describes what he calls "infotention": "intention added to attention, and mixed with knowledge of information-filtering … a coordinated mind-machine process" (17). Rheingold explores how digital, networked activity strains our attention in unique ways, and we should train our brain to be more focused when we do work online. Cathy Davidson suggests, on her syllabus for "This Is Your Brain on The Internet," an interdisciplinary undergraduate course at Duke University, that if the metaphor for the brain in the 20th century was the CPU, then the brain metaphor for the 21st century is the iPhone. Think about it. The iPhone works across multiple platforms and applications, it organizes networks, and it shares data in a variety of different forms. Its strength as a piece of technology is its ability to connect pathways among a variety of different programs and applications.

One of Rheingold's goals in *Net Smart* is to get people thinking about how to exercise control and focus over their attention during online work. Many of us have had the experience of sitting down "just for a minute" to Facebook, YouTube, or Tumblr and discovering two hours and multiple browser windows later that we have no idea where the time went. Consider our compulsive reaching for cellphones and our instinctive clicking on hyperlinks in a news story, just to satisfy curiosity or, deeper, to fulfill a less explicable psychological "need." In *Alone Together: How We Expect More from Technology and Less from Each Other*, Sherry Turkle studies the psychological complexity of human/computer relationships. She worries about the effect of "always on/always on you" networked devices on our ability to attend to others, to listen, and to empathize.

FOR THOUGHT AND DISCUSSION:

Our attention is demanded in our physical and virtual lives. How does a trip across the GSU quad focus our attention in ways that online activity does not?

The iPhone connects different media just like the brain makes connections among different languages, senses, social groups and activities. However, our brain works differently from a machine in that it can pay attention to only one process at a time when we ask it to complete something complicated. Before we begin an investigation of reading new kinds of media, it behooves us to acknowledge the challenges of that exploration. Do digital consumption and production encourage us, as Nicholas Carr writes in *The Shallows: What*

Kim, Judith. *The Associates*

the *Internet Is Doing To Our Brains*, "to dip in and out of a series of texts rather than devote sustained attention to any one of them," or is the abundance of information beneficial, according to Clay Shirky's *Here Comes Everybody*? Either way, as citizens of the virtual world, investigating the question becomes imperative. Rheingold writes that "[j]ust as the ancient arts of rhetoric taught citizens how to construct and weigh arguments, a mindful rhetoric of digital search would concentrate attention on the process of inquiry—the kinds of questions people turn into initial search queries" (64).

Explore

Activity 11.1

Is paying attention or staying focused while online difficult for you? Take a minute to examine your ability to monitor your attention online by trying some of the exercises below.

Find a friend who will let you study an "hour" of his or her online time. Take notes on where your friend goes, how many browser windows are kept open, and where links lead. Collect the raw "data" on what your friend consumes and produces (status updates, tweets, and emails count as "production"). After you are finished, try organizing the data: Into what categories can you divide the visited sites? Where did your subject spend the most time? Did activity seem linear (progressing along a logical path) or more organic or impulsive? Ask your subject to record the same "data" for you and discuss what you find. What does it teach you?

Research the Pomodoro Technique of time management and the application Focus Booster (www.focusbosterapp.com). Divide your time online into 25-minute segments according to Pomodoro and write realistic goals for what you are going to do during the time period (whether or not for academic purposes). How successful were you at staying on task for three different time segments?

Read John Tierney's article "When the Mind Wanders, Happiness Also Strays" in *The New York Times* (Nov 15, 2010) and Jocelyn K. Glie's post "10 Online Tools for Better Attention and Focus" on the productivity website *99%*. Experiment with some of the tools and compose a response to both texts that is personal to your own experiences online. Do Glie's and Tierney's pieces convince you that time spent wandering online is a problem to solve?

Participation

Our early uses of the Web involved an excited amount of access to information—information that was always available and timely. Schools, businesses, non-profit organizations, the government, any organized group could publish current data about its work. The Internet was supremely useful for checking movie times, ordering gifts, and generally just "finding things."

As time progressed, however, the Web became more dynamic. The O'Reilly Media Web 2.0 Conference, started in 2004, introduced the term "Web 2.0" into common usage. "Web 2.0" distinguishes between prior uses of the Web that were mainly consumptive and the evolving ability of digital citizens to *produce content.*

Plenty of people participated in digital culture before 2005, but after that time the Internet became more participation-friendly. Facebook, Wikipedia, and Flickr, among many others, signaled a new orientation for digital culture: they encourage user-generated content. Just think—what is Facebook without the pictures and text that its users contribute? Not much. It simply provides a very attractive and share-able frame that users are happy to populate with their own content. The shift in digital culture designated "Web 2.0" is significant, even if no one really agrees when it officially started (or if it has already ceded to some new model). Think of the stereotypical couch potato watching television for hours; this person illustrates the once passive media consumer. While being online may not appear any more physically active, online activity is now a thoroughly more interactive way to engage with media.

We can think of all this "production" actually as a new form of publishing; comments on an *Atlanta Journal and Constitution* editorial, posts to a blog, reviews of a book on Amazon, pictures to Picasa, or posting videos to YouTube represent dissemination of your thoughts. If everyone is publishing more, then everyone must be composing more; the inherent goals of first-year writing begin here. You may not think that a "writing" class has any relationship to how you interact with the Web, but think for a minute: is there another environment, apart from the web, where you write more?

Consider Wikipedia. Perhaps the most useful participatory experiment on the Web, Wikipedia presents an open model for knowledge production. We can all contribute to its vastness. In the early days of Wikipedia, teachers often scolded students for using Wikipedia in any scholarly way (many still do, in fact). However, Wikipedia has developed from a collection of thousands of dubious, argumentative posts to millions of entries that are constantly under revision by the citizens of the Web. Wikipedia is still not a recommended source in an academic essay, but it can be a great starting point when you begin to write something new. Wikipedia entries provide links to other, more verifiable sources, and these sources provide researchers additional places to search for credible content. If managed carefully and critically, mass-crowd participation can produce infinitely useful media on the Web. The lesson we learn from Wikipedia is this: our participation, as minor as it may seem, remains im-

Thompson, Fenton. *0100101001001*

portant to the digital environment because other people can quickly access it, comment upon it, remix it, or engage us in conversation about it.

FOR THOUGHT AND DISCUSSION:

Wikipedia, in its ability to open construction of "stable" knowledge to a variety of digital users, suggests a new culture of comment, revision, and re-imagination. What other websites offer new cultures to their users? Describe the "cultures" of these websites.

Because participation has become an integral component of Web culture, it behooves us to understand and assimilate it with our own behavior, if and when appropriate. This strategy means moving from a place of consumption (reading a restaurant review) to production (writing a review ourselves after our visit). The Internet has become such a useful collection of media *because* millions of people have taken it upon themselves to contribute to it. These discrete and numerous contributions to the content of the Internet result in enormous cultural changes to publishing, journalism, entertainment, and education. On a deeper level, they have an influence on how our culture defines "knowledge."

When we interact with the content of the Web, we encourage more interactivity and connection. When we post pictures or comments to our friends' content on Facebook, others can reply and we can start a conversation. We learn from social media, on an unconscious level, that the more we put into it, the more we get out of it. The content of our contributions to social media networks, and to the Web in general, has a large impact on response. If we type "great pics!" to a new album that someone has uploaded to Google+, we will probably not get much response. However, if we engage the photos in some creative or narrative way, other people on the network are more prone to participate with us. We might post "this picture reminds me of that time that we all met for dinner at Eats; when was that? who was there?" and with that, the digital "ball" starts rolling. Other people within the network are encouraged to answer the questions, link to more pictures, or make their own reflections.

The important lesson for the composition class, and any academic experience for that matter, is that participation increases our engagement in learning and connects us to other people. Discussion boards are a common feature of digital education portals (like Blackboard, Web CT, Desire 2 Learn, etc.), and teachers who use them are encouraging engagement and community. Rather than contributing an answer that is flat, we should approach a forum like we do a conversation—validating the opinions of others, making distinctions, and encouraging more response. Consider the following exchange in a hypothetical class:

Prompt: "How are the lessons of this lab useful?"

Melora: I found this lab useful because it helped me answer questions that will be on the test.

Jack: The lab was difficult because I kept getting different results from the tests. Was I doing it wrong?

Ahmad: I had the same experience as Jack, but I think that is part of the conclusion actually. If the results of the various tests are not consistent, doesn't that mean that we should consider outside variables?

Stephanie: I agree with Ahmad: like time of day, how the testing might change after multiple uses, temperature?

In this exchange, Melora interacts like a passive consumer. She gives the instructor back the answer that she thinks he is seeking. Jack, Ahmad, and Stephanie however, approach the forum with questions, suggestions, and connections. They express an intuitive value in the scholarly members of the forum community, and they participate in ways that foreground critical thinking, citation, and community. Our active and critical participation in digital environments, whether on the open Web or on classroom projects, are valuable to others. Digital culture invests knowledge sharing and knowledge production with more democratic potential, and we should take these opportunities seriously. On the next class discussion forum, peer review assignment, or information gathering trip across the Web, consider how your participation helps others. If you have something to contribute, think critically about how to provide comments in a detailed way that encourages community and interaction.

Explore

Activity 11.2

Do you have experience in the participatory culture of the Web or does it seem foreign to you? Here are some suggestions of how you can explore the dynamic capabilities of the Web.

Choose a recent online article in *The Atlanta Journal and Constitution* (www.ajc.com) or *Creative Loafing* (www.clatl.com) that includes a number of comments. Read through the comment chain, and post a response that agrees or disagrees with the contributions of previous commenters, citing their user names. See if you can get a discussion going between you and the community around the article to further explore the topic. Remember: engage in dissent civilly and carefully. Your goal is to encourage courteous, intelligent discussion.

Use an online discussion forum provided by your instructor to identify classmates who share your interest in a genre of music, film, or literature. Use the open-endedness of the prompt to practice community engagement: ask others to clarify statements that interest you and try to make overt connections between your interests and theirs. Analyze the thread in order to determine who makes the most engaging comments that move others toward participation.

Conduct a scavenger hunt related to material for your class via one social media network. Post the list of the items across the platform in a way that allows team members to share information (pictures of items acquired, interesting interactions, etc.) dynamically. Analyze which team's platform or use of the platform best supported the experience.

Audience

Audience has always been one of the trickiest issues for a writer to consider. Once, the audience for any text was limited to those who had economic access to the work, geographic proximity, and interest in the text. Whether it was the newspaper or a physics textbook, all three of those variables had to line up for us to begin to think about audience. Does someone have the money to buy the text or the ability to borrow it? Can someone physically get to where the text is located? Who is interested in this text? These questions acted as controlling factors, limiting and shaping an audience.

Richir, Courtney Jane. *Blue Maniac*

FOR THOUGHT OR DISCUSSION:
An artist often has to work hard to "find" her audience, even to the point of relocation. How does the Internet affect how a composition can find an audience?

The digital landscape has blurred or erased all of those variables. Certainly people still purchase texts, but the fact that texts *can* be obtained for free has resulted in millions of people writing content without asking for payment (consider the blogosphere, for example). The limits of physical geography are rendered almost irrelevant for readers with an Internet connection. Whether you buy a book on your Kindle or access articles on *The New Yorker* for free, that content is digitally available in seconds. Finally, there's the question of interest. Audiences are still limited to those who have an interest in the text, but because of the lowered thresholds of the first two (economic and geographic access) digital citizens can afford to be interested in more topics. The concept of digital searches (Google as the most ubiquitous, but not the only, example) has increased the amount of content to which an Internet user is exposed; consequently, we see that traditional limitations on a text's audience are dissolving.

But composers still have to consider audience, just as traditional writers have done. They just have to consider other factors as well. If the barrier to obtaining texts is dissolving and readers have more access to them, the new barrier that takes its place is *attention*. Every person who regularly spends time online knows that there are exponentially more free texts readily available and interesting enough to read than she will ever be able to read. So a reader's free time becomes a limiting factor. So, also does interactivity. Most users prefer to read texts with which they can interact—comment on, share, amend.

Composers in digital spaces should comprehend these new limits, motivations, and definitions of audience. Traditionally, anyone desiring to publish in a specific community needs to study the conventions, style, and content of that community. In the new media environment, that responsibility extends to forms of media. Specific composing platforms attract and engage unique audiences and construct unique community protocols. We are going to look at two of these in order to explore how they require a new definition of audience.

Blogs

The simplest tool for mass communication online is a weblog, commonly known as a *blog*. Multiple platforms (Wordpress, Blogger, LiveScribe, and many others) offer users a free space to construct multimedia compositions and publish them to the Web. Because blogging is so accessible and so many blogs exist, each successful blog speaks to a specific community and endeavors to cultivate that sense of community. Certainly, some blogs cater to a large, diverse audience—like blogs associated with CNN or the *New York Times*—but even those are tailored to specific readers within that network (example: the CNN religion blog).

Authors in the blogosphere spend time studying blogs addressed to similar audiences. In fact, most blogs feature a "blog roll" of other authors with whom they share affinity. This familiarity with similar digital spaces may not seem very much like academic "research," but it works the same way. Unless an author is lucky, he usually needs to discover and cultivate relationships with the authors within his interest network.

As all successful digital texts have become participatory, a blog is only partly the rhetorical territory of the author. The commenting space of successful blogs is alive with the responses of regular readers who voice support, critique, or extensions of the author's work. Different from a more traditional medium—the book—the authorial content of the blog is often influenced by the participation of its readers. Bloggers across a number of topics—academic, professional, or social—compose blog entries in response to the communities that develops around their sites. Active commenters on the blog form a dynamic audience that most bloggers appreciate and, to a great or minor degree, study.

Twitter

First launched in 2006, Twitter is the most popular microblogging platform online and is currently the second most popular social media site on the Internet. Like most social media sites, Twitter forces composers to consider audience in new and dynamic ways. Twitter users construct their own audience through an open network of other users and "hashtag" searches. More importantly, as is the case with most social media networks, Twitter users are both authors and audience members. As they post tweets, they cultivate the attention of other users. Twitter's unique place in the social media sphere is defined by its mostly open network and the compressed size of each tweet.

Twitter has evolved into a mostly public network, different from other platforms where users choose others who can see their content. While Twitter users have the option to "lock" their tweets, the platform encourages sharing information openly with the Web at large. Most Twitter users compose tweets with the understanding that they might be read by anyone, potentially lots of people they don't know. Twitter's "retweet" function permits a user to send a tweet to all of his followers with one click; if any of those readers also retweet that content, one author's contribution to the open network can quickly become viral.

Kim, Judith. *Update.*

The size of tweets also contributes significantly to an understanding of audience. A post to the Twitter network is limited to 140 characters, a limit which demands brevity. As we discussed before, the free access to information on the Web means that users are limited by the amount of media they can realistically digest. Blog posts and news articles can take minutes to digest, whereas a Twitter user can realistically read dozens of tweets during a five-minute period. This kind of reading is not thorough, but it does not need to be. Twitter users quickly develop an understanding of the usefulness of the network and can discard large amounts of what they read in order to get to information that is personally or professionally valuable. Because tweets can include links to more developed content, Twitter can become a suggestion board for longer texts.

FOR THOUGHT OR DISCUSSION:

Twitter messages can reach a ready audience in seconds with updated information about a local gathering, news worthy event, or protest. Police have used Twitter in order to keep informed of mounting protests or safety issues. What are some other professions that use social media like Twitter extensively? Why is audience an important consideration when using social media, especially in the professional realm?

The new media available to digital composers require a revised understanding of audience. When we compose for online spaces, whether a long-form blog post or a short tweet, we should do so with an appreciation for their potential interactivity and reach. Active digital readers want to participate in the texts that interest them, and the best Web compositions court that kind of participation. If you are assigned to compose a digital text for your class, pose questions that invite the replies of your readers. Open questions will suffice, but your post should steer readers toward a particular understanding and ask pointed questions about it. For example, your professor may ask you to respond to a reading from the textbook in a discussion forum open to the class; compose a text that explores the trickier questions of the reading. Do not be afraid to "think out loud" about what seems contradictory in the reading or about what terminology is unclear. Discussion forums, blog posts, and tweets are never intended to be closed circuit communication. They engage in constructing knowledge through participation and engagement.

Explore

Activity 11.3

Consider how these exercises prompt you to rethink the idea of "audience" across the Web.

Choose a regular blogger in a topic you enjoy (fashion, film, religion, politics, travel) who also maintains a Twitter presence. Spend some time researching who follows the author's Twitter account and who follows the blog. Are they the same people or are there some clear differences? Is one group significantly larger than another? What contrast exists between the topics of the blog posts and the content of the blogger's tweets? Often you will find that bloggers use Twitter to inform readers of new posts, but often the tweets will wander into different topics. Contrast the author's interaction with audience members between the blog and Twitter account.

Explore

Activity 11.4

Read Clive Thompson's *Wired* article "How Twitter Creates a Social Sixth Sense," published only a year after Twitter's launch. Then read Katrina Gulliver's "10 Commandments of Twitter for Academics," published in 2012 in *The Chronicle of Higher Education*. Thompson's article displays no comments (this feature has been closed by *Wired*), but Gulliver's article includes long responses. How do each of these authors attend to the idea of audience within the Twitter platform?

Choose a YouTube video that you find hilarious—you know, one of those memes that everyone sees within a 2-week period—and a blog post from any regularly posting author. How do the comments attached to one relate to the comments attached to the other? Analyze the difference between the two groups. While the video may have thousands of comments, evaluate the amount of engagement each audience has with the content. How does the composer's relationship with the audience affect its engagement?

While the use of new media in your composition classroom may be new to you, many professors are beginning to use new media sites or practices. College students have always had to embrace their identities as writers to be successful. New media spheres encourage us to think of ourselves as composers, too: of conversations, of visual images, of research projects. Digital learning, whether in a physical class that uses an online portal or a hybrid or fully online course, asks us to employ skills that we have already learned and to evaluate them critically. Exploring the definitions of *attention, participation*, and *audience* within a new media context helps us make sense of an increasingly digital world. Gaining new media fluency is an essential part of our development as critical thinkers, writers, and composers.

FOR CLASS DISCUSSION

By the time this edition of the *Guide to First-Year Writing* goes to press, the media examples included in it may be outdated. Discuss how your relationship to the media in this chapter is different to the characterizations made here. What types of media should be included in this chapter for the fourth edition?

By now you have discussed the value of applying the Rhetorical Situation to the materials you read and write. Think of three media literacy vehicles you use in your daily life (Facebook, Twitter, Vimeo, etc.) and apply the components of the Rhetorical Situation to each one. Use this information to discuss with your classmates the different cultural and communication value of something like email versus Twitter.

For further reading:

For more on digital media and on the production of digital texts in the Web 2.0 environment, take a look at these sources:

The Agenda with Steve Paikin: *The Myth of Digital Literacy* (video)

John Brockman: *Is the Internet Changing the Way You Think?* (book)

Collin Brooke: *Lingua Fracta* (book)

Nicholas Carr: *The Shallows: What the Internet Is Doing To Our Brains* (book)

Tyler Cowan: "Three Tweets for the Web" (article)

Cathy Davidson: *Now You See It* (book)

David Eagleman: *Six Easy Steps to Avert the Collapse of Civilization* (video lecture)

Howard Rheingold: *Net Smart: How To Thrive Online* (book)

Clay Shirky: *Here Comes Everybody* (book)

Sherry Turkle: *Alone Together* (book)

Student Work:

To find out more about producing digital texts, please visit www.guidetowriting.gsu.edu. Click first on "Community" and then "Companion Digital Projects. Here, you will find student examples of digital composition. Produce your own digital creations and share the links with the webmaster. She will add your work to our website to expand your audience.

James, Kaylin. *Round.*

12
CIVIC ENGAGEMENT AND COMMUNITY-BASED WRITING

At Georgia State University, writing assignments aim to develop your critical thinking, reading, and writing skills, and reflect a broader role for writing as responsible, purposeful social action.

The goal of a GSU education is broader and more encompassing than just getting a degree or getting a job: it should help you to become an informed, engaged citizen of your world and your community. In first-year composition classes, that engagement will often begin with community-based writing. *Community* can be loosely defined as a group of people who live, work, or study in close proximity to each other and/or who have shared values or interests. Your community could include your neighbors, people who play pickup basketball at the same park as you, people in your place of worship, or people who believe in a particular social cause. As you can see, you have many different communities in your life, and some of those communities will overlap. For example, one person you know may be a member of both your social and school communities; another may live in the same geographic area but not be part of your particular social community.

Georgia State recognizes the importance of community and strives to promote "the socioeconomic and cultural climate, education, health care services and other resources available throughout the city, as well as in communities across Georgia and beyond" (http://www.gsu.edu/about/). Some GSU English instructors adopt *community-based writing* to help meet this goal by linking writing assignments with service that benefits a community. In these classes, you might work in a particular community or in service to community members as part of your course requirements. The various types of service you undertake can help you develop specific writing skills and/or make progress toward certain course objectives. Some community-based writing activities focus on the person or people being served (i.e. the community), while others might address the person providing the service (i.e. you, the student). The primary goal in academic community-based writing projects is to come as close to complete reciprocity–an equal balance between the service and the served–as possible.

You may have already participated in some form of community service or volunteerism. *Volunteerism* is when one gives time, energy, or skill to benefit a specific cause or organization, without being compensated. The emphasis of volunteerism is on the entity being served, that is, the community that receives most of the benefit (Deans 10). While you might volunteer for community service or charity work through a campus or community organization, it is uncommon for volunteerism to be part of course requirements. (Deans 17).

On the other end of the spectrum is *internship*--also known as apprenticeships, work-study, and co-operative education programs--where you take a position with an organization in order to obtain on-the-job experience in your desired field. While your work as an intern will provide value to the organization with which you are interning, the ultimate goal is for you as a student to gain work experience.

Community-Based Writing

Between these two bookends (volunteerism and internships) exists a range of meaningful ways to engage with a community, some of which might be a part of your first-year writing class at GSU. Service activities may involve writing within the community, or community activities may serve as the subject for in-class writing activities. For example, you may be assigned a community-based research project which requires you to conduct interviews in your community or research local history in order to write a paper. One specific type of community-based research where researchers study and record information related to human culture is called *ethnography* (see below). If you are assigned such a project, you will want to refer to the information in the chapter 19 on interviewing, creating primary sources, and crafting a culture-based research question.

First-year writing courses may also employ community-based writing to address community literacy, civic literacy, and public literacy. *Community literacy* relates to reading and writing skills (in a general sense) as they develop outside of educational institutions. Work done in the area of community literacy might include efforts to understand and overcome obstacles in the reading, writing, and comprehension capabilities of a particular population, mentoring a particular community in an effort to improve literacy, or raising awareness of illiteracy within a particular community.

Civic literacy is best defined as knowledge surrounding the civil affairs (politics, policy, and governance) of a community. The community could be very small, as in a local school board, or it could be very large, as in the United Nations or the United States Congress. Community-based writing surrounding the area of civic literacy might involve letters to the editor of a newspaper or to a politician supporting or opposing a particular issue. You might write newsletters, pamphlets, or flyers for community distribution in order to, for instance, raise awareness about a candidate, issue, or pending piece of legislation. Or you might write an essay or research paper on how an issue impacts a particular community.

Public literacy "designates written language, including written language that is read aloud, that appears in a public sphere and deals with issues of concern to a group of people. Bumper stickers, newspapers, tax forms, and petitions are all examples of public literacy" (Ervin 1). If your instructor chooses to embrace public literacy in your composition class, you might be asked to write in an effort to address public issues.

Community literacy, civic literacy, and public literacy are sometimes lumped together under the heading "civic engagement." Ultimately, *civic engagement* involves meaningful interaction with the community and focuses on social or political issues. Working to improve the quality of life in your community, becoming involved in community events, or making others aware of community issues all fall under the umbrella of civic engagement. If you take a class that incorporates civic engagement, you might be required to serve at community or cultural events or for community organizations. You might be asked to write reflections about your experience, do research to support an organization or cause, or produce writing that would be useful to the community with which you interact. Unless your instructor specifies the type of engagement she or he has in mind, you may approach your project in any of these ways.

Some community-based writing activities involve *advocacy* for a particular cause, issue, political candidate, or proposed change. If you are required to write to promote social or political change, thereby calling on individuals or entities to act, your writing could be linked to activism, defined as "behavior designed to increase individual and collective human dignity, value, and quality of life" (Fleckenstein). Terms like "social justice" or "community action" also describe some kinds of advocacy.

When thinking about ways to engage in the community, assess your views of community, your skills and talents, your personal goals and values, and how you perceive your own role within the community. Consider the following ideas that can cause tension or "push and pull at each other" as you decide where you fit into the picture:

Engaged citizen	⟵———→*	Solitary self
Community as nurturing	⟵———→*	Community as constraining
Common good	⟵———→*	Individual freedom
Shared goals	⟵———→*	Personal opportunities
Responsibilities	⟵———→*	Rights
Shared norms and values	⟵———→*	Self-expressions and individualism
Common life	⟵———→*	Privacy
Consensus	⟵———→*	Dissent

Fig. 1. Kirp's Continuum, Community Tensions (2003). Source: Thomas Deans, *Writing and Community Action* p99.

Writing skills correlate in many ways with community activity or engagement. Thomas Deans, professor of English and author of *Writing and Community Action* (2003), identifies three paradigms for *community-based writing*: "writing *for* the community, writing *with* the community, and writing *about* the community." The chart on the next page helps illustrate the distinctions between the three:

	Writing *for* the Community	Writing *about* the Community	Writing *with* the Community
Primary Site for Learning	Nonprofit Agency	Classroom	Community Center
Privileged Literacies	Academic and Workplace Literacies	Academic and Critical Literacies	Academic, community, and hybrid literacies
Most Highly Valued Discourse	Workplace discourse	Academic discourse	Hybrid discourse
Primary Learning Relationship	Student-agency contact (instructor as facilitator)	Student-Instructor (service as facilitator)	Student-community member (instructor as facilitator)
Institutional Relationship	Instructor-agency contact person	Instructor-community site contact	Instructor/department-community center
Goals	(1) Students learn nonacademic writing practices and reflect on differences between academic and workplace rhetorics. (2) Students reflect on service experience to attain critical awareness of community needs. (3) Students provide needed writing products for agencies.	(1) Students serve at schools or community sites and reflect on their experiences. (2) Students develop critical consciousness and habits of intellectual inquiry and societal critique. (3) Students write journals and compose academic-style essays on community issues and/or pressing social concerns.	(1) Students, faculty, and community use writing as a part of a social action effort to collaboratively identify and address local problems. (2) Students and community members negotiate cultural differences and forge shared discourses. (3) University and community share inquiry and research.
Assessment	Can the students move ably between academic and workplace discourses? Have students critically reflected on the writing and service processes? Did students produce documents that will be of real use to the agencies?	Have students provided adequate service to the community site? How sophisticated a critique of social concerns can students demonstrate in academic discussion and writing? Has student academic writing improved?	Have local and academic community members engaged in collaborative writing or research? Can students reflect critically on issues such as cultural difference? Has the local problem been effectively solved, addressed, or researched?

*"Three Paradigms for Community Writing." From *Writing Partnerships: Service-Learning in Composition* (p. 17). NCTE, 2000.

What Does Community-Based Writing Look Like?

As noted above, there are many different approaches to community- based writing. The following are some examples of what community writing might look like if assigned in particular departments or disciplines.

Discipline-specific projects

Botany	During a visit to Arabian Mountain, students in a biology class photograph many kinds of wild plants that grow there. They do research and create a seasonal guide that will be printed by the mountain's nature center, so visitors know what kinds of plants to look for in which seasons and can learn their characteristics.
Political Science	Class members create an awareness-raising campaign reminding fellow university students to register to vote in Atlanta or to obtain absentee ballots for their home districts. Students write an article for the school newspaper, design flyers, and create a public service announcement to be aired on WRAS campus radio.
History	Students interview members of Atlanta's Veterans of Foreign Wars organization about their experiences returning to Atlanta after serving abroad. Students compile interviews into a booklet of stories, which is printed by the university print shops and distributed free to VFW members and placed in libraries around the state.
Spanish	Service-learners team up with a local nonprofit serving families impacted by domestic violence. Students translate documents, directories, forms, training manuals, and pamphlets from English into Spanish to serve the growing population of Spanish speaking clients and staff-members of the nonprofit.
Art	Art students apply for permission to create a mural on a disused bridge support, and write an application for a grant to cover the cost of materials. Then they work with a group of elementary school students to design and paint the mural. Students create leaflets and public notices to advertise the new public art and bring pride to the community.

Ethnography

Atlanta is a city rich in history and cultural diversity, leading many GSU instructors to create writing assignments that have an ethnographic research component to encourage involvement with our state capital and GSU's home. If you are assigned an ethnographic project, you might choose to research one of the many influential figures in the community: for example, Congressman John C. Lewis, who was engaged in the Civil Rights Movement of the 1960s; Alveda King, Martin Luther King, Jr.'s daughter, noted pro-life activist; Russell Simmons, hip hop mogul; or Don Cathy, CEO of Chick-fil-A. Each of these people provide a rich foundation for an academic paper, but the person you choose to study doesn't need to be such a high-profile individual, particularly if you're hoping to gain access to him/her for an interview. Regardless of whom you choose, if you investigate your community through the eyes of a researcher, you will have little trouble finding people with interesting stories and claims to the history and/or community of Atlanta.

Another option is to research local history: the Margaret Mitchell house; the structures that comprise the Atlanta History Center in Buckhead; the campus of Morehouse College; the city of Decatur (a prominent site for General Sherman to wage his campaign on Atlanta during the American Civil War); or any structure or plot of land that is considered significant to Atlanta history or the history of a smaller community. If you choose to research local history, you will want to visit the site to gather pictures, personal observations, and other information that might not be as accessible in books or on the Internet.

Ebenezer Baptist Church is located o Auburn Avenue in downtown Atlant Because this is the church where Dr. Kin preached his message of nonviolenc throughout the Civil Rights Movemen Ebenezer is now a Martin Luther Kinj Jr. National Historical Site.

Alternatively, you might choose to focus on a particular cultural group or practice in Atlanta in order to increase intercultural awareness and communication. Selecting a group to which you already belong may appeal to you more than working with a group where you are only an interested outsider. Consider researching refugee families at the Clarkston Community Center; Islamic Mosques in metro-Atlanta; the Atlanta Greek Festival and Greek Orthodox Church; the gay, lesbian, transgendered, and queer Pride Festival at Piedmont Park; or the annual sci-fi festival Dragon*Con. The Georgia State library also houses a nationally-recognized archive of Southern labor documents and materials. In each of these cases, the purpose of your study is to better understand a culture or cultural practice and share what you've come to know about that culture or practice through writing.

Ethnographies typically involve a great deal of research, so be prepared to investigate library resources, historical journals and databases, as well as best practices in conducting interviews. The Atlanta area is also rich in archives that make ethnographic studies particularly inviting.

Tips for Interviewing for Research

Keep all communication professional. Be sure to use proper grammar and spelling in all written correspondence (emails, letters).

Be aware of the interviewee's schedule. Make an appointment, arrive on time for the interview, and conclude the interview at the agreed upon time.

Dress appropriately for the interview. If in doubt, dress more professionally/formally.

Arrive with a list of questions, but don't be surprised if the conversation leads you down a different path.

Make sure your most critical questions are answered.

Ask permission to contact the interviewee for follow-up questions or for clarification as you write up the interview.

Ask open-ended questions (questions that can't be answered with a simple *yes* or *no*).

Take notes during the interview. If you plan to record the interview with video or audio, be sure you get permission first.

After the interview, send a thank you note.

Share your article or essay with the interviewee (if appropriate) prior to submitting it, in case she or he wants to correct any misunderstandings or misrepresentations.

Ask your professor about interviewing anyone who might have reduced ability to make decisions about what to tell you, or feel pressured to cooperate with your interview. For example, children under 18, prisoners, residents of medical or personal care facilities, adults with developmental or cognitive differences, or anyone whose answers could put her or someone else in danger (refugees, homeless people, women in shelters, etc).

Service Learning

Assignments for community-based and civic engagement writing might ask you to use your experiences as the basis for writing, including reflective writing, expository writing, and research essays. While community work can serve as a great basis for writing papers, there is another type of community-based writing that focuses on reciprocity between student-writer and community group. This writing is part of a broad field of study activities called service learning.

Service Learning is an educational approach that links academic objectives with course-related service in a way that benefits both the community and the student. Essentially, it is service with an academic purpose. When you take a class with a service learning component, you will apply specific course objectives to service. For example, you may learn about writing formal or business letters, then be assigned to write a letter on behalf of a non-profit organization requesting support or donations.

Service learning courses might also encourage you to work directly with a group in your community to produce documents that serve that group or organization's purposes. Instructors might ask for a "deliverable" piece of writing that fulfills two criteria: 1) satisfies a course writing assignment, and 2) serves an existing and ongoing need in the community. The goal here is *reciprocity*. Some examples of service learning deliverables might be instruction manuals or policy/procedure manuals, public relations/marketing literature, flyers, brochures, web content, newsletters, or communication templates.

Other types of service learning activities for English classes include service in the community that is specific to reading and writing. Working with reluctant readers in an elementary school, tutoring middle and high school students on essay writing, holding a resume-writing workshop for unemployed adults in the public library, or coordinating a book drive for a low-income neighborhood are all forms of service learning that work toward increased literacy in the community.

Service learning isn't specific to English classes, however. You can participate in service learning in virtually any course imaginable. University students in theater and women's studies programs all over the country have worked together to put on productions of the play *The Vagina Monologues* to raise awareness of violence against women as well as funds that benefit victim's advocate groups. Students in music appreciation classes have partnered with music therapy programs at a community hospital. Local Atlanta students in a geology class have recently worked to compile a database of the historic stone carvings located all over Stone Mountain. This "carving database" is now available online and has contributed to the historical and geological scholarship of the landmark.

Sometimes service learning projects–like those named above–involve class-wide assignments your instructor selected before the start of the semester. Other times, you will be given a requirement to complete a service learning project and asked to choose a topic and then find a community partner on your own. Don't feel anxious about this request. It can be challenging, but it can also be quite an adventure. Take advantage of the resources available here at GSU and on the Internet to help you identify a potential partner. A quick Google search of the terms "service learning" and your course ("physical education," for example) will yield results that show what other students have researched. You don't have to reinvent the wheel; if someone else has completed a service learning project on another campus, in another community, and was successful, why not try to replicate it here in the Atlanta-GSU community?

Finally, your instructor will be a great resource for you, so schedule some time for the two of you to brainstorm together on project ideas. The success of your project will depend, in large part, on the quality of communication you have with your instructor and your community partner along the way.

Activism

While some assignments require you to research a project and report your findings, you might also be asked to write to make a change. If you are assigned an activist project, you will work to make a change that improves life for an individual, a group, or the community as a whole.

While it may seem overwhelming to think of engaging in activism in a college class, you don't have to try to solve all the world's problems in a single semester. You could start by merely working to increase awareness about one specific issue. Or you might work to implement a change in policy that will

help a particular population within the larger community. Whatever you decide to do, remember that your activist work could motivate someone else to work for change, and, in turn, their work could motivate someone else. This impact is called the "snowball effect" because what you started as a small class project keeps growing and growing and, just like a snowball, it increases in mass as it rolls down a snow-covered hill.

Before starting any activism assignment, first consider which specific causes you care the most about. Are there some areas on campus where you see room for improvement? What issues in the community concern you? Can you target a group who would benefit from changes in policies or conditions? Look around you, find something that you feel passionate about and for which you are willing to work.

Once you have chosen a cause, determine what you can do to influence the situation. You might decide to work on increasing awareness of the problem by creating posters to put up around campus. Or you might want to write letters to implore the drafting of legislation or to voice support for a law or policy that would benefit your cause. No matter what you decide, make sure you are realistic about what you can do in the time you have, especially if it is a class project that is limited to a single semester. And don't think that your project is too small. You can't help every homeless person in Atlanta, but you might be able to increase awareness of the challenges that homeless people face, and as more people become aware of those challenges, they may offer help.

Whatever you decide to do, Georgia State University is a very supportive environment for activist work. GSU has many organizations that you can collaborate with when undertaking an activist project. For example, GSU Bikes is an organization that works to make the campus more bicycle-friendly in order to encourage more people to ride bikes to school, thereby reducing emissions and helping the environment. GSU's Nutrition Student Network works to increase nutrition awareness and promote healthy eating habits both on campus and off. And the Sustainable Energy Tribe at Georgia State addresses issues around sustainability and works to teach students and faculty about environmental issues.

If you want to go outside of the college campus, Atlanta offers plenty of opportunities for activist work. The Atlanta Community Food Bank helps fight hunger in the Atlanta area by distributing food to local non-profit agencies. Pets for Vets is a local organization that matches military veterans with shelter pets, giving the veterans a companion and giving the once-abandoned pet a second chance. Chastity House in Atlanta serves teens who suffer from sexual abuse, sex trafficking, and sexual exploitation. The possibilities are numerous.

Conversely, you may decide to work on an activism project without being tied directly to an organization. If a cause or issue interests you, then perform your own activist work. For example, you might notice that there are limited recycling bins on campus, and you may decide to write letters to the municipal waste service companies requesting more bins on campus to increase recycling activity. Or you might see that many students don't use the recycling bins and instead toss their plastic water bottles in the trash; you could create signs to post around campus to help students realize the availability of recycling on campus.

For any of the above causes, you could complete several different composition assignments for class. Assignment possibilities include writing letters asking for donations, making flyers to improve awareness, conducting research and using that research to write argumentative essays for a particular organization, or even creating a proposal for a fundraiser. Regardless of the assignment, the overall goal is the same: to work for a positive change while improving your writing skills with assignments that are specific and enjoyable.

Digital Civic Engagement

While it's exciting to be off-campus and in community spaces, you don't have to "go" anywhere in order to be actively involved with a broader, off-campus community. With the advent of Web 2.0, an increasing amount of civic discourse and community engagement is conducted online.

Many of you already actively engage in online communities–*Pinterest, Facebook, Twitter,* blogs, etc. You are most likely using social media, usually in the form of social networking sites, which you likely use for the purposes of communicating with friends and family or strangers with shared interests, such as football teams or community events. One of the distinctions between Web 2.0 and the previous Internet technology is the participatory or "social" nature of this newer media. Instead of users simply downloading or receiving information from the Internet, we now share and exchange information using the Internet as a medium for interaction.

Thanks to the social, participatory nature of Web 2.0, users can choose a wide variety of ways to engage with each other and myriad purposes for this engagement. Much like gathering in the library plaza on campus, students can choose to use the public space to socialize about weekend plans, share pictures of friends and family back home, or talk about a proposed increase in tuition across the University System of Georgia. You can continue to discuss these kinds of issues in the plaza daily or weekly, ultimately deciding to take some sort of action on the proposed tuition increase. You might create informational flyers and distribute them to others gathering in the plaza. You might make posters and recruit other concerned students to march together down to the State Capitol building and hold signs on the steps proclaiming your opposition to the proposed increases.

The same types of activities occur in the digital world. You have equivalent social interactions with your peers online through various social media, and you can choose to use that forum for social, community, or political purposes. The Internet provides a variety of public spaces specifically devoted to certain types of discourse (*Pinterest* for the crafty, DIYers, *sportlobster* for the sports enthusiasts, *volkalize* for the political debaters, *LinkedIn* for professionals) and more general public forums for crossover discourse (*Facebook, Twitter, Wordpress, Blogger, YouTube*).

The key to civic engagement through new media is to first join the conversation and observe. You need to have a fairly good understanding of the tool you are using to engage, and then you need to learn exactly how users interested in that cause or issue are already interacting with one another. Are users announcing and promoting in-person events, or are they using the media to inform and increase awareness? Do certain kinds of messages get more responses or shares? Just like in-person communities, see what you can learn about how a community works before you get involved.

Georgia State University Resources

GSU Office of Civic Engagement - service.gsu.edu

Devoted to helping students at GSU find service projects to work with here in Atlanta, this office is a good place to start if you want to get involved with our community but aren't sure how to begin. 428/429 University Center. 404.413.1550

GSU Student Organizations - gsu.orgsync.com

This website is home to the many student organizations at GSU involved with community service inside and outside the university. Search for "service" to see numerous opportunities to get involved. 330 Student Center. 404.413.1580

Service-Learning in the GSU College of Education - http://education.gsu.edu/outreach

Thinking of a career in an education-related field? Get involved in one of the on-going service projects in the GSU College of Education.

Community Engagement in the GSU College of Arts and Sciences - www.cas.gsu.edu/community

No matter what your major (from biology to music), the College of Arts and Sciences has opportunities to get involved in the Atlanta community and learn more about your chosen field.

Internet Resources

Campus Compact - campuscompact.org/resources-for-students

This organization is a coalition of more than a thousand colleges and universities all committed to campus-based civic engagement activities. The website offers a variety of resources to help students get actively involved in their communities.

Corporation for National and Community Service - nationalservice.gov

CNCS is a federal agency that exists to coordinate service opportunities with citizens who wish to put their time and talent to service.

National Service-Learning Clearinghouse - servicelearning.org

Start here for an explanation of what service-learning is (and what it is not), and then explore the rest of the site for ideas for service-learning projects, articles about the theory behind service-learning, and service-learning success stories.

VolunteerMatch.com and NobleHour.com

These sites match students with community organizations that have a specific need.

Major Issues and Ethical Concerns

Consider special ethical and safety questions as you prepare to undertake a service learning or public writing project. These include, but are not limited to, protecting the autonomy and safety of the community members with whom you work, navigating organizational background checks, protecting your safety while traveling to and serving in community sites, learning professional behavior and protocols, staying true to your personal convictions, and considering legal liabilities.

Remember that quality service learning and public writing projects are contingent on reciprocity. Your project should be an opportunity for all involved to learn from each other: beware the idea of a 'fortunate' group bestowing service on a 'less fortunate' group. These misperceptions of privilege and advantage can undermine the benefits of service and sour community relationships.

If the project you wish to undertake involves research with community partners, you may be asked to submit a proposal to the Institutional Review Board at Georgia State. This independent group of scholars and administrators is charged with protecting the welfare of research subjects. To have your project approved, you will have to verify that your research will not harm any human subjects, that you can protect the confidentiality of any data collected, that all qualified participants will have an equal opportunity to be involved, and that subjects may withdraw at any time without penalty. Your instructor will be able to help you determine whether or not you need IRB approval, and will assist you with the process of obtaining approval.

Some organizations you wish to work with may require background checks or extended training. If you are working with a protected class of people, such as children, prisoners, or persons with disabilities, you may be required to submit to a background check. This check may include questions about places you have previously lived or worked and fingerprinting to verify your identity. You should feel free to ask a community organization about their background check procedures, how long they will take, and who will be responsible for any costs. Consider this information in your project timeline and budget.

Be sure you understand the safety procedures and organizational protocols for working on-site, and ask questions if you are unsure what is expected of you. Only go to the service-learning site when you are expected by the organization and when your instructor knows where you will be. Wear appropriate shoes and clothing, do not provide or accept personal information from the community members you work with, and be cautious when travelling to and from service sites. Take precautions to protect your personal property, including a vehicle, from theft or damage when working in unfamiliar parts of the city. If you have special safety concerns, communicate them to your instructor or organizing faculty member as soon as possible. An instructor may also require you to provide emergency contact information, in case you are ill or injured while working off campus.

Be sure you understand the liabilities, legal and ethical, associated with your project. Do not assume that the instructor, organization, or university will be able to protect you legally or financially. Ask questions and communicate openly about insurance, safety, behavior, policies, best practices, and if necessary, alternative placements or opportunities.

Things to Remember...

When Taking Classes that Include Community-Based Writing

Course objectives do not change in classes that use community action; you will be required to complete some type of community action, but you will still be evaluated on meeting course objectives, including strengthening your writing and thinking skills.

While community service classes do generally require work outside of the classroom, they are not designed to require more hours than the same course without a community service component.

Your instructor is your point of contact if you have questions or concerns about the community service project.

Community service classes can provide you with opportunities to explore different careers, cultures, and situations. With an open mind, you might find that a class with a community-based component gives you more than just course credit; it can give you the chance to make a difference in your community or in someone's life, along with a better understanding of audience, rhetorical situation, and purpose-driven writing.

What Students Say About Their Community-Based Writing Experiences

"Service learning combines community-based service with classroom instruction, focusing on critical, reflective thinking as well as personal and civic responsibility. Service learning programs involve students in activities that address community-identified needs while developing their academic skills and commitment to their community."

The American Association of Community Colleges

Although you may be uncertain about service learning, most students find the experience rewarding.

"My time spent in service learning has been so rewarding that I plan to continue to find ways to serve others."

"Service-learning at Peachtree Elementary became one of the things I looked forward to most every week. I have come to realize how much I actually enjoy writing when the topic is something I am invested in and feel passionately about."

"I am truly a believer of what service learning does for one's own personal growth and development."

"It was helpful to engage in activities outside of the classroom environment and to be able to reflect on real life experiences."

FOR THOUGHT AND DISCUSSION

Use these activities as prompts for discussion or thought that will get you and your classmates talking about ways to engage in the local community.

Separate a sheet of paper into three columns. In the first column, make a list of five communities that you consider yourself a part of. In the second column, make a list of five things that you are passionate about. In the third column, make a list of five things that concern you. Once you've finished, look for connections between items on your lists. These intersections are potential opportunities for community involvement. Discuss your findings with classmates in a small group to identify causes or organizations that surround your personal values and passions.

Make a list of at least five people or groups in your community or school who you feel would benefit from a new policy. For each group, identify what policy change would benefit them and list why they would benefit from the change. Then consider what other groups might be affected by the change. When you have your list, compare it to the lists of your classmates and decide which causes you would be willing to do activist work for.

Sample Assignment

McNeil 1

Sample Assignment: Argumentative Research Essay

Purpose and Description:

This semester our course has been focused on the question "What's my stake?" We have explored and researched local social issues (such as gentrification, socioeconomic upshots of public transportation, racialized medical access, rap and hip-hop music culture and opinions, and community involvement in primary public education) and many local non-profit organizations that have been created in response to these issues. We have used writing as a tool of understanding how citizenship requires an engagement of community through critical awareness.

Using your chosen non-profit as a lens, you will assert an argument considering one or more of the following questions: How does the role of non-profit organizations depend on, intersect with, and reflect the responsibilities of citizenship? What is the role of non-profit organizations in communities? What is the state of non-profit organizations in Atlanta? How vital is your chosen non-profit organization to the city of Atlanta? Why it is (or is it not) important for Atlanta citizens to be aware of these organizations and/or engage them?

You are encouraged to incorporate your research from your Annotated Bibliography and other sources as needed to ground and support your argument. Likewise, the final thesis presented in your essay should reflect the multiple revisions conducted through your Thesis Group's discussion board.

Requirements:

- A thoughtful and sustained argument that clearly takes the above prompt into consideration and is backed by critical research of outside sources
- Full 6 to 8 pages, not including Works Cited page
- Reference to one primary source of your non-profit organization, one scholarly source, and two popular sources

General Checklist for Content:

- A main claim or thesis that is sustained throughout the essay (main point to which everything refers back and which is relevant to an audience)
- Reasons for the main claim or thesis (thoughtful analysis of and reflection on the issue)
- Support of the main claim or thesis (use of at least one properly cited, scholarly sources)
- A scholarly conversation (sources are woven into the body of the essay)
- A discussion of counter arguments
- Direct quotations from your sources
- Conclusions (referring to the "global" importance of the issue)

MLA format:

- 1" margins on top, bottom, left and right; left justified

- Name block is single spaced and includes your name, instructor's name, the class (ENGL 1102 and section number), and the date of submission
- Header should be ½" from the top right margin and include your last name and page number
- Descriptive title centered at the top of the first page
- The entire document should be double-spaced and in 12-point Times New Roman font
- A correctly formatted Works Cited page in MLA style

Assessment:

- Clarity and strength of thesis
- Development of ideas
- Organization
- Mechanics, grammar, and style
- Quality of exposition and persuasion
- Engagement with one primary source, one scholarly source, two popular sources
- Use of support in the form of quotations and referencing of sources
- MLA format (including a Works Cited page)

Sample Student Work

Jessie Giles

McNeil

ENG 1102

11/5/13

Living Walls, The City Speaks

Dubbed the "City Too Busy to Hate," by former mayor Ivan Allen in the 1960s, Atlanta has a vibrant, diverse community. Be it culinary, artistic, musical or theatrical, there is always something exciting to experience. In 1996, Atlanta was chosen to host the Olympics. This led to a massive clean up of the city and a rush to buy up property in the blighted downtown area. The popular opinion was that Atlanta would continue to thrive after the Olympics and that these businesses would be well poised to reap the benefits of this growth and expansion. As a result of the Great Recession that began in the early 2000's, however, this boom was not realized. According to numerous articles published by CNN and the Atlanta Journal-Constitution at the time, the city did continue to grow, but at a much slower pace than anticipated. Streets that had been cleaned up became littered again and social issues that had been swept under the rug began to reappear. At the same time, people started moving back into the historic neighborhoods, drawn by the low prices and historic charm. Then came the businesses, slowly at first and then by the dozens. Historic neighborhoods were suddenly in demand and housing prices rose, forcing the current residents into poorer neighborhoods farther away from downtown Atlanta. This cycle of gentrification repeated itself in neighborhood after neighborhood, creating racial and economic tension between the more affluent people who had moved into these neighborhoods and the people that struggled to remain. This tension, which often manifests itself in fear, petty crime, and anger, still remains in a few transitional neighborhoods and threatens to emerge in neighborhoods that are gaining popularity. While I believe Atlanta will continue to grow and that gentrification is most likely inevitable, I also believe that an alternative approach to these negative aspects of gentrification is not only possible, but also essential to the future growth of the city of Atlanta. Through a community-building effort to beautify the streets of Atlanta we can ease the strain and estrangement between neighbors and ensure that Atlanta not only grows economically, but also in a socially responsible way.

I moved into one of these transitioning neighborhoods, Cabbagetown, in 2005, at age 19. I still remember with perfect clarity the awe I felt the first time I drove down Powell Street. It was so absolutely different than where I had grown up, thirty minutes north of Atlanta, in the suburbs. Here, the streets were lined with colorful shotgun houses with bathtub gardens sprouting mannequin legs in the front yards and wrought iron fences littered with all sorts of kitschy knick-knacks. Within a few months, I began working at a locally owned pizza place in Cabbagetown. My co-workers were punk rockers, skateboarders, and graffiti artists, but they were like family to me. The place was an absolute mess but the neighborhood embraced its unassuming charm with a sort of maternal acceptance. I lived in Cabbagetown for years, working and immersing myself in the neighborhood, and gained a sense of what it means to be a member of a community.

As strong as our community was, however, there was one divisive issue that could not be agreed upon by Cabbagetown residents, and that was graffiti. Transitioning neighborhoods around us were also experiencing this struggle, split almost fifty-fifty with half the residents supporting and cherishing the thriving street art scene and half the residents resolutely against it. One of the neighboring areas, the Old Fourth Ward, went so far as to start a "graffiti task force" in conjunction with the Atlanta Police Department. In a March 2011 email listserv forwarded to me by a resident of the Old Fourth Ward, inhabitants of this neighborhood were encouraged by

Matthew Garbett, president of Fourth Ward Neighbors, Inc., to take photos of any new graffiti

and to keep a sharp watch: "EARS OPEN! You've probably seen the majority of key taggers in

your favorite establishments. They bus tables and wash dishes. They get hammered after work,

grab some cans and head out on their bikes. Even the legend 'Vomet' is some dishwasher around

here. Tips, heresy, whatever it's all valuable." The author even went so far as to suggest residents

"friend" suspected graffiti artists under fake Facebook accounts to gather intel. While surely

some graffiti artists at this time were working as bussers and dishwashers, Garbett is manifesting

an unwarranted suspicion of local, low-wage restaurant workers--a group that already receives a

fair amount of disdain for not having a "real" job; a group to which I then belonged.

According to Rosalind Bentley in an article appearing in the Atlanta Journal-Constitution

in December 2012, Living Walls had recently taken steps toward gaining community approval

for pieces in their 2013 conference, such as going door to door in Old Fourth Ward and meeting

with various neighborhood associations. Living Walls even enlisted the help of City Council

members to help navigate the permitting process (Bentley). Having lived in both Cabbagetown

and Pittsburgh, two very different neighborhoods, each with its own strong sense of community,

I understand the enthusiasm that these neighborhoods are capable of. Living Walls has definitely

taken a step towards harnessing this strength, and Living Walls is still a very young organization.

With a deeper commitment to community involvement, a little more manpower and continued

funding, I believe Living Walls could evolve into the organization that this city needs, just as

young "taggers" sometimes mature into talented young street artists.

Works Cited

Bentley, Rosalind. "Lessons Learned in Mural Dispute: Provocative Painting Draws Ire of Residents. Art Spurs Debate on how Much Say the Public should have." *The Atlanta Journal - Constitution.* Dec 23 2012. *ProQuest.* Web. 10 Jan. 2014.

Garbett, Matthew, et al. "[Fourth_Ward_Neighbors] Graffiti Information." Message to Fourth Ward Neighbors. 17 Mar. 2011.

"Ivan Allen." *NPS.gov.* National Park Service U.S. Department of the Interior. Web. 19 Nov 2013.

Johns, Myke. "Living Walls Starts a New Conversation." *WABE.org.* 14 Aug. 2013. Web. 13 Nov. 2013.

Kramer, Ronald. "Moral Panics and Urban Growth Machines: Official Reactions to Graffiti in New York City, 1990-2005." *Qualitative Sociology* 33.3 (2010): 297-311. *ProQuest.* Web. 10 Jan. 2014.

Living Walls Website. Living Walls Atlanta. Web. 19 Nov 2013.

Roti. Crocodile mural, University Avenue. 2012. Living Walls. *Google Images.* Web. 22 Oct 2013.

Semenza, Jan C, Tanya L March, and Brian D Bontempo. "Community-Initiated Urban Development: An Ecological Intervention." *Journal of Urban Health: Bulletin of the New York Academy of Medicine* 84.1 (2007): 8-20. *MEDLINE.* Web. 20 Oct. 2013.

Wheatley, Thomas. "Living Walls splits community." *Creative Loafing Atlanta.* 14 Nov. 2012. Web. 19 Nov. 2013.

Terms for Increased Understanding

The following terms, though they do not appear in the chapter, may come up in discussions or supplemental readings surrounding community-based writing.

Action research: a variation of community-based research whereby the researcher is an actively engaged participant in the organization being studied or an activist working toward change through this organization or community that is at the center of the research study. (Also called activist research or participatory research).

Counterpublic: a subaltern group that is aware, to some degree, of its subordinate status in relation to a dominant group or "public" (Warner 117). A counterpublic "comes into being through an address to indefinite strangers [...] in a magazine or sermon," for example, where it seeks to "supply different ways of imagining general or dominant public" (Warner 118).

Dissensus: a tool for communication that values difference and resists the normalizing force of consensus as an end goal.

Intercultural communication: the way in which people from a variety of geographical, socio-economic, religious, educational, and social backgrounds work to better understand and interact with one another.

Externship: similar to an internship program, an externship offers a student an opportunity to acquire professional experience by "shadowing" a professional in the industry they wish to work in, while simultaneously earning college credit.

Literacy: having knowledge of a specific subject or in a particular area (i.e., digital literacy means understanding of digital technology; sonic literacy means knowledge of the role of sound in composition; information literacy is the ability to navigate through the vastness of data and information available, evaluate it for quality, and use it appropriately, etc.).

Praxis: the cycle between action and reflection that is fundamental for social change.

Public Rhetoric: Public rhetoric involves communication (writing, speaking, and/or other modes of communication) that is situated within a public context, often for purposes of civic engagement or social change.

Public Writing: "written discourse that attempts to engage an audience of local, regional, or national groups or individuals in order to bring about progressive societal change" (Weissner 90).

Publics: According to Michael Warner, a public is self-organized group of strangers, a contextual "social space created by the reflexive circulation of discourse (67–118).

Rivaling: a strategy for communication that seeks out perspectives that differ or contradict one's own position in order to challenge assumptions.

Story-behind-the-story: a literary strategy that utilizes the situated knowledge in order to reveal speakers/writers' under-acknowledged agency or power.

For Further Reading

Addams, Jane. "The Subtle Problems of Charity." *The Atlantic*. August 1899. Web. 4 Nov. 2013.

Blanchard, Olivia. "I Quit Teach for America." *The Atlantic*. 23 Sept. 2013. Web. 11 Nov. 2013.

"Challenges to Free Speech and Academic Freedom at CCNY, 1931-42." *CCNY Libraries*. n.d. Web. 11 Nov. 2013.

Gladwell, Malcolm. "Small Change: Why the Revolution Won't Be Tweeted." *The New Yorker*. 4 Oct. 2010. Web. 11 Nov. 2013.

Nycz-Conner, Jennifer. "D.C.'s Miriam's Kitchen Rides Social Media Wave." *Washington Business Journal Online*. 20 July 2009. Web. 11 Nov. 2013.

WORKS CITED

Deans, Thomas. *Writing and Community Action: A Service-learning Rhetoric and Reader*. New York: Longman, 2003. Print.

——. *Writing Partnerships: Service-Learning in Composition.* Urbana, IL: National Council of Teachers of English, 2000. Print.

Ervin, Elizabeth. *Public Literacy*. New York: Longman, 2003. Web. 27 Nov. 2013.

Fleckenstein, Kristie S. *Vision, Rhetoric, and Social Action in the Composition Classroom.* Carbondale: Southern Illinois University Press, 2010. eBook Collection (EBSCOhost). Web. 27 Nov. 2013.

Warner, Michael. *Publics and Counterpublics.* New York: Zone Books, 2005. Print.

Media Credits

"Ebenezer Baptist Church." Photo. *National Park Service Digital Image Archives.* Wikimedia Commons. n.d. Web. 22 May 2014.

First year English student Narisha Ditmore helps unknown Atlanta-area elementary school student with literacy skills. Digital image. Georgia Perimeter College, Apr. 2012.

Man vyi. "Giant Snowball Oxford." 2007. Photo. *Flickr.com.* Web. 22 May 2014.

WORKS CITED

"20 Years Later, San Ysidro McDonald's Massacre Remembered." Web log post. *North County Times*. Lee Enterprises Inc., 2004. Web. 17 July 2004.

"A $300 Idea that Is Priceless." *The Economist* 28 Apr. 2011. Print.

Crue, Wuther. "Ordeal by Cheque." *Vanity Fair* 1932. Print.

Duggan, Paul. "In Sex-Crime Cases, Credibility a Thorny Issue." *The Washington Post* 1 July 2011. Print.

Echanove, Matias, and Rahul Srivastava. "Hands Off Our Houses." The New York Times 1 June 2011: A27. Print.

Fogarty, Mignon. *Grammar Girl: Quick and Dirty Tips for Better Writing*. New York: St. Martin's Press, 2008. Print.

Gillespie, Paula, and Neal Lerner. *The Longman Guide to Peer Tutoring*. Addison-Wesley Longman, 2008. Print.

Gleiberman, Owen. "Film Review: The Hangover." Rev. of *The Hangover*, by Dir. Todd Phillips. *EW.com* 2 June 2009. Web. 15 Nov. 2010.

Govindarajan, Vijay. "The $300 House: A Hands-On Approach to a Wicked Problem." Web log post. *HBR Blog Network*, Harvard Business School Publishing, 7 June 2011. Web. 22 Oct. 2011.

Greene, Andy. "All Star Rockers Salute Buddy Holly." *Rolling Stone*. Straight Arrow Publishers, 7 July 2011. Print.

Jayawardhana, Ray. "Alien Life, Coming Slowly into View." *The New York Times* 27 March 2011: WK10. Print.

Johnson, Judith. "The Truth about Writer's Block." *The Huffington Post*. HuffPost News, 25 July 2011. Web. 11 Nov. 2011.

King, Jr., Martin Luther. "I Have a Dream." Speech. March on Washington for Jobs and Freedom. Lincoln Memorial, Washington, D.C. 28 Aug. 1963. *Americanrhetoric.com*. Michael E. Eidenmuller. n.d. Web. 12 Nov. 2011.

Lincoln, Abraham. "Gettysburg Address." Speech. Dedication of the Soldiers' National Cemetary. Gettysburg, Pennsylvania 19 Nov. 1863. *Ourdocuments.gov*. n.d. Web. 15 Nov. 2011.

McGrath, Charles. "The Lexicon." *NYTimes.com* 8 Sept. 2011. Web. 9 Sept. 2011.

Meyers, Justin. "How to Make a Kindle Cover from a Hollowed Out Hardback Book." *Wonder How To*. n.p., March 2011. Web. 12 Nov. 2011.

Murray, Donald. "Teach Writing as a Process Not Product." *The Leaflet* 71.3 (1972): 11-14. Print.

Neil, Dan. "BMW 1M: Miniature, Mighty and Miles of Fun." *The Wall Street Journal* 3 Sept. 2011. Print.

Obama, Barack. "Remarks by the President on Osama bin Laden."
    Speech. Address to the Nation that Osama bin Laden is
    dead. The White House, Washington, D.C. 1 May 2011. *The
    White House Blog.* Macon Phillips. 2 May 2011. Web. 29
    Sept. 2011.

Rosen, Jeffrey. "The Web Means the End of Forgetting." *The New
    York Times* 25 July 2010: MM30. Print.

Schalet, Amy. "The Sleepover Question." *The New York Times* 23
    July 2011: SR9. Print.

Scham, Sam. "Top Ten Distractions for Writers, or Any Job Really."
    Yahoo.com 12 Aug. 2008. Web. 12 Nov. 2011.

Shemtob, Zachary, and David Lat. "Executions Should Be
    Televised." The New York Times 31 July 2011: SR4. Print.

Skinner, E. Benjamin. "People for Sale." *Foreign Policy.* March–April
    2008. Print.

Thornburgh, Nathan. "Violent Rhetoric and Arizona Politics."
    Editorial. *Time* 9 Jan. 2011. Print.

Wynn, Craig. "Take a Leap Into Writing." Student essay. Used by
    permission.

Young, Neil. "Let's Roll." *Are You Passionate?* Reprise Records, 2002.
    CD.

Zuniga, Janine. "San Ysidro Shooting Survivor Lives His Dream of
    Being a Cop." *San Diego Union-Tribune* 18 July 2004. Print.

Index

A

academic credibility 199
accuracy 199
action verbs 175
Action verbs 175
Activism 402
Ad hominem 88
ad populum 89
ad verecundium 89
Aesthetic reading 48
alphabetic literacy 287
Aniston, Jennifer 27
Annotated Bibliography 221
APA citations 223, 241, 242, 243, 245, 248, 255, 256, 258, 259
commonly used sources 257–258
online sources 255–256
print sources 252–253
References list 248
Sample References list 259
Appeals 82
appropriation 294
Appropriations 285
argument 6, 21, 199
Aristotle 2, 9, 10, 110, 146

Aristotle's persuasive appeals 82
arrangement 112
artifacts 309, 330, 341, 342, 349, 350, 353, 354, 355, 356
artistic proofs 110
attention 378
audience 285, 292, 293, 294, 296, 297, 299, 300, 307, 308, 309, 311, 312, 313, 317, 318, 325, 329, 343, 344, 378, 386, 387, 388, 389, 390, 391, 409, 418
authorship 299, 307

B

begging the question 89
Begging the question 89
block quotations 245
Blogger 387
Blogs 387
Brainstorming 134

C

Cheating 211
Cicero 146

Civic literacy 395
cliché 173
Clustering 134
Cohen, Sacha Baron 27
common ground argument 147
Community 391, 393, 394, 395, 396, 397, 399, 404, 406, 407, 409, 418
Conclusion 86
confirmation 146
Confusing Cause and Effect 89
Content 289
Cook, Tim 103
critical thinking 34
cultural specificity 288
culture 329
Culture
hyperliterate 287
pre-literate 287
currency 199

D

deductive fallacy 88
Deductive reasoning 86
delayed construction 173
delivery 112